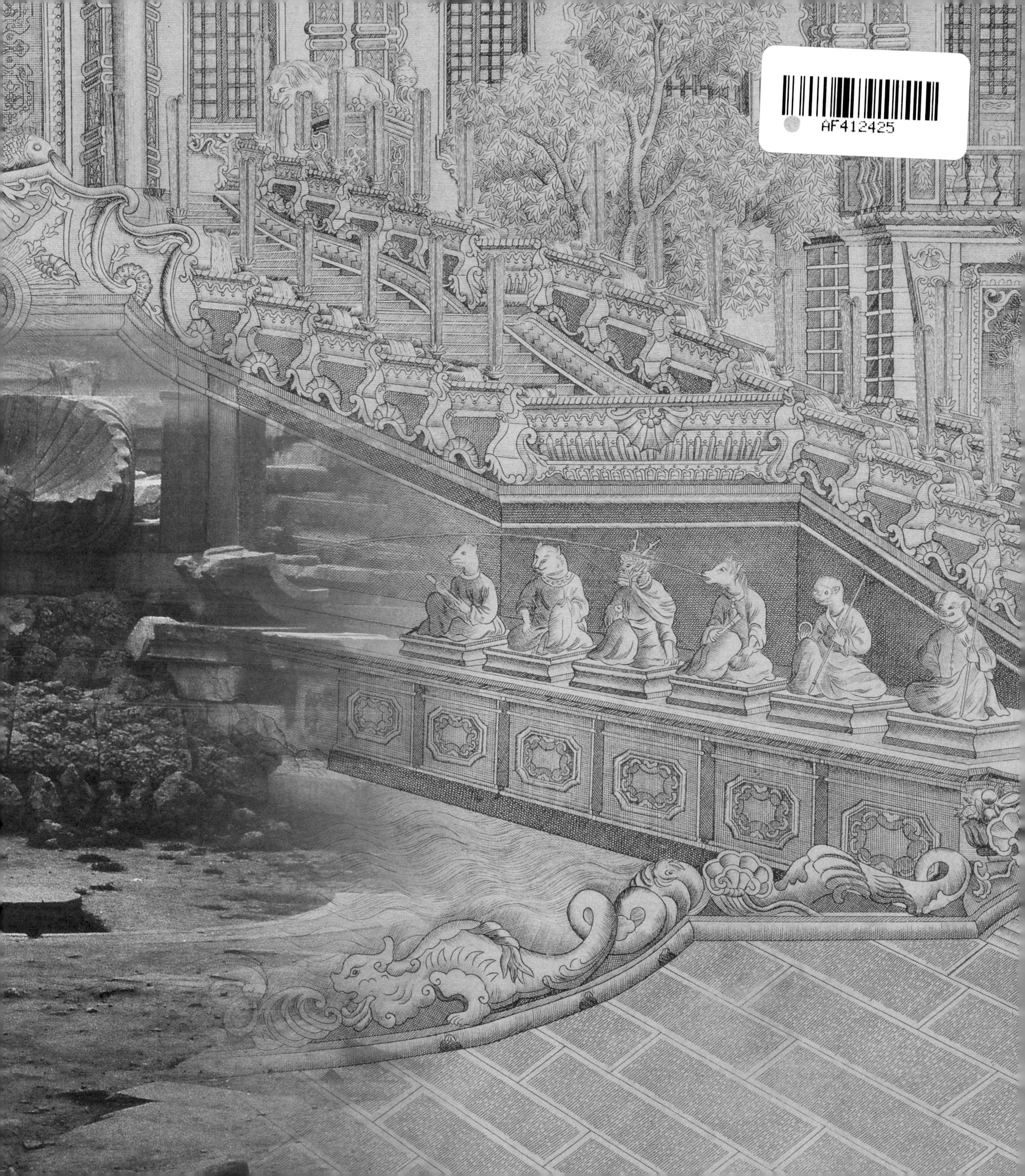
AF412425

艾未未

Ai Weiwei

Circle of Animals

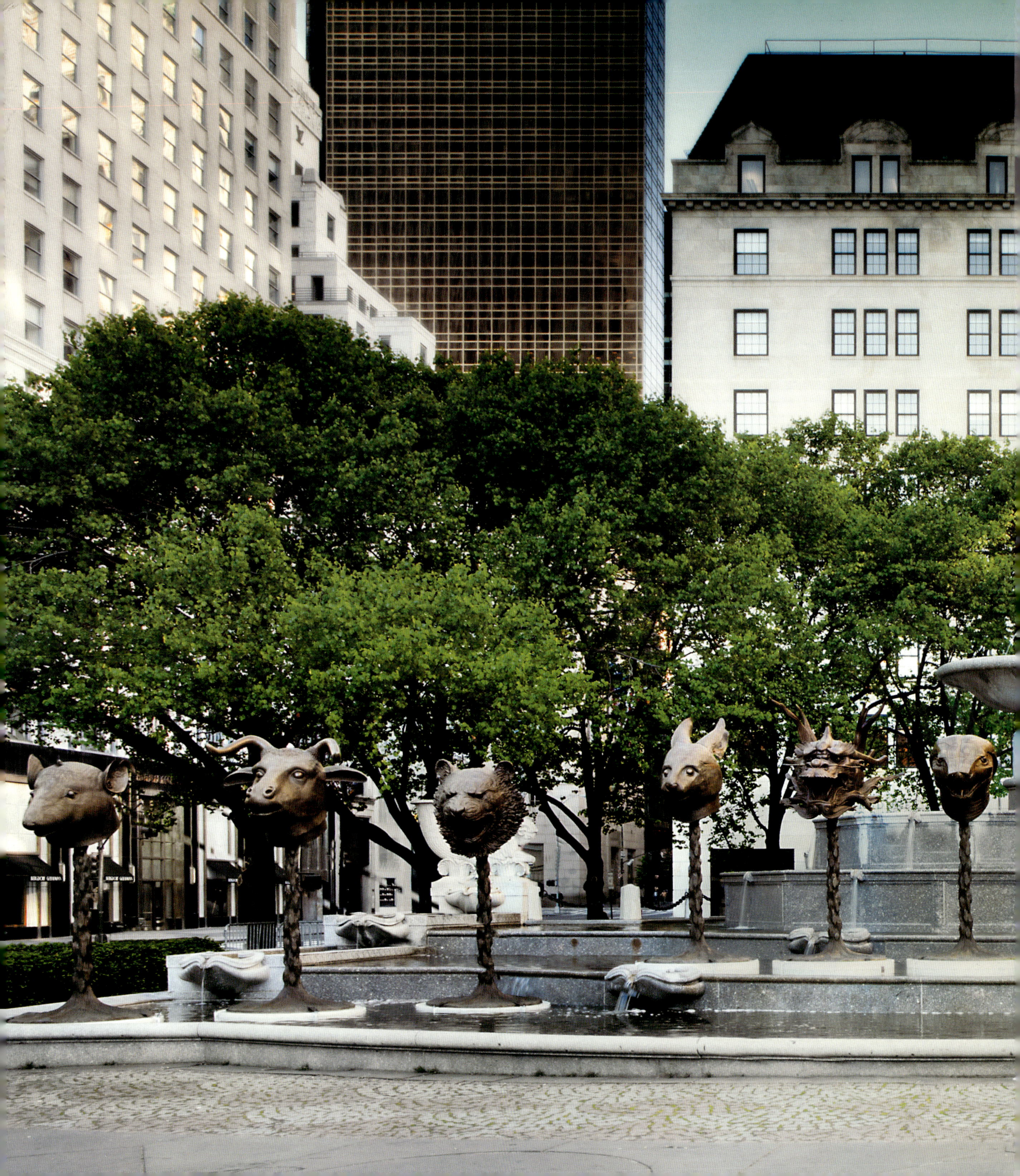

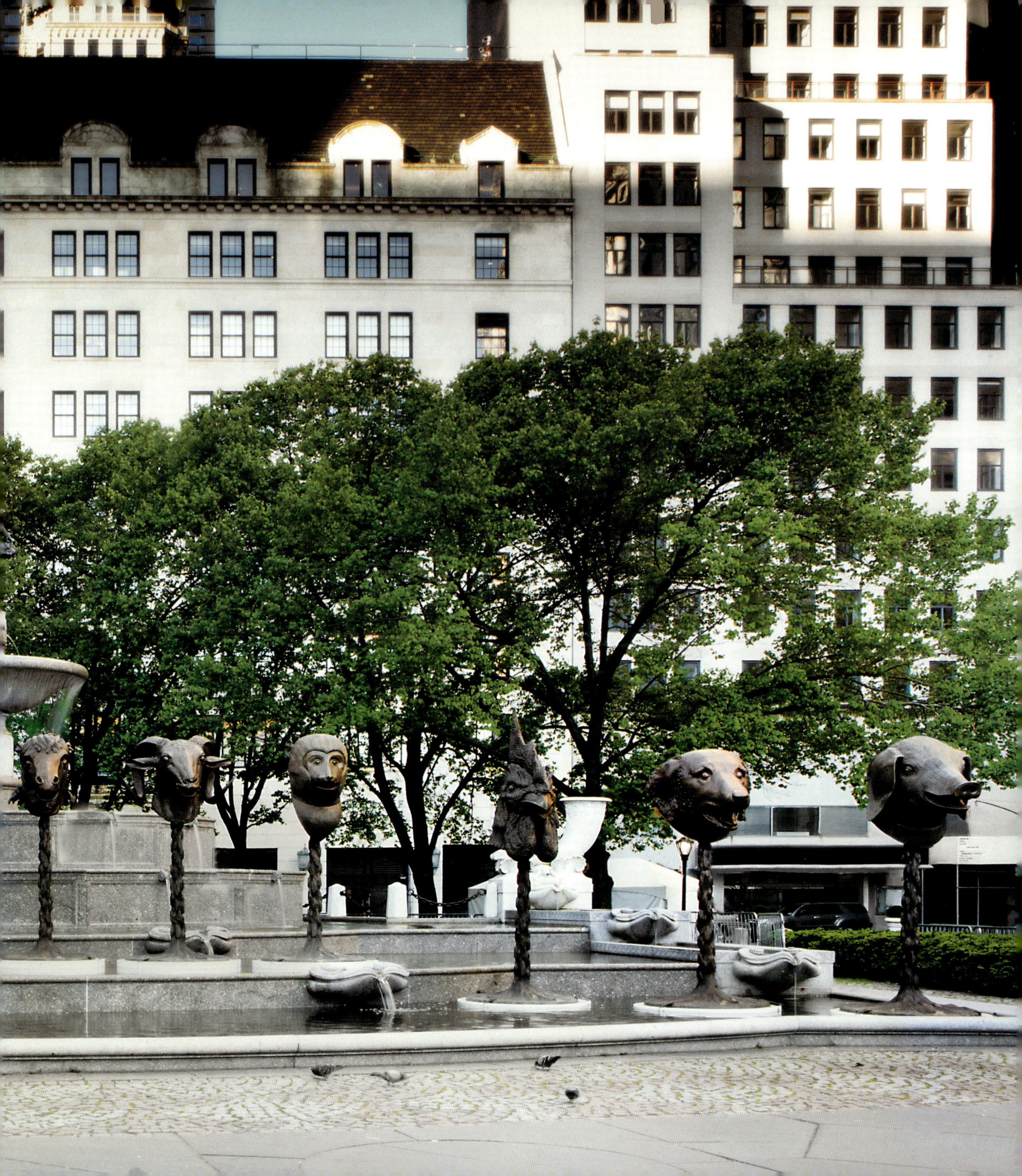

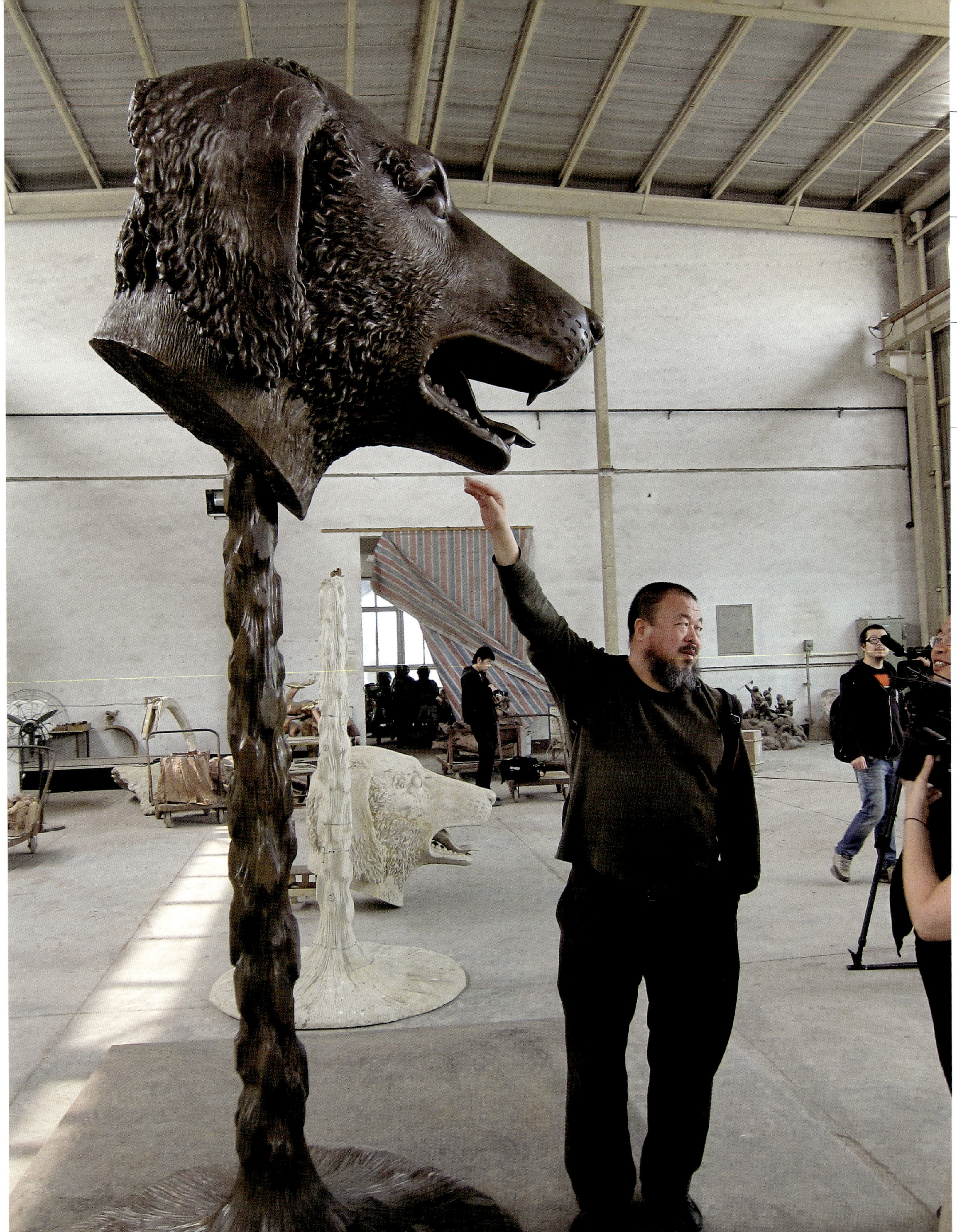

艾未未

Ai Weiwei

Circle of Animals

Edited and with an Introduction
by Susan Delson

PRESTEL Munich London New York

Published in association with AW Asia, New York, on the occasion of the traveling installation *Circle of Animals/Zodiac Heads* www.zodiacheads.com

Prestel, a member of Verlagsgruppe Random House GmbH

Prestel Verlag
Neumarkter Strasse 28, 81673 Munich
Tel. +49 (0)89-4136-0 Fax +49 (0)89-4136-2335

Prestel Publishing Ltd.
4 Bloomsbury Place, London WC1A 2QA
Tel. +44 (0)20 7323-5004 Fax +44 (0)20 7636-8004

Prestel Publishing
900 Broadway, Suite 603, New York, NY 10003
Tel. +1 (212) 995-2720 Fax +1 (212) 995-2733

www.prestel.com

Prestel books are available worldwide. Please contact your
nearest bookseller or one of the above addresses for information
concerning your local distributor.

Library of Congress Control Number: 2011933708; British Library
Cataloguing-in-Publication Data: a catalogue record for this book is
available from the British Library; Deutsche Nationalbibliothek
holds a record of this publication in the Deutsche Nationalbibliografie;
detailed bibliographical data can be found under: http://dnb.d-nb.de

Editorial direction: Christopher Lyon
Copy editing: John Farmer
Editorial assistance: Ryan Newbanks
Proofreading: Ashley Benning
Design and layout: Triboro
Production: The Production Department
Origination: GHP, West Haven, Connecticut
Printing and Binding: Paramount Printing, Hong Kong

The FSC-certified paper 157gsm NEO matte art
has been supplied by Moorim Paper Co. Ltd., Korea

ISBN 978-3-7913-4636-6

ENDPAPERS: Photocollage of a modern reproduction of the
eighteenth-century engraving by Yi Lantai, *West Façade of the Hall
of the Calm Seas (Haiyan Tang ximian)* and a recent photograph
of the ruins of the fountain depicted in the print. For the original
engraving, see pages 14–15.

PAGES 2–3: Installation view of *Circle of Animals/Zodiac Heads*
at the Pulitzer Fountain, New York City, May 2011

FRONTISPIECE: Ai Weiwei in the fabrication studio with
Circle of Animals/Zodiac Heads: Bronze – Dog, 2010

to Ai Weiwei

Contents

Foreword

IT WAS IN EARLY 2008 THAT THE IDEA OF A PUBLIC art sculpture for New York City first came up in conversation between Ai Weiwei and myself at his studio in Beijing. This was not unusual—ideas for intriguing projects were often part of our conversational flow. This one, though, stayed with us. Later that year, I arranged for Weiwei to come to New York, where we made an informal tour of public parks and other possible installation sites. We continued to discuss the project whenever we met, in cities all over the world. But it wasn't until February 2009, in the wake of the aborted sale of two bronze heads from the Yuanming Yuan fountain, that *Circle of Animals/Zodiac Heads* began to take shape.

At first glance, *Circle of Animals/Zodiac Heads* appears to be a simple, straightforward work: a playful exploration of the Chinese zodiac, easily enjoyed by anyone passing by. This is deliberate. Ai Weiwei firmly believes that a work of public art should address as wide a public as possible. But in *Circle of Animals/Zodiac Heads*, as in all of Weiwei's art, there are complex levels of meaning below that simple surface. As a re-interpretation of an eighteenth-century Qing imperial fountain later pillaged by invading Europeans, *Circle of Animals/Zodiac Heads* raises issues of international looting, the nature of cultural patrimony, and contemporary China's relationship to its own history. Ai Weiwei cares deeply about his country, its past and its future. As China continues to emerge as a global economic power, much of his art is concerned with the alignment of that power with a concomitant social progress. In its questioning of China's history and how it is understood today, *Circle of Animals/Zodiac Heads* is part of that inquiry.

On April 3, 2011, Ai Weiwei was detained by uniformed officers at Beijing Capital Airport as he was boarding a plane for Hong Kong. Aside from a brief interview with his wife, he was held incommunicado for eighty days. These circumstances lent an urgency to the presentation of *Circle of Animals/Zodiac Heads* in New York—which Weiwei describes as a "zodiac city"—and London in late spring 2011. Now, the work not only represented Ai Weiwei's thoughts on an episode in China's complicated history, on a certain level it represented the artist himself. In the uncertain weeks before his release on June 22, it was as though the animals spoke for him.

Working with Ai Weiwei to make *Circle of Animals/Zodiac Heads* a reality was a remarkable experience. Presenting it to the public without him has been sad beyond description. Over the years Weiwei and I became friends and, in a wonderfully companionable way, fellow dreamers. *Circle of Animals/Zodiac Heads* is only one of several projects we've undertaken together. It is a testament to an intensely creative life brought to a standstill by a government that does not understand or accept the profound patriotism that Ai Weiwei embodies. I am overjoyed that Weiwei's detention has ended, but I cannot help but want more than that on his behalf: a sense of freedom that encompasses not only his physical release but also his freedom of thought, expression, and activity. I look forward with all my heart to the day when Ai Weiwei is truly at liberty, in China and in the world.

Larry Warsh
FOUNDER, AW ASIA

Introduction: Headlong into History

i

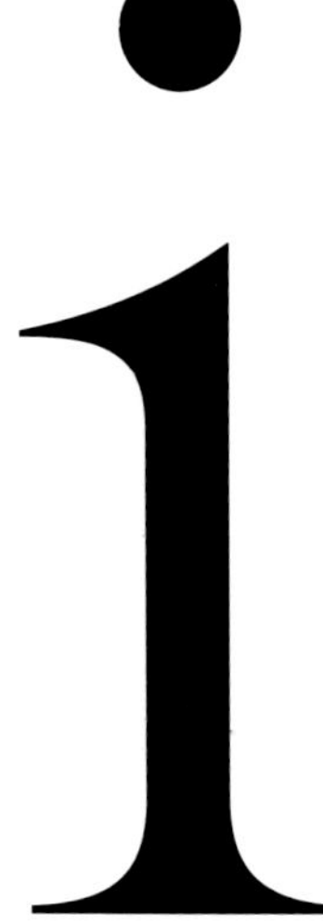

Installation view
of *Circle of Animals/
Zodiac Heads*
at Somerset House,
London, May 2011

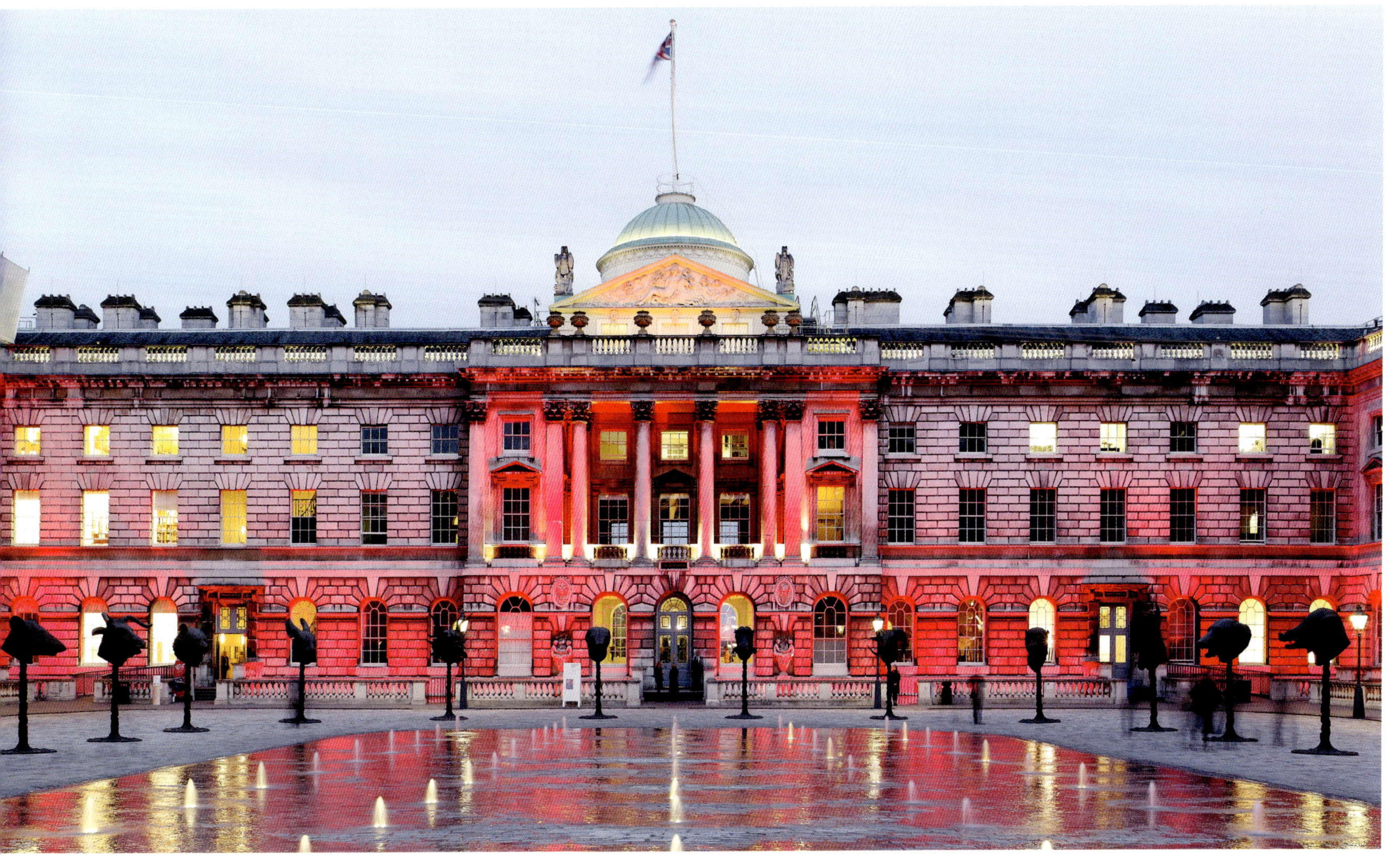

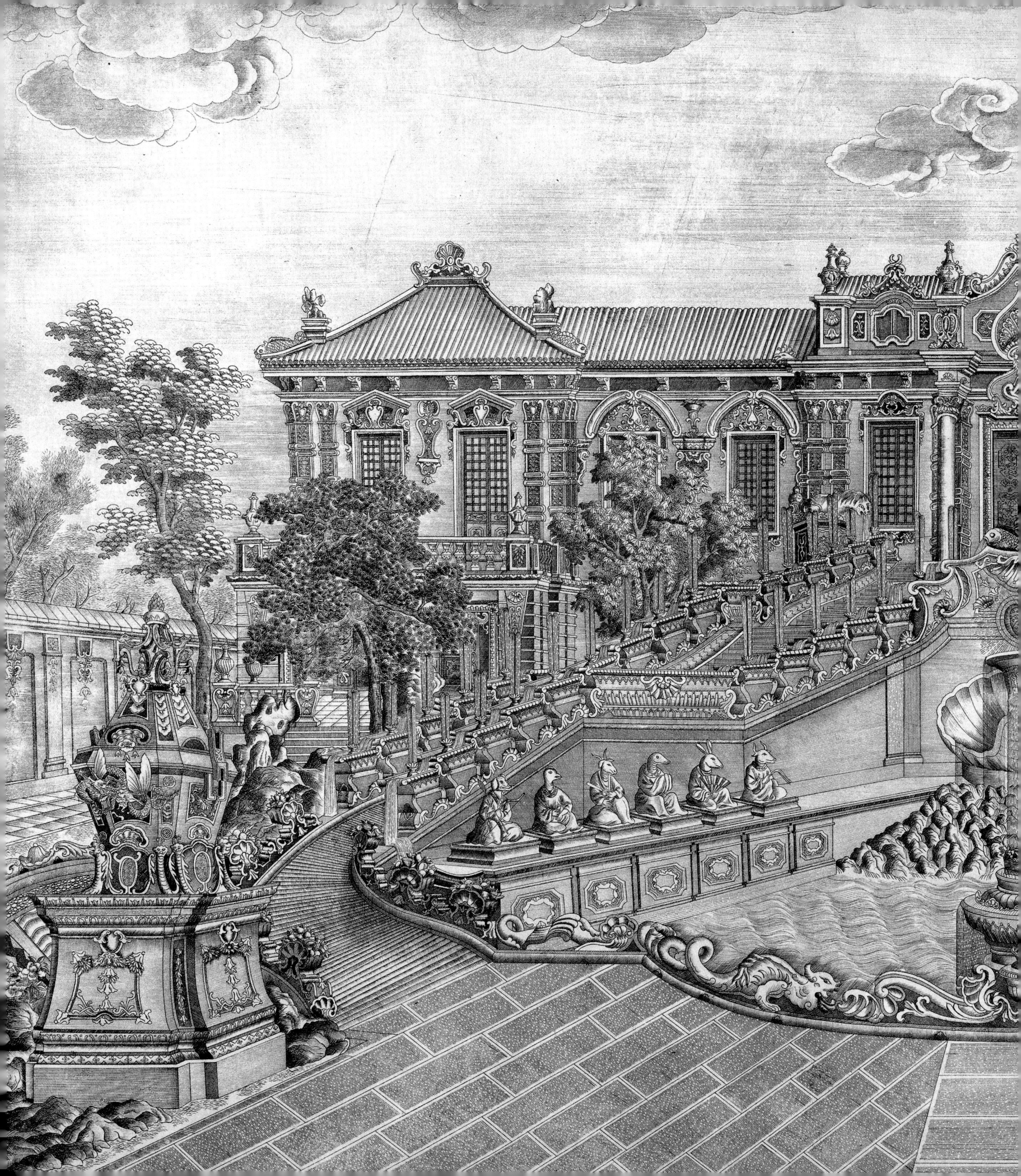

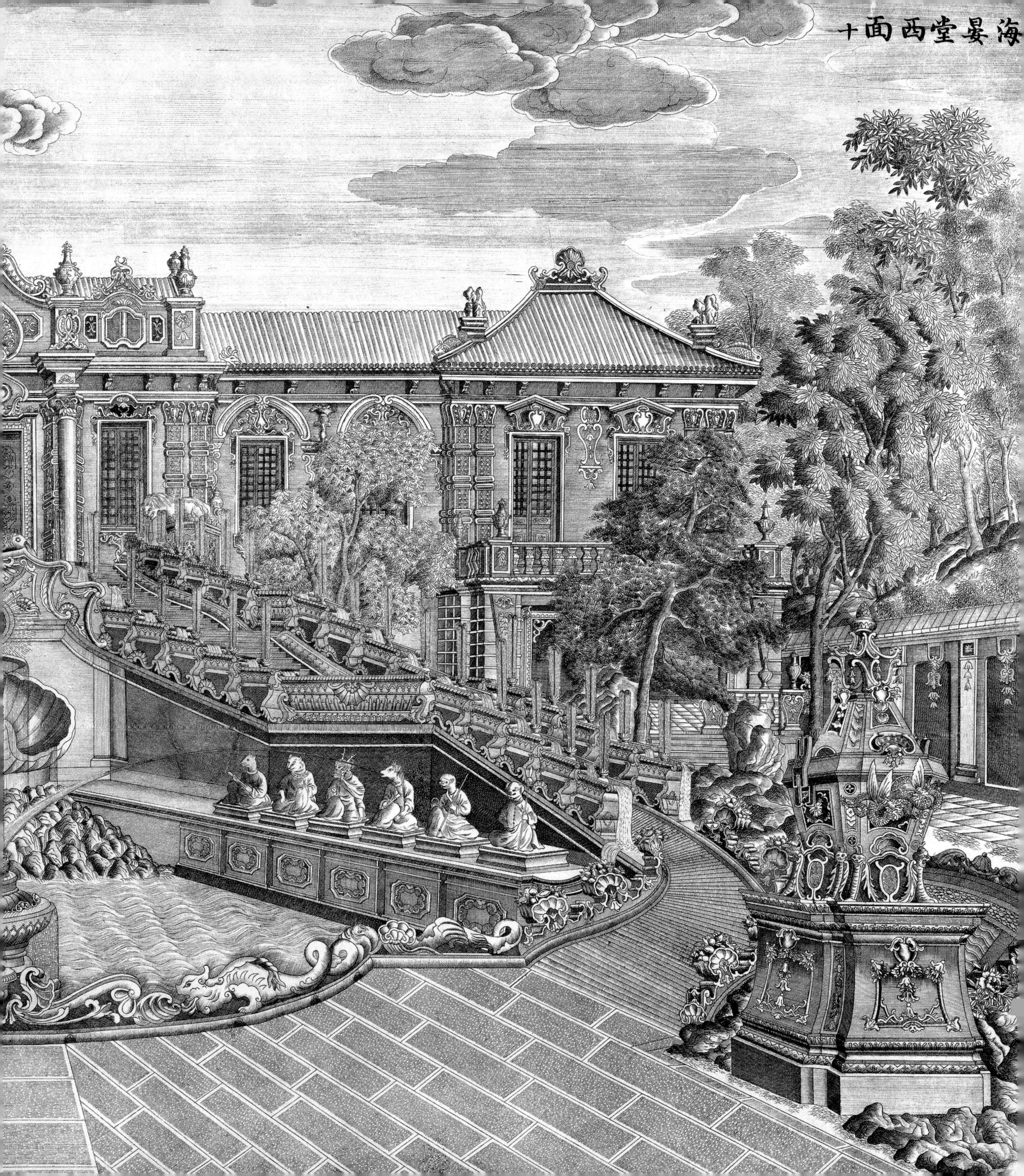
海晏堂西面 十

THE PAST IS NEVER DEAD. IT'S NOT EVEN PAST.[1]
William Faulkner's often-quoted dictum is hardly common
parlance in contemporary China, but it might as well be.
In recent years, a vivid sense of outrage over the injustices of
history—certain injustices in particular—has fueled vehement
expressions of nationalism by the Chinese government and many of
its citizens. As China continues its ascent as a world power
and its self-identity undergoes sustained transformation, the drive
to rectify past iniquities gains a parallel strength and intensity.

Much of the fervor centers on a time known in China as
the "century of national humiliation." Spanning approximately
1840 to 1945, this era saw the Chinese suffer repeated defeat
and domination by other nations, beginning with the First
Opium War (1839–42). It ended with the expulsion of foreign
powers from the mainland after World War II, or according
to some sources, with the founding of the People's Republic in
1949. The century of national humiliation is a defining episode
of Chinese history, akin to the Civil War in the United States or
the Elizabethan Era for the British. A staple of the public-
school history curriculum, it is common knowledge to virtually
all Chinese. Its locus of memory and most potent symbol is a
parkland and historic site on the northwest side of Beijing: the
Yuanming Yuan, or Garden of Perfect Brightness.

An imperial retreat established in the early eighteenth
century by the Kangxi Emperor (r. 1661–1722), the Yuanming
Yuan was enjoyed by a succession of Qing dynasty rulers,
including Kangxi, his son, the Yongzheng Emperor (r. 1722–35),
and his grandson, the Qianlong Emperor (r. 1735–96).
It was the Qianlong Emperor who, in the mid-1700s, initiated
the ambitious architectural project for which the Yuanming
Yuan is best known: a series of grand European-style fountains,
gardens, and palaces designed to house and display imperial
treasures, especially those from the West. Created under the
direction of Italian and French Jesuits serving at the emperor's
court, the European-style buildings and grounds occupied only
a small fraction of the Yuanming Yuan's vast acreage; the

greater part was filled with Chinese-style gardens and
traditional architecture constructed largely of wood. In 1860,
a century or so after Qianlong began building his European
palaces, the Yuanming Yuan was looted and burned by foreign
troops in the Second Opium War (1856–60). Ironically, it
was the ornately carved stone fountains and palaces of the
European section that survived, albeit in ruins. The Yuanming
Yuan was destroyed, its treasures carted off by invading forces,
its usable fragments scavenged by nearby residents.

Of the many works carried away from the Garden of
Perfect Brightness, one set of objects lies at the crux of this
volume: twelve bronze heads depicting the animals of the
Chinese zodiac, which had been designed as spouts for an
elaborate zodiac water-clock fountain. Positioned before the
largest of the European Palaces—the Haiyan Tang, or Palace
of the Calm Seas—the bronze heads were the defining element
in a complex set-piece that combined sculpture, hydraulics,
and Chinese and European aesthetics (fig. 1). In an interesting
twist of history, the heads have assumed a symbolic burden
far beyond their original modest function. Over the past two
decades, they have been transformed into a metonymic
shorthand for the cultural achievements of the mid-Qing era,
the losses suffered in 1860, and the humiliations that followed.
Their monetary value on the international art market has
soared, and despite their hybrid aesthetics, they have become
touchstones of a fervent and at times contentious nationalism.
Today, seven heads are accounted for; the whereabouts of
the remaining five are unknown.[2]

The zodiac heads of the Yuanming Yuan fountain are the
inspiration for *Circle of Animals/Zodiac Heads*, the 2010
sculpture by Ai Weiwei that is the impetus for this book. In
Circle of Animals/Zodiac Heads, Ai Weiwei again unites the
twelve animals, reinterpreting the extant heads and re-
envisioning those that are missing. In place of the seated
human figures, carved of stone, on which the original bronze
heads rested, he presents each animal head on a slender
column of metal, of a piece with the head itself, almost as if it
were being buoyed by a jet of water. He conceived *Circle of
Animals/Zodiac Heads* in two distinct versions: *Bronze*, a set of
oversized heads intended as outdoor public art, and *Gold*, a
smaller set for museum display, closer in size to the originals
and gilded to a bright gold finish. In *Circle of Animals/Zodiac*

PAGES 14–15: FIG. 1 Yi Lantai (active 1749–86), *West Facade of
the Palace of the Calm Seas (Haiyan Tang ximian)*, plate no. 10 in
a suite of twenty engravings entitled *The European Pavilions at
the Garden of Perfect Brightness*, 1783–86. Engraving mounted on
heavy paper, 19 ¾ x 34 ½ in. (50 x 87.5 cm)

Heads: Gold, a spirit of playfulness extends to the treatment of the bases. Most reference the original Yuanming Yuan fountain with motifs evocative of water—the dragon rising out of a magnificent whirlpool, the tiger emerging from concentric circles that echo the fur of its ruff—with one head, the snake, resting on what could be seen as a column of golden coins. In *Circle of Animals/Zodiac Heads: Bronze*, the imposing heads are positioned above eye level, inviting viewers to contemplate them from an entirely different perspective. This public art version debuted at the Bienal de São Paulo in autumn 2010; an international, multi-year tour launched in New York and London in 2011.

A WILLINGNESS TO ENGAGE WITH HISTORY, AND TO examine the uses to which history is often put is characteristic of Ai Weiwei's art. He himself has experienced something of history's vicissitudes. His father, Ai Qing (1910–1996), was one of the country's most revered modern poets. Jailed and tortured as a leftist by the Kuomintang in the 1930s, he became a key literary figure in the early days of the People's Republic, only to be swept up in a purge of intellectuals in the late 1950s. When Ai Weiwei was an infant, the family was sent to Xinjiang, a remote region in the far west that was, in terms of exile, the equivalent of Siberia. With the first wave of the Cultural Revolution in 1966, the family was further banished to a camp on the edge of the Gobi Desert, where they lived in a damp, seeping room dug from the earth. There, Ai Qing was forbidden to read or write and was pressed into daily labor cleaning latrines. After five years, the family was permitted to return to Xinjiang; Ai Weiwei was then a young teenager. In 1975, after five more years in Xinjiang, Ai Qing and his wife and children were allowed to return to Beijing.[3] Three years later, Ai Weiwei enrolled in the Beijing Film Academy, where his classmates included internationally acclaimed Fifth Generation directors Chen Kaige (*Yellow Earth, Farewell My Concubine*) and Zhang Yimou (*Raise the Red Lantern, The Story of Qiu Ju*). Ai Qing was publicly exonerated in 1978; in 1981, Ai Weiwei left for New York, where he remained for more than a decade.

It is not simply China's past, but China's ongoing relationship to its past that engages Ai Weiwei. In his oeuvre, pinballing historical references can invest even the most unassuming objects with layers of meaning, bringing a richness and unexpected dimension to the work. For viewers unfamiliar with the nuances of Chinese history, such allusions can slip by unnoticed, leaving an at-times unsettled, off-kilter sense of the work—as though something were perhaps missing, not from the art but from the knowledge one brings to it. This volume was conceived in response to that sense of "something missing." It offers a focused look not only at Ai Weiwei's art but at historical references that resonate powerfully in both versions of *Circle of Animals/Zodiac Heads*. In Western countries, China's century of humiliation is not the stuff of history textbooks, and few have heard of the Yuanming Yuan or its zodiac fountain. Fewer still understand the importance of the zodiac and its animals in Chinese cosmology and in the traditional structuring of time in hours, days, months, and years. Yet these historical factors come to bear not only on *Circle of Animals/Zodiac Heads* but on contemporary China's concept of itself as it assumes an increasingly prominent role on the world stage. For Western admirers of Ai Weiwei's art, and for those with an interest in contemporary China, the essays in this volume have much to say.

The text of *Ai Weiwei Circle of Animals* is organized in three parts, in a chronological arc that begins from and ultimately returns to the present time. The opening section looks at *Circle of Animals/Zodiac Heads* and its place in Ai Weiwei's oeuvre; the final section focuses on the meanings that contemporary culture has assigned to the original zodiac heads, as objects of value circulated on the international art market and as icons of nationalist sentiment. Between them, part two examines three historical topics, commencing with an exploration of the zodiac and its role in Chinese cosmology, progressing to an account of the creation of the Yuanming Yuan in the eighteenth century, and culminating with its looting and destruction in the nineteenth century. With the possible exception of the first topic, it would be inaccurate to assume that any of the essays pertain only to China. Indeed, one of the book's revelations is the extent to which its themes, both historical and contemporary, are international in scope; another is the degree of sophistication that characterized cultural exchanges between China and the West in the seventeenth and eighteenth centuries. While several of the authors analyze or reference the same historical events, each does so from a distinct perspective. The result is a multifaceted, overlapping portrayal, somewhat cubist in nature, of Ai Weiwei, his art, his engagement with history, and the historical events at play in *Circle of Animals/Zodiac Heads*.

The book opens with a photo gallery of *Circle of Animals/ Zodiac Heads*: *Bronze*, a suite of images of the individual heads. This suite is followed by "My Work Is Always a Readymade," excerpts from a series of interviews with the artist about *Circle of Animals/Zodiac Heads*, which were conducted in 2009–10 by Phil Tinari, Larry Warsh, Evan Osnos, and Alison Klayman, and recorded by Klayman for her feature-length documentary *Ai Weiwei: Never Sorry* (2011). In these interviews, Ai Weiwei's voice comes through clearly: good-natured, at times wry, but intensely focused and articulate about the issues that are touched on by *Circle of Animals/Zodiac Heads*, and the history that resonates through the work.

The interview excerpts are followed by Karen Smith's "Monkey King Makes Havoc: Ai Weiwei Conducts a Carnival of the Animals." In this essay, Smith approaches core themes of the work through a consideration of nineteenth-century British imperialism and the events leading to the looting and burning of the Yuanming Yuan in 1860. She casts the specifics of Ai Weiwei's art and life against the broader context of Chinese history, examining the cultural currents that have helped shape his outlook as well as his art. Smith takes a holistic view of Ai Weiwei's practice, seeing his blogging and micro-blogging as being of a piece with the rest of his art, all of it poised to question China's relationship to its own history, and the role that art can and should play in contemporary Chinese society.

Charles Merewether's essay, "The Original and the Copy: Ai Weiwei and the Fate of the Zodiac Heads," also takes a historical episode as its point of departure—in this case the creation of the Yuanming Yuan under a succession of mid-Qing emperors. Adapted from his book *Ai Weiwei: Under Construction* (published by the University of New South Wales Press in 2008 and now out of print), Merewether's essay approaches Ai Weiwei's use of history from a somewhat different perspective, examining in depth the artist's subtle play with concepts— Duchampian, Warholian, and otherwise—of the original and its reproduction, and the potential for an object's meaning to be radically transformed in a contemporary context. Following

Merewether's essay is a suite of images of the individual heads that comprise *Circle of Animals/Zodiac Heads*: *Gold*.

From an initial focus on Ai Weiwei and *Circle of Animals/ Zodiac Heads*, the book turns to explore the circumstances surrounding the original bronze zodiac heads of the Yuanming Yuan fountain. Stepping far back into history, Paola Demattè opens the second section with an examination of the zodiac and its role in Chinese cosmology. For many Westerners, the Chinese zodiac is little more than a light diversion, something one might encounter in a New Age bookstore or Chinatown restaurant. Demattè's essay, "*Circle of Animals/Zodiac Heads* and the Twelve-Animal Cycle in China," meticulously restores the animals to their key role in the structuring of time in Chinese tradition, examining their function across multiple chronological cycles. In an added boon, Demattè takes a close look at the engraving of the Haiyan Tang fountain reproduced as fig. 1, analyzing it from a traditional chronological perspective, down to the hour of day that it depicts.

Marco Musillo's "Mid-Qing Arts and Jesuit Visions: Encounters and Exchanges in 18th-Century Beijing" focuses on the origins of the Yuanming Yuan's European section in the Jesuit mission at the Beijing court and in the voracious appetites of Qing emperors for knowledge of the West. In chronicling the cultural exchange that, over decades, led to the creation of the European section of the Yuanming Yuan, Musillo draws detailed portraits of three rulers, their personal preferences, and their intellectual pursuits. What emerges is a fascinating account of a sustained cross-cultural collaboration, and an illuminating perspective on the European Palaces and their symbolic importance in the Qing imperial worldview.

Picking up the historical thread, Kristina Kleutghen's "Heads of State: Looting, Nationalism, and Repatriation of the Zodiac Bronzes" offers a glimpse of the Yuanming Yuan's European section as a marvel of eighteenth-century innovation and cross-cultural exchange, then examines in detail the events leading to the Yuanming Yuan's destruction in 1860 and the heads' subsequent commodification on the open market. She traces their shifting fortunes in the context of China's century of humiliation and its continued reverberation in contemporary Chinese culture, a national narrative as yet unfinished.

The original zodiac heads and their value, symbolic and monetary, in contemporary global culture are the subject of the book's third section. It opens with "The Heads at Auction: Two Experts Weigh In," excerpts from filmed interviews by Alison Klayman and Colin Jones with Chinese art experts Lark E. Mason, who conducted groundbreaking research on the heads at Sotheby's in the 1980s, and Joe-Hynn Yang, a senior vice president at Christie's at the time of the sale, in 2009, of the rat and rabbit heads. Both Mason and Yang personally handled individual heads in preparing them for auction, and their insights encompass not only the heads' histories as art-market prizes, but their characteristics as objects and the craftsmanship that went into their creation. Rounding out this final section, Jones's "The Zodiac Heads and the Auction Block" recounts the recent sale history of the seven known heads, focusing in detail on the rat and rabbit heads owned by the late fashion designer Yves Saint Laurent, which were at the center of the auction that Yang describes: the highly controversial and ultimately aborted sale by Christie's in February 2009. Jones's survey of the heads' auction histories reveals how their soaring art-market value coincided and is interwoven with their emerging significance as nationalist icons, and with China's increasing stature as a world power. As he observes, these linked dynamics continue to exert a powerful influence on the global art market, which is likely to grow stronger as the century unfolds.

THE AUTHORS WHO CONTRIBUTED TO THIS VOLUME are not only scholars but by necessity translators, each arriving at English equivalents for the Chinese terms that are commonly cited in these texts. For the ease of Western readers, we have rendered these phrases in a common vocabulary, and have taken up the suggestion by China scholar Geremie Barmé to use the term "Yuanming Yuan" rather than "Yuanmingyuan"—the latter being more consistent with Chinese grammar but more challenging for English-reading eyes. The same is true for "Haiyan Tang," which is also presented in this text as two words rather than one. Virtually all of the contributors sharply rejected the terms "Summer Palace" or "Old Summer Palace," which have been used since the nineteenth century in referring to the Yuanming Yuan. Though common in French as well as English, the terms are erroneous. Sited just outside Beijing, the Yuanming Yuan was a year-round imperial retreat, and in some instances—notably for the Yongzheng Emperor—the primary imperial residence. (As Kristina Kleutghen points out, the true imperial summer retreat was located 250 kilometers north of Beijing.) For these reasons, throughout the book the Yuanming Yuan is called by that name, or by the translation the "Garden of Perfect Brightness." The terms "Summer Palace" and "Old Summer Palace" appear only in direct citations of Western historical references.

AW ASIA IS PLEASED TO HAVE TAKEN A LEAD ROLE in the development of *Ai Weiwei: Circle of Animals*. As a private organization dedicated to promoting the field of contemporary Chinese art through publications, educational programs, curatorial projects, and institutional loans and acquisitions, AW Asia actively seeks out publishing projects that advance its mission. This volume, with its focus on a major public artwork and its ambitious historical scope, reflects AW Asia's interest in advancing an understanding of contemporary Chinese art that goes beyond media headlines and art-market dynamics. Like *Circle of Animals/Zodiac Heads*, the book looks to draw greater attention not only to the zodiac fountain of the Yuanming Yuan, but to the complex ways in which the past remains with us and continues to shape the future.

---

1. William Faulkner, *Requiem for a Nun* (New York: Vintage Books, 1975), 80.

2. The missing animals are the dragon, snake, ram, rooster, and dog.

3. Some sources, including the *New York Times*, have reported the year of the family's return to Beijing as 1976. In an email to the author dated March 25, 2011, the archivist at Ai Weiwei Studio confirmed the year as 1975.

Circle of Animals/

Zodiac Heads

BRO

NZE

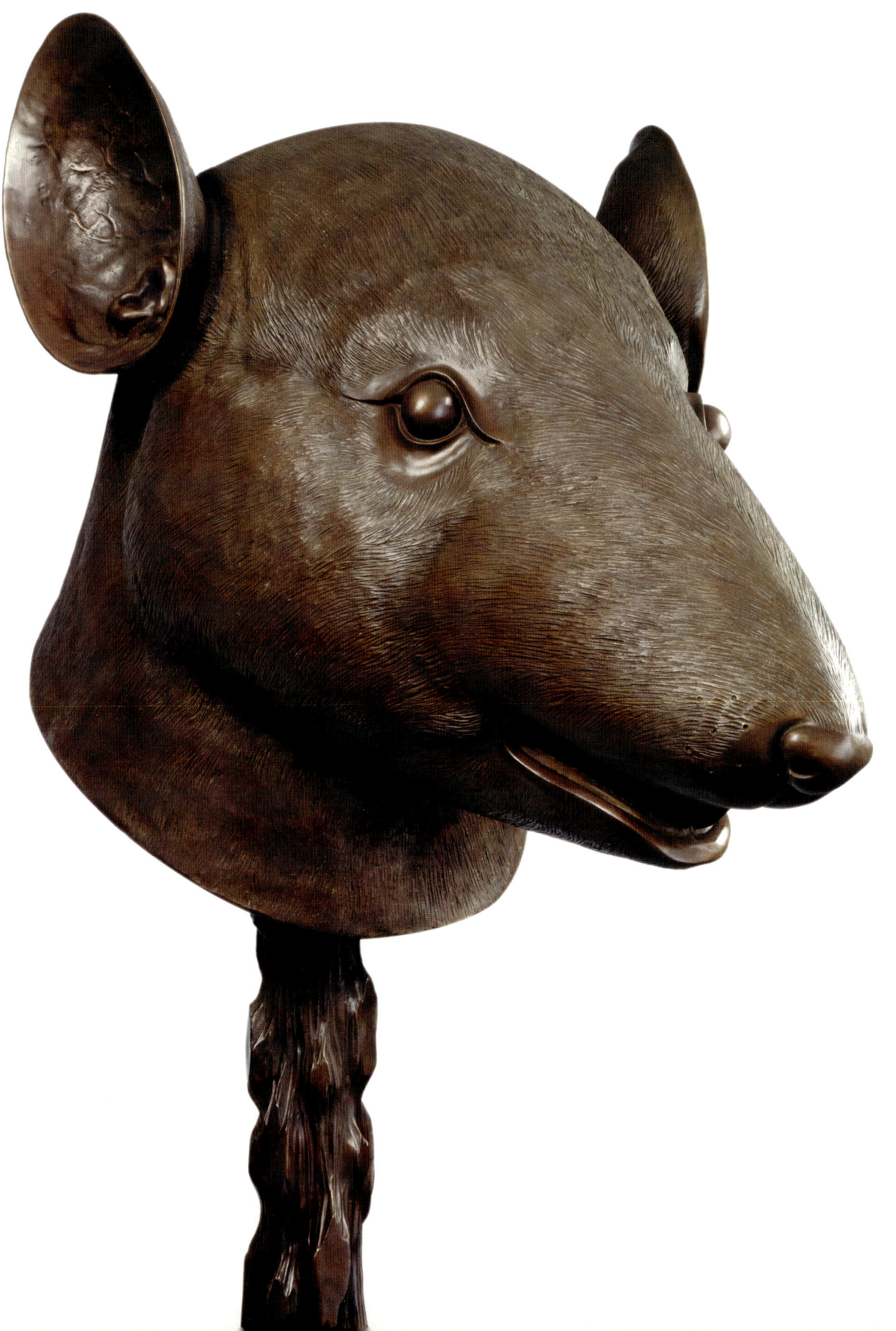

Rat

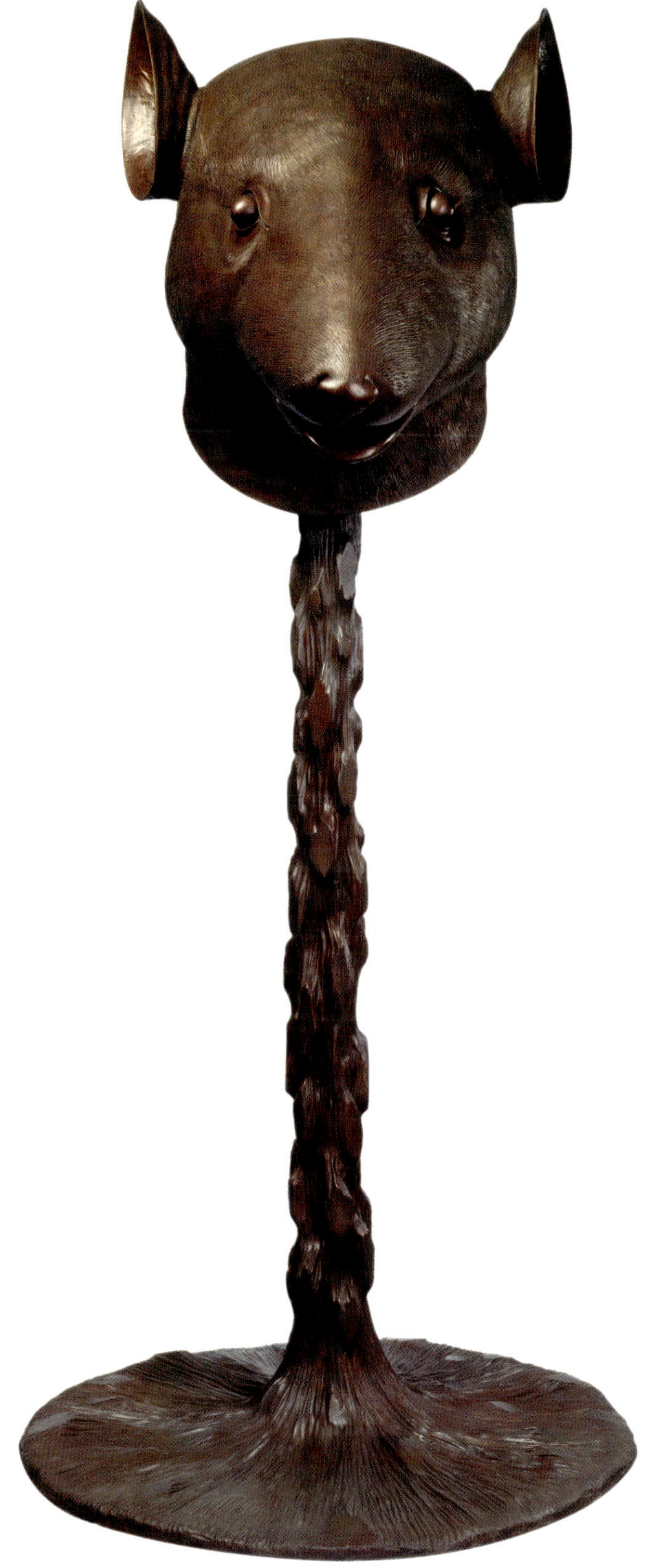

(*laoshu* 老鼠) 11 p.m.–1 a.m.

According to a Chinese fable, the rat came to
be first in the twelve-animal cycle because, in a
race set up by the Buddha to determine the order
of the twelve animals, the rat surreptitiously
rode on the ox's back, dismounting just before
the finish line to rush ahead and win the race.
This story highlights the qualities of the
rat, an animal generally believed to be shy and
mean, but which in China is also a symbol of
intelligence, innovation, industry, and wealth.
The good qualities that Chinese tradition
attributes to the rat (or mouse) stem from these
animals' uncanny ability to find and hoard
food—qualities that also can be seen in a negative
light, and so the rat sometimes appears in
Chinese fables and paintings as the emblem of
corrupt officials or profiteers.

2010
Bronze
119 x 53 x 62 in.
(302.3 x 127.2 x 157.5 cm)

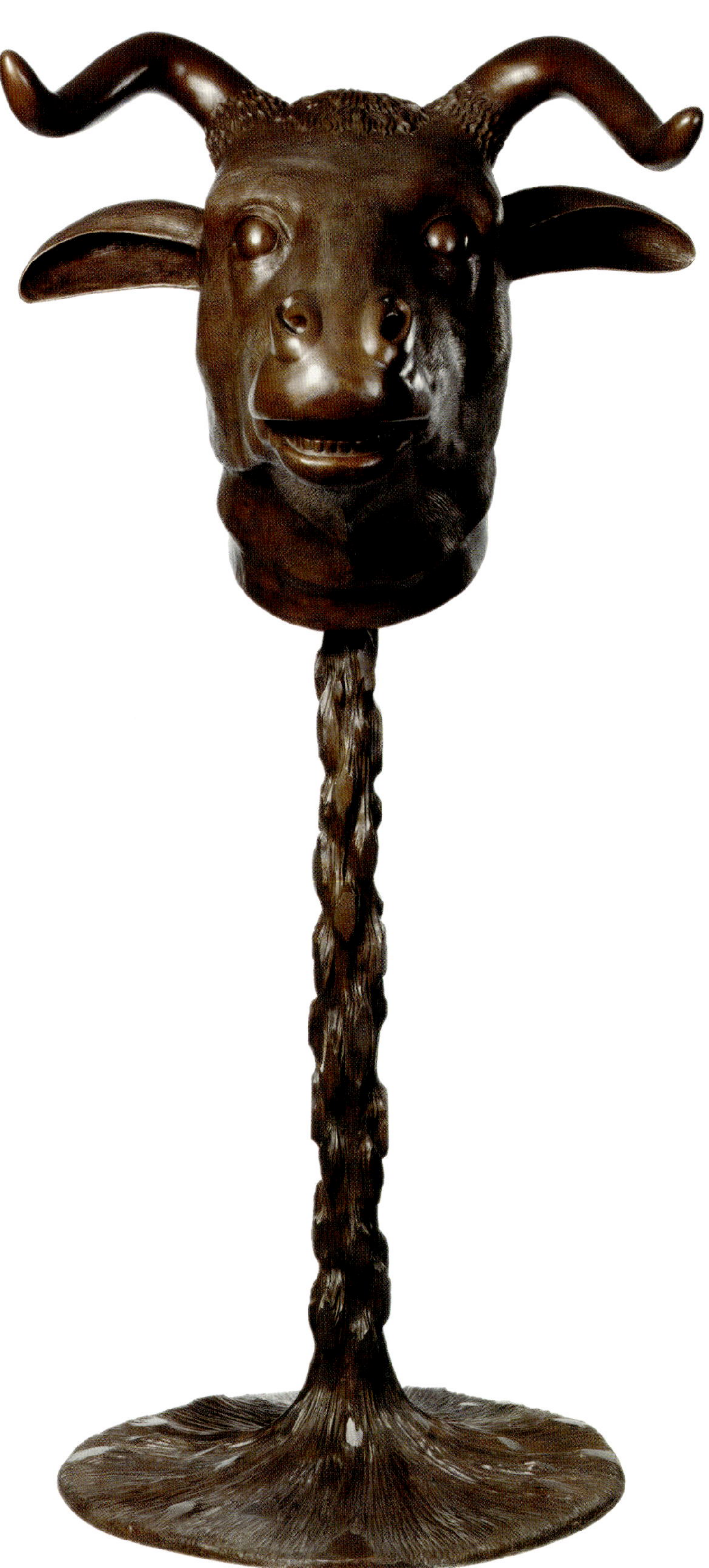

Ox

(*niu* 牛) 1–3 a.m.

The ox (or water buffalo, which is common in China's southern regions) played a key role in agriculture and by extension in agricultural rituals and religion in China. Its association with the plowing of fields in springtime made the ox a symbol of that season and the earth. Archaeological evidence shows that since antiquity this animal was employed in ritual sacrifices to natural deities or royal ancestors and that its bones (particularly the shoulder bones) were used in divination by fire and as writing surfaces (the so-called oracle bone inscriptions). Aside from being an important agricultural symbol, the ox and ox herding were adopted by Chan (Zen) Buddhists and Taoists alike with reference to the patient training of the mind towards greater awareness and as symbolic of the return to the source. The legendary Taoist philosopher Laozi is often represented riding an ox or a water buffalo, because legend has it that he wrote the *Daodejing* (Tao Te Ching) on the back of this animal.

2010
Bronze
128 x 62 x 63 in.
(325.1 x 157.5 x 160 cm)

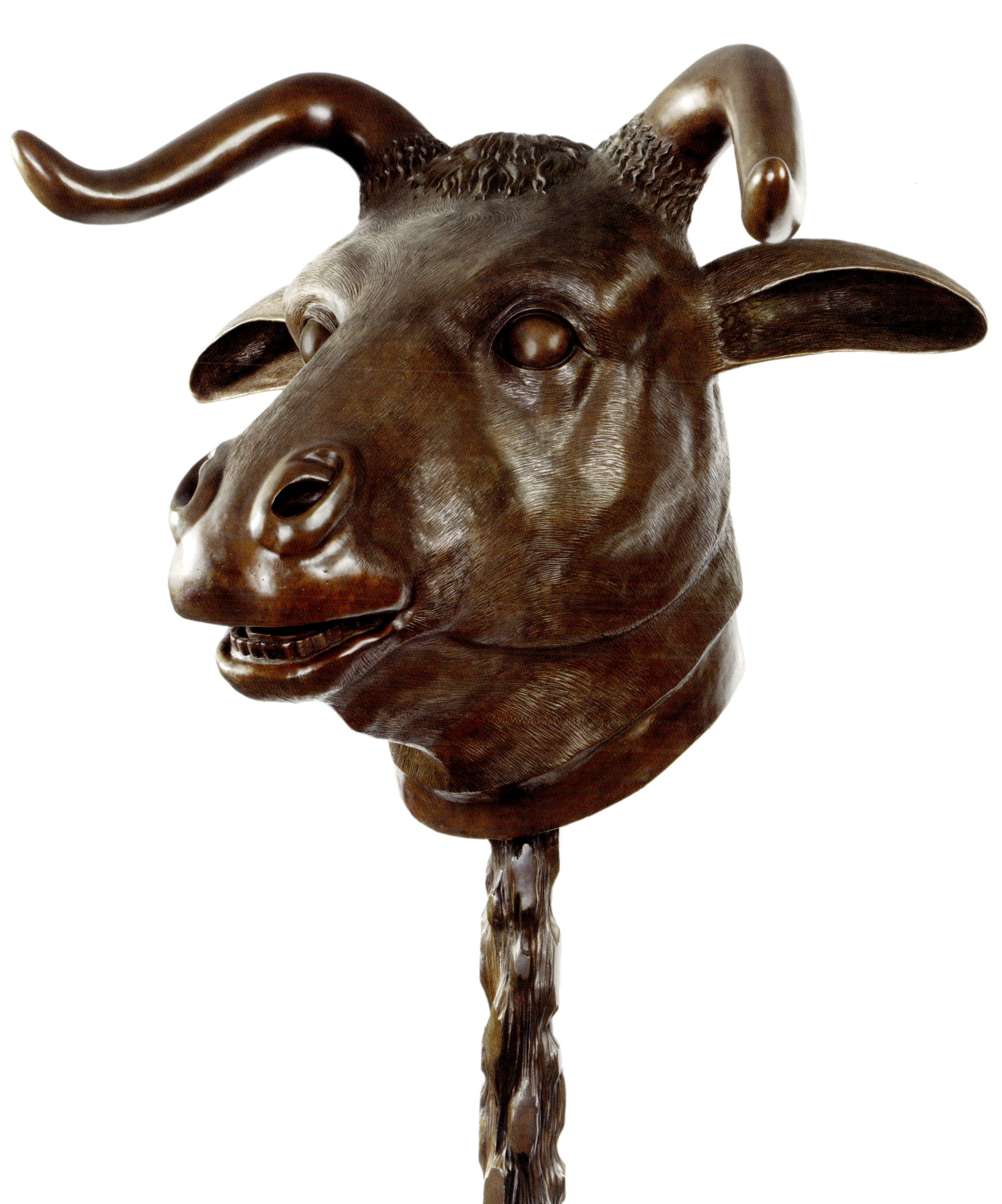

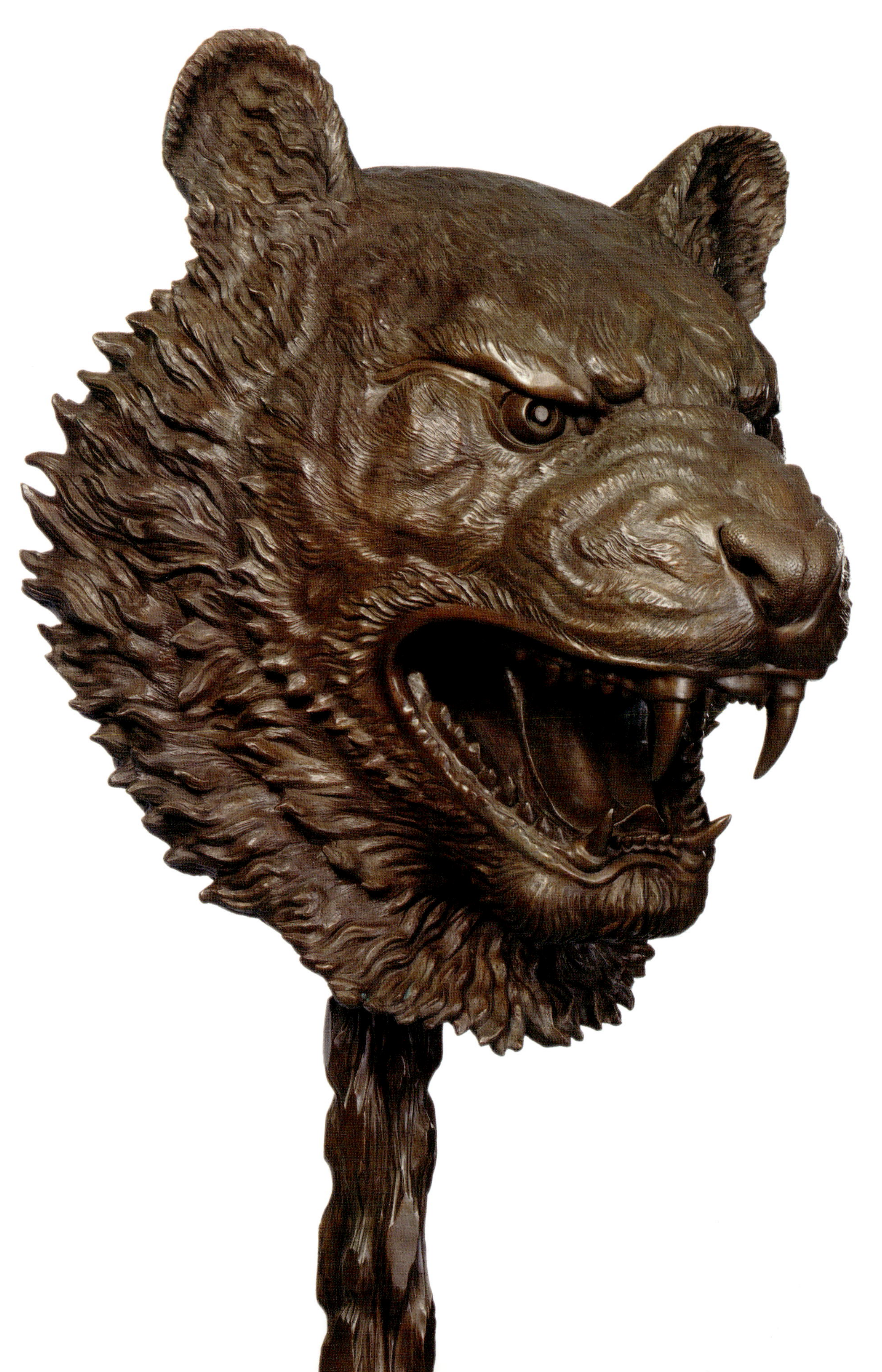

Tiger

(*hu* 虎) 3–5 a.m.

The tiger appears often in Chinese literature and art and is considered the king (*wang*) of animals. In a Neolithic tomb in central China, a tiger and dragon mosaic was found arranged around the body of the deceased. This is one of the earliest representations of the mythical white tiger (*baihu*), the emblem of the west and a symbol of the constellation by that name that occupies the western quadrant of the sky (as a pendant to the green dragon of the east). In one story, the immortal Xiwangmu (Queen Mother of the West), who presides over the orchard of longevity peaches, is shown either sporting a tiger tail or accompanied by a tiger. Tigers are also represented in schematic designs on Bronze Age ritual vessels and are frequently seen in Taoist paintings, either alone or accompanying immortals and sages.

2010
Bronze
129 x 53 x 62 in.
(327.7 x 134.6 x 157.5 cm)

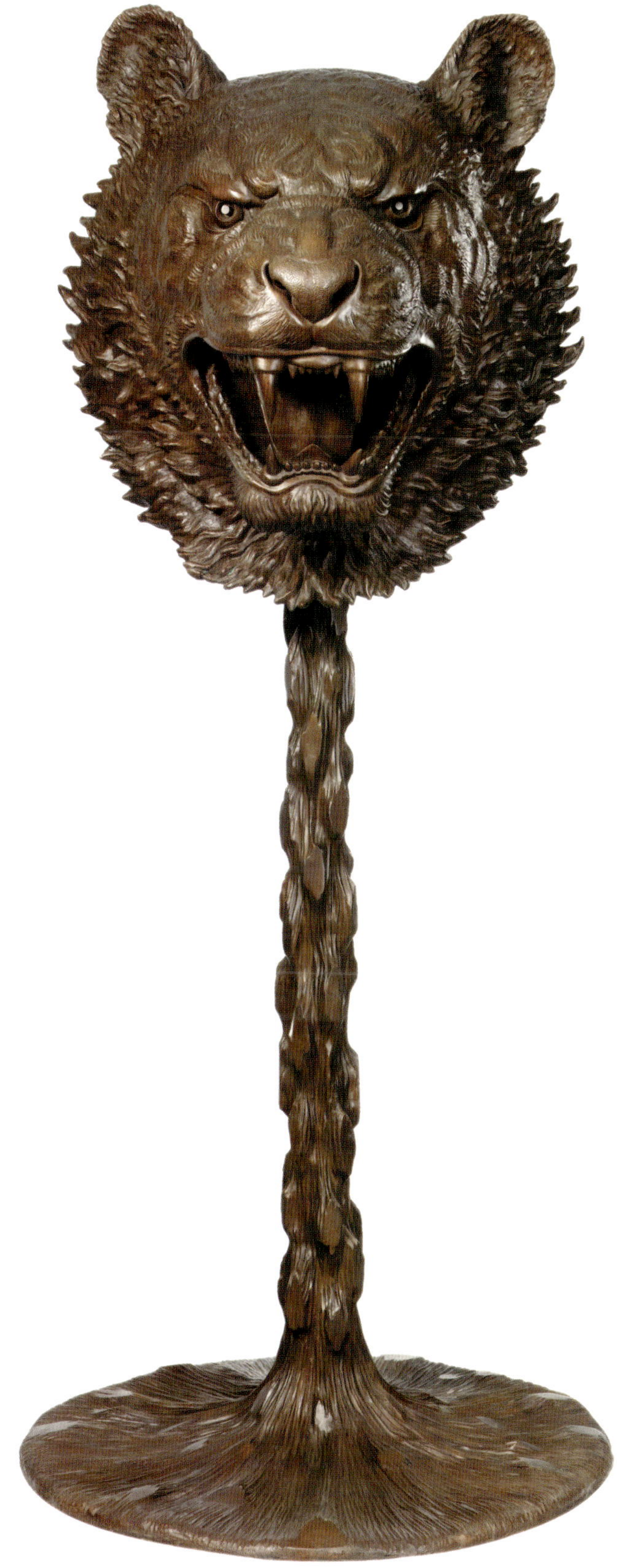

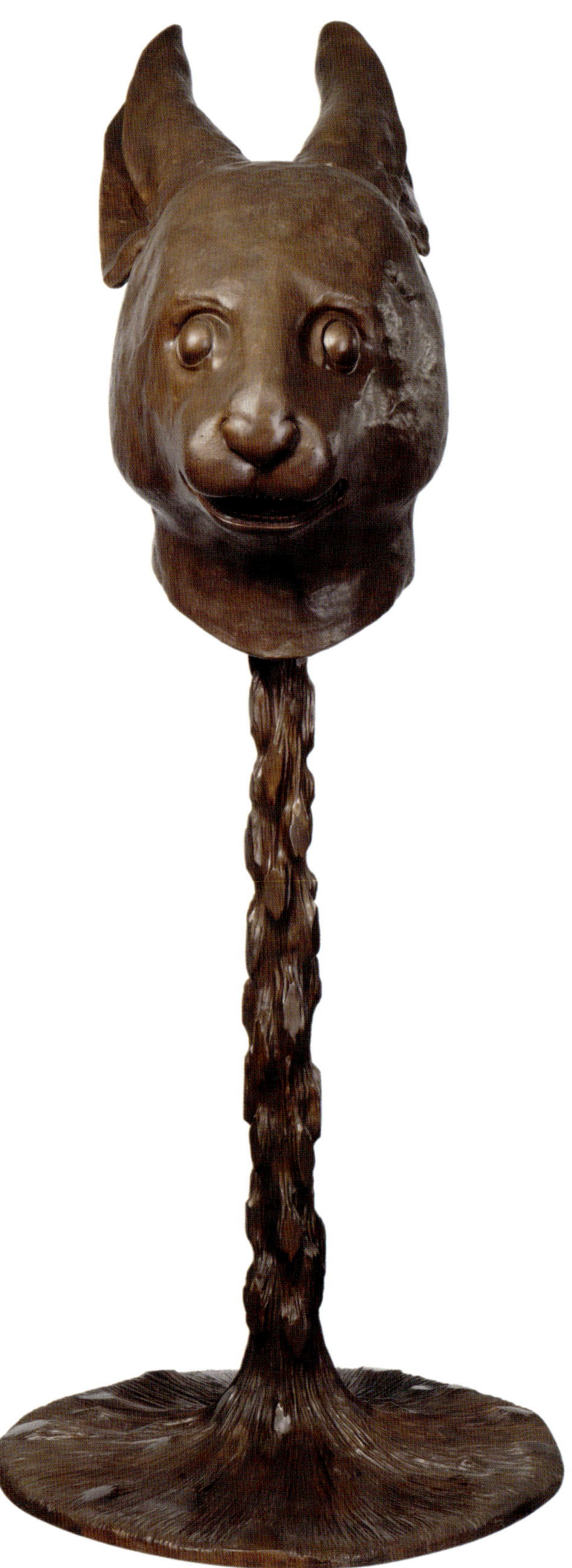

Rabbit

(*tu* 兔) 5–7 a.m.

The rabbit or hare has in Chinese lore a close connection with the moon, of which it is thought to be an emanation. According to a famous fairy tale, on the moon there is a jade rabbit (*yutu*), who stands at the foot of a cassia tree pounding a pestle in a mortar to crush the ingredients for the elixir of immortality. A Buddhist story tells that the image of the rabbit was placed on the moon as a reward for this animal having offered its body to feed a hungry beggar who turned out to be a god. In China, the rabbit is also shown preparing its elixir in the company of the Queen Mother of the West, the female immortal. This animal is a symbol of longevity and, for obvious reasons, of fertility. Legend has it that rabbits conceive by looking at the moon and that they live to be one thousand years old. Once they reach five hundred years of age, they turn white and, if seen, are omens of good things to come.

2010
Bronze
129 x 53 x 62 in.
(327.7 x 134.6 x 157.5 cm)

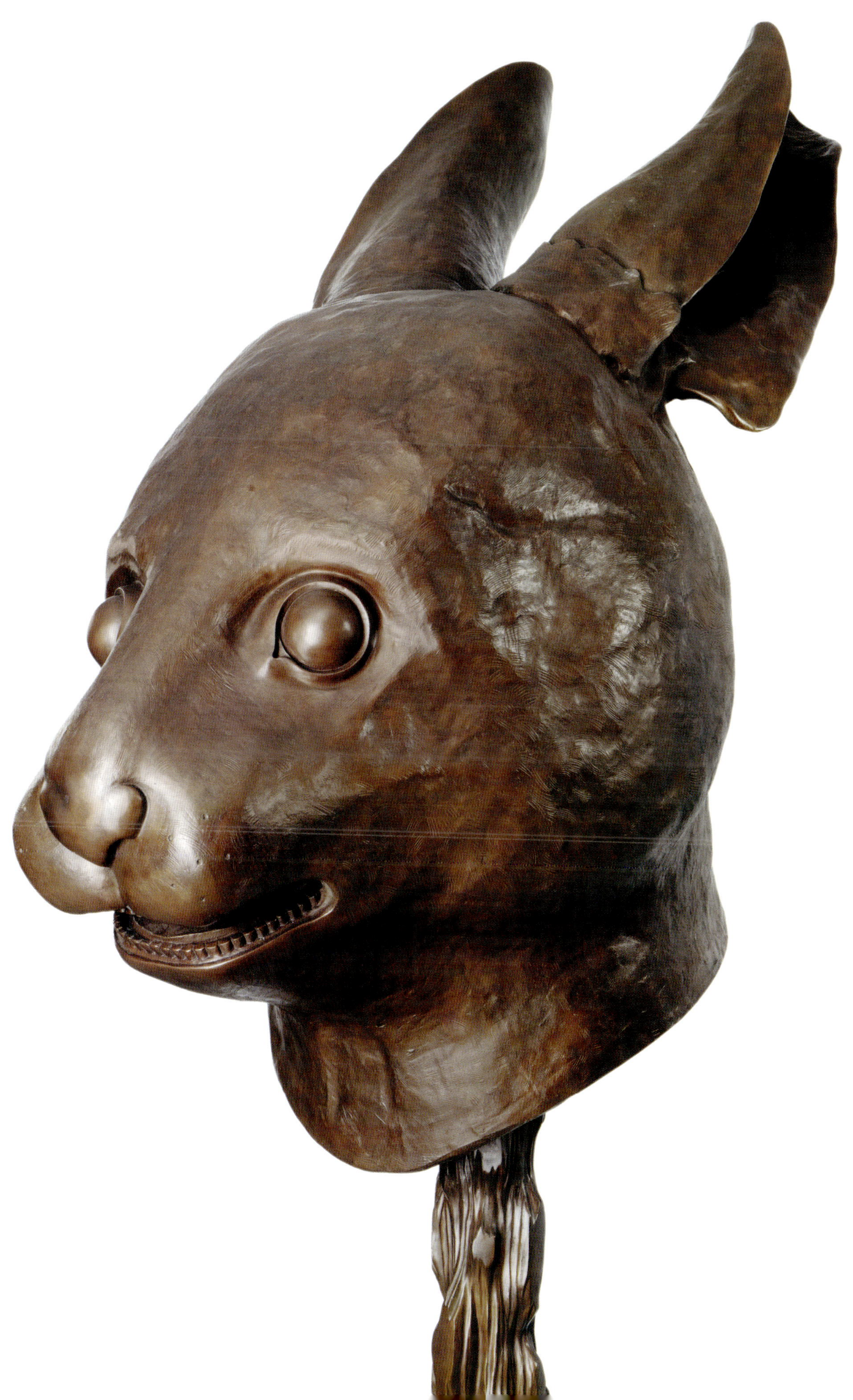

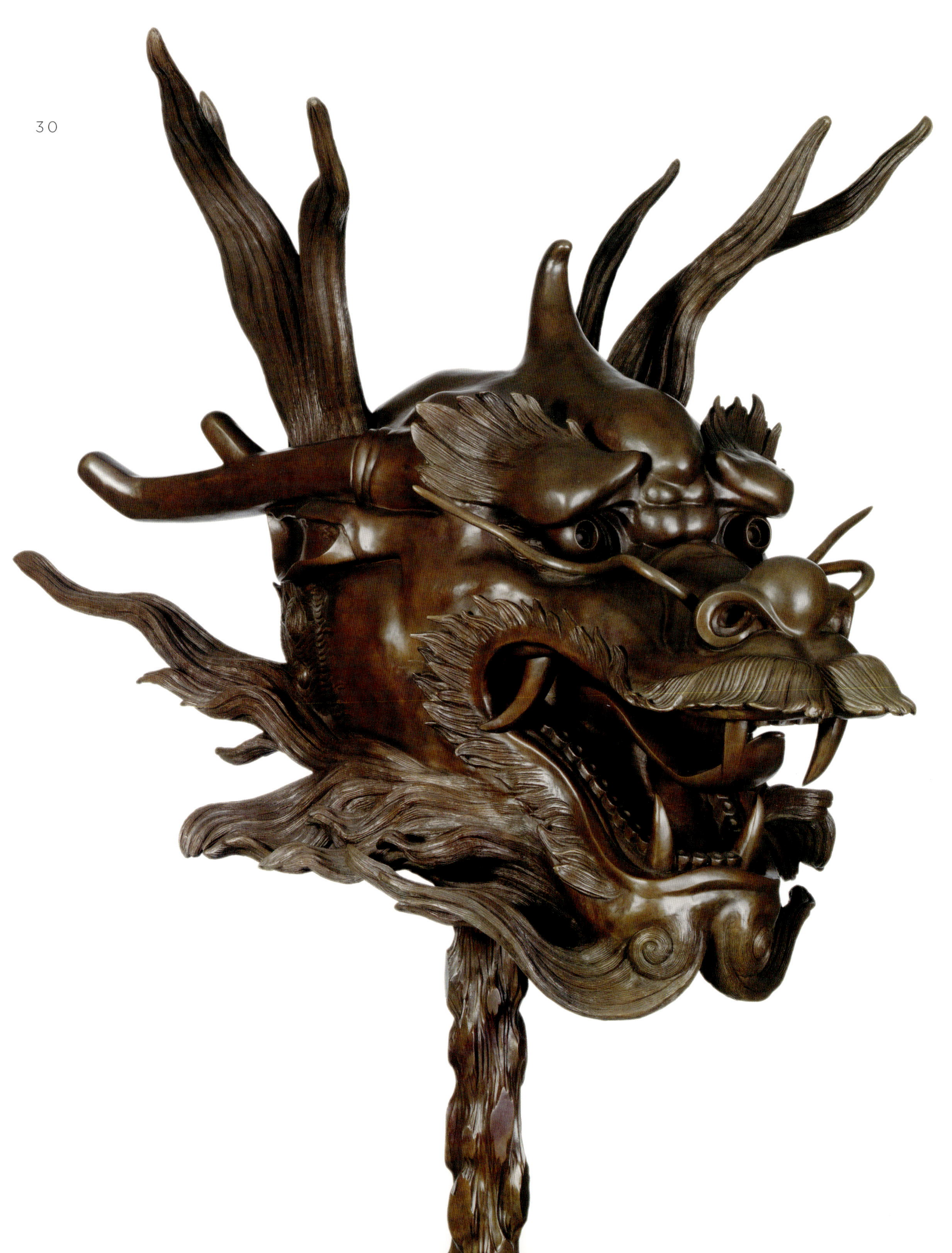

Dragon

(*long* 龙) 7–9 a.m.

The dragon, the most auspicious of the twelve animals, was a symbol of the emperor's power in dynastic China. Its origins are very ancient and its image was prominent on imperial robes and porcelain. Archaeologists have traced the earliest images of the dragon to the prehistoric period, when they were painted on pottery or fashioned into jade pendants. The dragon, the only imaginary creature among the twelve, is said to be a composite with the horns of a deer, a camel's head, the eyes of a demon, the body of a snake, and the scales of the carp. The dragon has 117 scales, 81 of them *yang* and 36 *yin*. The dragon is also linked with astronomy because the green dragon (*qinglong*) constellation is a symbol of the east and thus of the rising sun. A dragonlike creature with one horn, known as the *qilin*, announced the birth of Confucius by carrying a jade tablet with a message to the mother of the philosopher. In modern China, this creature is still perceived as fortunate, and the year of the dragon often causes an upsurge in birth rates.

2010
Bronze
134 x 66 x 77 in.
(340.4 x 167.6 x 195.6 cm)

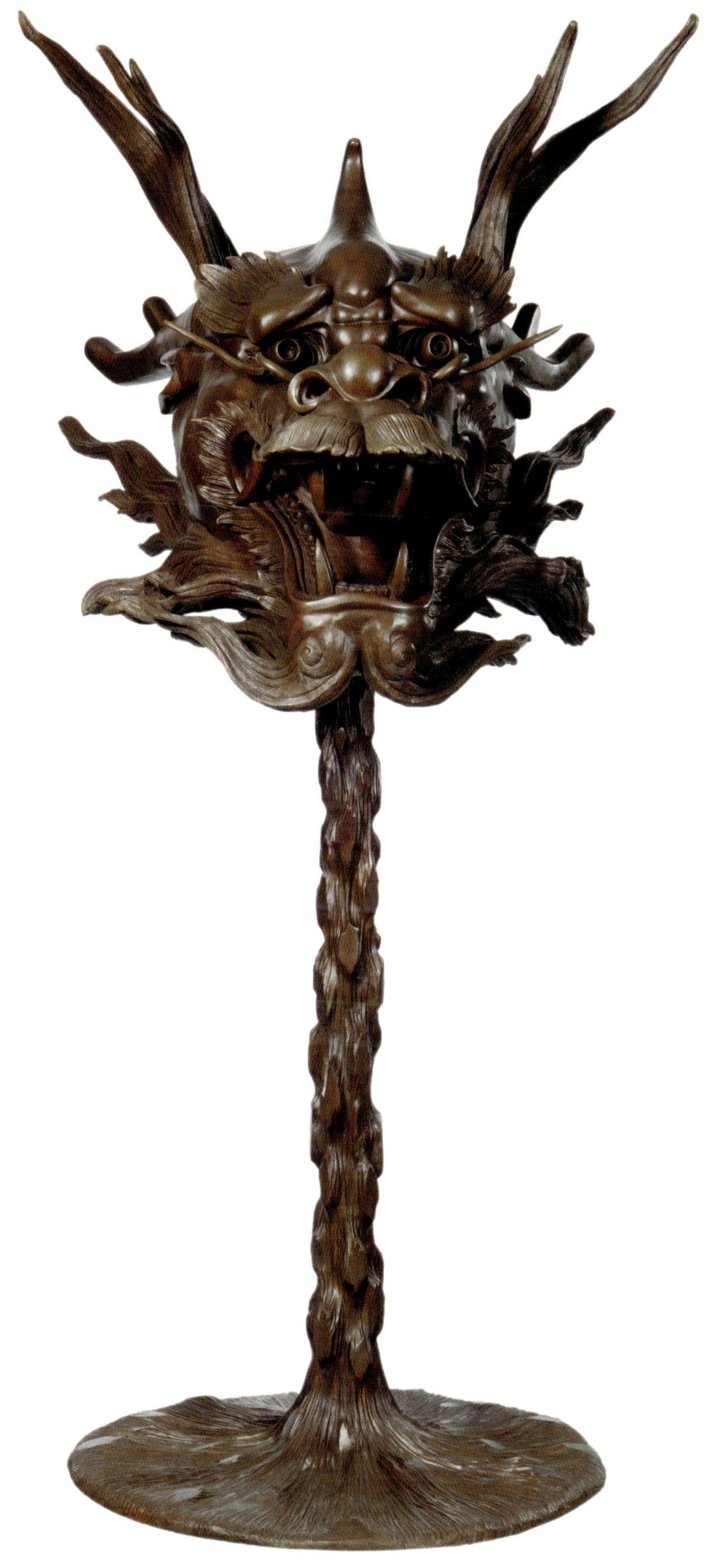

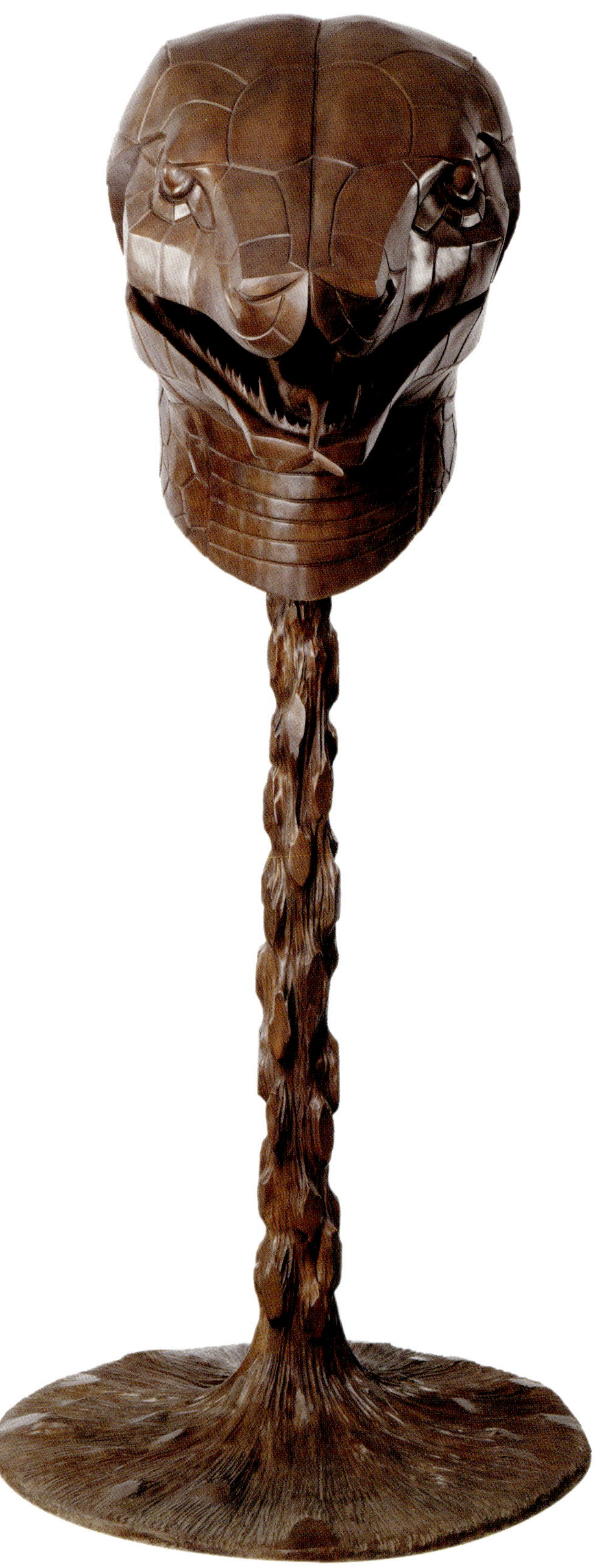

Snake

(*she* 蛇) 9–11 a.m.

The snake is believed to be closely related
to the dragon, and though its image is not as
benevolent, it is said to have supernatural
powers. In fact, though snakes are considered
cunning and even evil, they are venerated and
feared because they are thought to be the
embodiments of demons and spirits. Therefore,
to buy a captive snake with the intention of
liberating it is a virtuous action, even though
Chinese tales caution against befriending these
creatures. According to the legend of the White
Snake, a young scholar fell in love with a
white snake demon that had turned itself into a
beautiful maiden. When her true identity was
revealed, disaster ensued and the snake demon
was thrown into a well. Not all images of the
snake are so daunting. In antiquity, immortals
were thought of as half-human, half-animal
creatures featuring long snake tails. Images
of such creatures appear often in the interior
decoration of early dynastic burials. Similar
to the immortals are Nüwa and Fuxi, the
Chinese creators of the world, who are
represented with human upper bodies and
interlocking snake coils.

2010
Bronze
118 x 53 x 63 in.
(299.7 x 134.6 x 160 cm)

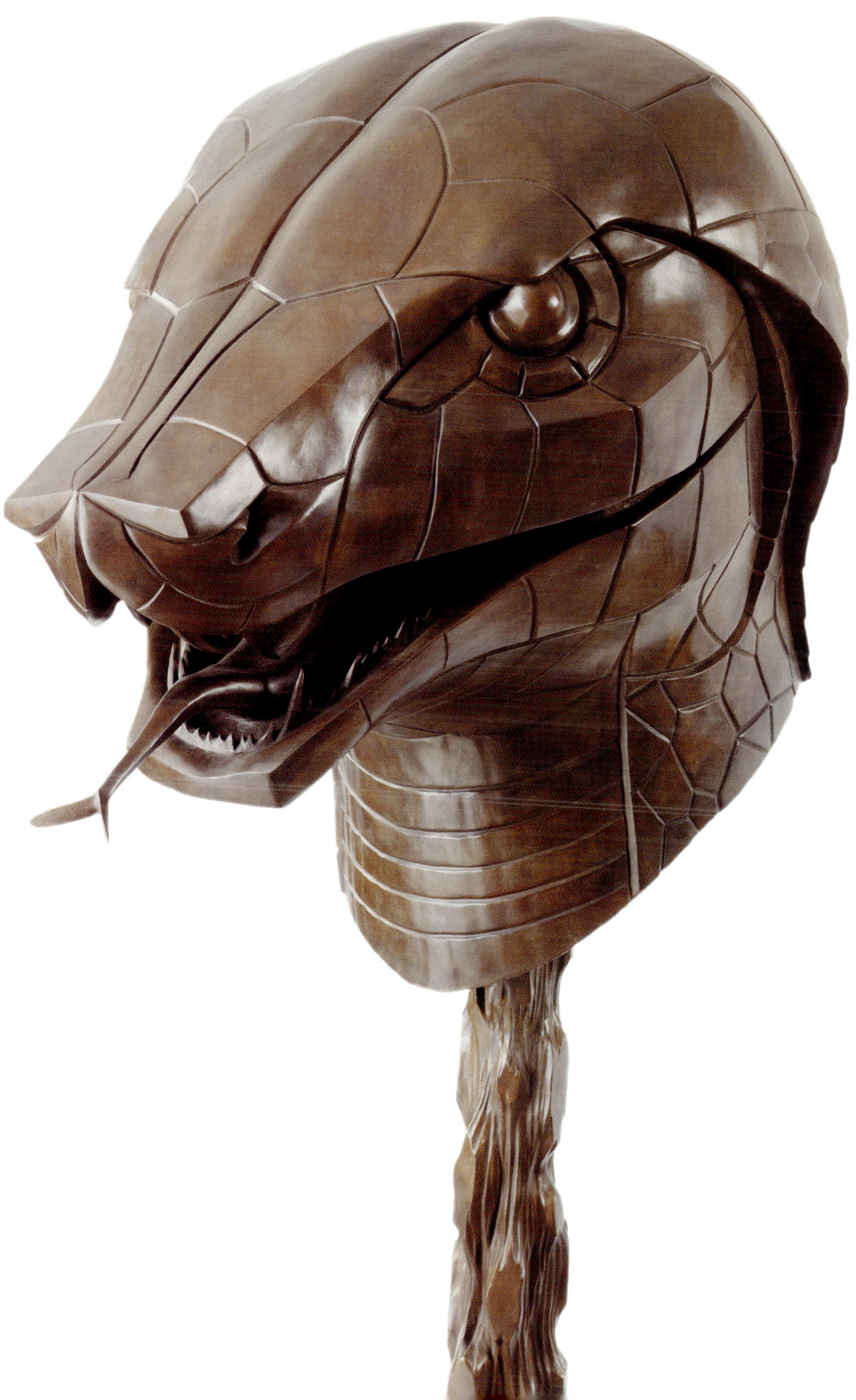

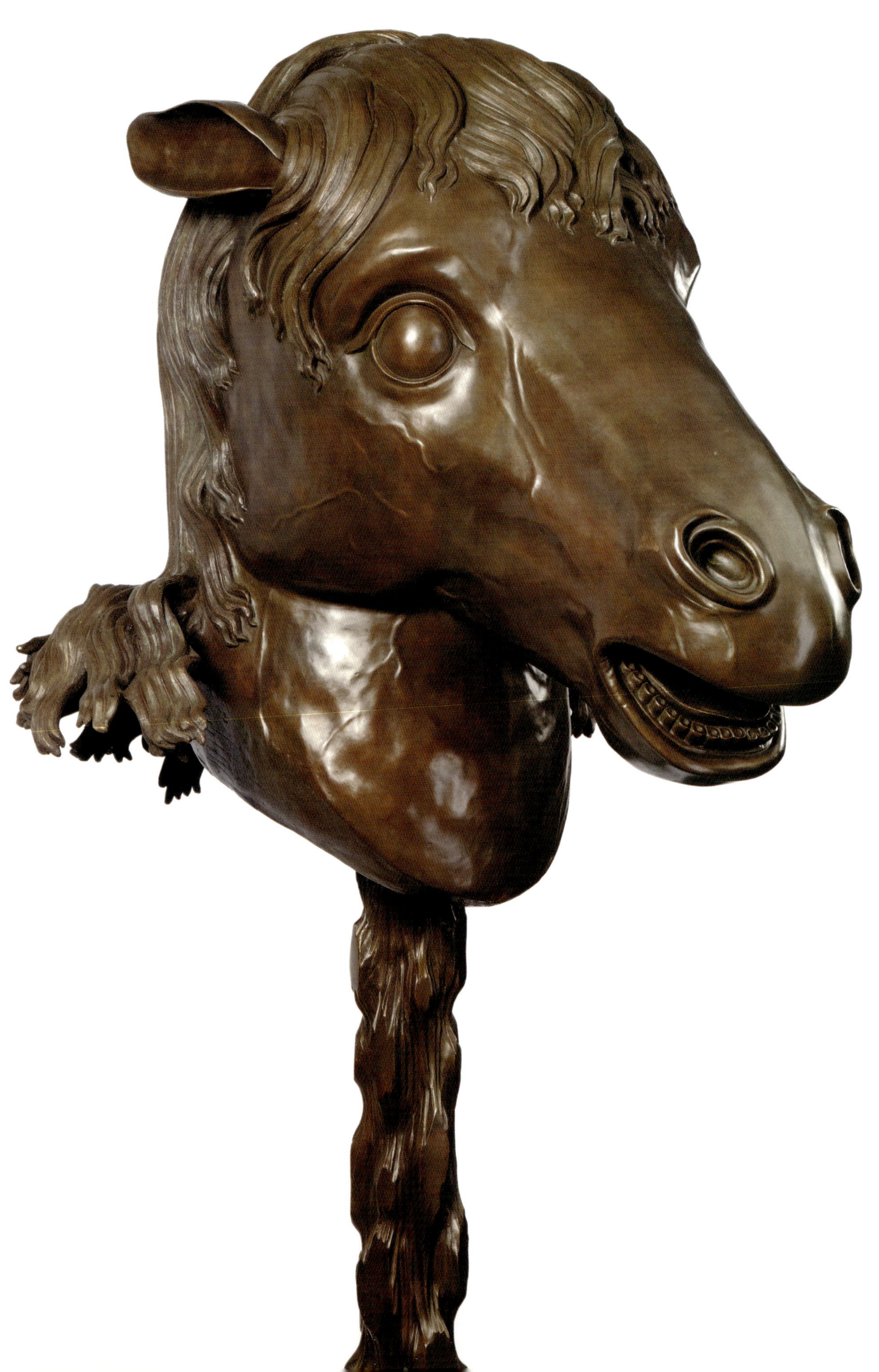

Horse

(*ma* 马) 11 a.m.–1 p.m.

The horse appears for the first time in the Yellow River valley during the Bronze Age alongside the chariot, having been introduced probably through contacts with inner Asian nomad pastoralists. As witnessed by the numerous life-size statues of horses in the terracotta army of the first emperor of China, among other evidence, horses played a paramount role in China's history. Notwithstanding their strategic importance, good horses often had to be imported from Central Asia at great cost because of local breeding difficulties. For these reasons, the horse was seen as a valuable and, to a certain extent, exotic animal. Tang dynasty writers often marveled at the fabled heavenly horses of Ferghana, hardy and fast animals thought to sweat blood. The famous ceramic Tang horse figurines, which are much appreciated by collectors, represent this breed. Horses also were commonly portrayed in paintings.

2010
Bronze
119 x 53 x 61 in.
(302.3 x 134.6 x 154.9 cm)

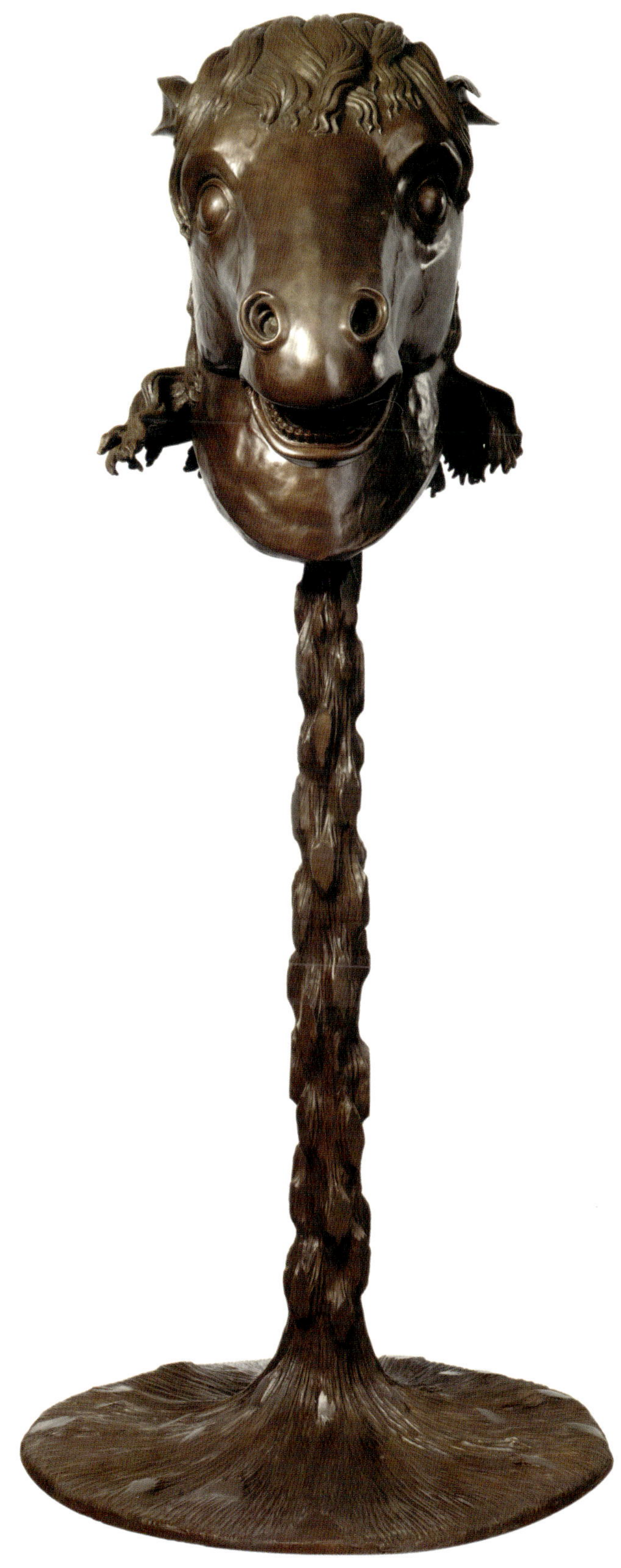

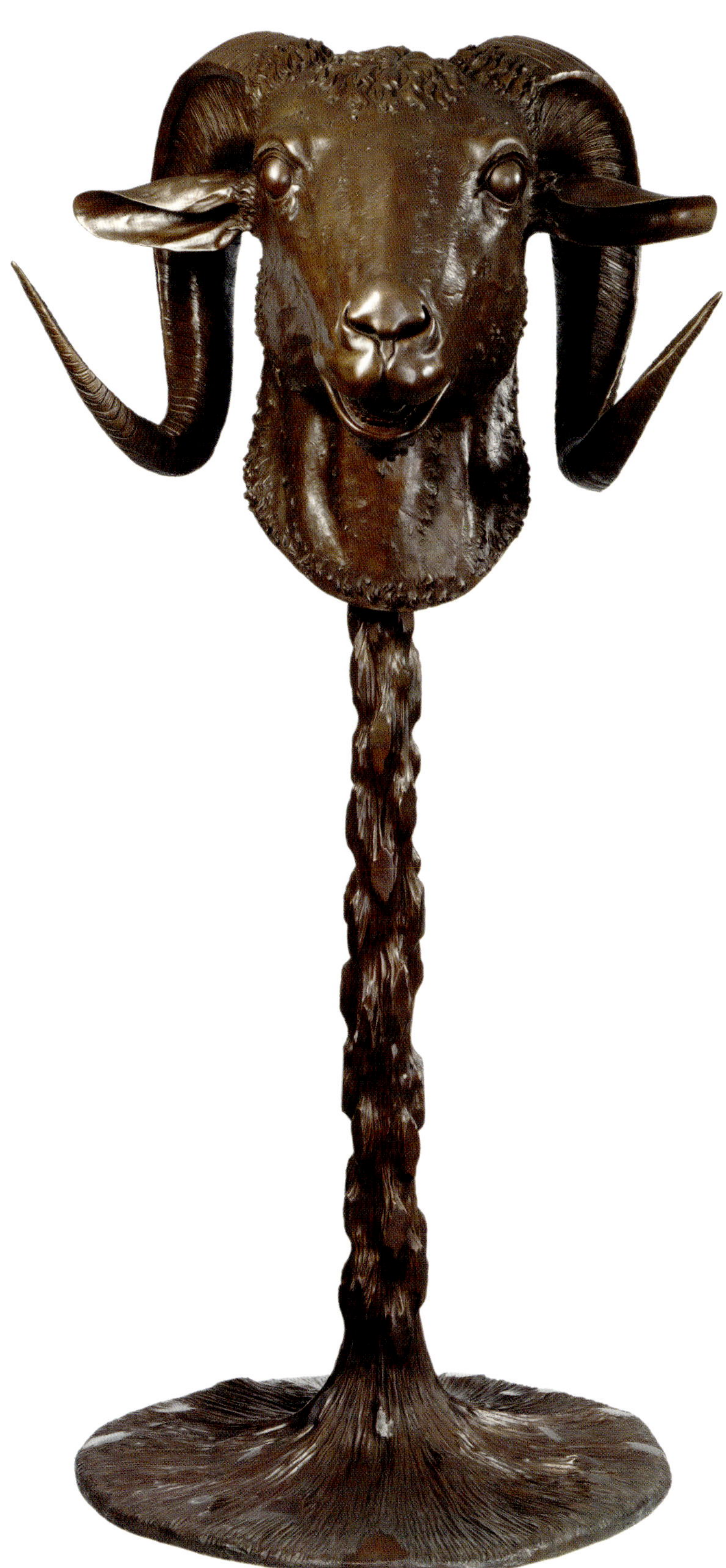

Ram

(*yang* 羊) 1–3 p.m.

The ram or goat is a domestic and sacrificial animal that appears very early in Chinese history. The character for its name is seen in the earliest Chinese inscription, its likeness is found on Bronze Age ritual vessels, and ancient books mention its use in ceremonies in honor of ancestors. This animal is also linked to the pastoral nomads that lived on China's northern and western frontiers. Simply carved images of various types of sheep and mountain goats abound on the rock cliffs of these territories, which are now part of China. The ram is sometimes associated with justice because a legend tells that the mythical emperor Gao Yao had in his court of law an insightful one-horned ram who would strike only the guilty and not the innocent. These animals are represented, though not frequently, in Chinese painting.

2010
Bronze
120 x 60 x 62 in.
(304.8 x 152.4 x 157.5 cm)

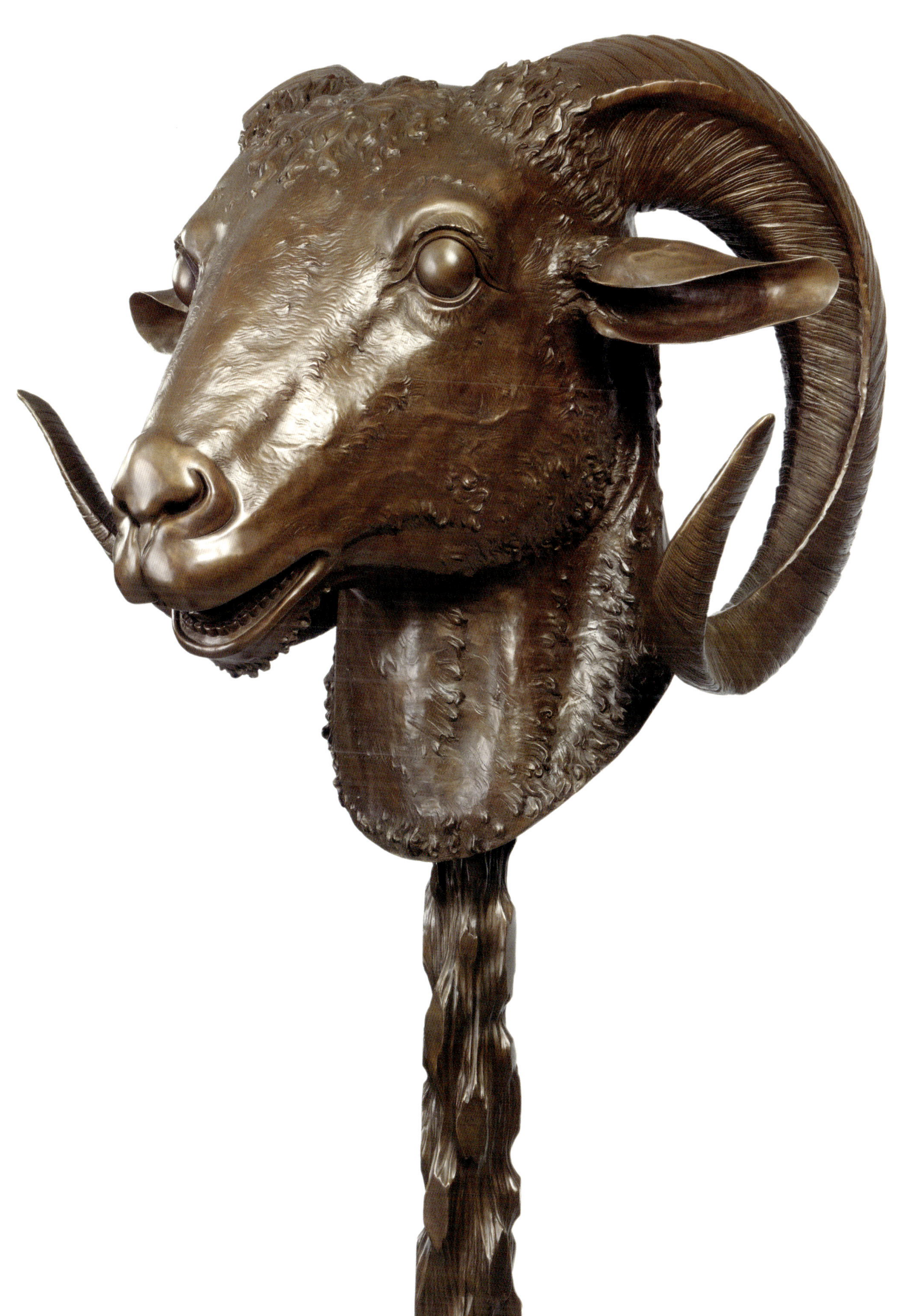

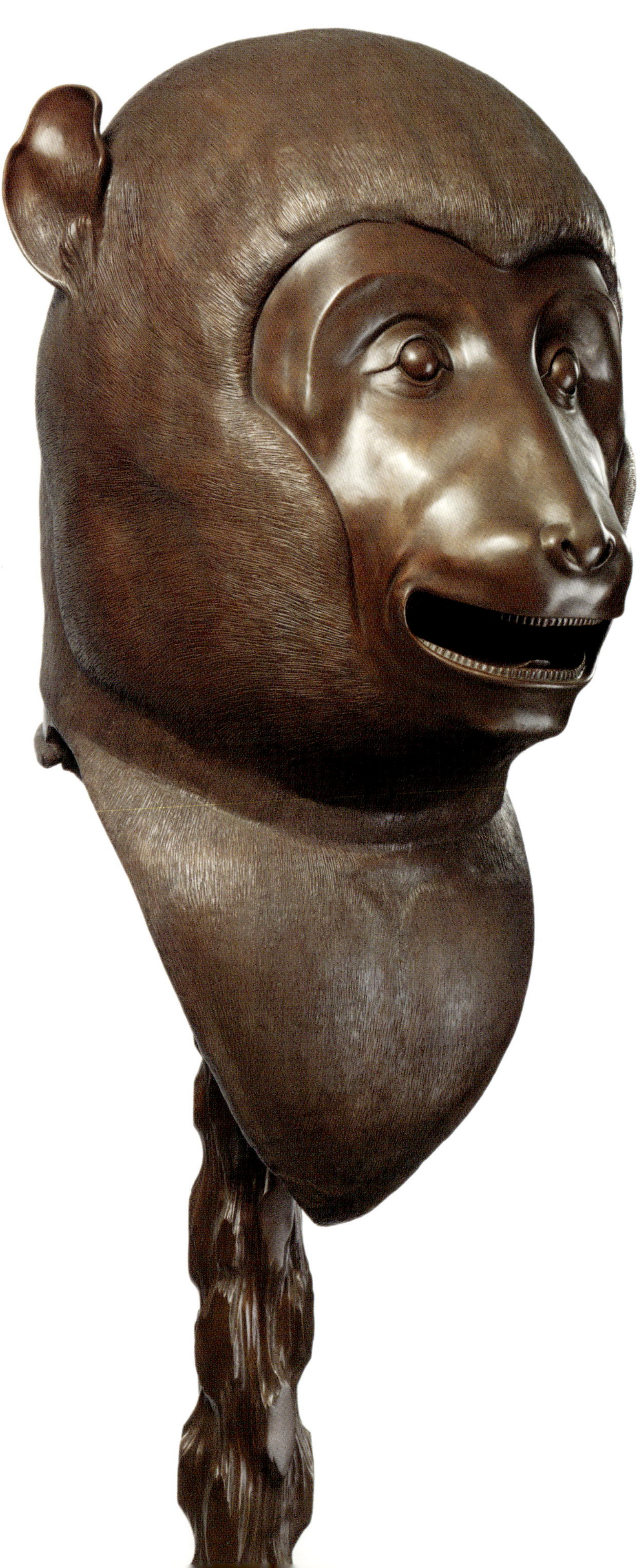

38

Monkey

The monkey is a complex figure in Chinese animal symbolism. Praised for its ability to drive evil away by controlling spirits and demons, it is also thought to be a trickster and a clown. Some consider it an emblem of deceitfulness and ugliness, while others, Buddhists and Taoists in particular, regard it as a clever animal very close to humans and a sign of humanity's link to nature. In Daoism, the gibbon's long arms were thought to be conducive to absorbing the universal *qi*. In Chan (Zen) Buddhism, the monkey is the mark of the as-yet-unenlightened mind. A well-known monkey figure is Sun Wukong, also known as Monkey King, the main character in the sixteenth-century Chinese classical novel *Journey to the West*, which tells in fantastic terms the story of the Buddhist monk Xuanzang's pilgrimage to India.

2010
Bronze
119 x 53 x 56 in.
(302.3 x 134.6 x 142.2 cm)

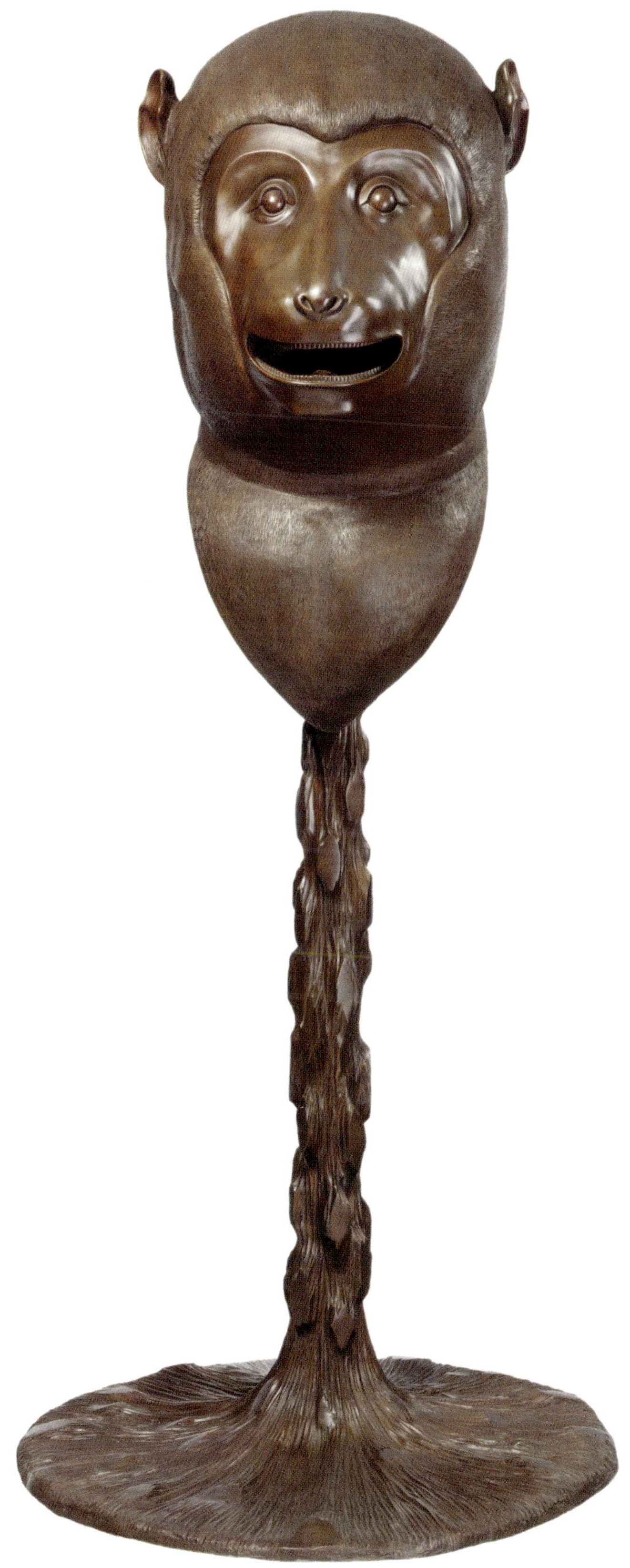

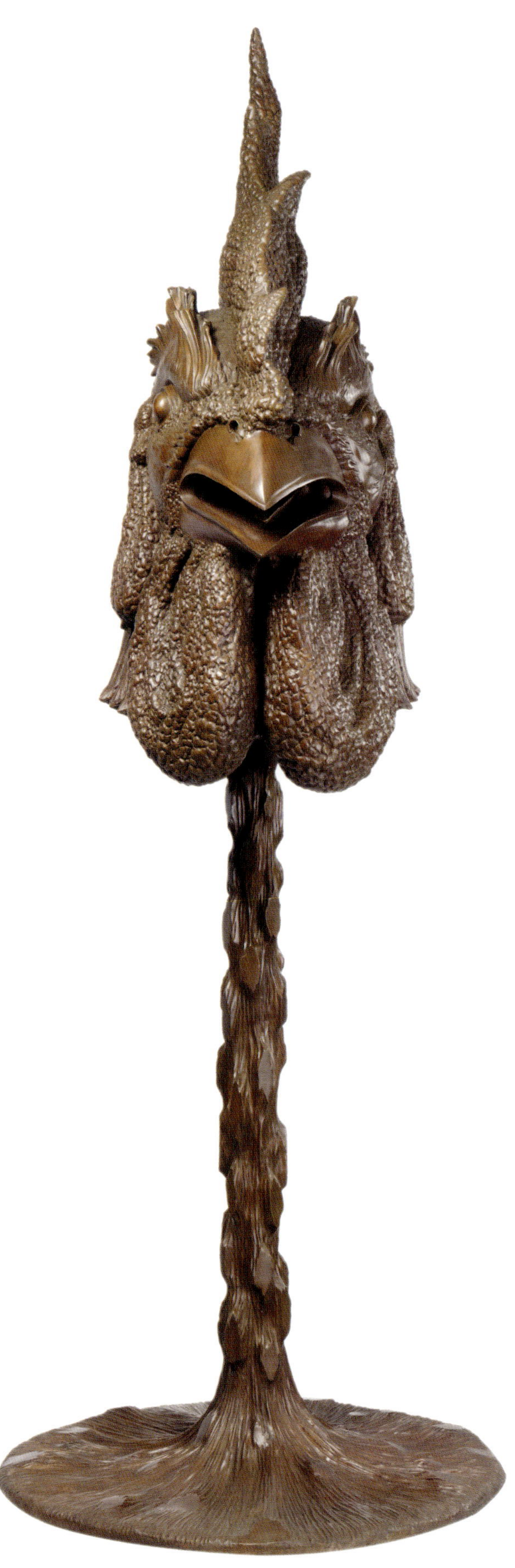

Rooster

(*ji* 鸡) 5–7 p.m.

The rooster is a revered animal in Chinese lore because it is thought to be able to ward off evil influences (probably because it eats poisonous pests). It is also said that a picture of a red rooster attached to a wall can protect a house from fire. The rooster is in fact the principal embodiment of *yang*, the male and active force, and the force of fire. The association with yang, fire, and ultimately the sun, links the rooster to the Vermilion Bird (*zhu que* 朱雀), which is the symbol of the south and a constellation. The connection with the cosmic sphere extends to the chicken's eggs, which are emblems of the universe. The body and qualities of the rooster are emblems of the five virtues: the rooster's crown, which resembles the cap of Confucian officials, symbolizes its scholarly and literary ambitions; the spurs indicate its military prowess; its propensity to fight is a sign of courage; its ability to rule the henhouse is a mark of benevolence; and its early morning crowing is a sign of reliability and faithfulness. Paintings of roosters are auspicious, and paintings of roosters, hens, and chicks are symbols of caring parents.

2010
Bronze
114 x 53 x 55 in.
(289.6 x 134.6 x 139.7 cm)

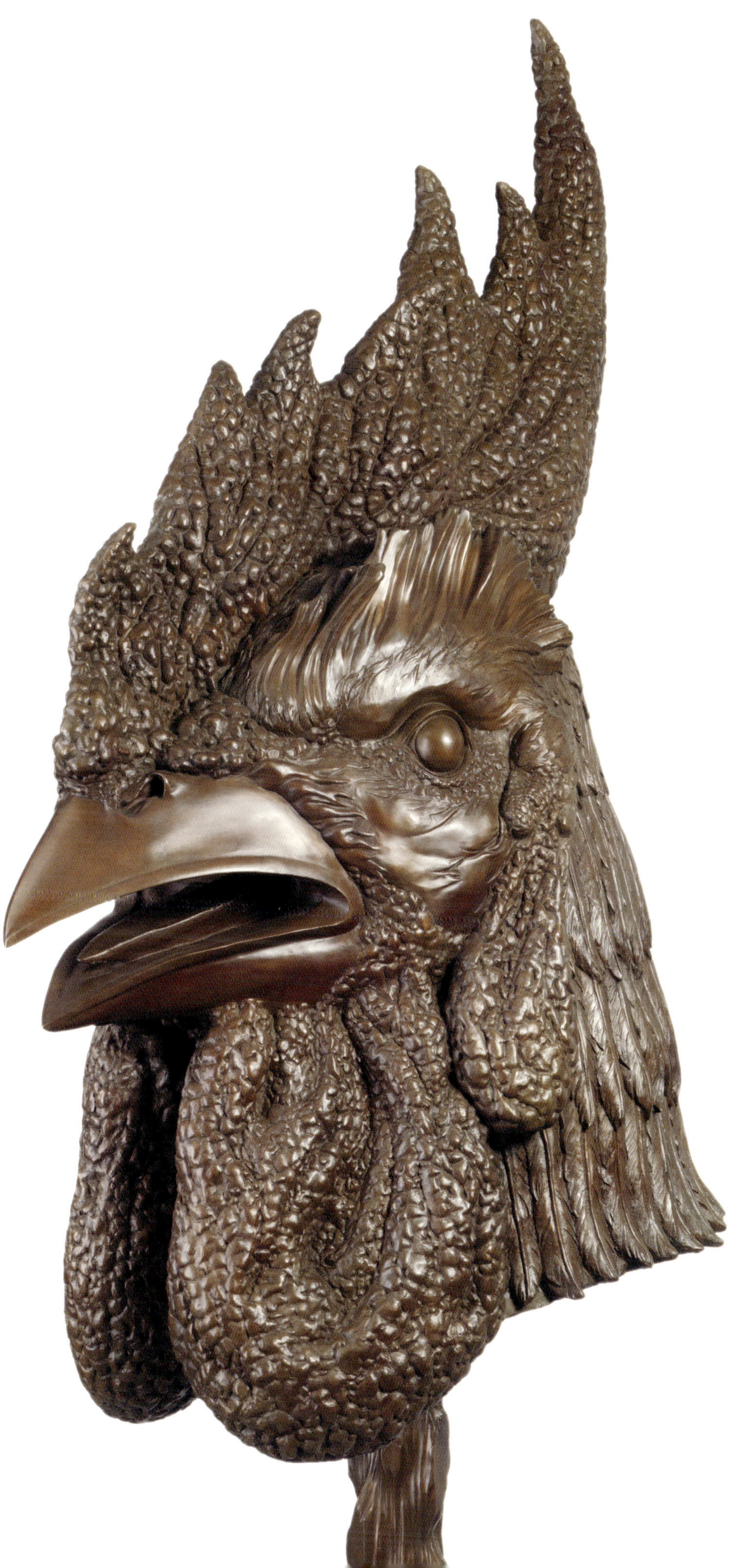

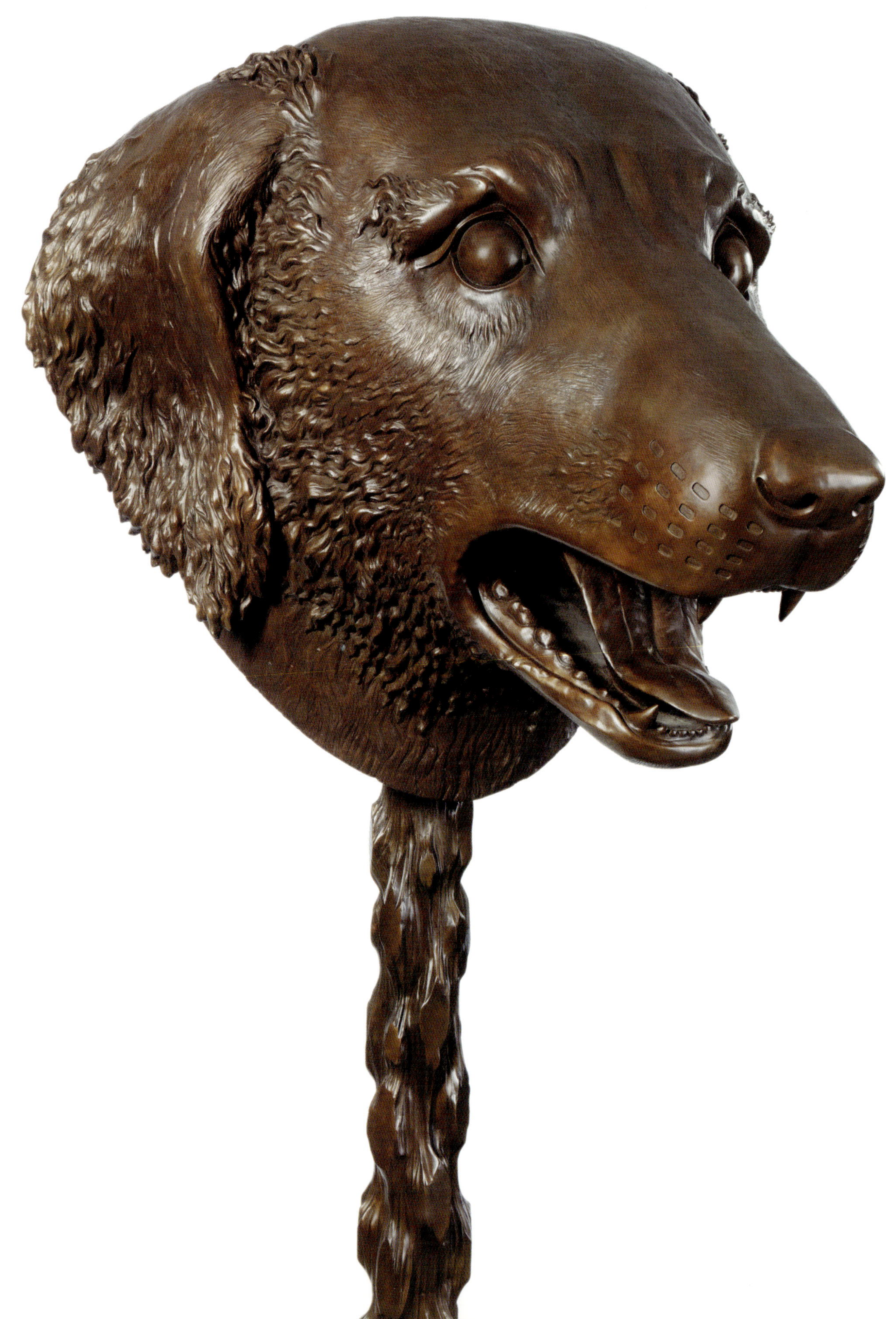

Dog

(*gou* 狗) 7–9 p.m.

When a wandering dog chooses to settle down in a home, it is thought that that family will prosper. The dog also is considered a symbol of loyalty. Possibly for this reason, dogs were buried in Bronze Age tombs as sacrifices at the bottom of the pits, below the coffins. A Chinese legend holds that in the sky there is a Heavenly Dog (*Tiangou*), which is the spirit of a woman who died unmarried and without children. The Heavenly Dog is said to steal the souls of infants in order to adopt them or, according to other accounts, to have a chance to return to earth. For this reason, newly married women keep in their rooms the image of a spirit in the act of shooting an arrow to the Heavenly Dog. The Heavenly Dog, which is actually a star (*Tiangou xing*), was also supposed to devour the moon and cause eclipses. Dogs appear in various guises in Chinese art. Ceramic or porcelain figures were formerly buried in tombs as protectors. Statues of lion-dogs often guard the entrances of temples or important buildings. Paintings may represent favorite pets or the imperial hunting dogs.

2010
Bronze
119 x 53 x 68 in.
(302.3 x 134.6 x 172.7 cm)

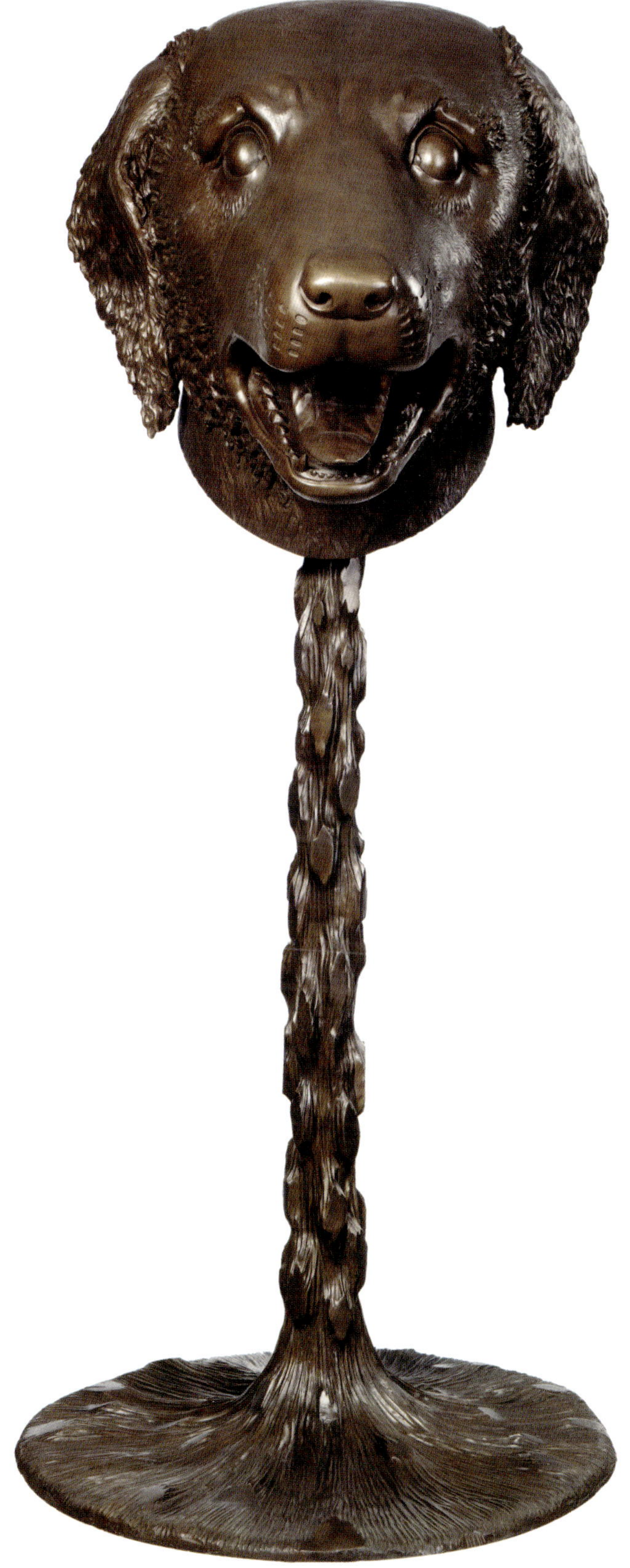

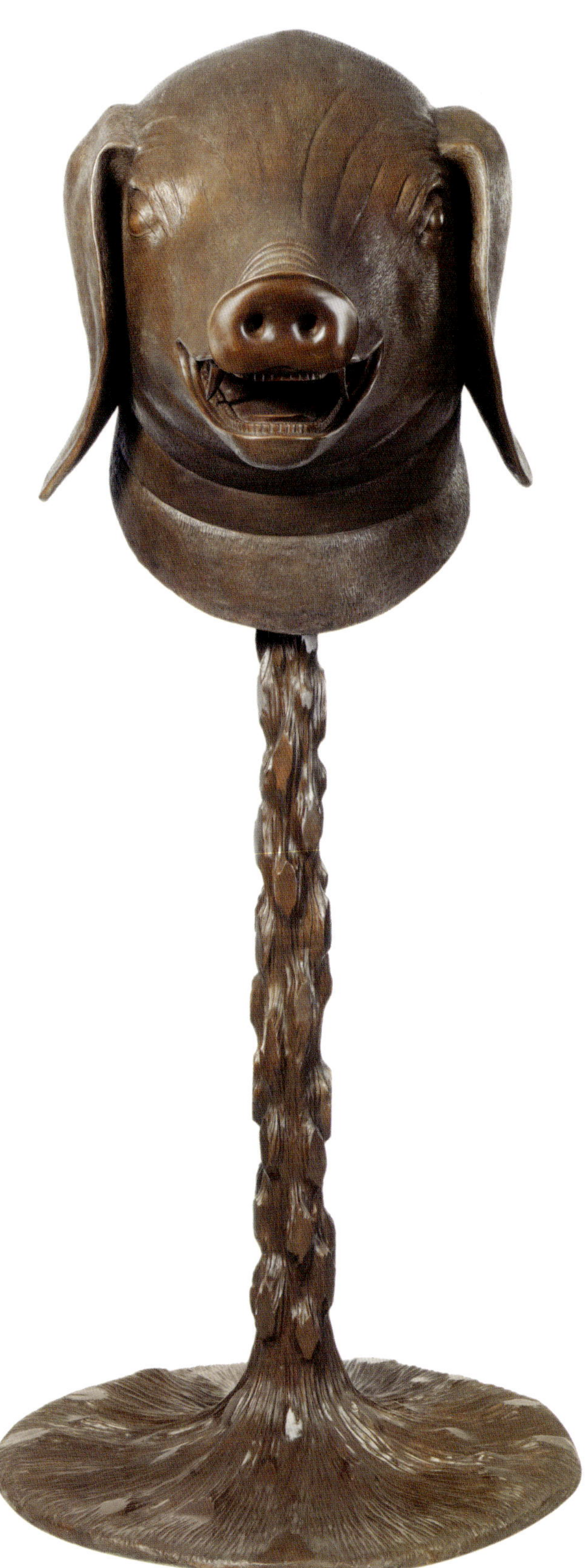

Boar

(*zhu* 猪) 9–11 p.m.

The boar, one of the earliest animals to be domesticated in China, played an important role in both Chinese culture and diet. It was a symbol of wealth in ancient China, and pigs' heads are found as offerings in some rich Neolithic burials of north China where the pigs presumably had been used as sacrificial offerings. Images of pigs or boars are not uncommon in prehistoric art, and in tombs of the early dynastic period archaeologists often discover miniature pigsties filled with animals, a reference to the earthly wealth of the deceased. The pig also appears in stories and legends. Zhu Bajie or Monk Pig, a half-man, half-pig creature, plays an important role in the novel *Journey to the West*, which narrates the pilgrimage to India of the Buddhist monk Xuanzang. According to the tale of the twelve-animal race by which the Buddha determined the order of the zodiac animals, the boar arrived late at the finish line, but in its last few steps managed to trample the cat, who, having just awakened from a long sleep, was trying to rush ahead. The boar thus earned the twelfth place, beating the cat who arrived in thirteenth place and was left out of the twelve-animal cycle.

2010
Bronze
119 x 53 x 67 in.
(302.3 x 134.6 x 170.2 cm)

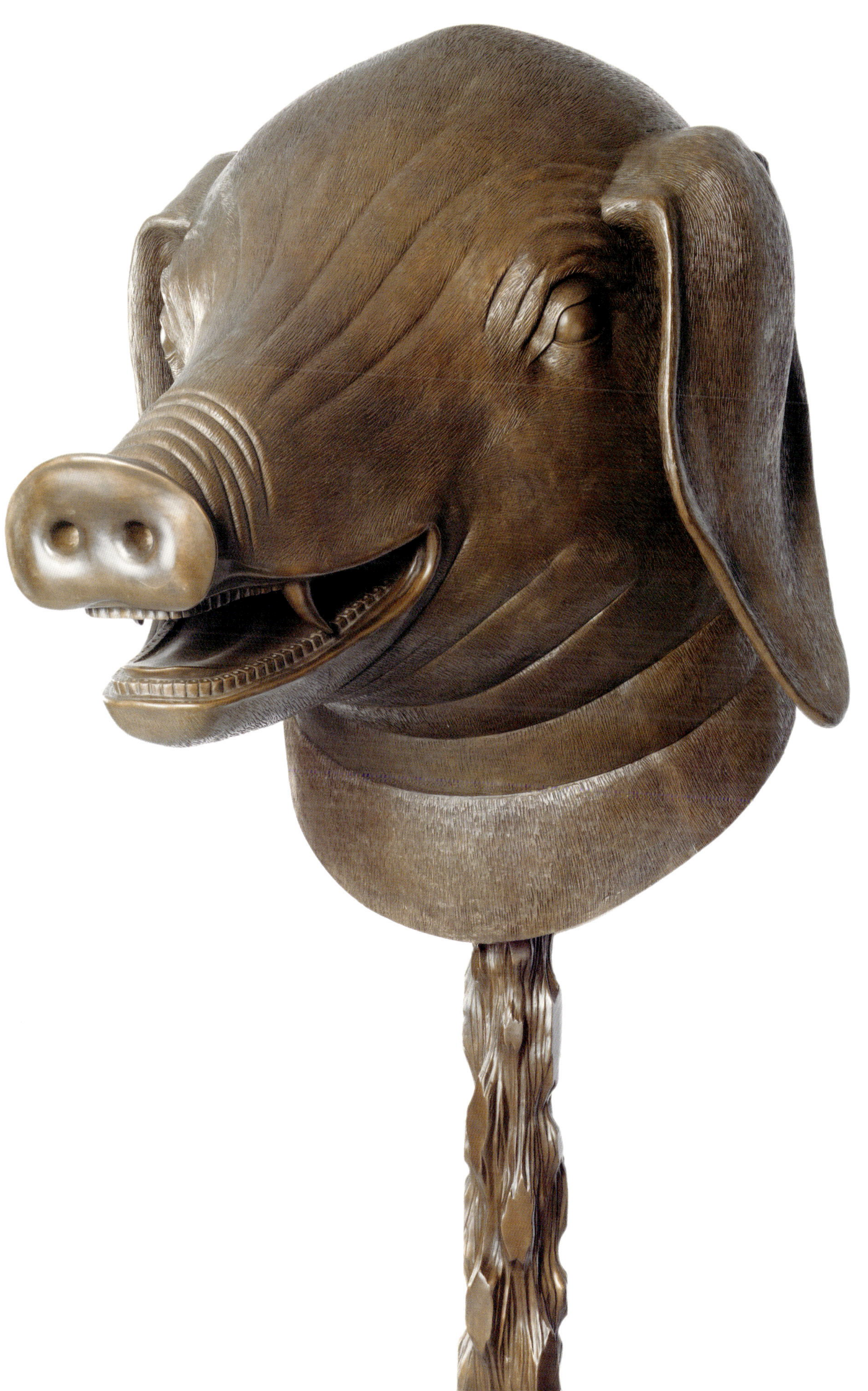

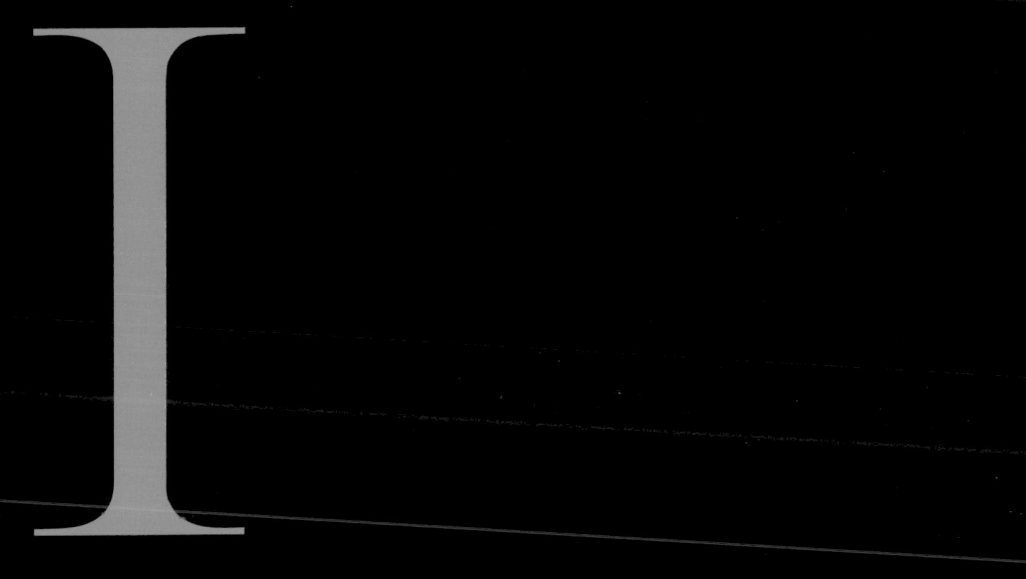

I

Part One

"My Work Is Always a Readymade"

1

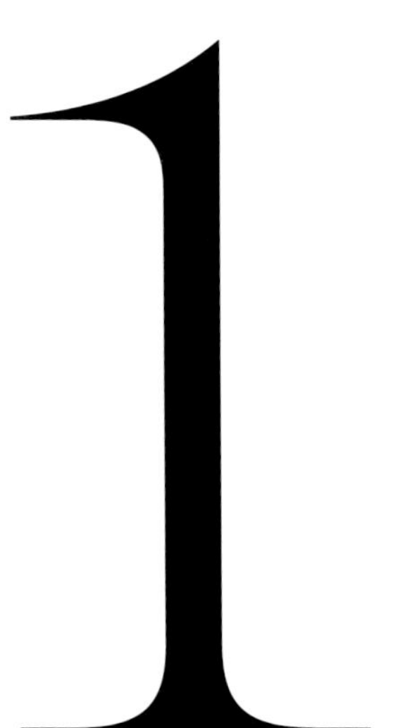

FIG. 2
Ai Weiwei in the studio
with an early version of
*Circle of Animals/Zodiac
Heads: Gold – Rooster,*
2009

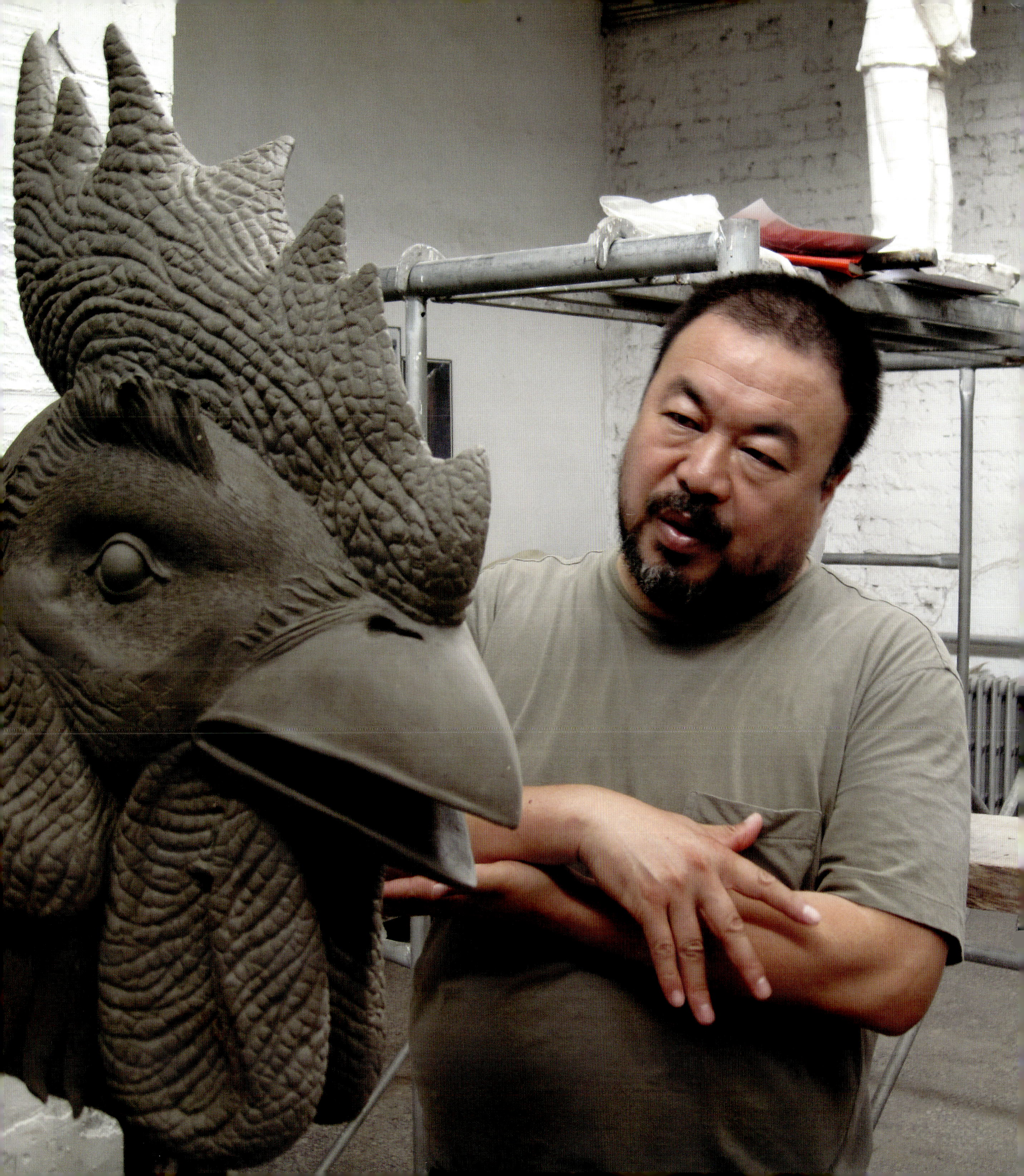

Ai Weiwei's art reflects his profound and wide-ranging interest in China's history and art. Here, he discusses his concept for Circle of Animals/Zodiac Heads, *the process of making the work, the original zodiac fountain that inspired it, and aspects of Chinese history that are reflected in it. His responses have been excerpted and edited from a series of interviews conducted in 2009 and 2010 by filmmaker Alison Klayman, magazine editor and contemporary Chinese art expert Phil Tinari, Larry Warsh of the art organization AW Asia, and Beijing-based* New Yorker *correspondent Evan Osnos.*

On Making a Work of Public Art

Circle of Animals/Zodiac Heads is your first public artwork to be shown in a major U.S. city, and is being shown at Somerset House in London as well. What's challenging about a project like this? What's interesting?

To make a work as public art interests me because you are confronted with very complicated conditions. "Public" in the real sense is not the museum public. It's art for people passing by or for having in a children's playground. How to use public space is always an interesting topic. But I don't like most public sculptures. Too much ego without much humor. They're more like landmarks in the city—you know where they are , so you know where you are.

How did the project first come about?

First, Larry Warsh and I had a long discussion about public sculpture, and I went to see the possible sites in New York City. He explained what other artists did, but still no interesting concept. Until one day I thought, this zodiac concept could be interesting. And Larry liked it very much, and Phil Tinari, too. So we started to develop it, and I found my friend Li Zhanyang, who was happy to make the first mold for me.

What sort of things do you keep in mind when you're creating a work like this?

You can't do something that's completely foreign to people, or they won't be interested in it. Maybe they won't like it, or won't be comfortable with it, or they'll say it's too distant from themselves. But it can't be completely foreign to them. That would become problematic.

How do you hope it will be received by the public?

I want this to be seen as an object that doesn't have a monumental quality, but rather is a funny piece—a piece

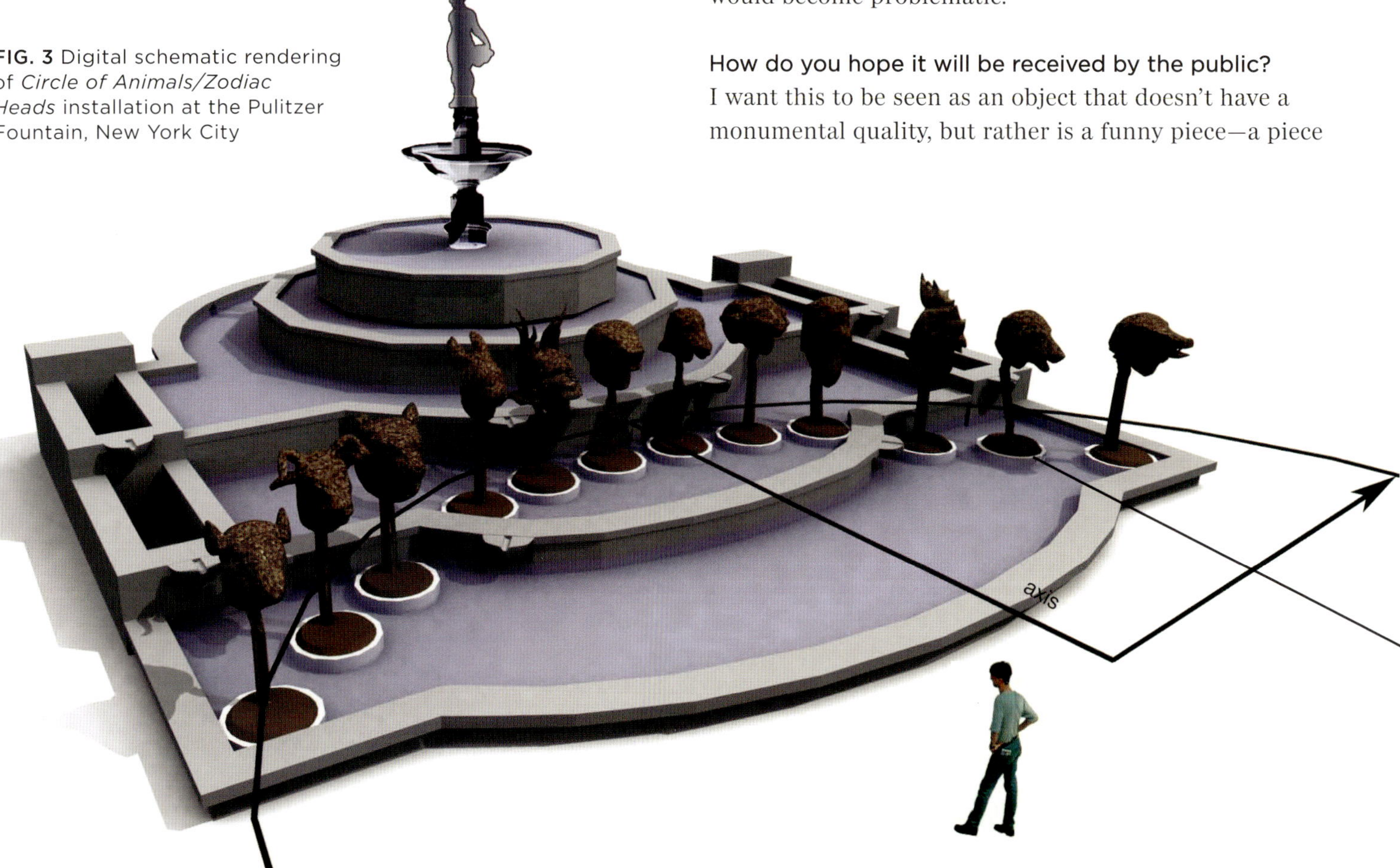

FIG. 3 Digital schematic rendering of *Circle of Animals/Zodiac Heads* installation at the Pulitzer Fountain, New York City

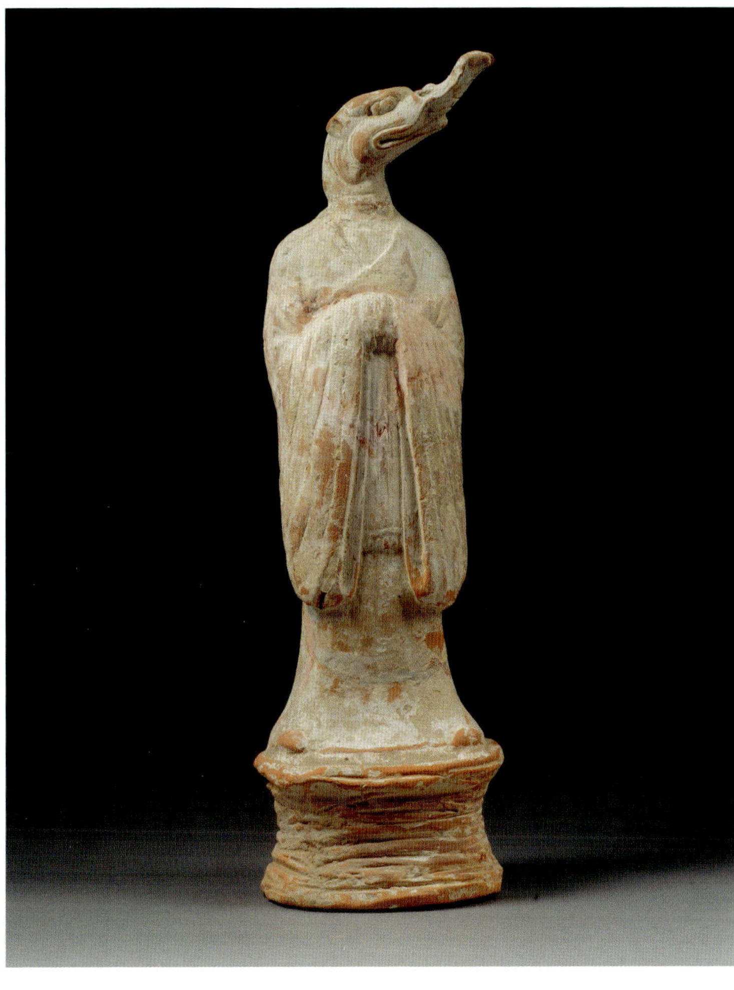

people can relate to or interpret on many different levels, because everybody has a zodiac connection.

A sculpture always functions as an object that people would question the meaning and content of. They're just objects that could suggest something else. No matter if it's ancient or contemporary, it's 3-D. The only difference is that now people think you shouldn't touch it.

I think the public deserves the best. Before, only a pope or an emperor could see these kinds of things. Now you can see them in a public garden. People don't have to have too much information about the work. They should just look at the objects and see the connection through their own experience. If the work can do that, it will already be successful.

You lived in New York City for more than a decade in the 1980s and early 1990s. How does it feel to be bringing *Circle of Animals/Zodiac Heads* to New York?

I think to have a public art installation in New York is a good idea. New York is the first cosmopolitan city I'm familiar with. It's not one kind of people, it's people from everywhere, and a lot of minorities. So I think it's a perfect place for *Circle of Animals/Zodiac Heads*. It's a zodiac city.

Visual Thinking: The Ideas Behind Circle of Animals/Zodiac Heads

When you started on this project, how familiar were you with the twelve zodiac animals? How common are they in Chinese culture?

All twelve images are familiar to me, because I was a collector, and in history they appear in different objects—jade, stone carvings and two-dimensional designs, everywhere. In the process of envisioning the missing dragon head, for instance, we looked at all kinds of dragons, such as the ones embroidered on fabrics. Every dynasty has its own way to make dragons, and they all look different (fig. 4) So we have to be very knowledgeable about this.

It's very common in Tang dynasty art to see the zodiac group, with the body of a man, with a long shirt and with a hat on. It's very lovely, very intense. The strange thing is, everybody talks about tradition, but every dynasty clearly has a different style to it. In the sense of carving the shape—even materials and textures. Completely different.

How would you describe the design of the original zodiac fountain at the Yuanming Yuan? What was it that caught your imagination?

The style is very interesting—Chinese, but mixed. It is a Western understanding of a Chinese way. You can see those things happening during the eighteenth century. The West had Chinese gardens and Chinese pagodas in their parks and houses. And images. It was always about illusions of Oriental-ness, or Chinese-ness.

Five of the original zodiac heads are missing and may never turn up again. But *Circle of Animals/Zodiac Heads* includes all twelve. Why? What was it like to envision those missing heads?

I think it's a good idea to have a complete set: these seven that exist and the five that are unknown. Without twelve, it's not a zodiac. So the idea was first, to complete it, and more important, to complete it the way I think it should be. Then that becomes solid, because I did it. The new event of my twelve zodiac heads becomes a new factor.

Circle of Animals/Zodiac Heads relates to some very complicated issues. Who made the original zodiac fountain, for what reason? And why were the heads lost? Are they truly lost, or at the auction house? Who is buying and for what reason?

One of the missing zodiac heads may just show up next season, so we will see how it compares to our version of it. You try to imagine the existing zodiac image, but your imagination can't really "meet" the real one. Of course, we want the missing heads to be seen as part of the same group. But at the same time, we have the liberty to make them what we think they should be, and will make more sense. So there's not much creativity there. It's about how to interpret the missing heads into a similar visual language as the existing ones.

In envisioning the animals for *Circle of Animals/Zodiac Heads*, what sorts of sources did you draw on?

My dragon is more an early Ming dynasty dragon. Some details are Qing dynasty, so it's a mixture. The ram is taken from a ram I have, a stone ram in my courtyard here. The basic model is from the Ming dynasty. The snake is more of a modern, scientific look—we did a bit of fantasizing there. For the rooster and the dog, we took a more realistic approach. It's fun to work with the existing models, and to imagine the non-existing possibilities.

Why make *Circle of Animals/Zodiac Heads* in two sizes? What do you see as the differences between the two versions?

We needed two sizes because of the process. We needed the small set for study—to make it possible to compare the existing heads with the imaginary ones. And that's the only way to do it.

The smaller ones I wanted to be proportionally as close to the originals as possible, because it builds an argument as to why I'm doing the project. Because there's five of them missing, and I wanted to replace them, to fill the gap of our imaginations there. Also to gild the entire set into gold, and give it another visual language with that.

But to me, that's not enough. I think for different kinds of surroundings, the small ones are too personal, too close to our own size. I wanted to see how they looked in blowups, and in other possibilities. It's amazing how size changes it.

In the original zodiac fountain, the bronze animal heads sat on human bodies, probably carved from stone. But in *Circle of Animals/Zodiac Heads*, the heads rest on slender columns and bases. What did you have in mind with this?

The bases are really our own interpretation. Because in museums you have always just a box, a bare box. But we wanted some details, to really push the style of the bases that are supporting the sculptures, so each piece has a unified language. I think it's more interesting this way. In the smaller set in particular, the rooster base relates to the rooster, and the dragon has its own style. All the bases were designed according to the characteristics of each head. That gave us a chance to redefine them. It's really a new set of creatures.

We added different textures to the bases, like roots or water—a few different types. Some of the supporting columns are even curved (fig. 5). If you have textures, you need to have some movement in there. Even the base cannot be flat, or it'll be like a mirror. I told the sculptor, we need to sculpt the whole base. So they did.

Tell us about the process. Where did you start?

First, we cast into plaster. And from that we moved into rubber, then made a bronze model. Then with the first bronze testing piece I saw the problems with the bronze, because there are different problems with the different materials. So we fixed them. And then we had the gilding process for the smaller heads.

Plaster is the most classic sculpture-casting material. Using it as a mold will capture all the details. Before, we used fiberglass, which failed—so harsh, and hard to fix. So plaster is one important part of the process. Clay doesn't work—it won't endure, it changes shape when it shrinks, and it cracks as it dries. So it's not possible.

When I saw the first examples of bronze back from the foundry—so beautiful—I was surprised. I never thought it would turn out so well, with all the details. Sculpting feels different from casting. Once you cast, it comes out whole. A very different feeling. I was very satisfied and gave the signal to do all twelve.

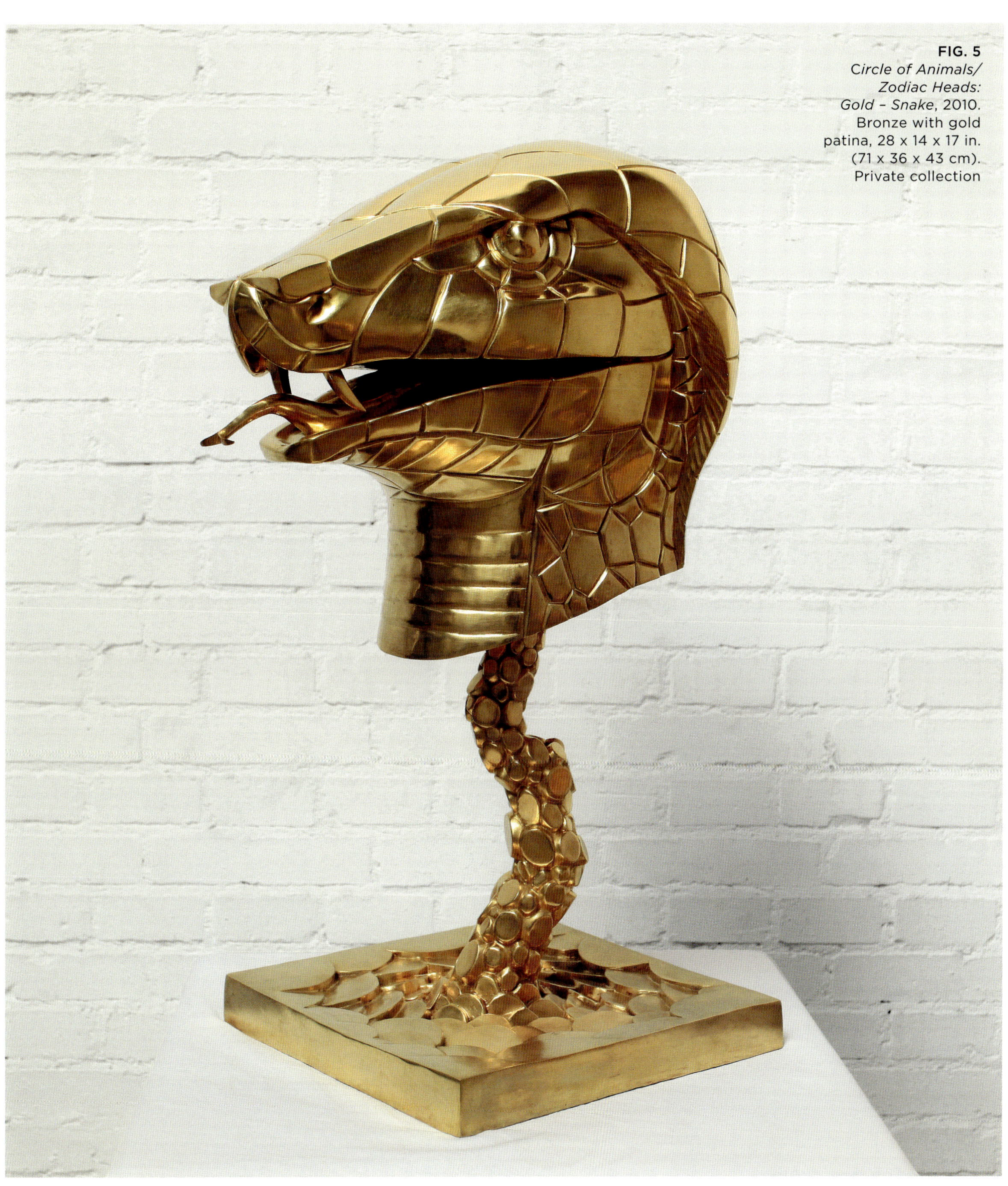

FIG. 5
Circle of Animals/
Zodiac Heads:
Gold – Snake, 2010.
Bronze with gold
patina, 28 x 14 x 17 in.
(71 x 36 x 43 cm).
Private collection

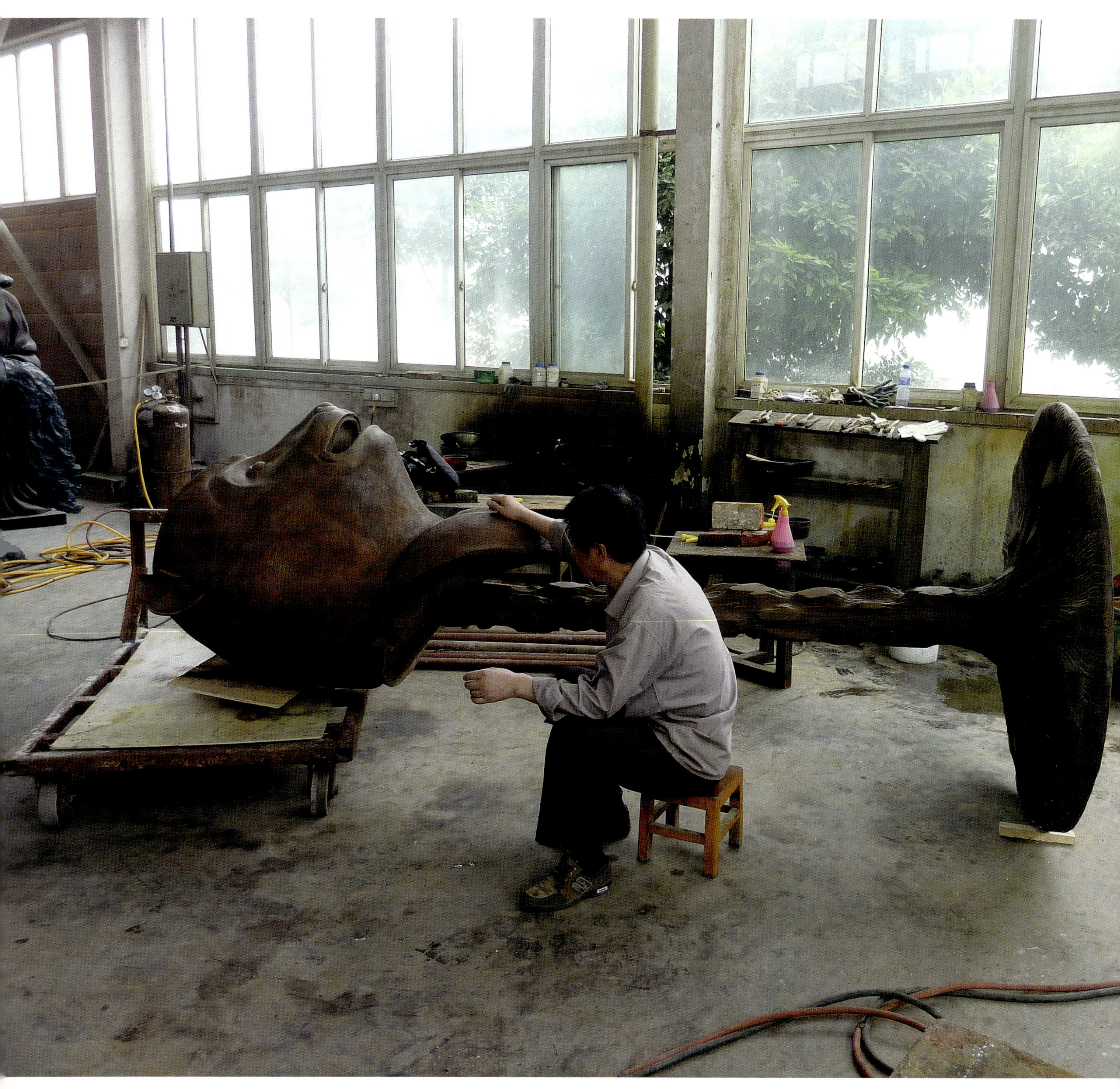

You felt strongly that the smaller version of *Circle of Animals/ Zodiac Heads* should be done in a gilded gold patina. What was the thinking behind that?

I didn't want *Circle of Animals/Zodiac Heads* to appear exactly like the original heads. But at same time, it is exactly like the original. But it has a completely different shine. I think that's very, very important. The gold really can give greatness and a sense of environment. We have a completely different way of looking at something if it becomes shiny, because the reflection destroys the original forms and shapes. That's very important.

Gold objects have been recovered from tombs dating from the Han dynasty or even earlier. But especially in the Tang dynasty, under the Persian influence during that era, everything became gold and silver. And in that time, Chinese jade completely disappeared. So gold, from a very early time, symbolizes power and richness, and a luxury lifestyle. I don't think that meaning has changed today. I think gold still reflects that.

In making *Circle of Animals/Zodiac Heads,* you worked with a team of highly accomplished artists and craftspersons. What was that like? How did that enrich the work?

I control the work, but I don't want it to be exactly my taste. I give the basic structure, then give it space to grow. I always work with my old friend Li Zhanyang. I like his workmanship— that's my style. I hate to work with someone with no sense of humor, and he has the right kind of humor for me.

It's strange to work with others, with sculptors—good friends—and have to give them guidance. To tell them to produce something that is a copy of an original, but not an exact copy—something that has its own sensitive layer of languages, which are different, and that bears the mark of our own time. The communication has to be back and forth: if it's right or not right, will it have a base, what is this base going to be, do we need to gild it, do we need a small one and not a large one and why, and factoring in different locations in terms of money, time, craftsmanship. All those issues are mixed together. You have to maintain your presence, so that the people working on it realize that this is important, that it's absolutely very fine work. They have to believe in it; otherwise it will change tone and become something different. So how to work with others and how to make people feel this is something worth doing, is always a question.

It's very much like today's musicians. You don't have to write each tune, you just bring in different—you design the space, the beat, and the structures to be designed, rather than the craftsmanship. In that way, the process can free me from very much involvement. I can make my choices much more freely. I won't be limited by specific skills, but can instead make a much more liberal choice.

I think art today is really more like communicating between artists, discussing and talking about who's doing what and how to put those elements together to create something different. So I have a very good time doing those things with them.

What are some of the challenges you encountered?

With all my projects, even when I work with the most superb craftpersons, it is still difficult because I always have to explain what exactly is in my mind. And that's hard to explain—even for me, it's hard to know. I have to go through the process and learn, to find the possibilities, to become familiar with the possible conditions. So we have to make a lot of mistakes, do a lot of testing. I need to find things out. People often say I'm not certain about what I want, which is true. I know the basic direction, but I don't know if I'm going to find a mountain or a river there. I know why that situation is going to be, but I have to go through it; otherwise I'll never experience it. That gives me the pleasure in doing art. Otherwise, why do it?

Looking Back: The Zodiac Fountain and the Twelve Bronze Heads

The zodiac fountain was created in the 1700s for the Yuanming Yuan, an imperial retreat just outside Beijing, where it was part of a separate section of European-style gardens and buildings. It was designed by European Jesuits in the court of the Qing-dynasty Emperor Qianlong. Why was the emperor so interested in the West?

I don't know much about the history of the Qing dynasty, but I think Europe must have been very cool to them. At that time, the West was relatively well developed, very scientific. They gave the emperor a lot of clocks to make him happy. At that time, Chinese people still looked at the sun's rays and water to determine the time. So I guess they yearned for that kind of civilization.

But Chinese people at that time weren't that interested in foreign countries. The center of their lives had always been China itself. That is to say, if you are a central empire, the

FIG. 6 *Circle of Animals/Zodiac Heads: Bronze – Monkey,* 2010, in production at the foundry in Chengdu, China

wealth of people all around you is dedicated to you. This kind of thinking prevailed until the Opium Wars and invasions, which eventually proved this thinking to be misguided.

The decorative elements of the fountain—including the bronze zodiac heads—were designed by Giuseppe Castiglione, an Italian Jesuit at the imperial court. His designs for the animal heads—how do they strike you?
I think from the images of the existing seven, they are not exactly Chinese in appearance. You know, we have all sorts of animals in Chinese painting and sculpture, but none close to this. This is a more realistic approach. Especially the tiger—you can see that it looks more like a bear than a tiger. That really shows traces of being made by a foreigner. It's not really Chinese culture.

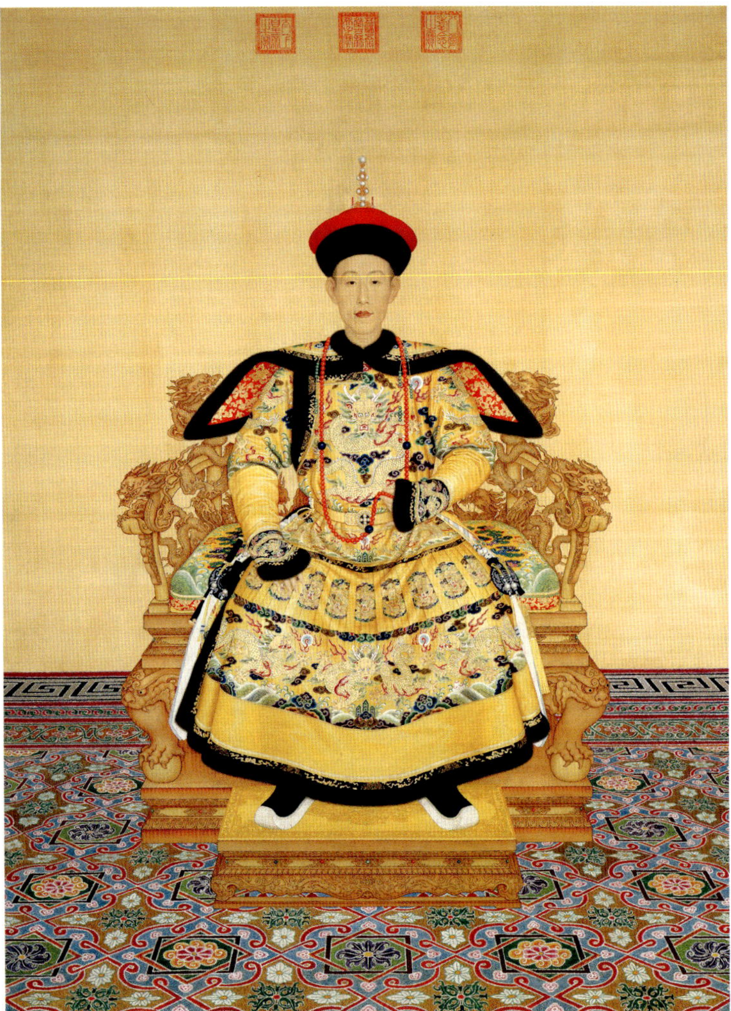

Giuseppe Castiglione felt that no one in the Qing court was capable of making these kinds of things. But in reality, China's sand-casting technology even at the time of the Bronze Age was the best in the world. However, China wasn't always as good at realistic sculptures—a copy of so-called reality. They were never really interested in it. They thought, Reality is reality and you should never try to understand what reality *means*. Maybe they felt that what we see is not true reality, or that what we see is actually a limited version of reality. So they just made representations of the world in their hearts. Their hearts interpreted the world, and these artists would just create simple artworks, something personal to them. This kind of detailed feather, this kind of realistic carving—China wasn't all that into it.

One thing people talk about in China, in relation to these zodiac fountain sculptures, is how they're part of a period of national humiliation—that they were taken away by foreign troops in 1860, during the Second Opium War. Did you learn about that in school when you were growing up?
Yes, that's what we always learned—imperialism, and how China suffered under those pressures from the eight nations. And that's all we imagined in our textbooks.

Did you realize that it's already been 150 years from the day the sculptures were taken in October 1860?
Wow. That's amazing. Actually, 150 years is not too long. China has changed, China has changed so dramatically. And the world has changed. It's become so different.

Many people in China regard the original zodiac heads as national treasures. What are your thoughts about this?
I don't think the zodiac heads are a national treasure. They were designed by an Italian, made by a Frenchman for a Qing-dynasty emperor who was the ruler of China, but the Manchus of the Qing dynasty actually invaded China. So if we talk about national treasure, what nation are we talking about?

FIG. 7
Formal court portrait of the Qianlong Emperor, painted in 1736 by Italian Jesuit missionary and artist Giuseppe Castiglione. Ink and color on silk, 95 x 70 ½ in. (242 x 179 cm). Palace Museum, Beijing

The Yuanming Yuan was burned down in 1860, and those objects found their way into the auction market in the West. Then China became a new power, having risen in the global landscape. So people are using the zodiac heads to talk about patriotic passionate reasons. This company, Poly Group, which has a lot of money and is government-owned, is buying them back for the Poly Museum.

But they're not worth that much, and they're not Chinese, and they're not national treasures. So under this talk of national treasure being looted by Westerners, and now buying it back—it's political hype. Once people start to buy, the price jumps—doubles, triples, crazily high—and even becomes a national affair. First they wanted to stop the auction in 2009, which of course they couldn't. Then they want to buy the heads back. This is a little wrong, because once you buy from the auction, you admit this is just another art object and you lose your fighting position. So it's very dramatic and very crazy. There was a guy at the 2009 auction who wanted to show that he's patriotic, so he bought the heads and later refused to pay the money. It was a big controversy in China and in the international auction market.

Maybe after I deal with this matter through making this artwork, people will re-examine this whole issue. It does bring significance to these old objects. But just as decorative objects, the original heads stayed quiet for many years. They're just like a toilet seat, or anything else.

Among the Ruins: Ai Weiwei and the Yuanming Yuan

In the 1970s, you spent a lot of time at the ruins of the Yuanming Yuan.
It's the first place I went after I came to Beijing from Xinjiang in 1975. I immediately went to study art, and the Yuanming Yuan is a place I would go every week. I'd ride a bicycle from Xidan—it takes a little over thirty minutes if you ride very fast. There was no one there. I have a photo of myself standing right in front of this ruin (fig. 8).

That was post–Cultural Revolution. Probably the ruins are the only physical evidence you have of different elements of Western traditions. So a lot of poets and artists would go there to have a poetry reading or to do some paintings and sketches. In the photo, I was standing there, making a drawing. In front of me were people from Western embassies, having a barbeque. It was a really wild, overgrown place, with only a few people going there. A very wild place.

What attracted you to it?
I don't like the feeling of ruins, but as a young man I was always wandering in them, because they reflect a lot of things you could never imagine. It's very easy to understand how beautiful the garden could have been, because the remaining stones are so beautifully carved (fig. 9). Once I bought one piece, like a stool. Later, a collector bought it from me. It was so beautiful, I regret selling it. It was carved as a water lily leaf. I never saw a stone so beautiful. The person who sold it to me said it was from the Yuanming Yuan. Often we would still see stones from there sold in the market—not today, but a few years ago. It's the most beautiful carving a stone ever can have.

The Yuanming Yuan belongs to the past, to the 1970s. I hate to see how they truly destroyed it again. It should remain untouched. Now, everyone talks about rebuilding it or adding some tourist construction. They are trying to ruin it. It's really bad—not ruined by foreigners but truly by Chinese. You can see how Western people who looted it had such a high appreciation of those objects—maybe that's the reason they did the looting. But you'd never see Chinese who would write that sentence. In China, it was either part of the emperor's family or the uneducated poor, ready to take anything home to use. If a stone was too big, they would just chop it.

But to me, it's a very strange feeling, because all those things are not really in Chinese taste. It's really the Manchu Qing dynasty who had this kind of taste, who liked this kind of color and shape. Personally, I don't like it that much. I think

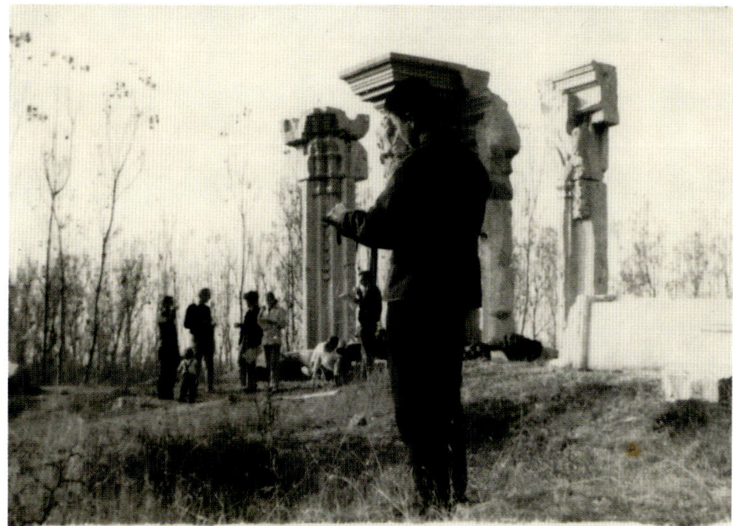

FIG. 8 Ai Weiwei at the ruins of the Yuanming Yuan in the late 1970s

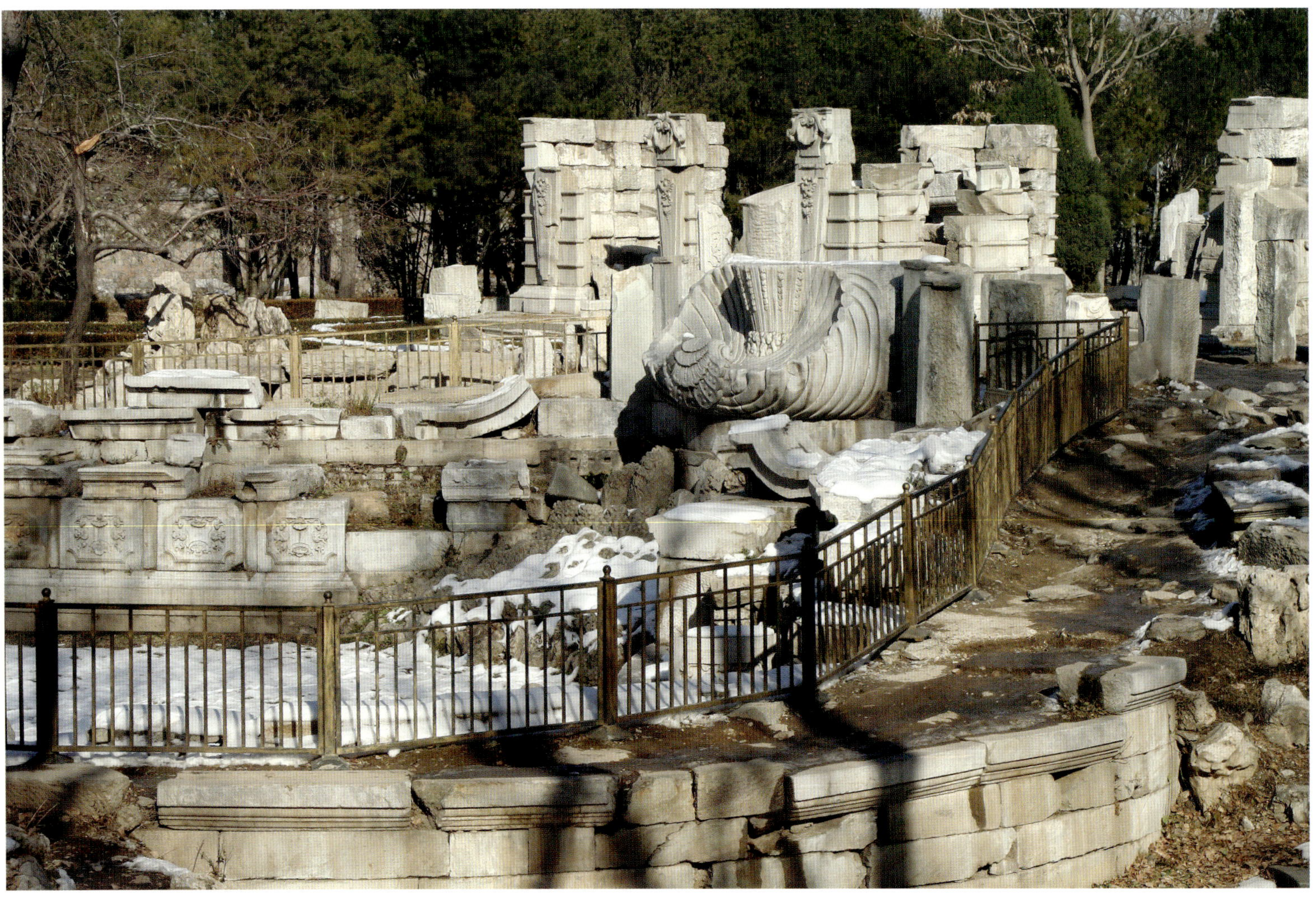

FIG. 9
The zodiac fountain
ruins, now part of
the Yuanming Yuan
Park in Beijing

it's worth a lot of money just because it belonged to emperors. None of the objects reflect ancient Chinese traditions. If you look at Chinese objects from the Ming or Song dynasty, it's nothing like this, really.

Were the ruins a magnet for artist communities in the 1970s? Or did that come later?
The painters' gathering in Yuanming Yuan village near the ruins was in the early or middle 1980s, not before that. Before that, it was a really rural village, just like a village anywhere. And you'd see those carved stones from the Yuanming Yuan being used by farmers for their pig houses, or some even for the foundations of their homes. You know, the destruction wasn't that bad in 1860—it was just burned, not completely destroyed. It was really destroyed by the local farmers, because everybody tried to take a piece home and use it for construction.

I think people want to point fingers at others. They never point fingers at themselves, they want to say, They destroyed it. They like that story, to say that their existence, or even their sadness or tragedies, are caused by others. They don't say, Because of me, because of myself, this happened.

On the Original and the Copy, the Real and the Fake

Do you see your new set as copies of the existing heads and new versions of the missing ones?
No. I don't think even the copies are exactly the same. It's a new understanding of the total project. It's not as if some are cast from the original. It's a new interpretation.

My work is always dealing with real or fake, authenticity, what the value is, and how the value relates to current political and social understandings and misunderstandings. I think there's a strong humorous aspect there. The Yves Saint Laurent zodiac auction in February 2009 really complicated the issues about art, about the real, about fake, resources, looting, about the appreciation of objects—all these kinds of issues.

The original zodiac heads were basically decorative objects, but *Circle of Animals/Zodiac Heads* is a work of conceptual art. Tell us about that.
The original heads were a functioning part of that fountain in the Yuanming Yuan. To remake that as a piece of art—conceptual art—is to question the whole act of appreciation and collecting, taking artwork and positioning it with you. And talking about the originality and the identity of the work, because it is very confused. It's pointing to many different issues—of course to China, to myself, to all the people who would question whether the work is valuable or not valuable, real or not real, or better than real, or not as good as real. And how it's going to be shown, why it's being shown, how it's being sold, and why people are paying for it. So it's a problematic object.

Anybody can make a set of zodiac figures. They actually date from the Tang dynasty. The zodiac fountain heads from the Qing dynasty are only a copy of Tang dynasty ones. We can see earlier ones from over 1,200 years ago. And you know, we never change the subject, we always change the interpretation, we change the platform, the base of the condition. To make *Circle of Animals/Zodiac Heads*, I had to first put it into the categories of my concerns, and whoever sees this work will relate it to what I did before. Dealing with fake and real, true

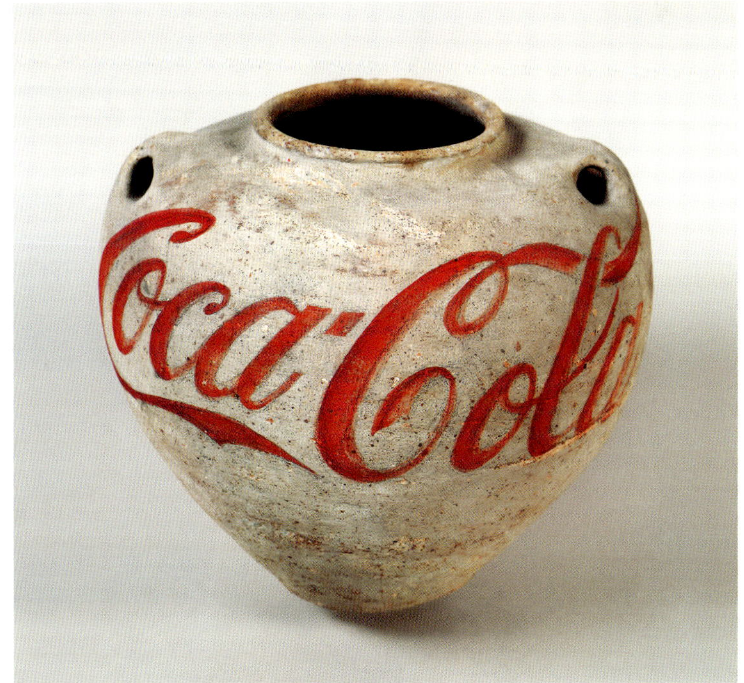

FIG. 10
Ai Weiwei, *Han Dynasty Vase with Coca Cola Logo*, 1995. Urn from the Western Han dynasty (206 BCE–24 CE), paint, 10 x 11 x 11 in. (25 x 28 x 28 cm). Sigg Collection

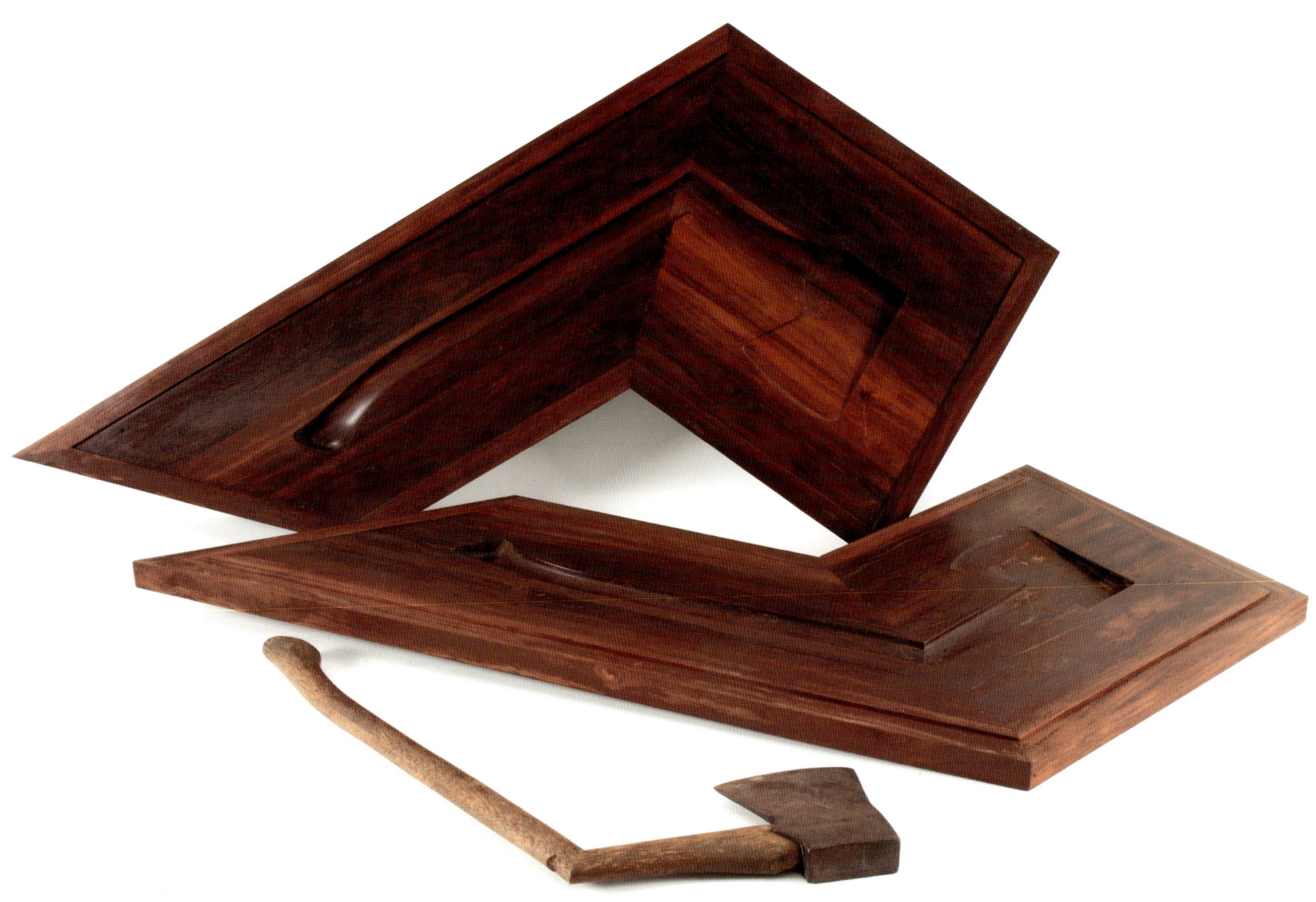

FIG. 11
Ai Weiwei, *Ax in a Box*,
1989. Ax, wooden box,
dimensions variable.
Private collection

FIG. 12
Ai Weiwei, *Mao behind
Bars I*, 1986. Oil on canvas,
96 x 72 in. (243.8 x
182.9 cm). Private collection

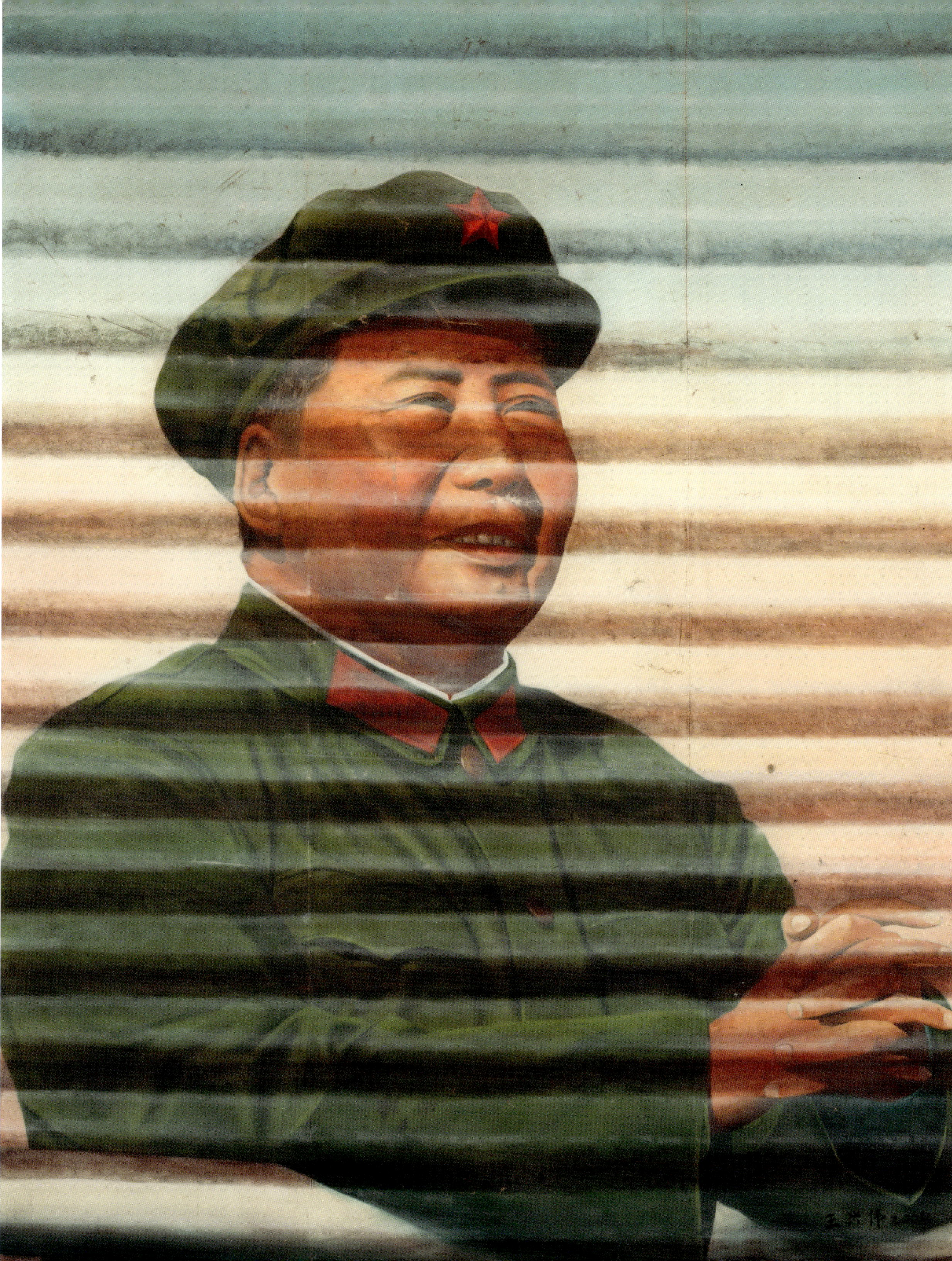

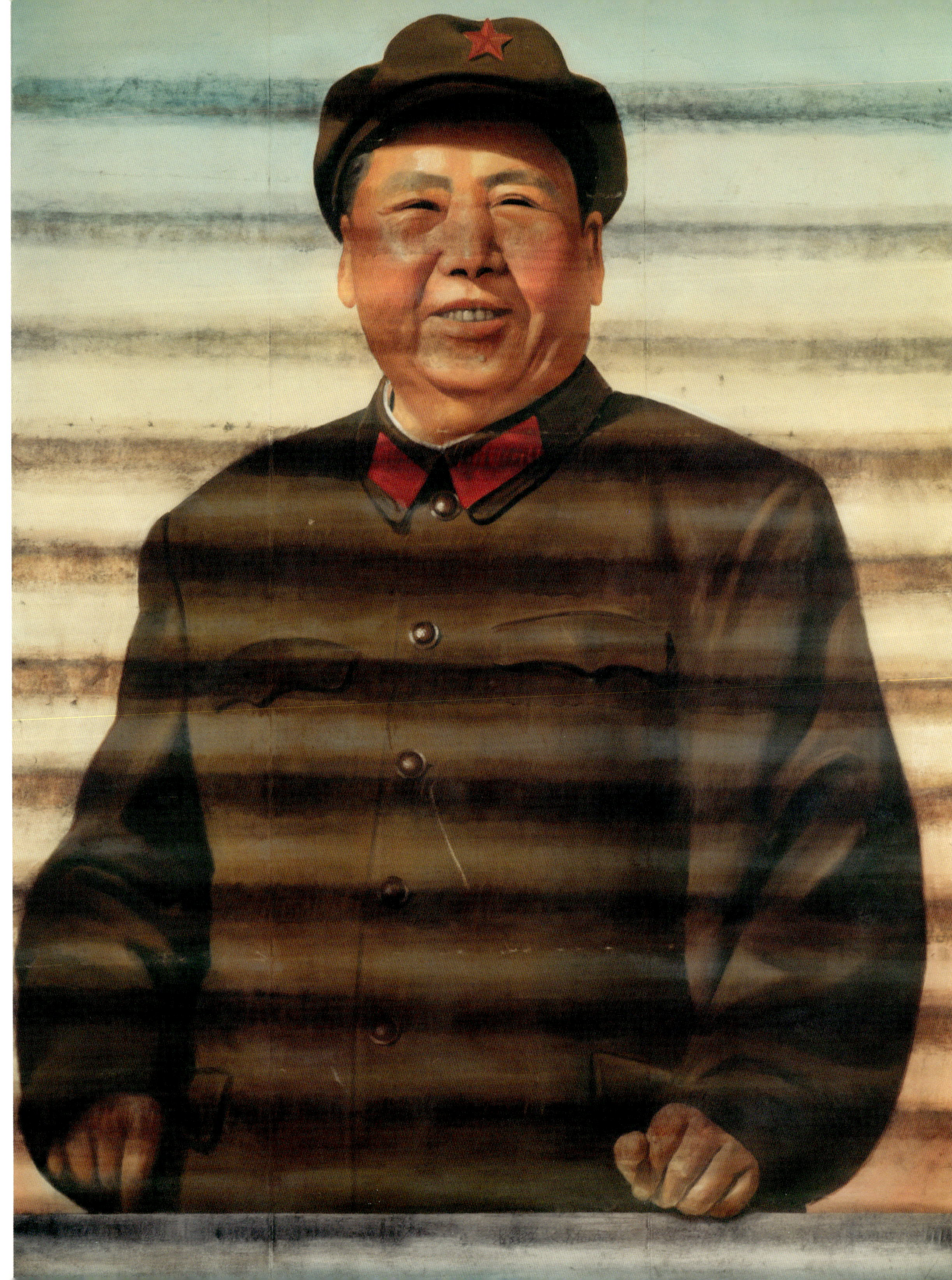

value, aesthetics—all those questions concern me. Also, as a contemporary artist, I have the possibility of putting the work in a museum. When that happens, the work itself will carry different meanings, its own experience.

I am always concerned with how we make judgments. And in questioning others' judgment, and also questioning my judgment. And always saying art is not the end but the beginning. Art is not the end. The product is never the end but should be the beginning. Otherwise art has no life.

The word "readymade" comes up in your work a lot. Do you think it's appropriate to use it in referring to the original sculptures, the original Yuanming Yuan fountain? In this case, are those readymades that you're dealing with, or is it something else?

My work is always a readymade. It could be cultural, political, or social, and also it could be art—to make people re-look at what we have done, its original position, to create new possibilities (fig. 11). I always want people to be confused, to be shocked or realize something later. But at first it has to be appealing to people.

The original bronze heads are readymades and at the same time they are not readymades. Every readymade I touch becomes different, not exactly the same. They always have another shade of lighting and completely different positions. I very much enjoy that game, because it plays with past and present and future, and it questions our own positions and our own judgment. That is very important for me. What I care about is how those things are carried forward, and how that plays an important role in our thinking.

The humor in an artwork is when you say something and it means something else. Also when you try to be sincere and it points to something else. It's hard to grab, but we all can sense it. You can fake the real. And you can fake the fake.

Ai Weiwei and the Chinese Zodiac

When you were growing up, did the Chinese zodiac play much of a role in your daily life? Do you know the signs for other family members, for instance?

I think that my dad was a dog. My mom is a rooster, like me. But I'm not sure, actually, because when we grew up, nobody talked about the zodiac. It's just not the kind of thing our family talked about, you know. My father, Ai Qing, was more of a modern person, and we were a kind of "new culture" family. I never met my grandmother or grandfather when I grew up. We were living in political exile in a remote area in Xinjiang, with no relatives. Everything was "new establishment."

I think today, the Chinese people care about the zodiac for fun. It doesn't have much impact or symbolic meaning. It's another way to look at humans as a species—you have a blood type, a Chinese zodiac animal, and a Western one. It doesn't have any meaning, really.

But because *Circle of Animals/Zodiac Heads* is animal heads, I think it's something that everyone can have some understanding of, including children and people who are not in the art world. I think it's more important to show your work to the public. That's what I really care about. When Andy Warhol painted Mao in the 1960s and 1970s, I don't think many people understood Mao, either—it was just this image that people knew, like Marilyn Monroe or somebody (figs. 12, 13). So they might see these zodiac animals like that—like Mickey Mouse. They're just animals. Eleven real animals and one mystic animal.

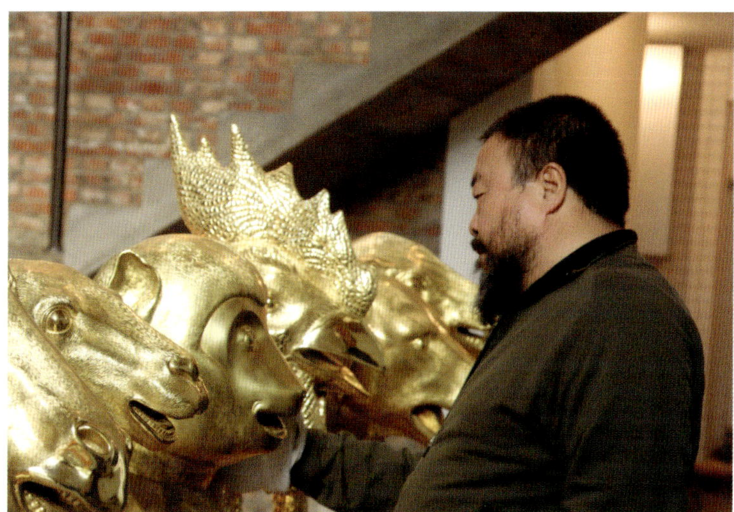

FIG. 13
Ai Weiwei,
Mao behind Bars II,
1986. Oil on canvas,
96 x 72 in.
(243.8 x 182.9 cm).
Private collection

FIG. 14
Ai Weiwei in his Beijing studio examining early versions of heads from *Circle of Animals/Zodiac Heads: Gold*, 2010

Monkey King Makes Havoc: Ai Weiwei Conducts a Carnival of the Animals

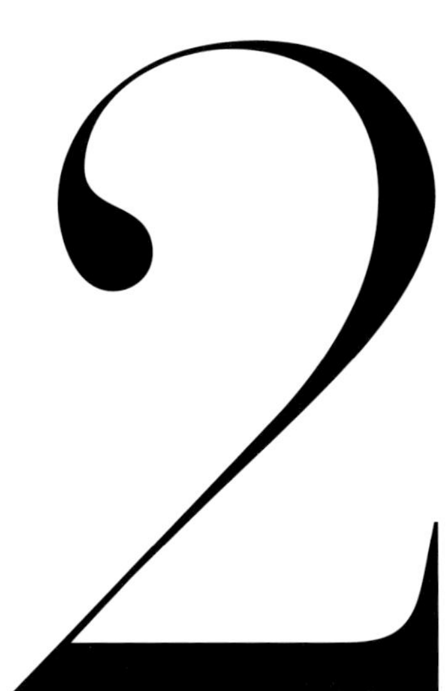

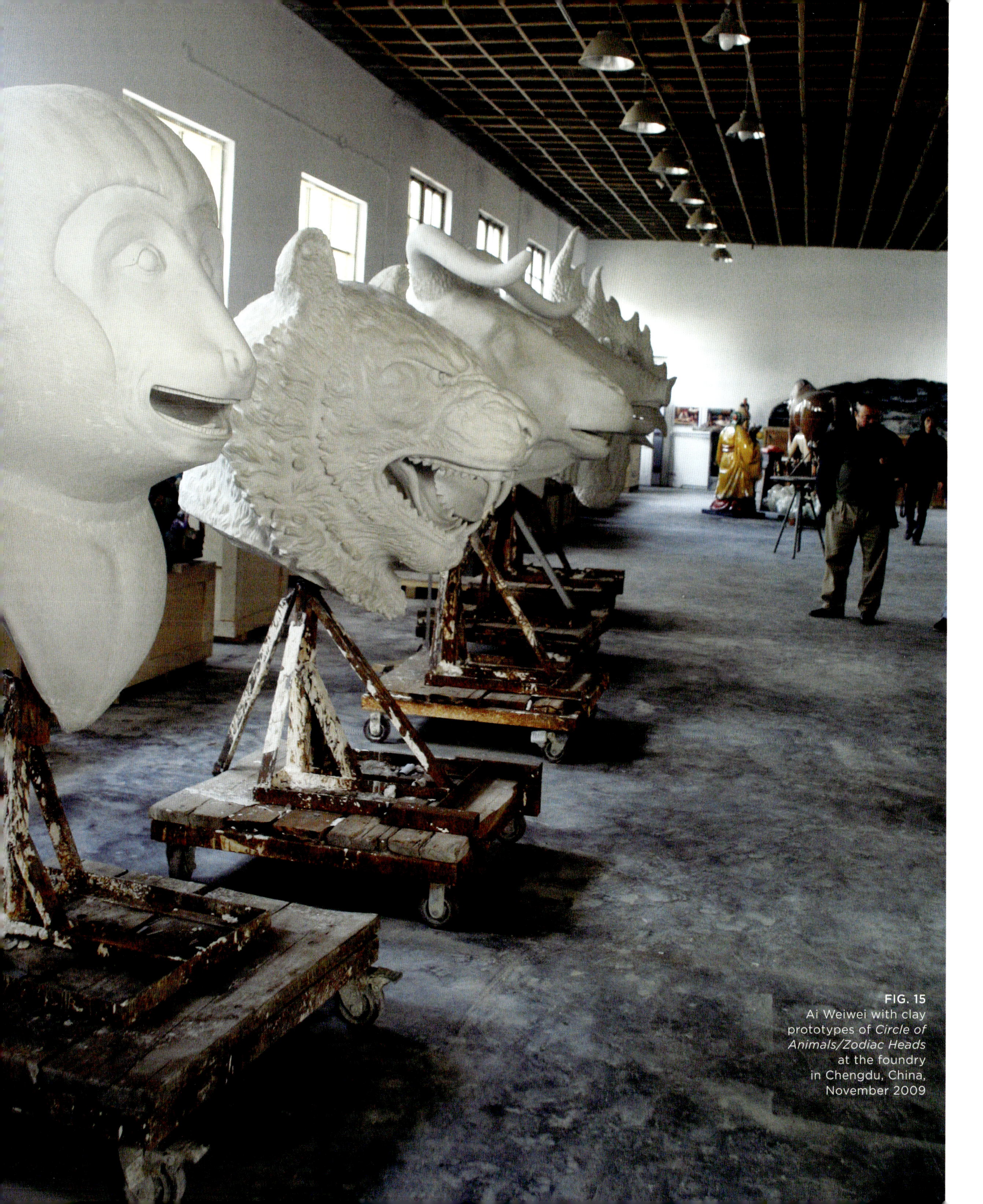

FIG. 15
Ai Weiwei with clay
prototypes of *Circle of
Animals/Zodiac Heads*
at the foundry
in Chengdu, China,
November 2009

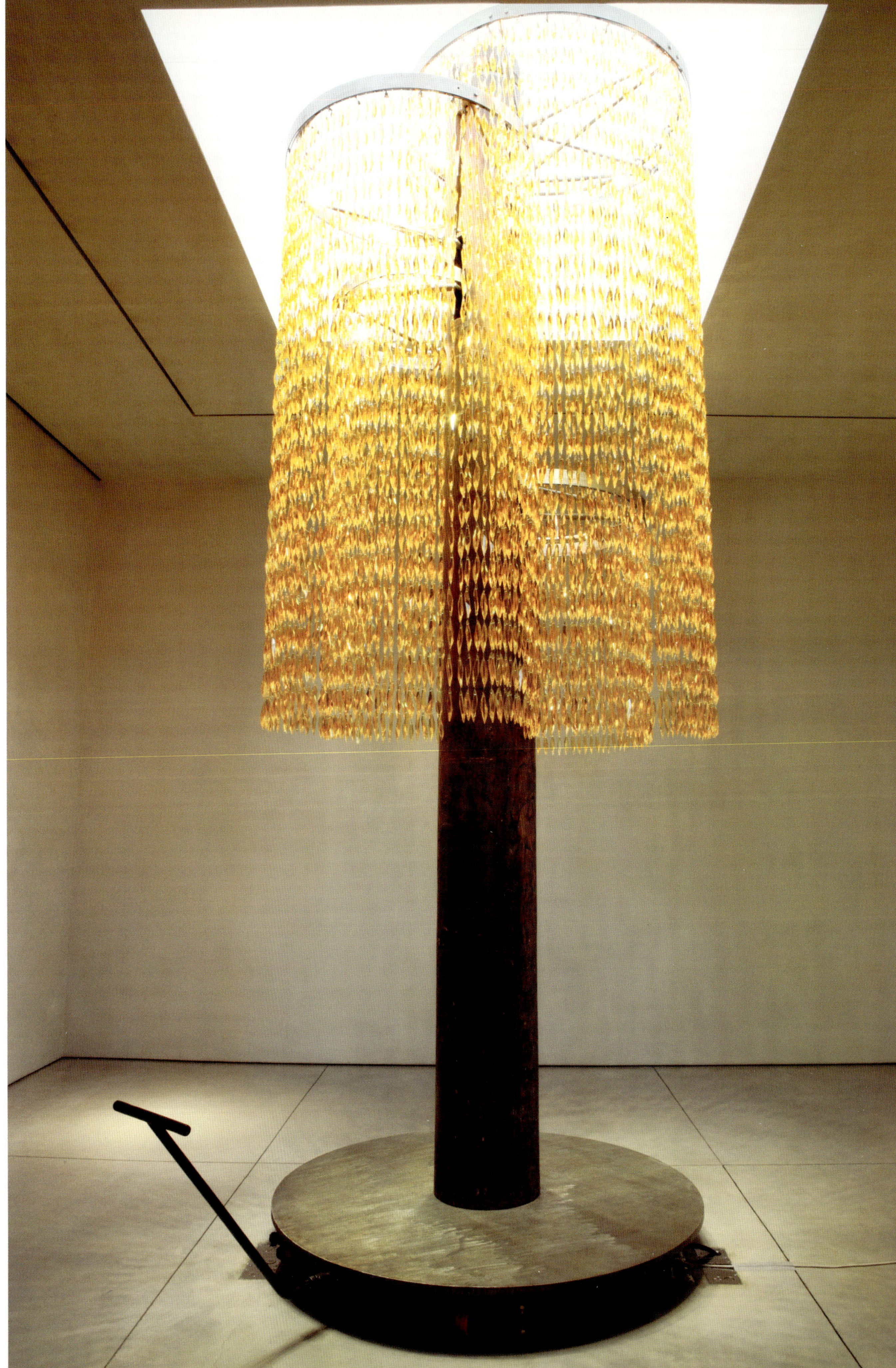

FIG. 16
Ai Weiwei, *Traveling Light*,
2007. Tieli wood, glass
crystals, lights, and metal,
187 ¾ x 88 ¼ x 69 ¾ in.
(477 x 224 x 177 cm)
Private collection

'I wonder why we hate the past so.'
'It's so damned humiliating.'[1]

— William Dean Howells and Mark Twain

HISTORY CAN BE A HORRIBLE THING. IN THE WORDS of Edward Gibbon, it is "little more than the register of the crimes, follies and misfortunes of mankind."[2] By the mid-eighteenth century, this British historian and parliamentarian was in a position to know: the British Empire's catalogue of "crimes, follies and misfortunes" committed, overlooked, and swallowed in the name of empire building was well documented. And even though some considered that "We as a nation are little better than brigands, murderers and poisoners in our dealings at this moment with half the population of the globe,"[3] those in favor of empire building were firm in their conviction that "half-civilized Governments such as those of China, Portugal, Spanish America, require a dressing every eight or ten years to keep them in order."[4] The destruction of the Yuanming Yuan, the Garden of Perfect Brightness, and the removal of the now infamous bronze animal heads was the result of one such "dressing" China required to ensure "order" was maintained.

Behind the arrogance intoned here lay a moral—Christian—rationale that was felt by the peoples living under those "half-civilized" governments as a righteous superiority. If there is truth in the notion that "He who has money, lives long; he who has authority, can do no wrong; he who has might, establishes right,"[5] then with the profits of burgeoning international trade in their pockets, and with the authority of military strength there to enforce their adventuring bravado, the British established a might that persuaded them wholly of the "rightness" of their cause, and, as exampled above, the requisite dressings were duly meted out.

That is, almost without exception, the tone in which such events have been passed down as history to generations of British high school students. In that era Britain happened to be ahead of the game, but the approach applies not only to British history. The same can be said of the way *all* histories are scripted, going back to the earliest civilizations, told in tales that are alternately heroic or villainous depending on which side of "civilized" we were fated to be born, and whether we are heirs to the heroes or to their victims. So if we "hate the past," as Howells believed, it is inevitably because we are taught to do so. And if it appears to be humiliating, as Mark Twain claimed, then it is because we are persuaded of that also: firmly persuaded, too, as in the case of several generations of Chinese in the 170-odd years or so since the humiliation suffered at the hands of imperialist invaders—which included France and Germany as well as the United States and Japan—commenced in the nineteenth century and that, to various constituents in China today, has yet to be redressed.

If, on the other side of the line—in present-day Britain or in any other nation perceived to have inflicted injustice upon China—the subject of humiliations inflicted is rarely spoken of or even alluded to, it is because history today is placed confidently within neatly defined politically correct boundaries, where "just moral causes" are reductively analyzed and unsavory aspects, such as the trade in opium, itself the cause of several wars fought in its name, are rephrased to suit modern, liberal democratic agendas.[6] Times change; history moves on. We are no longer the same people our forefathers were, even if our national identities continue to define us. But if nations don't actually change very much, at least their fortunes do: modern-day China is settling into a new role on the global stage, a position from which it currently appears to enjoy a wide range of advantages over its first-world ("Western") cousins. To date, and in spite of the advent of an avant-garde art scene in China which first emerged in the early to mid-1980s, these "advantages" remain largely economic. As Ai Weiwei is always quick to point out, art, creative freedom, and innovation have yet to make a significant appearance in real, practical terms, either within China or on its behalf. He goes further, questioning their very existence: "Even though China today has become such a power"—a miracle after so much time of struggle, as he readily admits—"in terms of creativity, or cultural values, there's no clear definition of what China today represents. We can't see how it contributes to the world, to the global situation, to new technology, or enriches ordinary people's daily life by offering some meaningful ideas."[7]

So here is the first answer to the question of what Ai Weiwei's art is all about: his attempt to "offer some meaningful ideas." Understanding that concept squarely places both the diversity of his artworks, and the more recent seam of "activism" with which he is credited, on the same page: a page that is itself directly linked to the situation of China today in all its myriad facets. And that brings us back to the past. History is not a subject in which empirical fact is de rigueur: victors embellish victories; victims strategically navigate their losses and humiliations. Both approaches have less to do with actual fact than with appeals to targeted constituents, to unite citizens in celebration or in dreams of redress. Nonetheless, with respect to the inspiration behind Ai Weiwei's monumental work *Circle of Animals/Zodiac Heads*, and a discussion of how the appropriation of the original bronze animal heads relates to his extraordinary body of work, the facts and fiction surrounding their history, and the nature of historic narratives constructed to account for it are paramount. So, let the story begin.

Once upon a time, through a series of unfortunate events and in the name of a just cause, in the mid-nineteenth century Britain and China were on the opposite sides of not one, but two Opium Wars. Lord Elgin, the man who led the British and French forces that destroyed the Yuanming Yuan on October 18 1860,[8] wrote that "War is a hateful business. The more one sees of it, the more one detests it."[9] Yet it was always *necessary* to achieving a desired end. Ergo, the destruction of the Yuanming Yuan in the cause of revenge, not only for the kidnap and torture of British diplomats[10] and the Chinese refusal to conform to the Treaty of Tientsin, which the British obliged Chinese officials to sign in June of 1858,[11] but—more to the point—to redress the unacceptable routing of British forces in China by *Chinese* forces in June 1859.[12] This astonishing defeat could not go un-"dressed." Thus it was that events were set in motion that would result in the demise of the Yuanming Yuan: a choice, explained in the *New York Times* some years after the event, of striking at "a government building to save the ordinary people from the 'blow' . . . without exposing the great city to the horrors of a bombardment."[13]

In the process, as has been vigorously described in historic accounts ever since, what could be pillaged was seized upon, that which was not deemed valuable or was too difficult to remove was destroyed, and then the whole lot torched. It took several days to complete the destruction.[14] The French were said to consider Elgin's decision "a Gothlike act of barbarism,"[15] but, as if countering this undignified charge, one British soldier was reported as quipping: "People don't plunder palaces every day."[16]

And in the midst of the destruction and pillage twelve bronze animal heads were removed: heads that had functioned as the focal point of an elaborate water clock, and which were, then, but glorified waterspouts, the modern equivalent of gold-plated taps—or, less flatteringly, "a worthless pile of faucet heads, as numerous Chinese bloggers have confessed they are."[17] Impressive yes, realistic certainly, and artistic as far as befitted

their utility, but since they were never intended to be viewed in close detail as artifacts independent of the water clock as a whole, they conform to a curiously simplistic aesthetic. Ai Weiwei might suggest that "what is really most bizarre is that objects like these can be misunderstood as a national treasure, when really they are not," yet without doubt, important they are. The heads are possibly the only unique feature of the Yuanming Yuan to have survived to the present. The aura of the original trauma of the 1860 destruction is seen to engulf them; it is a potent quality. That is why, today "The ruins of these pavilions and their fountains . . . are taken . . . as being representative of the Yuanming Yuan as a whole, even though in extent and architectural style they were of minimal importance."[18]

Indeed, since the offering of three heads at auction in 2000[19] in Hong Kong, for some portions of Chinese society the animal heads have become the rallying point for nationalist fervor. But as Ai Weiwei was quick to point out on his blog in February 2009, following the second wave of outrage ahead of the auction in Paris: "The rabbit and rat bronzes are not Chinese culture, and they have no artistic value. Patriotism is not a love of the Aisin Gioro family name, and twelve playthings manufactured in the West are not the quintessence of Chinese culture."[20]

THAT WAS NOT THE ONLY THING AI WEIWEI HAD TO SAY. The controversy that rose up around the animal heads demanded a response and, much to the delight of his blog followers, he rose to the challenge.[21] While he used the conservative Chinese position and actions that took center stage in the wake of the auctions as a timely opportunity to take on the entire gamut of contemporary Chinese cultural attitudes, for Ai Weiwei the response—in particular, the local response among those who expressed outrage in China—was simply the latest example of the cultural malapropisms that abound in modern China. The advent of blogging had already provided him with an irresistible means of taking a stand against them, his prose a blend of Futurist Manifesto, Guerilla Girl *j'accuse!* and British-tabloid satire, toned with irreverence, candor, and always with wit. His diatribes also provided particular insight into the mood of contemporary China. "Once you understand that lawyers are swindlers, the law is dubious, the media is low-down, and the system is fatuous," he opined in 2009, "then you will know why the Chinese pretend, and what

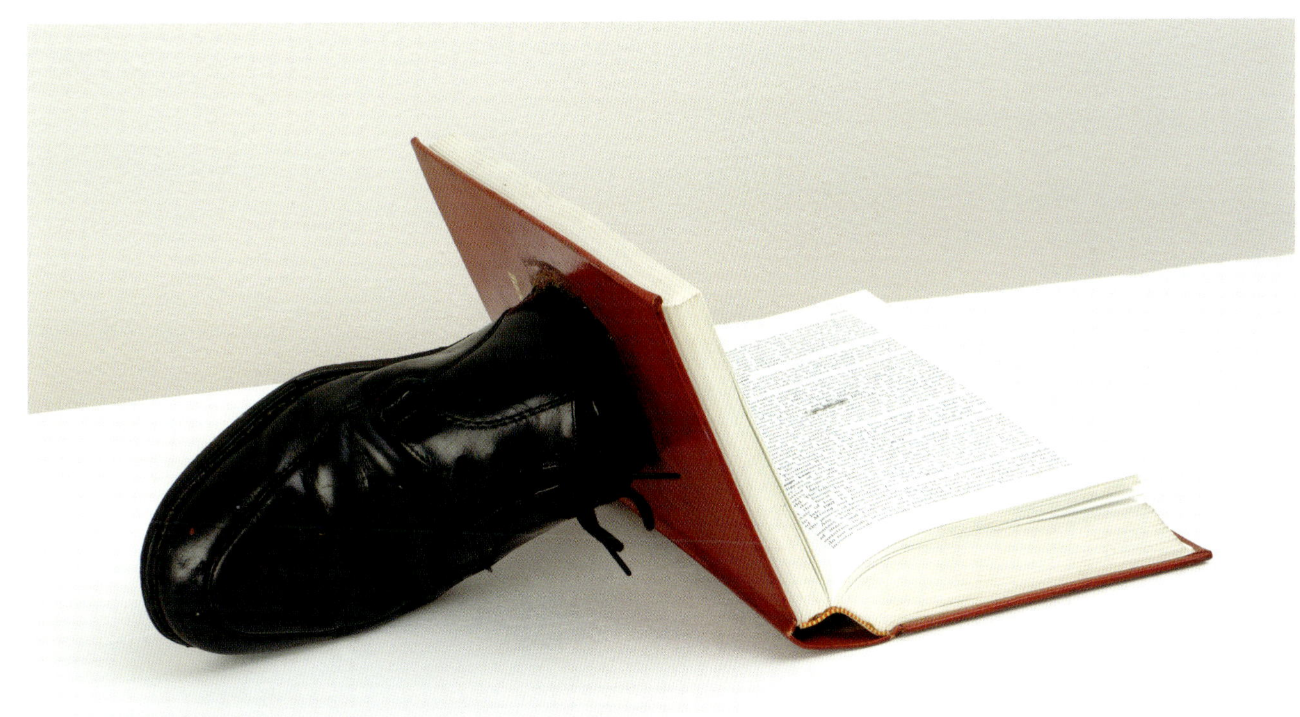

FIG. 17
Ai Weiwei, *Untitled*,
1986. Book with shoe,
17 x 9 x 6 in. (43.2 x
22.9 x 15.2 cm).
Collection Urs Meile,
Switzerland

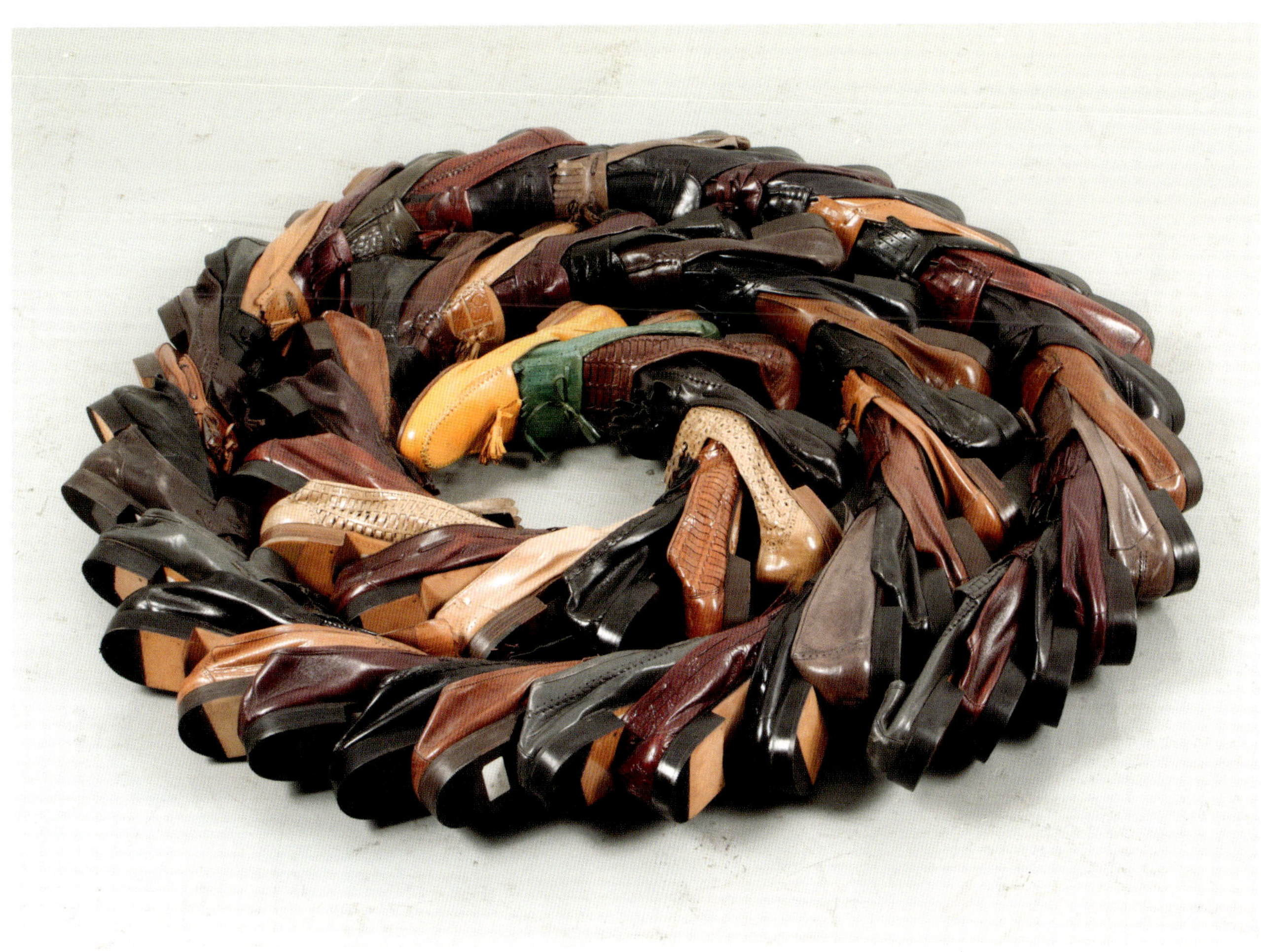

FIG. 18
Ai Weiwei, *Circle of
Shoes*, 1986.
Leather shoes,
12 x 92 in.
(30.5 x 233.7 cm).
Private collection

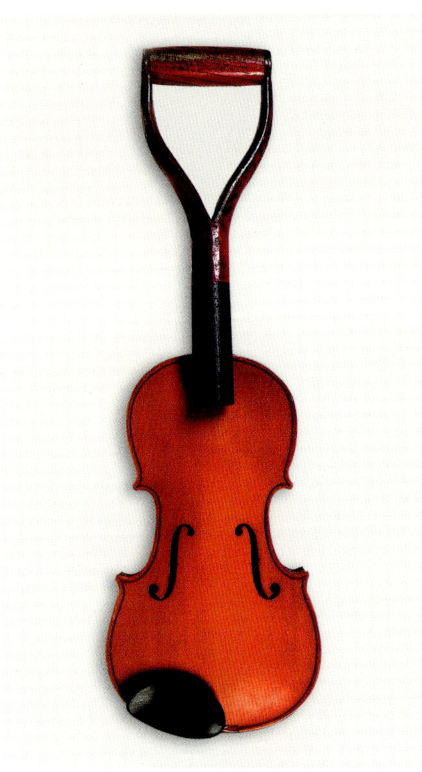

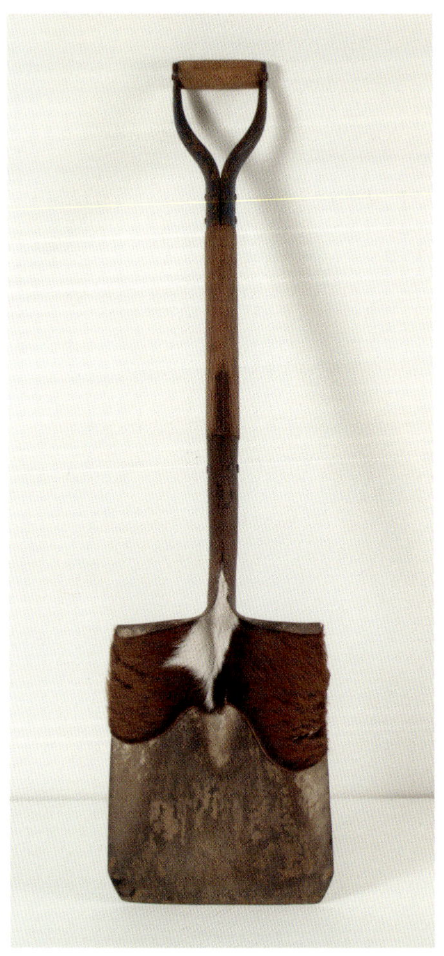

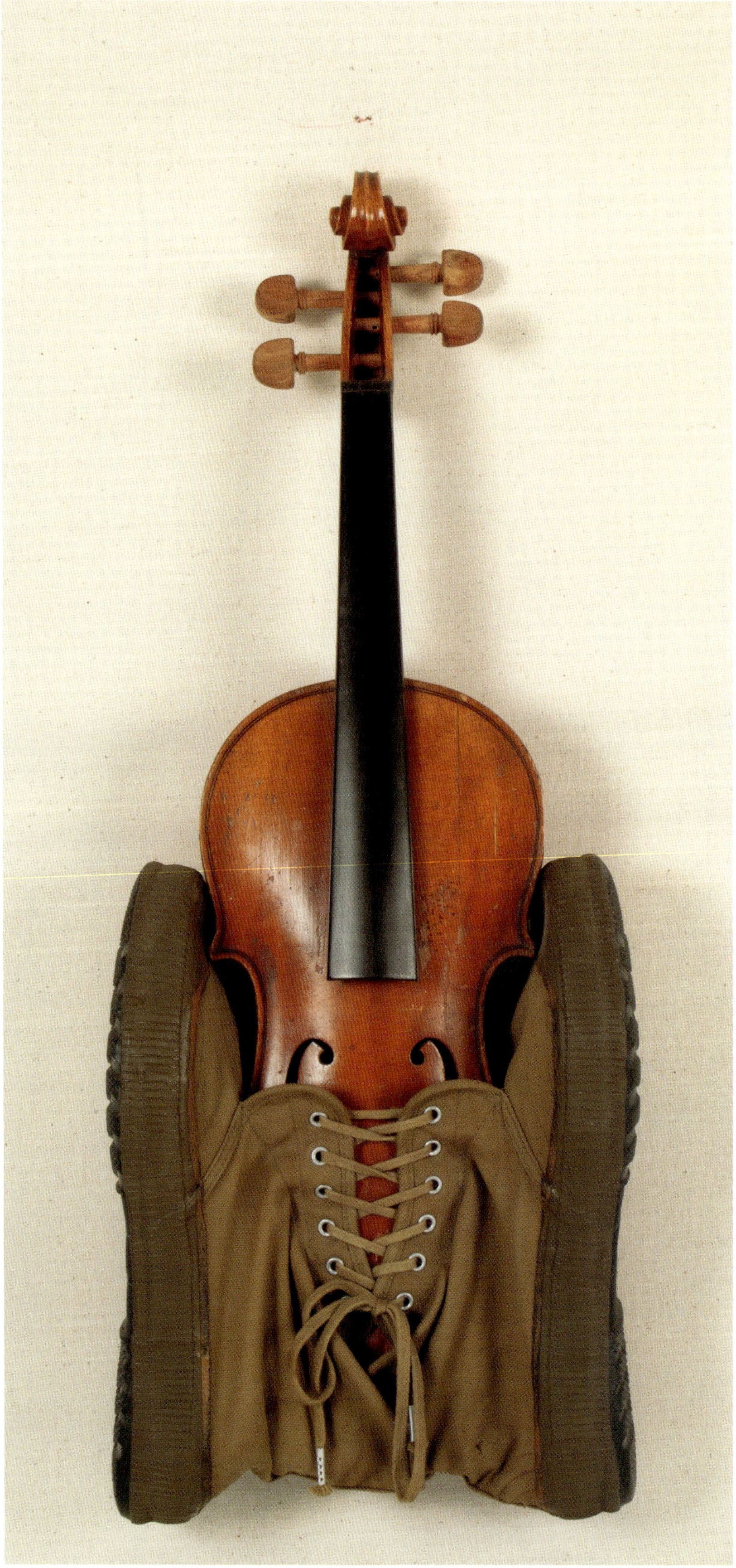

FIG. 19
Ai Weiwei, *Violin*, 1985. Shovel handle, violin, 25 x 9 x 3 in. (63.5 x 22.9 x 7.6 cm). Collection of the artist

FIG. 20
Ai Weiwei, *Shovel*, n.d. Shovel, cowhide, 39 x 12 in. (99.1 x 30.5 cm). Private collection

FIG. 21
Ai Weiwei, *Violin Shoes*, n.d. Violin, shoes, 23 x 9 in. (58.4 x 22.9 cm). Private collection

FIG. 22
Opposite: Ai Weiwei, *Mona Lisa in Space*, 1986. Oil on canvas, 59 x 53 ½ in. (151 x 136 cm). Courtesy André Stockamp & Christopher Tsai

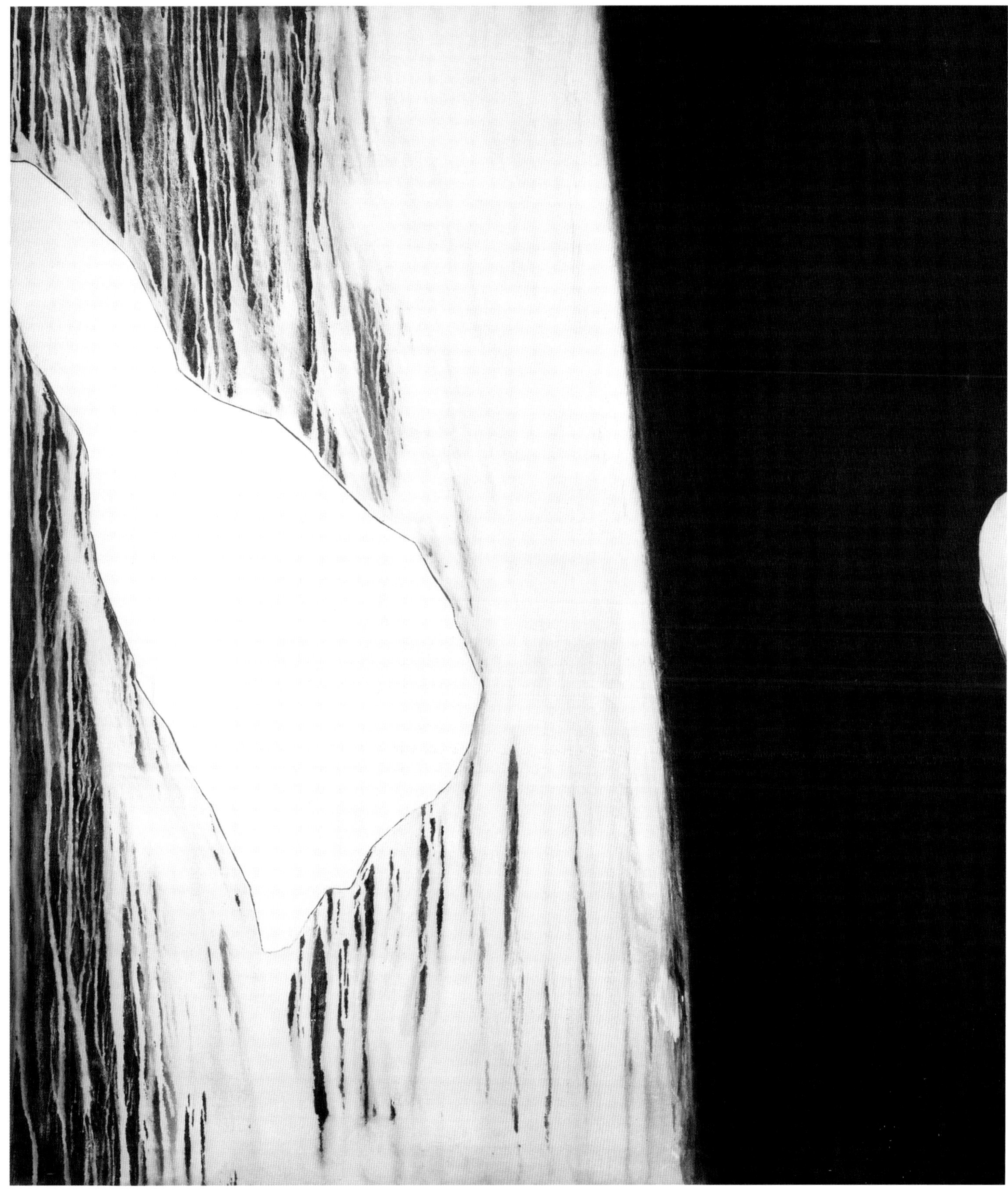

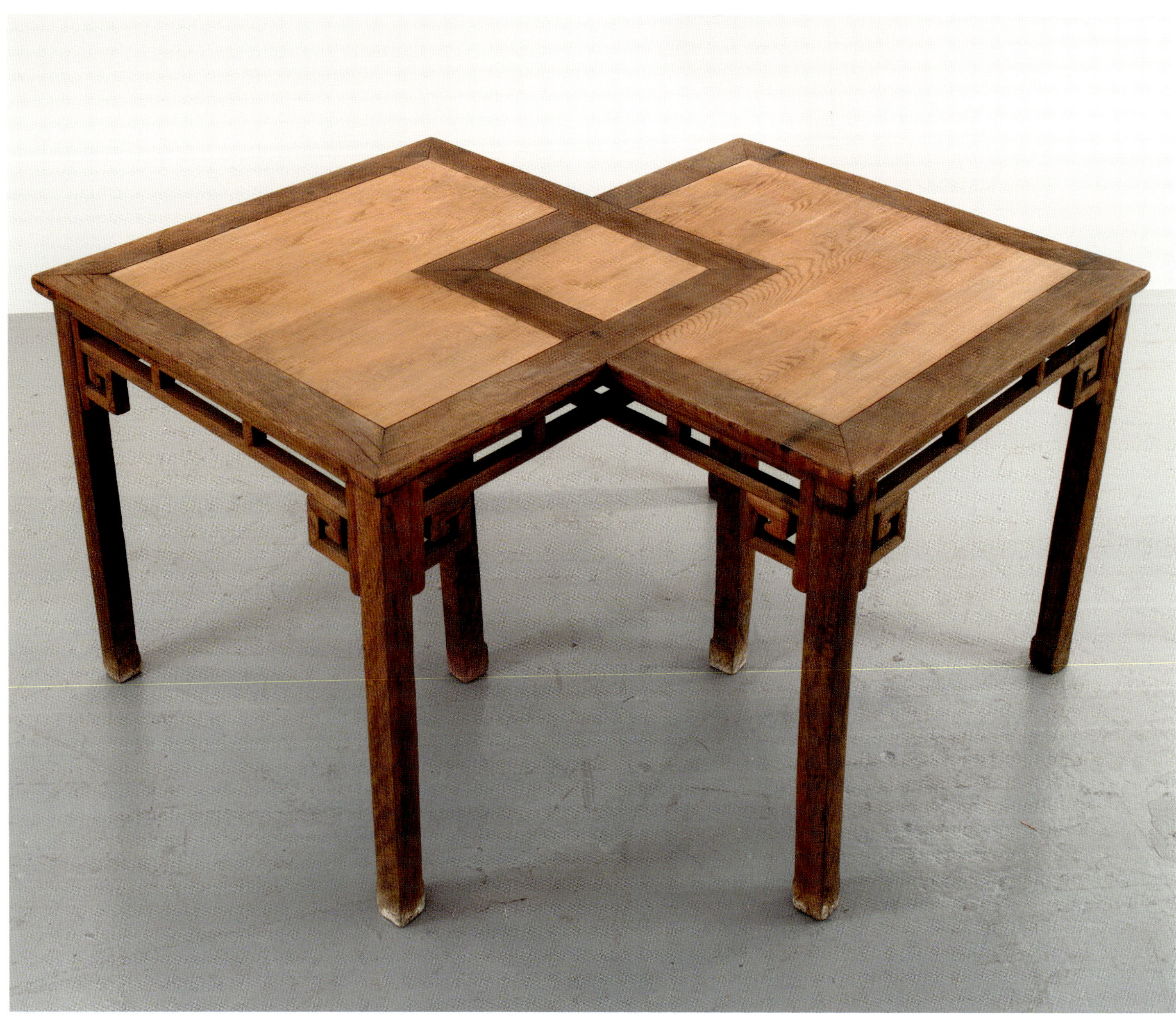

FIG. 23
Ai Weiwei, *Crossed Corners*, 1999. Wooden tables, Qing dynasty (1644–1911),
34 x 77 ⅜ x 51 in. (86.4 x 196.5 x 129.5 cm)
Private collection

they pretend. This is a nation that disregards fact and shamelessly grandstands itself."[22] The blog was where Ai Weiwei's life and art converged seamlessly as he demonstrated his belief that there is little if any difference between art and politics, between artist and politician. In retrospect, the blog was to Ai Weiwei's artistic career as a urinal in the hands of Marcel Duchamp.

The issue that fed his rhetoric in 2009 was the hollow ring to the so-called patriotic outcry against the auction of the rat and the rabbit animal heads in Paris and the politicized gestures on both sides that resulted.[23] That, and the fact that, while there was a violently emotional posturing on the part of some Chinese people, as well as damning criticism of them and of Western collectors and authorities by others, at no point was there a public discussion about what had *actually* happened in the past, about what value the heads *actually* represented, nor of the extent of the *actual* damage done by the interlopers in comparison to the destructive force of the Chinese people when they set their minds to it. It was not about who was right or who was wrong, but about the reality that judgment is impossible in the absence of debate.

It didn't take the arrival of British and French troops in China in the mid-nineteenth century to introduce the Chinese to cycles of death and destruction, and to the "crimes, follies and misfortunes of mankind" that Gibbon described: not in general, since every dynastic change beginning with the first Chinese emperor brought with it tumultuous upheavals, nor in specific. With respect to the Yuanming Yuan, locals were quick to loot the wreckage in the immediate aftermath of the Elgin attack, during the Boxer Rebellion at the turn of the century, and again after the collapse of imperial China in 1911. In that famous blog entry Ai Weiwei added that the Yuanming Yuan ". . . enjoys its current state of decline not merely because of the Western invaders; the contributions of our compatriots cannot be erased. That palace was a row of pigsties until the 1980s, and at that time there wasn't a home in the vicinity that wasn't using its richly ornamented white marble as bricks."[24]

Of course, there was also Mao Zedong, a man who wielded his enormous "might" with the aim of establishing "right" as he saw it. Or was he simply following in the footsteps of his forefathers if, as is claimed for him, he actually said "originality comes from destruction?"[25] History certainly appears to demonstrate the ways and means by which Mao put this claim into action (and the ferocious degree to which he believed he was right). In terms of the Yuanming Yuan this was reflected, if not in a direct attack upon the remains, then certainly in bungled attempts to arrest its ruination.

By the mid-twentieth century, Ai Weiwei was in a position to know all about the most recent "crimes, follies and misfortunes" for which his own people were responsible. For reasons of his birth that are well documented elsewhere,[26] by the time he became aware of his interest in art in the mid-1970s, he had pretty much seen all manner of destruction imaginable: of objects, of artifacts, of history, culture, values and ideals, as well as society, community, and individual human lives—none greater than those acts perpetrated during the Cultural Revolution (1966–76). He spoke from experience when he asked the following question: "Over the first few

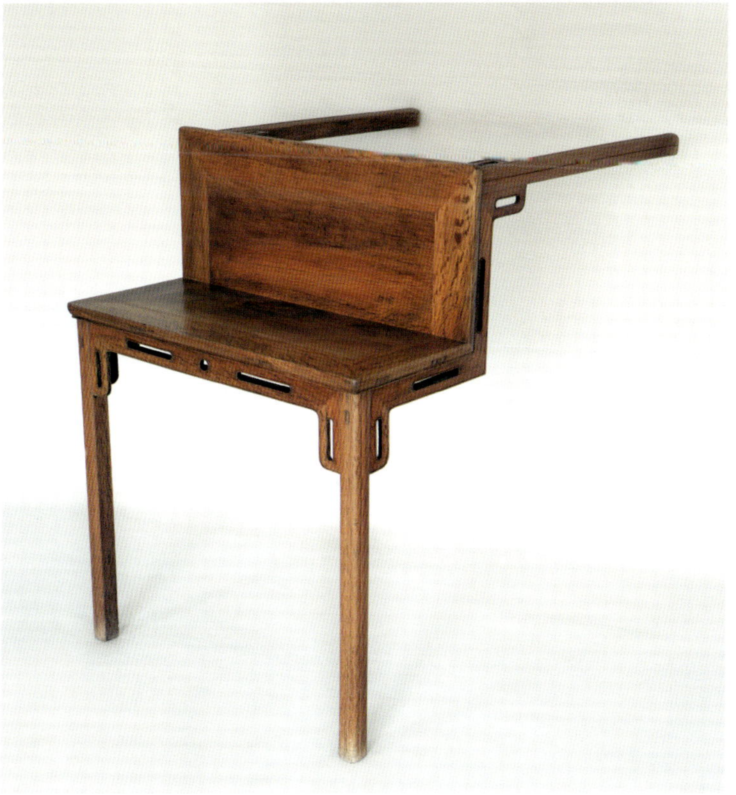

FIG. 24
Ai Weiwei, *Table with two legs on the wall*, 1997. Wooden table, Qing dynasty (1644–1911), 36 x 46 ½ x 48 in. (90.5 x 118 x 122 cm) Private collection

decades of New China, in the name of the revolution, and during the Cultural Revolution, across the entire nation and in Tibet, countless cultural relics were destroyed in the name of the people, the party, in [the name of patriots]. You [patriots] destroyed infinite numbers of temples, smashed thousands upon thousands of Buddha statues, melted inestimable numbers of wagons filled with gold-plated Buddhas—who will stand up today and tally their worth?"[27]

This, then, was one of the worst periods of destruction in China in living memory. And one that was not inflicted by external forces but carried out by Red Guards, a force of youth ignited by Mao, which turned the Chinese world upside down. "In Cultural Revolution we were all supposed to destroy everything from the past: to completely smash it," Ai Weiwei recalled. "So many paintings and artifacts destroyed. It became a real tradition."[28] If his own history had been different, Ai Weiwei would have had to swear allegiance to a Red Guard group too, but since his father had been proclaimed a rightist, he belonged to a "black element" of the new society and was excluded.

There is no small irony in the fact that the bronze animal heads should, in recent years, be perceived as representative of an ideal about Chinese heritage for the very generation that was told by Mao to destroy the "Four Olds."[29] Had the heads still been in place in the Yuanming Yuan in the 1960s, they would have been targeted and destroyed too; although, given the demand for iron that underpinned the 1957 Great Leap Forward—a mass movement aimed at bolstering steel production nationwide—the heads would probably have been melted down then, without a second thought, never to be seen again.

The destruction did not end with the Cultural Revolution, or with the death of Mao. "In the time of the opening and reform when houses, roads, neighborhoods were being destroyed and new ones built, the destruction was almost worse than Cultural Revolution. People have forgotten about historical truth, the real acts, the ways in which things were created," Ai Weiwei has said. "They [have no feeling for] the value of the past today, it's completely gone. . . . But how could it remain after all the things that were destroyed, the temples, the places, the art works, homes and materials,

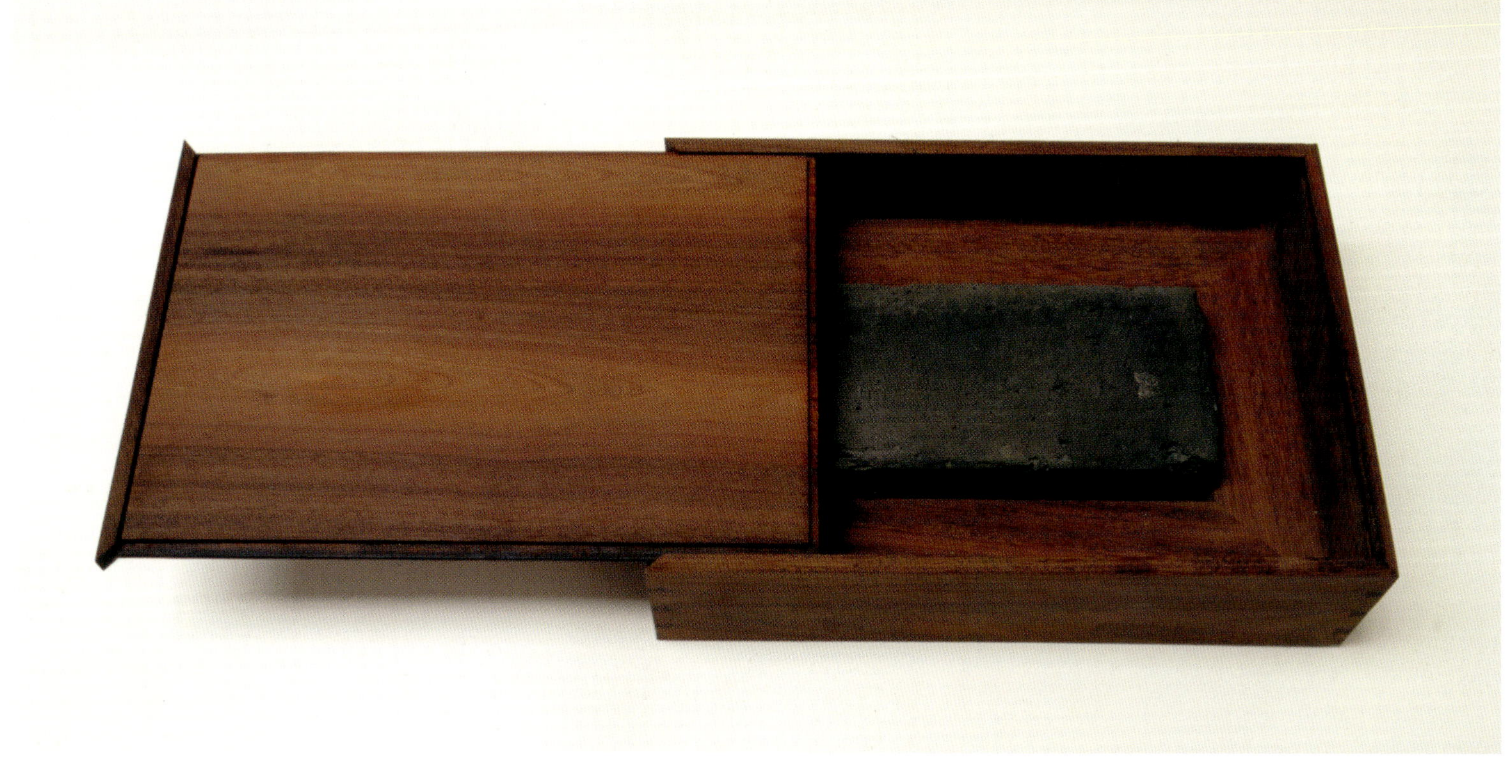

FIG. 25 Ai Weiwei, *Gift from Beijing*, 2002. Ancient brick from dismantled house, wood from destroyed Qing dynasty temple, 14 x 9 x 4 in. (35.5 x 22.5 x 9.5 cm). Private collection

the daily wares and images? On top of that, then the way of learning, of understanding, has been cut off, too."[30]

Ai Weiwei's own extensive body of work contains numerous examples of the pursuit of originality through destruction. These date from his earliest experiments in New York as he chopped up shoes, garden spades, and violins to fashion artworks (figs. 19–21). He created and then "destroyed" paintings by blasting them with sand or water to break back through layers of paint to achieve a new type of painting (fig. 22). Then there were the reconfigured furniture pieces he began making upon his return to China in 1993 (figs. 23, 24), his dropping of a Han dynasty urn in 1995, and many additional "abuses" to which he made other such precious urns subject: dousing them with paint and covering them with graffiti, for instance, or grinding them to dust. The end sought was always the same: that indeed, originality *could* be found in destruction and transmuted into an experience for the viewer that, in an encounter with a work, is shocking and breathtaking.

Ai Weiwei's acts were not, in their moment, the self-willed demonstrations of an anarchist, the artist engaged in destroying for destruction's sake, or for the thrill of it alone. They represent a direct, succinct conduit of his philosophy, which is that "art is the way we understand ourselves."[31] Through his art, Ai Weiwei asks that we understand what it means for an artistic, cultured, humanistic individual to turn into a destructive force. How ought we to respond? At what point do we stand up for something we believe in? Looking at Ai Weiwei's 1995 work, *Dropping a Han Dynasty Urn* (see fig. 37, pages 90–91), the blank, nonplussed expression on his face—seen in the sequence of photographs that document the piece as he does what the title describes—is striking. His face suggests a clinical awareness of the value of what is to be destroyed. But then, who cares? Did anyone try to stop him? Clearly not.

Art is, then, the means by which Ai Weiwei gives visual form to his understanding of his own culture and people, not merely from a personal perspective, or from personal experience during the turbulent era of his youth, but *now*, today. It is through art that he understands society, its ills and woes, the conflations of the cultural framework and history. It is here we find clues to his take on the follies and fallacies of the political field—the stifling of individual freedom—but also the crimes that the general lack of transparency inevitably encourages. Thus, in *Circle of Animals/Zodiac Heads*, Ai Weiwei reconfigures the original forms of the bronze animal heads as a cultural mirror in which the past becomes a reflection of the

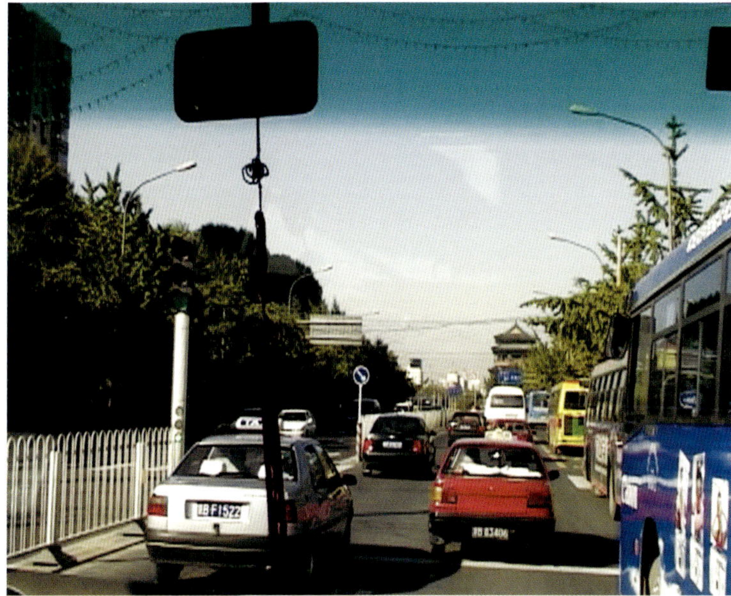
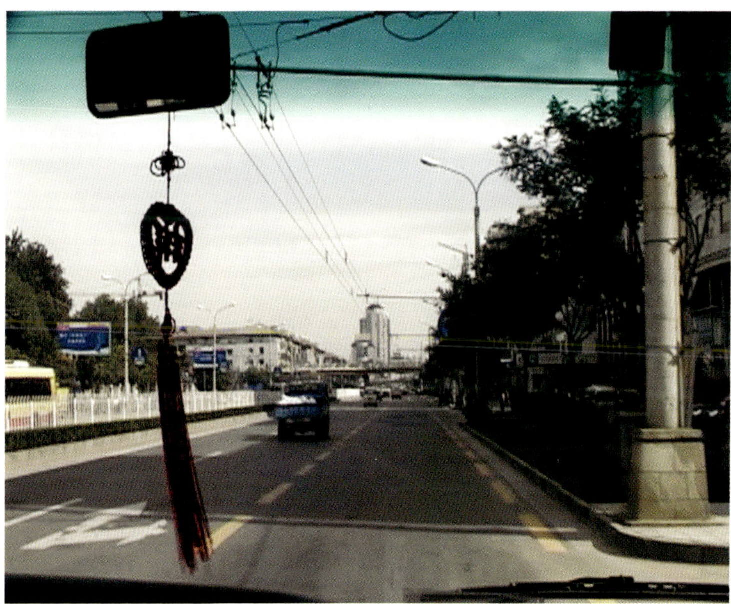

FIGS. 26 AND 27
Ai Weiwei, stills from *Beijing 2003*, 2003. Video, 153 hours

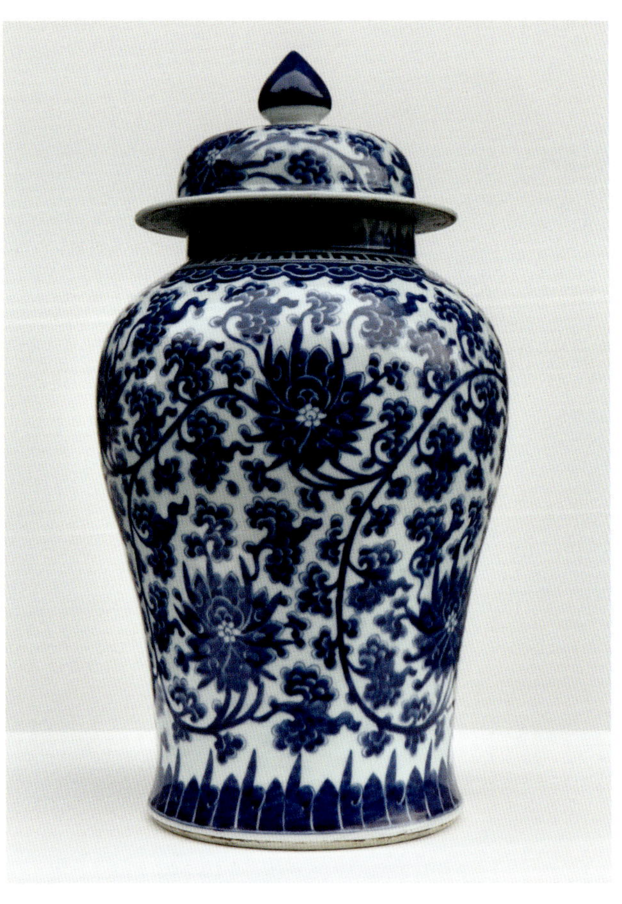

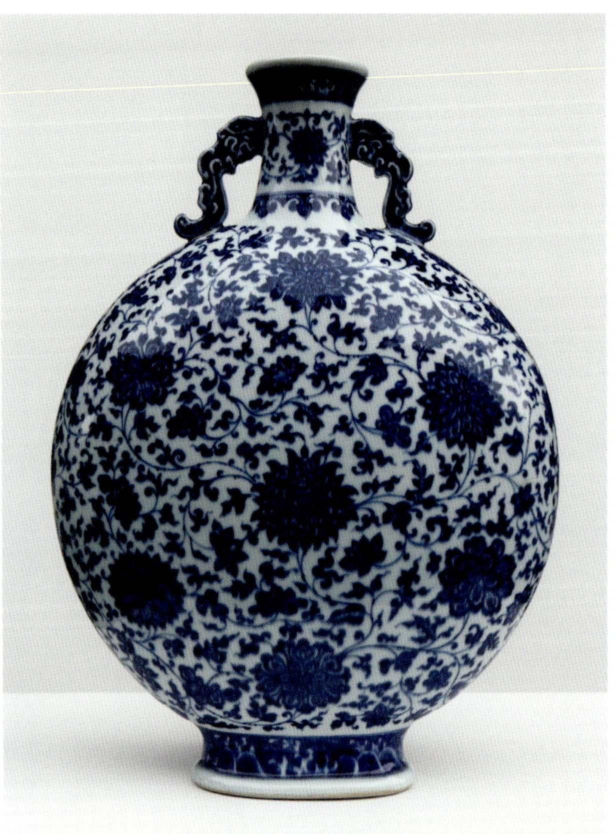

FIGS. 28 AND 30
Above left and opposite:
Ai Weiwei, *Blue & White Porcelain*, 1996. Two replicas in the style of the Qing dynasty, Kangxi era (1661–1722). Porcelain, glaze, and cobalt brushwork; left: 18 x 9 in. (45.7 x 22.9 cm) with lid; opposite: 18 ½ x 10 ½ in. (47 x 26.7 cm) with lid. Private collection

FIG. 29
Below left: Ai Weiwei, *Blue & White Moonflask*, 1996. Replica in the style of the Qing dynasty, Kangxi era (1661–1722). Porcelain, glaze, and cobalt brushwork, 20 ⅞ x 14 ½ x 3 in. (53 x 36.8 x 7.6 cm). Private collection

present. If we are able to detach ourselves from the emotional entanglement in which they have become mired, we might discern a distinct absurdity to the claims, actions, and counter-claims that surrounded the appearance of the rat and rabbit heads at the Paris auction in 2009 and that no doubt will continue until the remaining five are accounted for.

The absurdity lies in the ways in which the events of history are invoked; how history is used as a rallying cry, as a reason, as a call to arms or to action and, in the case of China, to deflect any questioning of issues closer to home. As leading Sinologist Geremie Barmé suggests, "The gardens, the exploitation of them and the debates surrounding them reveal in essence many of the central issues and lurking problems in China's quest to preserve its heritage."[32] Ai Weiwei is by no means alone in grasping this contradiction, but he is almost alone in holding it up for scrutiny in the public domain. This role is not one he sought for himself as he embarked upon his career, but insofar as it has assumed an increasingly important part in his art, the sociopolitical and cultural climate of present-day China are crucial to an understanding of Ai Weiwei's oeuvre and his activism. The "past in the present" is an intractable factor leading to the choice of the controversial bronze animal heads as the basis for *Circle of Animals/Zodiac Heads*.

THE APPROPRIATION OF "READYMADES" IN AI WEIWEI'S work can be traced back to his years in New York, from 1982 to 1993. But in spite of chopping up the occasional shoe, spade, or violin as he digested the ideas of Duchamp and of Warhol, his daily activity focused on absorbing the life around him. Photographs he took during this period reveal a poignant interest in the manifestations of social unrest: the riots in Tompkins Square in August 1988, for example, which recalled the struggle of The Stars painting group[33] a decade earlier and pointed to the lack of genuine "cause" felt by Ai Weiwei's generation in China, and for him personally once the heady romance of The Stars had palled.

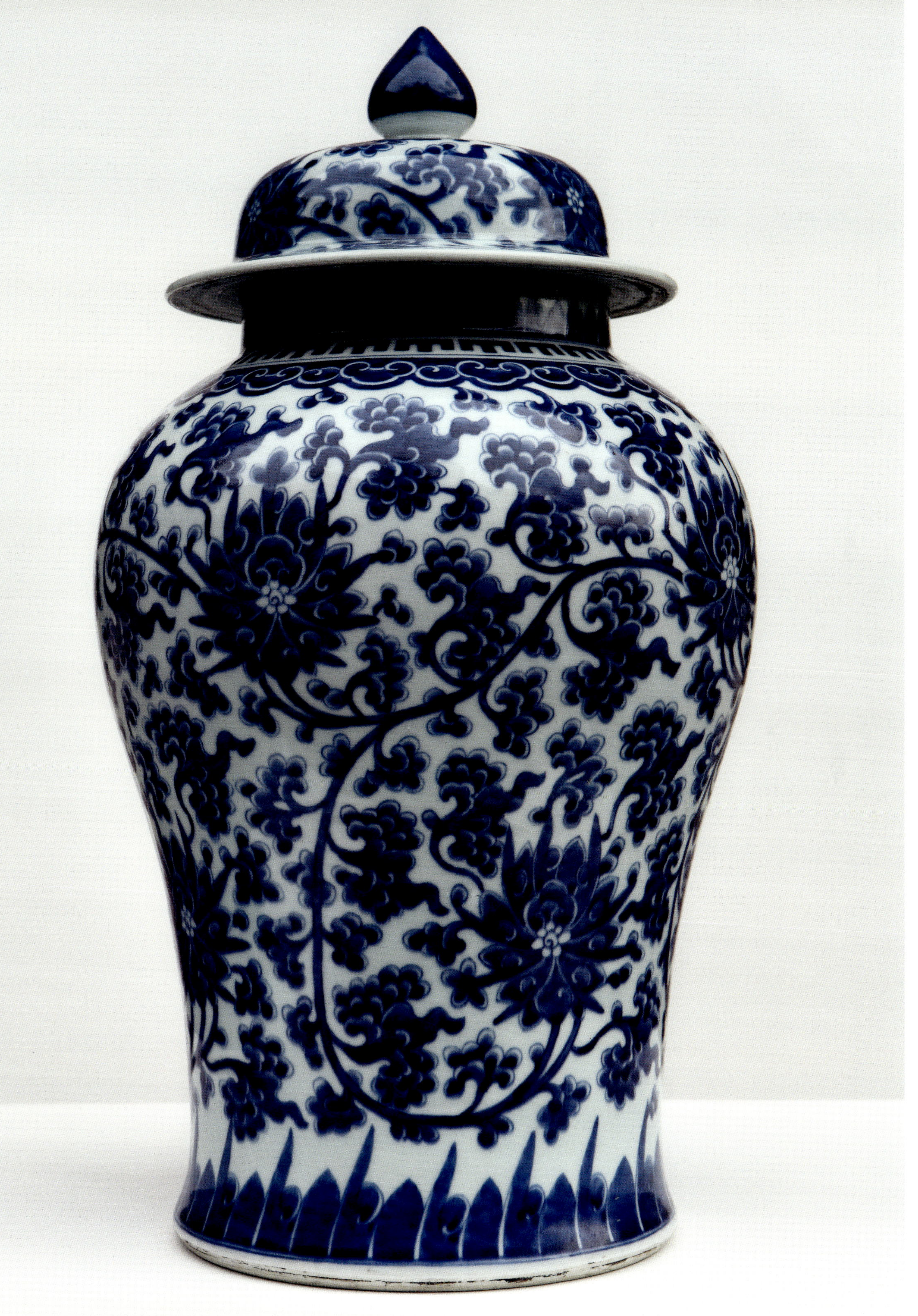

Back in Beijing, it was first craftsmanship that guided the development of early works, in a series of small elegant gestures: ethereal Chinese-style landscapes discerned in the polished facets of thin slices of marble and granite; experiments with furniture (figs. 23, 24); and a general gathering of materials that would become the foundation of numerous subsequent works. In tandem with his taste for destruction, Ai Weiwei also preserved a large quantity of similar antiquities, either by appropriating them in his art (temple wood in works such as *Through*, (2007–8), gray Beijing bricks (*Gift from Beijing*, 2002, fig. 25), or simply repackaging them as works (*White Stone Axes*, 2006).

There was apparently no cataclysmic moment that channeled Ai Weiwei's practice towards the political. He has described, with some irony, observing municipal workmen etching lines across the exterior walls of old houses in the *hutong* areas of old Beijing where his mother lives.[34] Such shoddy workmanship he observed daily, living with his mother from his return to China in 1993 until the completion of the studio-home that he designed and built himself in 1999. Since 1996, he had also observed the destruction of many parts of the city that first gained momentum during that time, and the poor quality of so many of the buildings that replaced those demolished. The shortcuts in evidence were born of the same greed and pragmatism, compounded with short-term egotistical ambitions, that would wreak devastation on the lives of so many children and families in the 2008 Sichuan earthquake, about which Ai Weiwei had much to say.[35]

The changing face of the city subsequently inspired several projects, in the course of which Ai Weiwei documented various

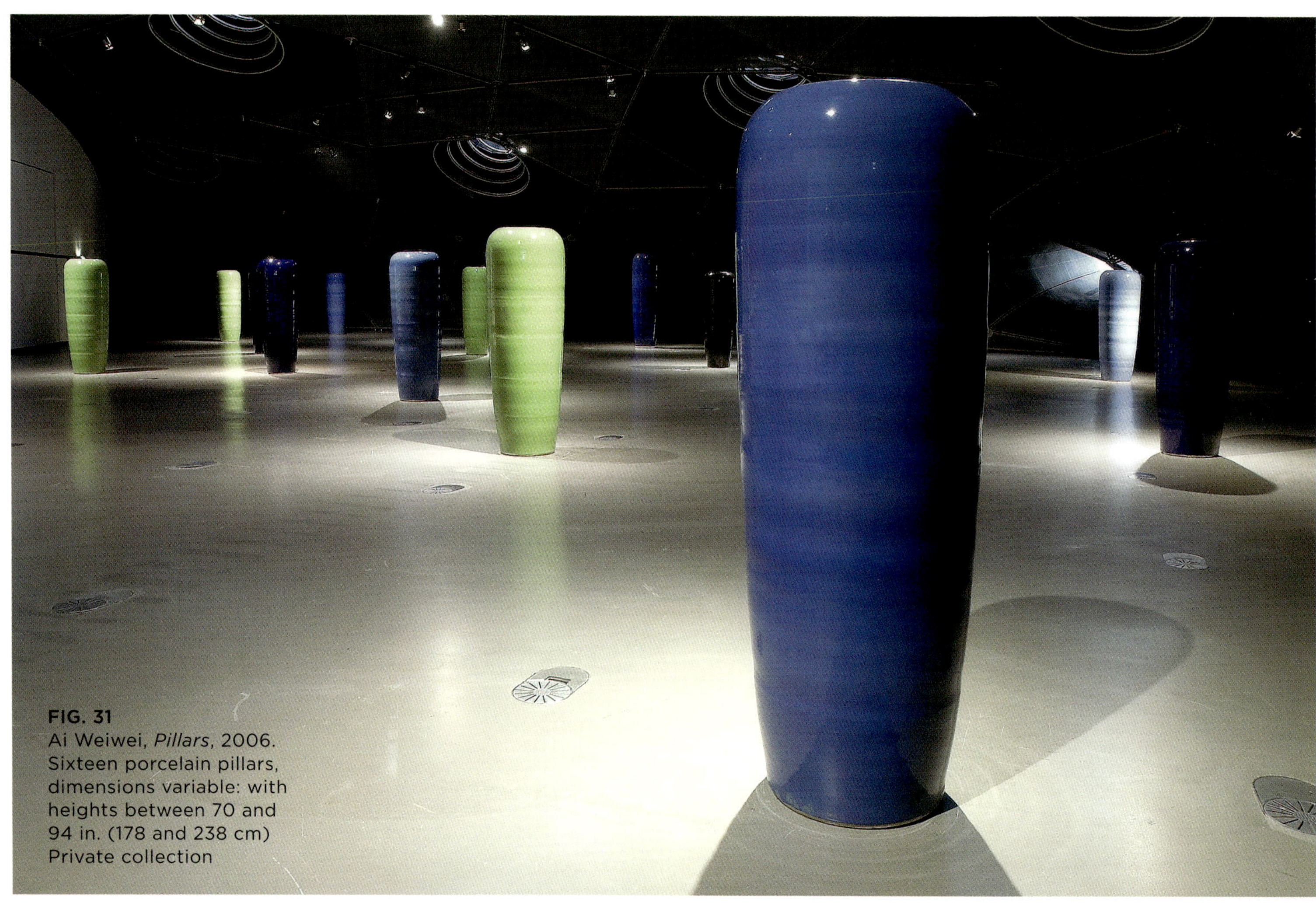

FIG. 31
Ai Weiwei, *Pillars*, 2006.
Sixteen porcelain pillars,
dimensions variable: with
heights between 70 and
94 in. (178 and 238 cm)
Private collection

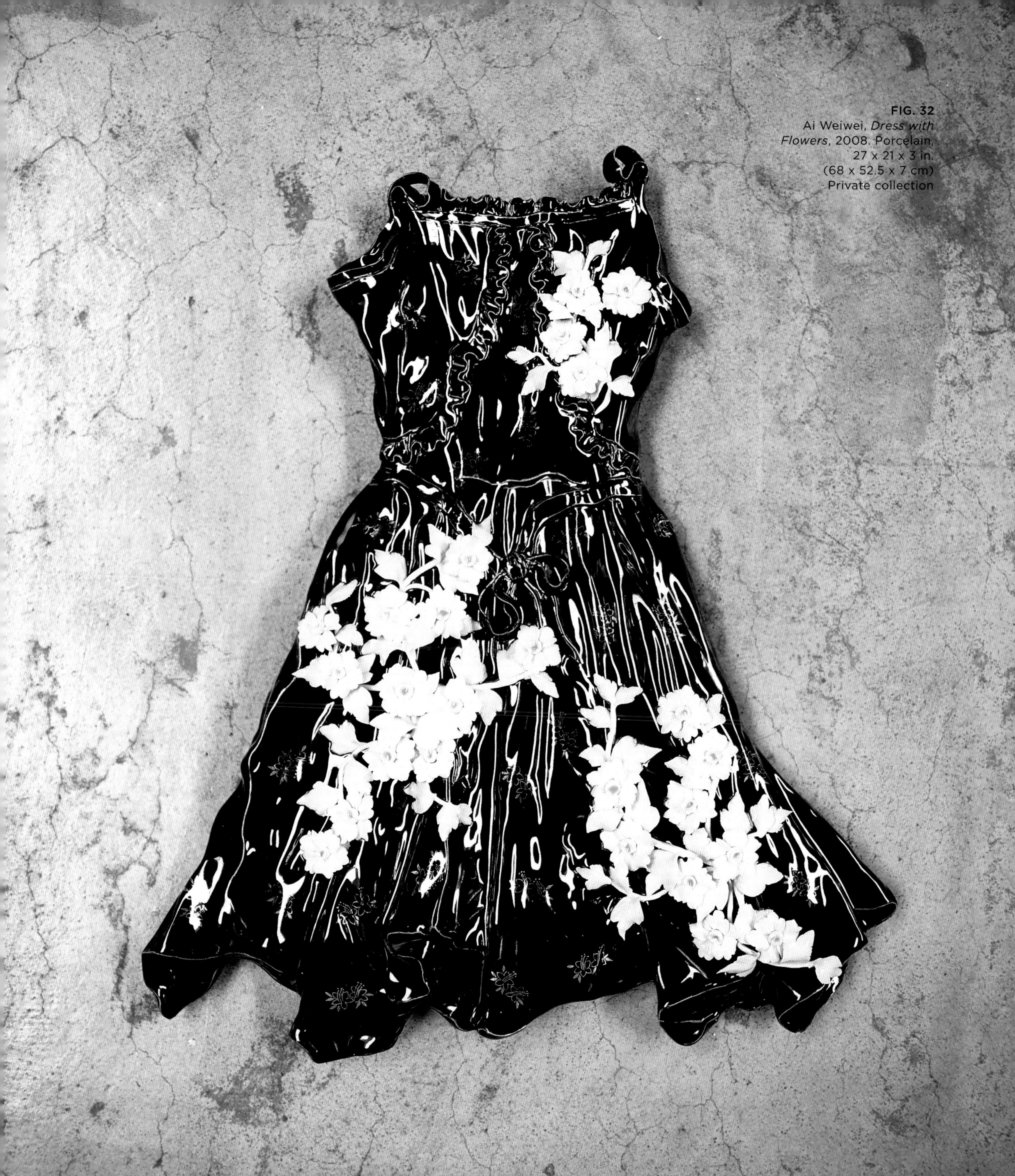

FIG. 32
Ai Weiwei, Dress with
Flowers, 2008. Porcelain,
27 x 21 x 3 in.
(68 x 52.5 x 7 cm)
Private collection

aspects of the urban center: video of roadways (*Beijing 2003*, 2003; *Beijing: The Second Ring*, 2005; and *Beijing: The Third Ring*, 2005, figs. 26, 27), and photographs of every street within the heartland of the city center (*Beijing 10/2003*, 2003). In the same period, working with a team of willing younger artists, he guided the compilation and publication of three books that are today best described as unique archives of conceptual art practice in China in the early 1990s (the *Gray*, *Black* and *White Cover* books). Following the initial foray into architecture designing his own home and studio, in 2000 he began to accept architectural commissions, which eventually made him a household name in China and a media darling around the world.

If any one element can be said to have changed both his approach and practice, it was the advent of the Internet—or more precisely, the social communications platform that morphed from the blogosphere. This amplified Ai Weiwei's voice in the community in ways not previously envisioned. At that point, art still had a limited audience in China—prior to the advent of art zones like Beijing's 798 in the early 2000s, there were few independent spaces in which to exhibit—but the word, via the private world of the computer user, proved mighty indeed. Thus, from 2005, blogging absorbed as much of

Ai Weiwei's creative energy as his "traditional" art practice. It made sense: in his words, "I am most interested in what we think about when we think about art. When does something become art? When we call something art, does that mean it is not something else? Why would a table be a "table" under some circumstances and not others? As an artwork, is it then not a table?"[36]

This comment was made as Ai Weiwei experimented with furniture, but this line of questioning led to *Emperor's Choice* (1996–98), a stunning collection of porcelain vases (figs. 28–30) that are perfect replicas of exemplary pieces from the Qing dynasty and the reign of Kangxi (1662–1723), which "represented the apex of China's porcelain tradition. . . . There was nothing more prized."[37] He realized that, working with the best artisans in Jingdezhen,[38] it was possible to reproduce the quality perfectly. Why do it? Because, he wondered, "If [the reproductions] are real in a modern context . . . exhibited in a contemporary art exhibit, does their original value continue to exist? If they are fake, then how do they differ from authentic period pieces when they are exact replicas with no recognizable difference? Can a museum exhibit a modern reproduction as an authentic piece?"[39]

This made me think of American philosopher Richard Shusterman, who asked: "What are the stakes in calling something art? Sometimes you can debate with people: Is it art? Isn't it art? And you get into an empty stalemate or circular bickering. Then it's worth asking: In calling this art, what is at stake? That you take the work seriously? . . . That you ascribe an eternal transcendent value to it?"[40]

In China, the stakes continue to be high. In light of this circumstance, what aligns Ai Weiwei's artistic expression with the tradition of "transcendent" art is the mindset of the artist: his questioning, his constant inquiry, and that fact that he always sees a new hurdle once one barrier has been crossed.

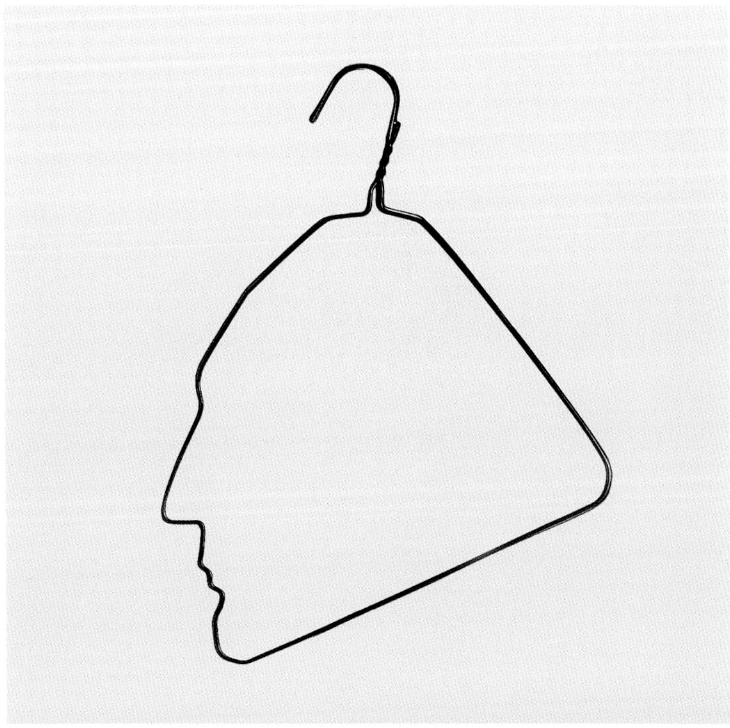

FIG. 33
Ai Weiwei, *Hanging Man*,
1985. Clothes hanger,
15 x 11 in. (38 x 28 cm).
Collection of the artist

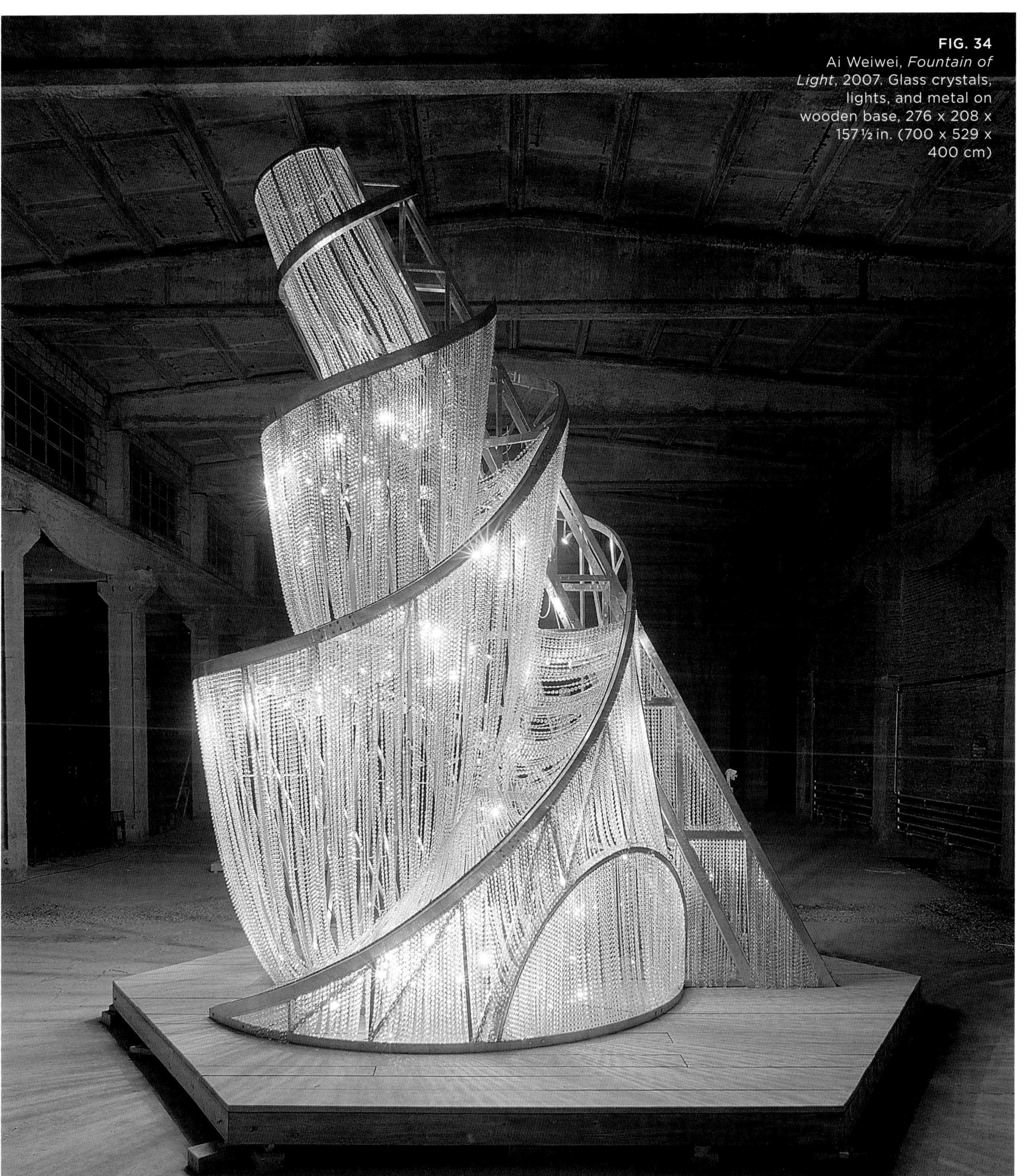

FIG. 34
Ai Weiwei, *Fountain of Light*, 2007. Glass crystals, lights, and metal on wooden base, 276 x 208 x 157 ½ in. (700 x 529 x 400 cm)

It's not just about achievement; failure often provides the best springboard into a new arena, evident in his use of traditional skills: of joinery and of porcelain making—think huge pots (*Pillars*, 2006) (fig. 31)—as much as girls' dresses (*Dress with Flowers* series, 2006–8) (fig. 32). His fascination with skills and how process infects and alters human thinking was recently demonstrated in the extraordinary commission he produced for the Turbine Hall at Tate Modern in fall 2010. Here, he used the simple form of a sunflower seed, direct from nature but also deeply embedded in the cultural experience of not just Chinese but multiple Asian peoples. To the production of one hundred million pieces, each individually handcrafted, fired, and painted on not one but *two* sides, he brought a technical process and skill of mind-boggling proportions and deft sophistication. Holding one of these life-size little seeds in the palm of one's hand, or between thumb and forefinger, it's hard to believe it's not real. Ai Weiwei's commitment to detail and will to perfection induced the residents of an entire village in China's Jiangsu province to rally round a communal activity: to commit themselves to the production of these minuscule artworks, a simple act of creativity that will remain etched on the collective memory for their lifetimes and beyond.

So, whether from nature or from art history, the act of appropriation in Ai Weiwei's practice is key. In New York, he had paid homage to Duchamp's profile (*Hanging Man*, 1985, fig. 33) and to the graphic style of Keith Haring, and in 2007, he appropriated Tatlin's *Monument to the Third International*, reworked as a monumental floating chandelier titled *Fountain of Light* (fig. 34). But the appropriation of readymades is not about building in clever references to great artists to elevate the artist's own work. "I am always dealing with the political situation in which objects reflect the political opinion of the time in a general and philosophical way," he has said.[41] It is here, then, in "the political opinion of the time" that we need to locate the 2010 appropriation of the original bronze animal heads to *Circle of Animals/Zodiac Heads*, which, more specifically than any previous work to date, is aimed at "changing the understanding of them and to encourage a discussion."[42]

Circle of Animals/Zodiac Heads might have begun when the possibility of having a public sculpture in New York presented itself, but the choice of the bronze animal heads was guided by the artist-as-politician role which Ai Weiwei had created for himself. "When Pierre Bergé said, 'If you give up Tibet I'll give them back to China,' then you see how cultural artifacts become important at different times for very different reasons. There is so much fiction around the structure. I felt this was the perfect set of forms for a public artwork."[43] That, and the fact that the work's debut in the São Paulo Biennial in September 2010 coincided, almost to the day, with the 150th anniversary of the theft of the original bronze animal heads—a milestone that would certainly place the issue once again in the news.

Art critics are always skeptical about whether "artists who attempt to make strong political statements . . . can successfully refuse the dynamics of capitalism and keep from becoming darlings of the world they seek to critique."[44] This point could well be raised by Ai Weiwei's *Circle of Animals/Zodiac Heads*. The reproduction of a controversial set of "national treasures" could be interpreted as cashing in on controversy in a world where controversy *always* sells, to which Ai Weiwei's international media profile attests. Especially since, prior to the media attention wrought by the auctions of individual heads, they were as good as buried and gone. Few people knew of their existence or had seen them:[45] all the heads that emerged for sale came from private hands, and there are (curiously) no known holdings in public museums in Europe or the United States, except those that have subsequently returned to China, to the Poly Museum in Beijing. Had people seen any of the heads, the majority would most likely have failed to recognize these "Western playthings," as Ai Weiwei has described them, as even being Chinese. "If they didn't appear in the auction sales everybody would have forgotten about them," he contends. "The auction made them relevant because of that period of history. Now you see different groups using them; to buy back those things as an act of nationalism or patriotism."[46]

Circle of Animals/Zodiac Heads might fool his compatriots—at least those not accustomed to reading between the lines—into embracing Ai Weiwei as their darling. Given the scale of the individual heads and the prominence of their placement in the Western art arena, *Circle of Animals/Zodiac Heads* could be construed as slapping the issue of stolen national treasures once again in the Western public face. Yet to Ai Weiwei, the animal heads are nothing other than what, in *Circle of Animals/Zodiac Heads*, he has transformed them into— remember he stated that they had no artistic value. In *Circle of Animals/Zodiac Heads* they are, for him, a new gesture in the conjoining of art and politics. The existence of the originals is immaterial beyond their innate ability to illustrate a powerful historic conflation in a very public arena. If, as one writer suggests, "the Chinese zodiac heads are not artworks with aesthetic value, but rather material witnesses to the looting of the [Yuanming Yuan],"[47] we might expect Chinese patriots to welcome *Circle of Animals/Zodiac Heads* in the way that other monuments to historic trauma have been embraced as vehicles for communal mourning and release. Of course, this is not Ai Weiwei's aim. To him, on this scale and to the degree that they have been perfectly replicated, they symbolize an attitude, an emotion, and a socio-political phenomenon—the impact and the consequences of history—that can be evoked, investigated, and unbalanced by such a reworking of the originals and the placing of *Circle of Animals/Zodiac Heads* in the public realm. That they have been replicated to perfection drives home the message to greater effect: in these heads, these faces, we see the expression of the past, we see history, but are forced to ask what has been learned from it. China is not alone in the charges of cultural destruction that are levied against it. *Circle of Animals/Zodiac Heads* will clearly test individual and collective attitudes towards the original bronze animal heads, towards appropriation in contemporary art practice, and towards Ai Weiwei.

Such public appropriation of national heritage is not without precedent in the Chinese art world. In a similar vein, Cai Guoqiang unleashed storms of criticism upon himself when in 1999 he 'borrowed' the *Rent Collector's Courtyard* for his work at the 48th Venice Biennale.[48] Many Chinese refused to see the 'replica' as art, and decried the theft of authorship as well as the blatant infringement of creative copyright. The tirade of anger directed toward Cai Guoqiang only served to highlight the attitudes that Ai Weiwei finds so irritating, and that *Circle of Animals/Zodiac Heads* was surely created to expose. After all, the significant difference between *Circle of Animals/Zodiac Heads* and his earlier *Emperor's Choice* is that the São Paulo Biennial, New York, and London as public stages are so much bigger and more public than that which has been afforded the porcelain reproductions. But in light of Ai Weiwei's domination of Documenta 12 in 2007, we can assume he has little fear of big stages.[49]

When discussing the original bronze heads with Ai Weiwei, he referred to *Circle of Animals/Zodiac Heads* as his "fountainhead." It suggested a direct allusion to Ayn Rand's titular epic, especially when we recall her take on the novel's theme: "Individualism versus collectivism, not in politics, but in man's soul."[50] Given Ai Weiwei's grasp of American culture, and his knowledge of the epoch-making authors of the mid-

twentieth century, the allusion is not entirely random. Towards the end of *The Fountainhead,* Rand writes: "Independence is the only gauge of human virtue and value. What a man is and makes of himself; not what he has or hasn't done for others. There is no substitute for personal dignity."[51] Independence, virtue, value, and personal dignity are qualities upon which Ai Weiwei's "meaningful ideas" are predicated. As he morphs from artist into "cultural politician," merging artistry with activism and demonstrating the interchangeable nature of art and politics, these qualities, above all else, appear to be most important to him. Like Rand, he believes that people should strive for excellence without fear of failure, and above all, abhor anything less than perfect work. *Circle of Animals/Zodiac Heads* is simply the most recent of "meaningful ideas" from Ai Weiwei. It shows us how he puts his energy behind his belief in striving for excellence as he ponders the nature of personal dignity, perhaps to make this period of history more palatable for the future readers of its narratives, less hateful to them; at the very least, less humiliating.

1. A question asked of Mark Twain by the writer William Dean Howells, and to which Mark Twain replied as per the above. William Dean Howells, *My Mark Twain* (Baton Rouge: Louisiana State University, 1967), Section VIII, 19.

2. Edward Gibbon (1737–1794), *The History of the Decline and Fall of the Roman Empire* (three volumes published 1776, 1781, 1788), cited in Volume One, "The Decline and Fall of the Roman Empire in the West," Chapter Three, "Of the Constitution of the Roman Empire in the Age of the Antonines."

3. British manufacturer and parliamentarian Richard Cobden (1804–1865), writing to his friend, John Bright, ironically in regard to the destruction of the Yuanming Yuan. Quoted in Edward Steele, *Palmerston and Liberalism* (Cambridge: Cambridge University Press, 1991), 121. Cobden owned the distinction of tumbling Palmerston's government with his views on the "utterly unrighteous" behavior of British forces in China.

4. Lord Elgin quoted in John K. Fairbank, *Trade and Diplomacy on the China Coast* (Cambridge: Cambridge University Press, 1953), 380.

5. German novelist and poet Gottfried Benn (1886–1956). In Ferenc M. Szasz, "Quotes About History," George Mason University's History News Network. http://hnn.us/articles/1328.html.

6. "It is worth remarking the extent to which the nature of this conflict (the Opium Wars)—it was indeed an opium war, fought to secure the fortunes of a trade that occupied a vital position in the economic life of the British Empire—is still either ignored or played down in otherwise reputable historic works. In a recent example—the *Oxford History of the British Empire: the Nineteenth Century* (Andrew Porter ed., Oxford, 1999) —opium barely makes an appearance in over 700 pages." John Newsinger,

"Elgin in China," *New Left Review* issue 15 (May–June 2002): 125.

7. Author interview with Ai Weiwei at his studio, July 10, 2010.

8. British and French troops entered the Yuanming Yuan on October 6, 1860. Much of the looting was done October 7–9. The fire was set on October 18.

9. Written by Elgin in his journal on October 7, 1860, in reaction to the partial pillaging of the Yuanming Yuan by an advance force of French troops. Quoted in John Beresford, *Storm and Peace* (Books for Libraries Press edition, reprinted 1967), 73.

10. A group of British diplomats that included Harry Parkes and Elgin's secretary, Henry Brougham Loch, was arrested on September 18, 1860. Elgin determined that there was no alternative to an assault on the capital itself.

11. Signed between China and Britain on June 26, 1858. This was one of a series of treaties imposed upon China by Russia, the U.S., Britain and France, and which were also known as the Unequal Treaties.

12. This followed the Chinese reaction to the manner in which newly appointed British Ambassador Frederic Bruce, brother of Lord Elgin, chose to "arrive" in Beijing, by marching on the capital with a large military entourage. The defeat was incurred at the Dagu Forts on the coast at Tianjin as the forces attempted to land and embark on the determined march.

13. "China, the Ruined Summer Palace, the Coolie Trade—Commission of Inquiry—New Printing Office—Visit of Prince Kung," *New York Times*, February 2, 1874, 2. The writer was identified only as "our own Correspondent in Peking," signed 'P.'

14. Newsinger, "Elgin in China," 138.

15. Ibid.

16. John Hart Dunne of the 99th Regiment, in a letter to relatives in England, recorded in John Hart Dunne, *From Calcutta to Pekin, Notes Taken from the Journal of an Officer Between those Places* (Elibron Classics, facsimile of the 1861 edition published by Sampson Low, Son & Co., London, 2005), 131.

17. Tamara Levitz, "Who Owns the Chinese Zodiac Figures?" *Proa - Revista de Antropologia e Arte* 1 (2009), n.p. http://www.ifch.unicamp. br/proa/.

18. Geremie Barmé, "Yuanming Yuan, the Garden of Perfect Brightness," Editorial page in *China Heritage Quarterly* 8 (December 2006): n.p. http://www.chinaheritagequarterly.org/editorial.php?issue=008.

19. The first heads at auction were the monkey and the boar, which appeared in New York in 1987. Three—the ox, the horse, and the tiger—were then offered in London in June 1989 (a moment when the Chinese people were distracted by the student demonstrations in Tian'anmen Square, and the government reprisal on June 4). The ox and the monkey heads were re-auctioned at Christie's, Hong Kong in 2000; the tiger head was sold soon after at Sotheby's, Hong Kong. All three were acquired by the Poly Museum in Beijing.

20. Ai Weiwei blog entry, "Give My Regards to Your Mother," February 27, 2009. The blog was closed down in 2010. The collected blog texts appear in *Ai Weiwei's Blog—Writings, Interviews and Digital Rants, 2006–2009*, edited and translated by Lee Ambrozy (Boston: MIT Press, 2011). Aisin Gioro was the family name of the Qing emperors.

21. During this phase of Ai Weiwei's blog, he was receiving tens of thousands of hits per day. The blog was considered one of the most popular in China.

22. Ai Weiwei, "Give My Regards to Your Mother" in Ambrozy, *Ai Weiwei's Blog*.

23. Winning Chinese bidder Cai Mingchao refused to pay; French owner Pierre Bergé, partner of Yves Saint Laurent, said he'd give them to China if China would significantly liberalize its policies toward Tibet.

24. Ai Weiwei, "Give My Regards to Your Mother" in Ambrozy, *Ai Weiwei's Blog*.

25. Though it sounds like something Mao could have said, this attribution has never been verified.

26. Ai Weiwei was the son of one of China's leading modern poets and writers, Ai Qing (1910–1996). In 1957, the year of Ai Weiwei's birth, Ai Qing was labelled as a rightist and exiled to China's remote western region of Xinjiang, where he was assigned to clean toilets. The family remained there until the mid-1970s, when Ai Qing was permitted to return to Beijing for medical treatment. See Karen Smith, "Ai: Giant Provocateur," in Karen Smith, Hans Ulrich Obrist, Bernard Fibicher, and Ai Weiwei, *Ai Weiwei* (London: Phaidon Press, 2009); Philip Tinari, "A Kind of True Living: The Art of Ai Weiwei" *Art Forum* 45 no. 10 (Summer 2007): 453; and newspaper articles such as Christopher Hawthorne, "An Exile Ascends China's Big Stage," *New York Times*, October 28, 2004, F1; and Adrian Searle, "Turbine Hall Commission," *The Guardian*, March 5, 2010, 38.6

27. Ai Weiwei, "Give My Regards to Your Mother" in Ambrozy, *Ai Weiwei's Blog*.

28. Interview with Ai Weiwei by the author at his studio on July 10, 2010.

29. The "Four Olds" refers to "old customs, old culture, old habits, old ideas."

30. Author interview with Ai Weiwei at his studio, July 10, 2010.

31. Alex Rauch, "No Fake: An Interview with Ai Weiwei," Portlandart. net (August 9, 2010). http://www.portlandart.net/archives/2010/08/no_ fake_an_inte.html.

32. Barmé, "Yuanming Yuan," http://www.chinaheritagequarterly.org/ editorial.php?issue=008.

33. The Stars painting group (*Xingxing Hua Hui*) was founded in 1978 and made famous by two exhibitions, one in 1979, one in 1980. Ai Weiwei was a (young) member of the group from 1979 and prior to his departure for the U.S. in 1981.

34. This work was part of the process of beautifying the capital in the run-up to the Olympic bid. Due to the urgency of the program, its very scale, and the lack of adequately skilled workers to complete it, numerous ill-conceived shortcuts were employed, such as the line-etching Ai Weiwei described, which was a poor imitation of the distinctive gray bricks traditionally used in *hutong* construction.

35. Ai Weiwei has been an outspoken critic of the authorities in Sichuan, which he accused publicly of shirking its responsibility to ensure the safe construction of public buildings, and thus indirectly allowing for substandard structures which uniformly collapsed during the devastating earthquake in May 2008, whilst private sector-built structures remained standing. When local authorities refused to release figures on the dead and wounded, Ai assembled a team of volunteers to gather the names of the victims, which were published on his blog. The blog was eventually shut down. Undaunted, Ai produced *Remembering* (2009), presented as one of the major works in his solo exhibition at the Haus der Kunst, Munich, in October that year. *Remembering* was created using thousands of children's backpacks to spell out in Chinese across the façade of the building the words of one grief-stricken mother speaking of her daughter: "She lived happily on this earth for seven years."

36. From "Ai Weiwei on CCAA, Identity and His Recent Work," an interview with Harald Szeemann, Chinese-art.com 1 no. 6 (January 1999): 9. *Chinese-art.com* was a website that became defunct in 2000. Texts from the site were published in limited runs by Art Media Limited between 1997 and 1999. Sourcing: Art Media Limited, AON Insurance Tower, 12th floor, 3 Lockhart Road, Wanchai, Hong Kong.

37. Ibid.

38. Located in Jiangxi province, Jingdezhen served as the imperial kilns through the Qing and Ming dynasties.

39. Szeemann, "Ai Weiwei on CCAA."

40. Richard Schusterman in conversation with Suzi Gablik, recorded in "Breaking out of the White Cube" in Suzi Gablik, *Conversations Before the End of Time* (London: Thames & Hudson, 1995), 259.

41. Interview with Ai Weiwei by the author in July 2010.

42. Ibid.

43. Ibid.

44. Carol Becker in conversation with Suzi Gablik, recorded in "Our Students Need the City," in Gablik, 358.

45. Two heads, the monkey and the boar, were placed on loan to the Metropolitan Museum of Art in New York for several years prior to their sale at Christie's, New York, in 1987. According to the Christie's catalogue entry for the monkey head, it was exhibited at the Metropolitan Museum of Art in 1981. Lot 516, Sale 2030, "The Imperial Sale," April 4, 2000. http://www.christies.com/LotFinder/lot_details.asp x?from=salesummary&intObjectID=1789539&sid=82bc93ee-9746-4f1f-881f-e99353a7ab27.

46. Author interview with Ai Weiwei at his studio, July 10, 2010.

47. Levitz, "Who Owns," http://www.ifch.unicamp.br/proa/.

48. *The Rent Collector's Courtyard* (1965) was a social sculpture, meaning a work produced under the needs and guidelines of socialist ideology to show the hard life suffered by the peasantry at the hands of the feudal landlords. For his play with this work Cai Guoqiang was awarded the Golden Lion, the top prize for an artist participating in the Venice Biennale.

49. Ai Weiwei's project for Documenta 12 was multifaceted in every sense, but centred on *Fairytale*, described by many as a "social sculpture" because in the course of the exhibition's run, the work transported 1,001 ordinary Chinese citizens to Kassel to experience life and culture in this German city. It was aimed specifically at poor people from remote communities, people without passports who had never traveled further than the boundaries of their provincial towns or even out of their villages. The dormitory that housed the Chinese visitors became a focal point of Documenta, but it was *Template*—a monumental sculptural piece, constructed from a multitude of wooden doors salvaged from old houses that had been demolished to make way for new highrises in China's burgeoning cities and suburbs—that made a lasting impression on all who saw it. Not least in the wake of a storm during which *Template* collapsed, after which Ai Weiwei declared himself more pleased with its new form.

50. Ayn Rand quoted in a back-cover description of *The Fountainhead* (New York: Signet Paperback, 1952).

51. Ayn Rand, *The Fountainhead* (New York: Signet Paperback, 1952), part 4, chapter 18, 681.

The Original and the Copy: Ai Weiwei and the Fate of the Zodiac Heads

3

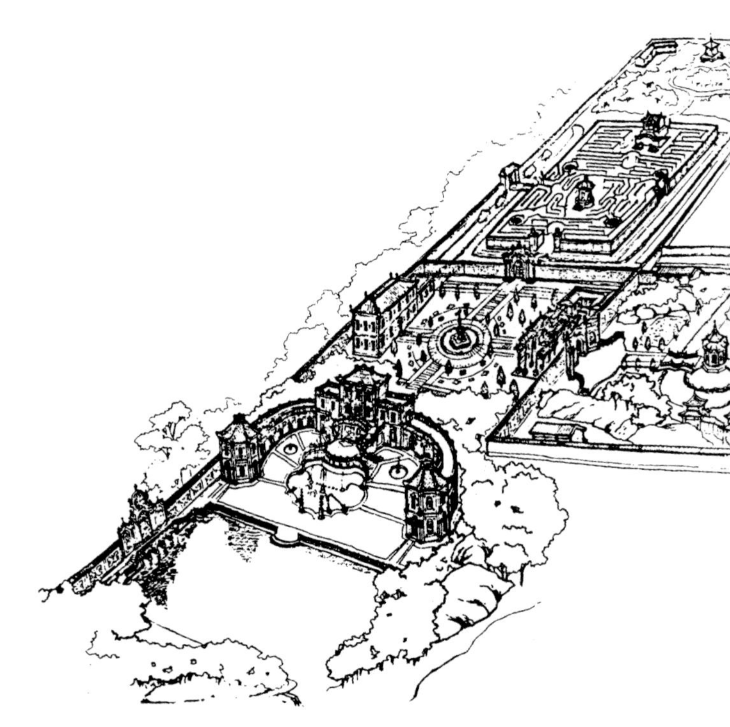

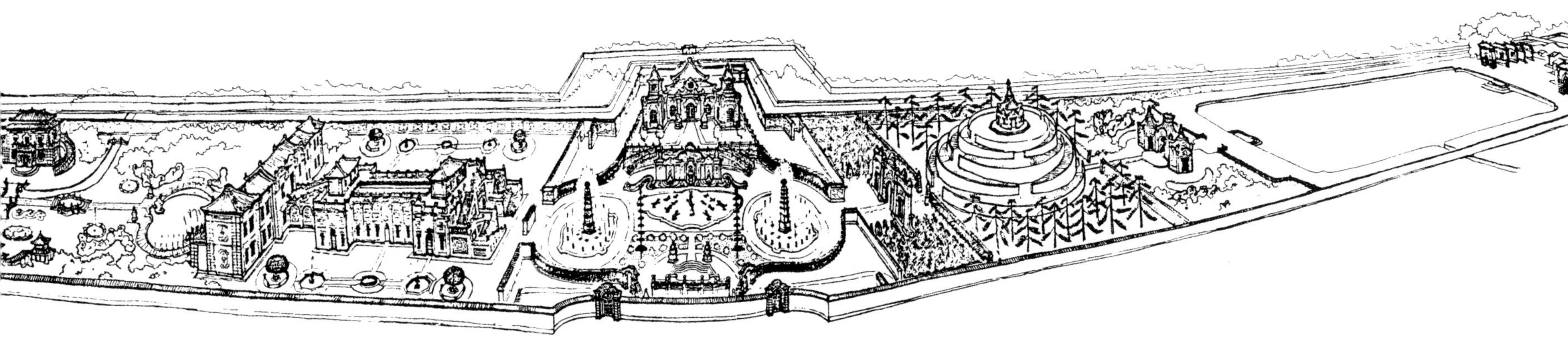

FIG. 35
Plan of the European
Pavilions, from
Jin Yufeng *"Yuanming yuan
xiyanglou pingxi"*

OVER THE COURSE OF THE PAST TWO YEARS, AI WEIWEI has produced *Circle of Animals/Zodiac Heads*, a series of twelve sculpted figures that represent the animals of the Chinese zodiac. Seven of these heads replicate those produced for the Yuanming Yuan.[1] But those eighteenth-century bronzes are no longer simply a representation of an important chapter in the cultural history of China and its relations of cultural exchange with the West. More significantly, the heads were looted, along with other cultural artifacts, at the time of the burning of the Yuanming Yuan in 1860. This led to the appearance of many of the objects, including several zodiac heads, in recent auction-house sales, accompanied by a rising call for cultural repatriation by the Chinese government. No matter their aesthetic value, the zodiac heads have become a lightning rod for the issues surrounding patrimony and the significance that the Chinese government has accorded this chapter in the history of the country and its people.

Throughout his practice, Ai Weiwei has followed various strands of inquiry into the object of the copy and, hence, a disengagement from the original. Rather than valorizing the concept of the original as the cornerstone and value of an artist's work, his art can be characterized by its constant exploration of issues around the readymade object, the recycling of existing found objects, and the concept of re-presentation through the copy. Through this exploration, his work has demonstrated the potential of the object to be constantly re-signified, embracing and transforming its meaning, significance, and value in the context of the contemporary.

From this perspective, it seems almost inevitable that Ai Weiwei should engage with the history of the Yuanming Yuan. He had been one of many students who had visited the grounds, as a place to meet as much as a site for drawing ruins. But his engagement with the zodiac heads is not a project of retrieval or restoration of a cultural and material history. Rather, it begins after the fact with what has persisted and can be recycled anew and differently.

Built initially as a private residence and retreat on the northwestern outskirts of Beijing, the Yuanming Yuan became the center for Chinese imperial power of the Qing dynasty, as distinct from that of Tian'anmen (Gate of Heavenly Peace) and the Forbidden City, initially built by the Ming dynasty in the fifteenth century. Rather, the development of the Yuangming Yuan, especially under the Qianlong Emperor (r. 1735–96), became emblematic of what Richard Strassberg describes as "the ruler's sense of his place at the center of a symbolic microcosm of the universe (that) . . . embodied native cosmographical concepts"[2] (fig. 35). This project of extension and building represented an extraordinary history of cultural exchange and collaboration between East and West that begins in the sixteenth century. Initially driven by trade interests and the propagation of Christianity, the French monarchy influenced the arrival of French Jesuits in China in the seventeenth century. The Jesuits were not only missionaries; their work as intellectuals created an opportunity for a much richer environment of cultural exchange. This development was interrupted by the fall of the Ming dynasty in 1644, which was overthrown by the Manchus of northern Asia. The succeeding Qing dynasty was seen as the imposition of foreign rule that lasted more than two hundred years, until the early twentieth century. And while the character of the cultural exchange shifted over this period, the imperial relationship with the Jesuits continued to grow in a number of ways, particularly in the fields of scientific and artistic knowledge and application.

Most significant was the mutual interest and admiration between the Europeans, especially the French, and the Chinese emperors, who had seen illustrations of Versailles and Italian baroque villas. Between 1747 and 1783, at the behest of the Qianlong Emperor, the Jesuit lay brother and artist Giuseppe Castiglione (1688–1766) designed a small part of the vast imperial gardens complex into the Garden of Perfect Brightness. Castiglione in turn was asked to recommend someone who could design fountains in the manner of the European palaces that the emperor had seen in illustrations. He invited Michel Benoist, S.J. (1715–1774), trained as a mathematician and astronomer, to design and build the fountains that would ornament the European pavilions and surrounding gardens of more than three hundred hectares.[3] The European pavilions were designed not for habitation so much as for exhibition, as halls for the display of the emperor's collections—including those given him by European visitors and courts—and as backdrops for the fountains. In particular, the design of the Haiyan Tang, the Palace of the Calm Seas, embodies a perfect example of how this vision was made manifest. Featuring a water-driven clock that marked the hours of the day, it was framed by a semicircle of sculptures made of stone and bronze heads that symbolized the twelve earthly branches, or zodiac signs, of Chinese astrology. The fountain's waters would jet out of an animal's mouth when the hour it represented arrived.[4]

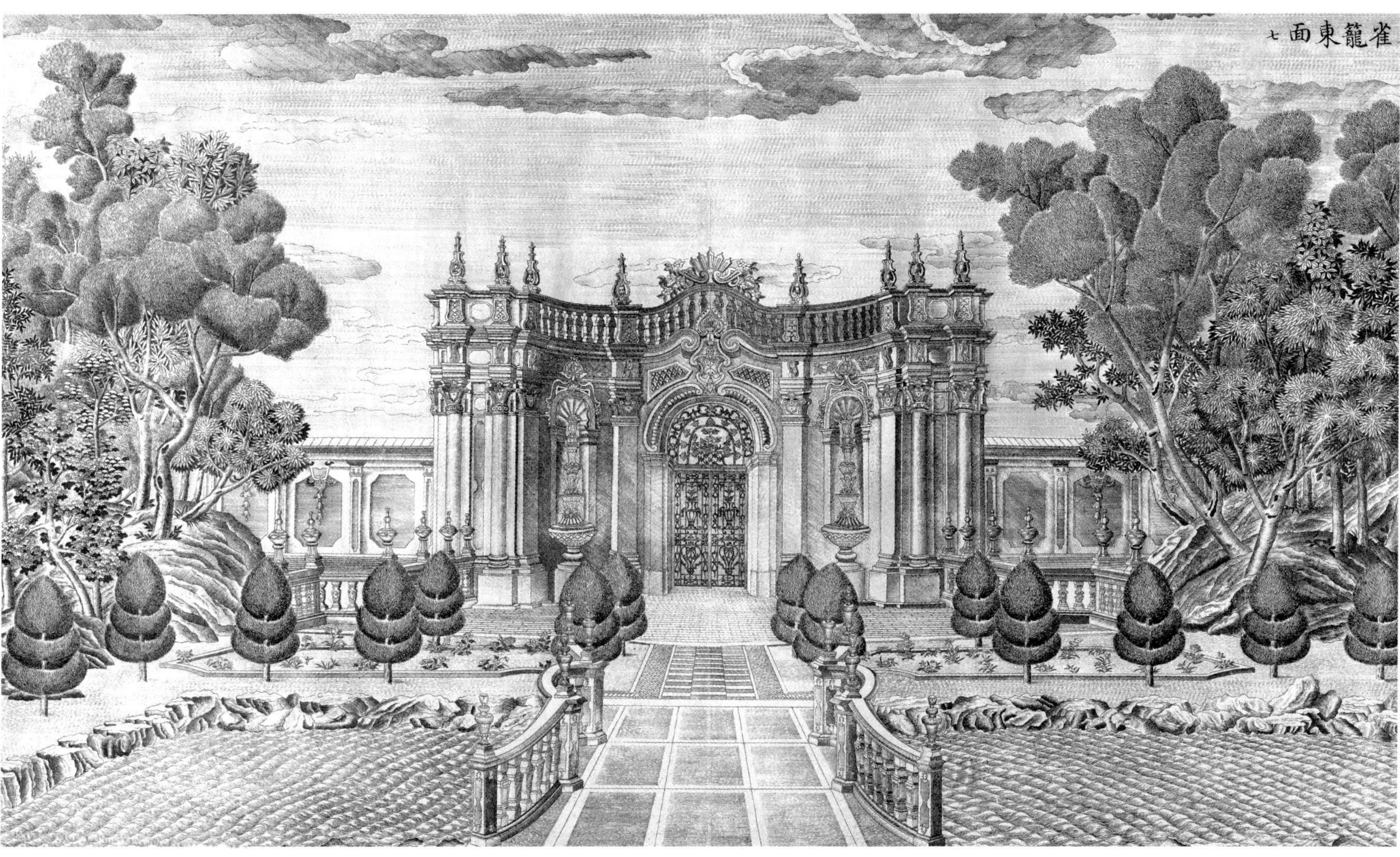

FIG. 36 Yi Lantai (active 1749–86), *East Façade of Aviary (Yangquelong dongmian)*, plate no. 7 from *The European Pavilions at the Garden of Perfect Brightness*, 1783–86. Engraving mounted on heavy paper, 19 ¾ x 34 ½ in. (50 x 87.5 cm)

Following the construction of these pavilions, a set of twenty engravings was commissioned by the Qianlong Emperor in 1783. Made by the Manchu court artist Yi Lantai, who may have studied under Castiglione, the engravings are an extraordinary example of an intercultural approach to rendition (fig. 36). Using both Chinese and Western modes of depiction, the artist rendered visible not only different perspectives, but the intricate design and detail of the construction.[5] However, less than one hundred years later, the value of the engravings became inestimable with the destruction wrought upon the Yuanming Yuan in 1860 by the English and French armies, which burned and destroyed the palaces and grounds. The result was devastating, leaving little intact. Vast treasures disappeared at the hands of the invading army officers, foot-soldiers, and nearby residents, for whom such treasures were a means of income if not quotidian use.

It is now ironic that the zodiac sculptures, designed precisely within a space of intercultural collaboration and exchange, have become a touchstone not only in the subsequent fate of Yuanming Yuan, but equally in the cultural heritage of China and its relations of exchange with the West. Ai Weiwei opens the door to this history by referencing the fact that some of these zodiac heads have not simply survived a history of destruction, but have gathered another meaning and significance by entering the circuit of the global commodity trade. Their circulation highlights the role of auction houses in providing, in effect, a clearinghouse, creating a market of private and public collections for such objects.

A Contemporary Valence

In 1993, Ai Weiwei returned to Beijing after having spent more than a decade in the United States. The primary purpose was to see his father, who had fallen ill, but he decided to stay. The artist's homecoming was to a China that had both changed and remained the same. The end of the Mao era had allowed for an opening of China to the rest of the world, especially in terms of economic development. The expansion of trade brought with it considerable interest in forms of cultural exchange, especially for the Western market. This meant the opening of galleries run by Westerners and the export of work for museum and gallery exhibitions and sales. At the same time, the changes that occurred under Deng Xiaoping also led to a slow transformation of cities and people's lives, entailing an overturning of the past. Nowhere was this more evident than in the second-hand markets that had become vast trading depots for old China: objects and artifacts recycled and sold off as relics of the past and as new luxury commodities for those who hung on to the glories of a former China.

Early on after his return, Ai Weiwei began visiting these markets and found evidence of the extraordinary wealth and aesthetic refinement achieved under different dynasties, now for sale. He discovered that the markets were selling vases whose authenticity was impossible to confirm scientifically. Old or new, copies or not, they were nonetheless exquisite examples of craftsmanship and skill. The copies clearly required a level of expertise equivalent to that of the craftspersons who had made the originals. Travelling to Jingdezhen, a region famous for its kilns and the production of imperial porcelain, Ai Weiwei discovered that such craftsmanship still existed.

Moreover, he recognized that the concept of authorship and notions of the original or copy were radically distinct from those in the West. This distinction must have been most pronounced in the context of his recent experience of having lived in the

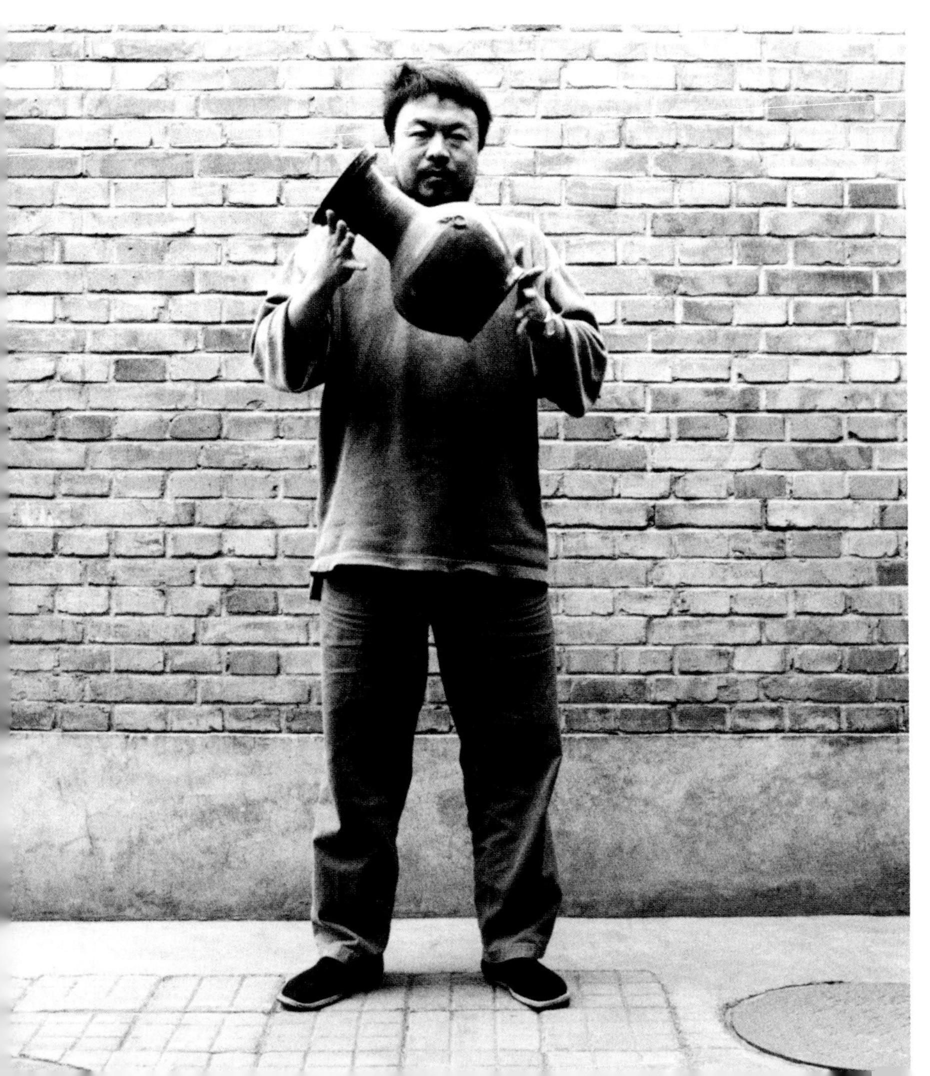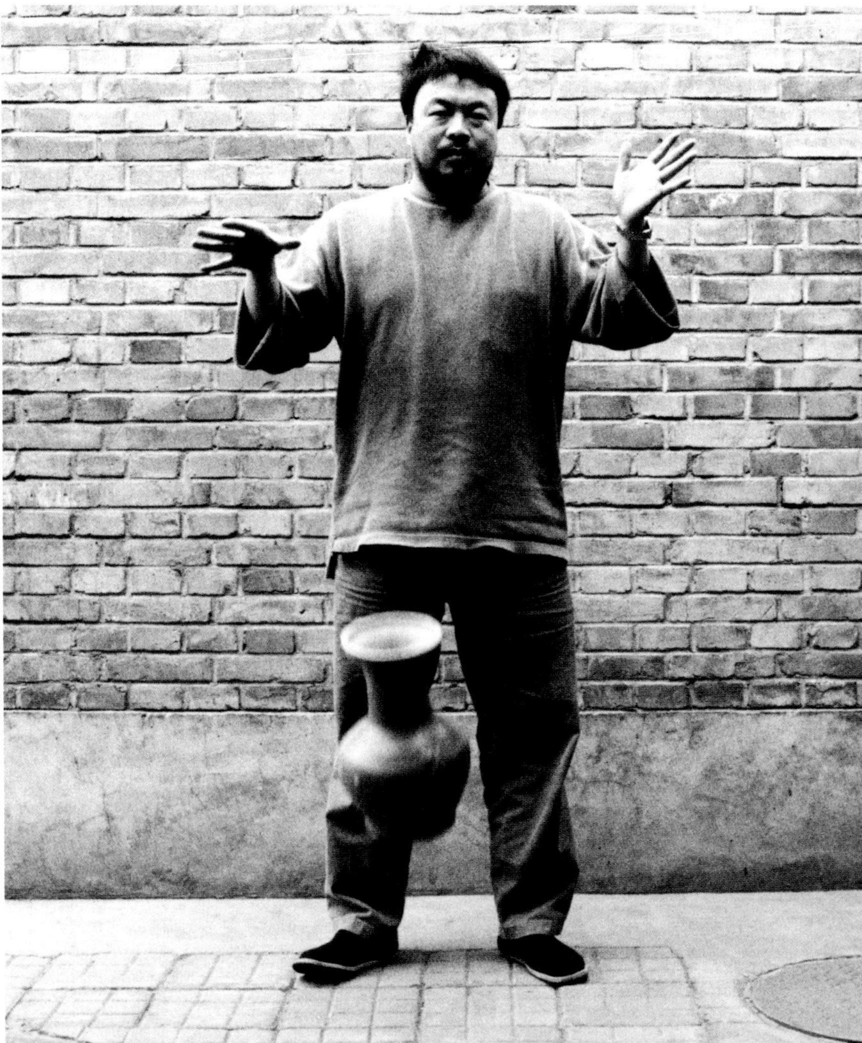

West, especially in New York, where the approach of artists like Marcel Duchamp and Andy Warhol had had such a tremendous impact on the definition and course of modern and contemporary art. For each of them, the idea of the readymade, and the copy or reproduction, respectively, had as much, if not more, validity than the concept of the original. In point of fact, Warhol had conceived of his own work in the context of the "Factory," a term that implied that the concept of reproduction or the copy was essential to the logic of mass production. The difference in China was in essence one of value. Mass production there did not mean in any sense a diminishing of quality or status, and there were artisans who conceived the original in the context of its mass production. Responding to this tradition, Ai Weiwei conceived of making replicas of ceramic pots or porcelain vases from different dynasties. And yet, in making replicas, he gave a contemporary valence to the work, not simply by provoking a revaluation of the concept of value but, in its transformation, the question of the use and abuse of this concept. He perceived

the potential of a contemporary artist making copies or replicas as not dissimilar to the practice of Warhol, but in the context of China. And yet, he was not simply mimicking a Warholian or Pop Art gesture. In making replicas or copies, Ai Weiwei did not make clear whether he was also using originals; moreover, he showed the objects as contemporary works by himself as the artist. These works appeared, first and foremost, as a series of different forms of engagement with the idea of the original, raising issues about their value.

Two years after Ai Weiwei returned to Beijing from his twelve years' residence in the United States, he produced what was to become a key work: *Dropping a Han Dynasty Urn* (1995), a photo-triptych that marks a significant shift in his perspective on the role that contemporary art could take in China (fig. 37). Little in contemporary Chinese art paralleled this form of practice, except that of the Xiamen Dada group in the mid-1980s. These artists had incorporated performative acts in which they destroyed the products of their practice, which

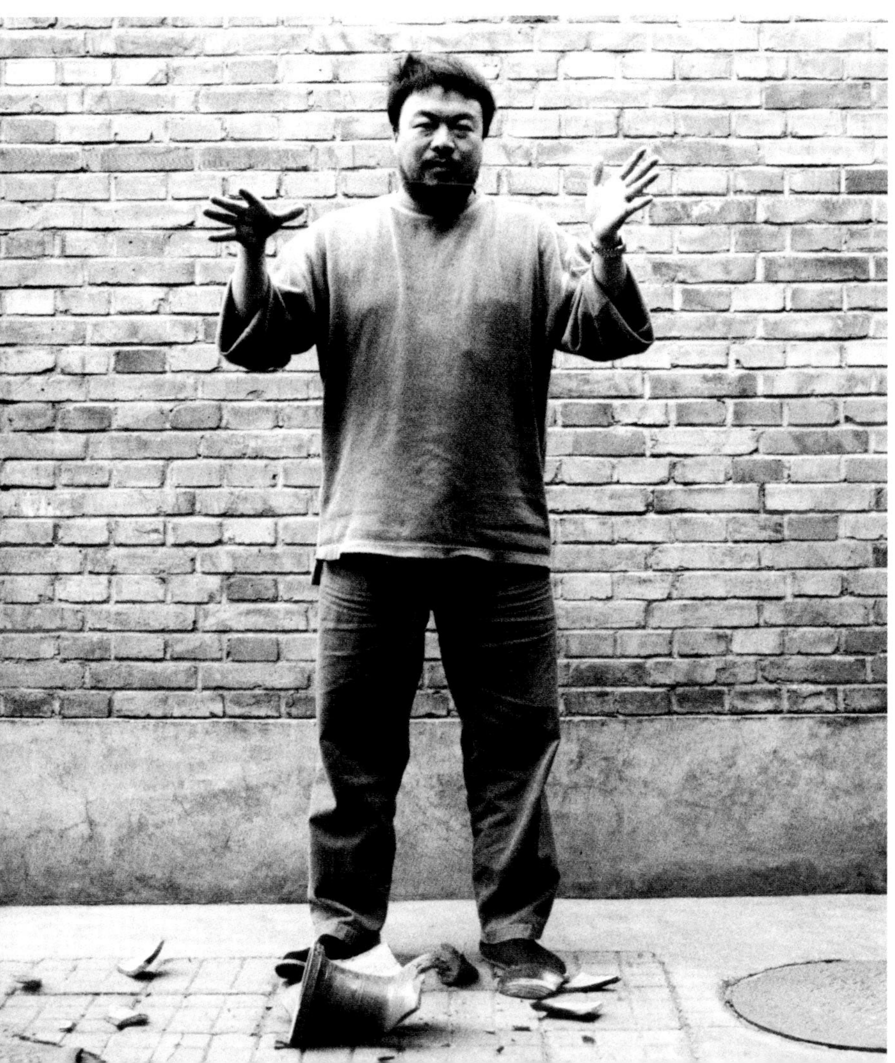

FIG. 37
Ai Weiwei, *Dropping a Han Dynasty Urn*, 1995. Gelatin silver print triptych, 50 x 43 in. (125 x 110 cm) each. Collection of the artist

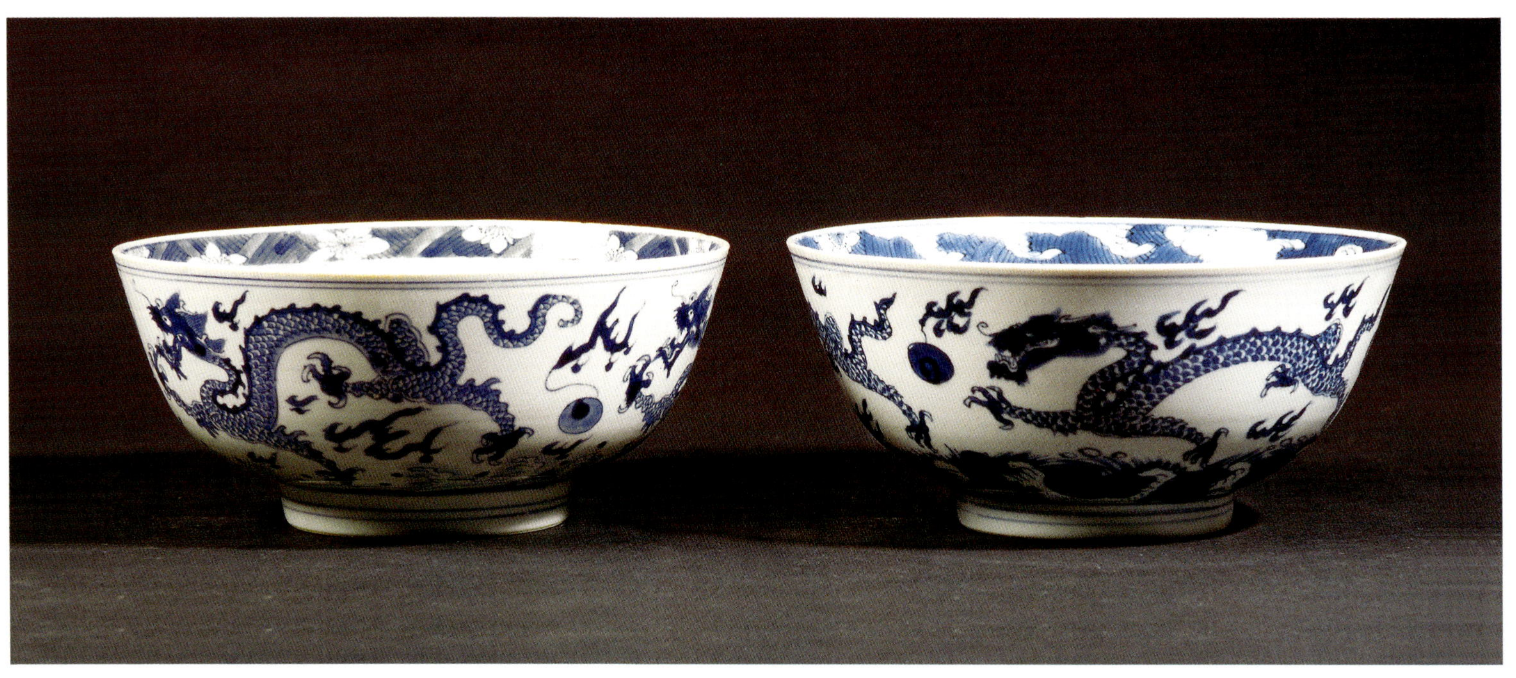

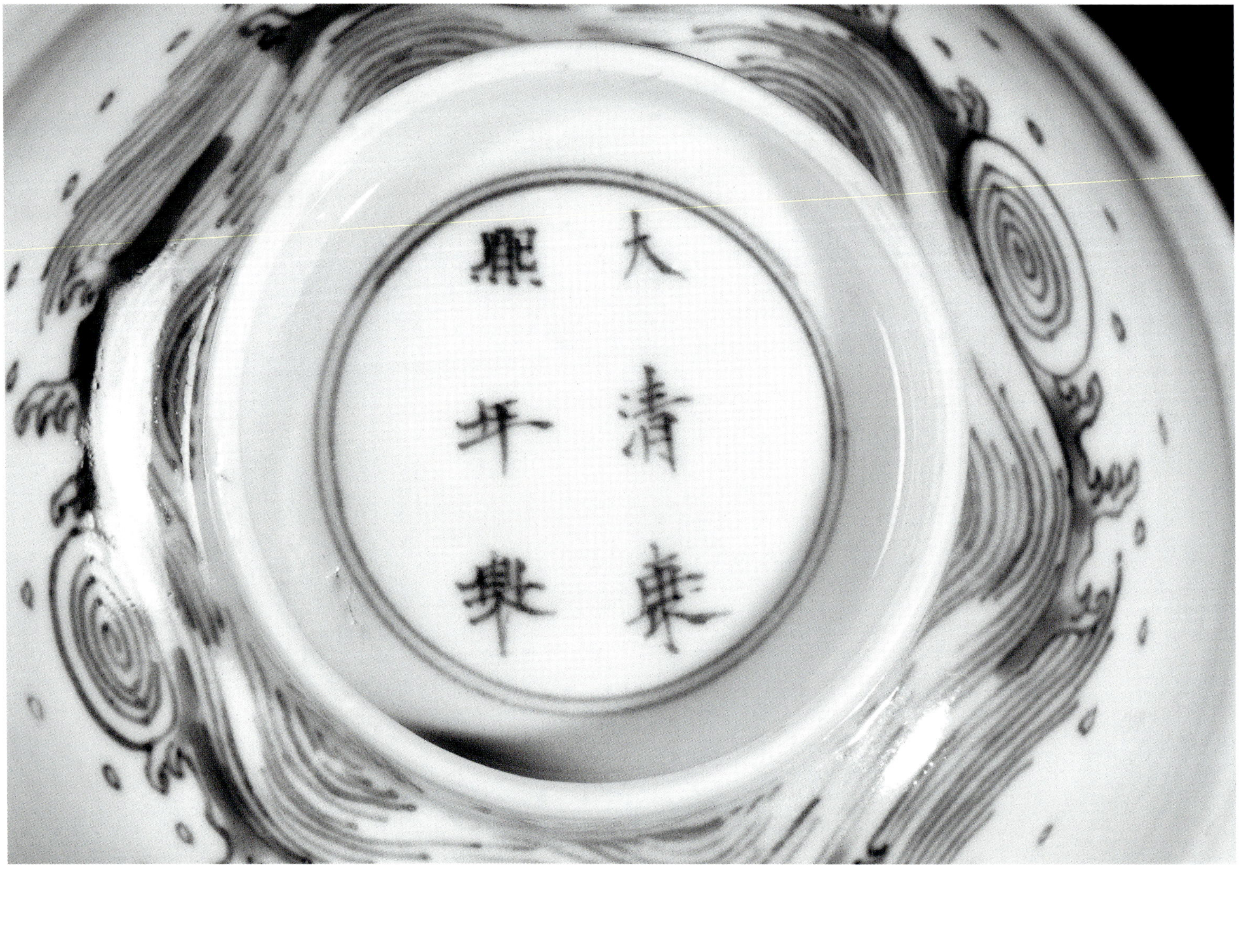

FIG. 38
Opposite, above:
Ai Weiwei, *Breaking of Two Blue-and-White "Dragon" Bowls*, 1996. Photograph of two blue-and-white "dragon" bowls, Qing dynasty, Kangxi period (1662–1722). Private collection

FIG. 39
Opposite, below:
Ai Weiwei, *Detail*, 1996. Photograph of bowl, Qing dynasty, Kangxi period (1662–1722) showing Kangxi mark. Private collection

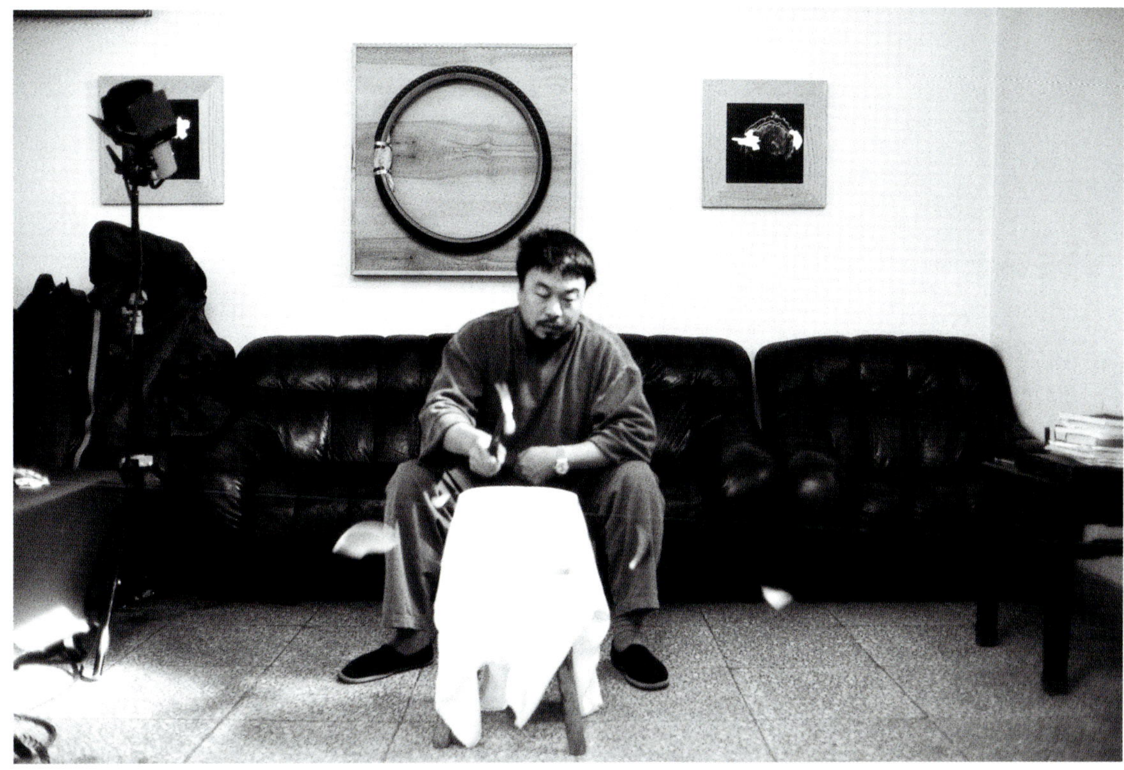

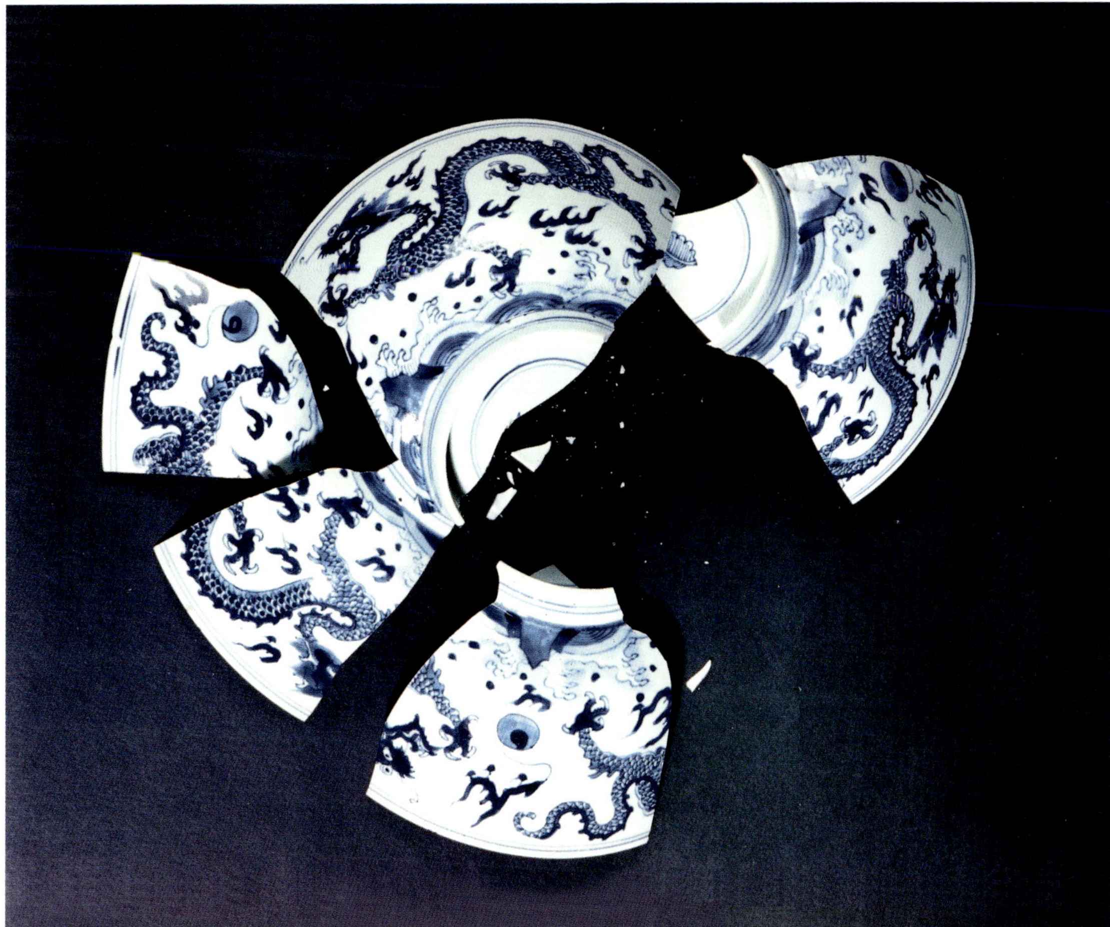

FIG. 40
Ai Weiwei, *Documentation of "Breaking of Two Blue-and-White 'Dragon' Bowls,"* 1996. Photograph of performance. Private collection

FIG. 41
Ai Weiwei, *Detail*, 1996. Photograph of broken bowl, Qing dynasty, Kangxi period (1662–1722). Private collection

FIG. 42
Ai Weiwei, *Wok with Violin Bow*, 1986. Metal, wood, 31½ x 28 in. (80 x 70 cm). Collection Urs Meile, Switzerland

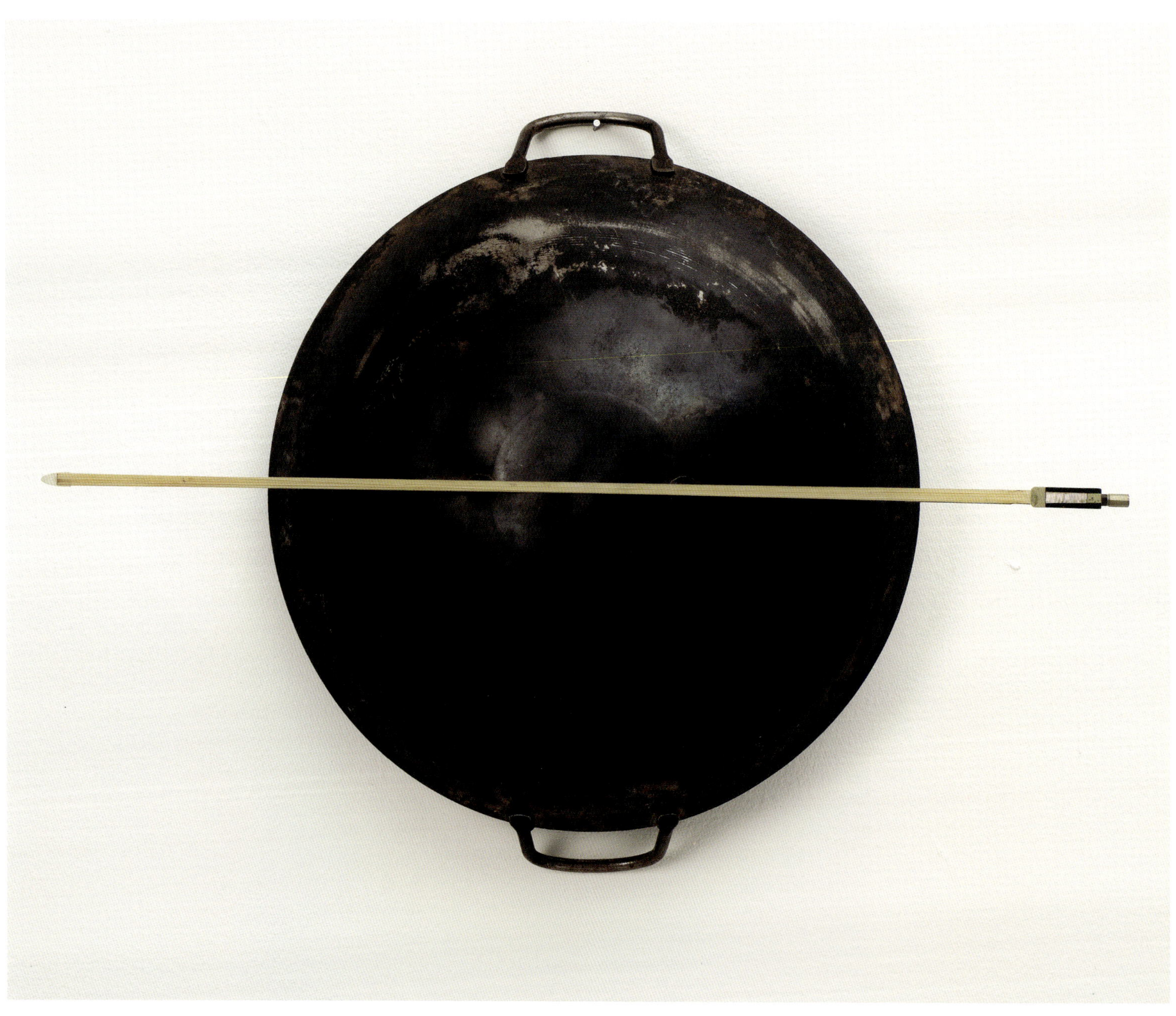

corresponded to some of the more radical dimensions of Berlin Dada after World War I. Ai Weiwei had been in New York at that time, and on his return to China, his approach took on a different valence. This shift was not only in response to his own new line of development, but equally to the changes that had occurred in China in his absence, in which "commodity fetishism" had become increasingly important to the conduct and development of a new life for the Chinese individual.

In *Dropping a Han Dynasty Urn*, Ai Weiwei uses photography to document his own performative action, which takes place in front of a brick wall: he holds an antique urn, then lets go of it, and finally allows it to smash onto the ground. Taken individually, each of the three photographs records a particular relation to the urn as a symbol of China's antiquity. One could say that the first represents the survival of the urn within the present moment, a relic of great symbolic value embodying the material, aesthetic, and cultural history of China. The second records a gesture of letting go, not only of the urn but also of history. The artist's pose in the third photograph is no different from that of the second, even though the urn is smashing into pieces at his feet. There is no evident surprise on his face, nor is there an expression of shock or dismay. The destruction of the urn is presented as an ordinary action and, together with the purely descriptive title, suggests a conscious diminishment of its significance. In this act of negation, there appears to be little appreciation or recognition of the knowledge and craftsmanship of the materials used to produce an object of aesthetic refinement and beauty.

To a certain degree, this action and the resultant work of photographic documentation extend Ai Weiwei's exploration of the readymade that had characterized his approach in the 1980s. In the instance of the 1995 work, however, nothing, in effect, remains except the photographic document. This becomes the work, displacing the concrete materiality of the urn and, with its capacity to be infinitely reproduced, transferring its value to the modern form of mass reproduction. In the following year, Ai Weiwei offered a further elaboration of this scenario. Under the title *Breaking of Two Blue-and-White "Dragon" Bowls* (1996), he presented a photograph of two antique bowls (fig. 38). A second photograph, *Detail* (1996, fig. 39), was a closeup of a blue-and-white Kangxi bowl showing the Kangxi mark; a third, also titled *Detail* (1996, fig. 41), depicted the fragments of a smashed blue-and-white "dragon" bowl. A black-and-white

photograph, *Documentation of "Breaking of Two Blue-and-White 'Dragon' Bowls"* (1996, fig. 40), showed the artist, hammer in hand, in the process of breaking the bowls.[6] It is a literal visualization of the expression "going under the hammer," referring to the auction-house practice of hitting the podium with a hammer when a sale of a work is confirmed.

Two years later, Ai Weiwei produced a group of so-called performance remains entitled *Dao Guang Blue and White Porcelain and Hammer* (1998), displayed in a small vitrine-like frame mimicking a museographic form of presentation. While similar to the *objet trouvé* format used by the Surrealists, this work offers a dramatic critique of the archival (museal) logic by which the act of historical effacement is recast as an act of preservation.[7] By displaying the hammer alongside the porcelain bowl, the artist highlights the performative agency of the object's production. That is, the treasured fragments of porcelain become evidence of the violent mutuality of patrimonial desire and the patricidal impulse.

While the breaking of the bowls suggests the transmutation of value within the structure of the international art market, the significance is now pointedly turned toward China and its policies, in which acts of destruction and preservation seem to go hand in hand. Even as the Chinese government can speak of the cultural patrimony of the nation—that is, of "national treasures" and the need for their preservation—it appears oblivious to the widespread looting, devastation, and ongoing process of cultural deracination.[8] Paradoxically, what appears to be an act of iconoclasm is, in fact, Ai Weiwei's critique of the ideological appropriation of the objects. At the same time, he casts a longer shadow still on the imperial despotism of particular dynasties that made possible some of the highest achievements in the arts and sciences. Seen in such terms, his action provokes consideration of the degree to which such skills and refinement could be fostered only under the authority of a regime that invested this amount of time and labor in the production of such a highly demanding craft. This is clear in the instance of the Yuanming Yuan.

Ai Weiwei's gesture doubles the irony of state discourse around cultural refinement to expose it as also a discourse of power. Rather than seeking the violent overthrow of an aesthetic tradition that symbolically stands for the past, Ai Weiwei proposes an inversion of violence against the past by challenging the ideological reconstruction of aesthetic value. Perhaps the only way of changing the value and meaning of the urns as objects of great beauty is to free us of the values inscribed upon them: to destroy, paint, or copy them. The urns, and indeed the zodiac heads, propose the possibility of a coexistence of other regimes of art—as opposed to their appropriation or negation—and the values for which they stand. It is from this vantage point that we see them again and, hence, can begin to appreciate them differently.

By virtue of his actions, Ai Weiwei seeks to liberate our perception of these objects in order that they become visible again. This approach was pointedly instanced in 1997, when he painted a Coca-Cola logo on a Tang dynasty vase that was shown at Max Protech Gallery in New York. It was then shipped back to Beijing with an attached letter stating that it was not authentic but a copy.

The Copy

To better understand Ai Weiwei's engagement with the zodiac heads, one need look no further than his own work, casting back more than twenty-five years to his early readymades. Produced while he was living in New York, works such as *Untitled* (Book with shoe, 1986, fig. 17) or *Wok with Violin Bow*

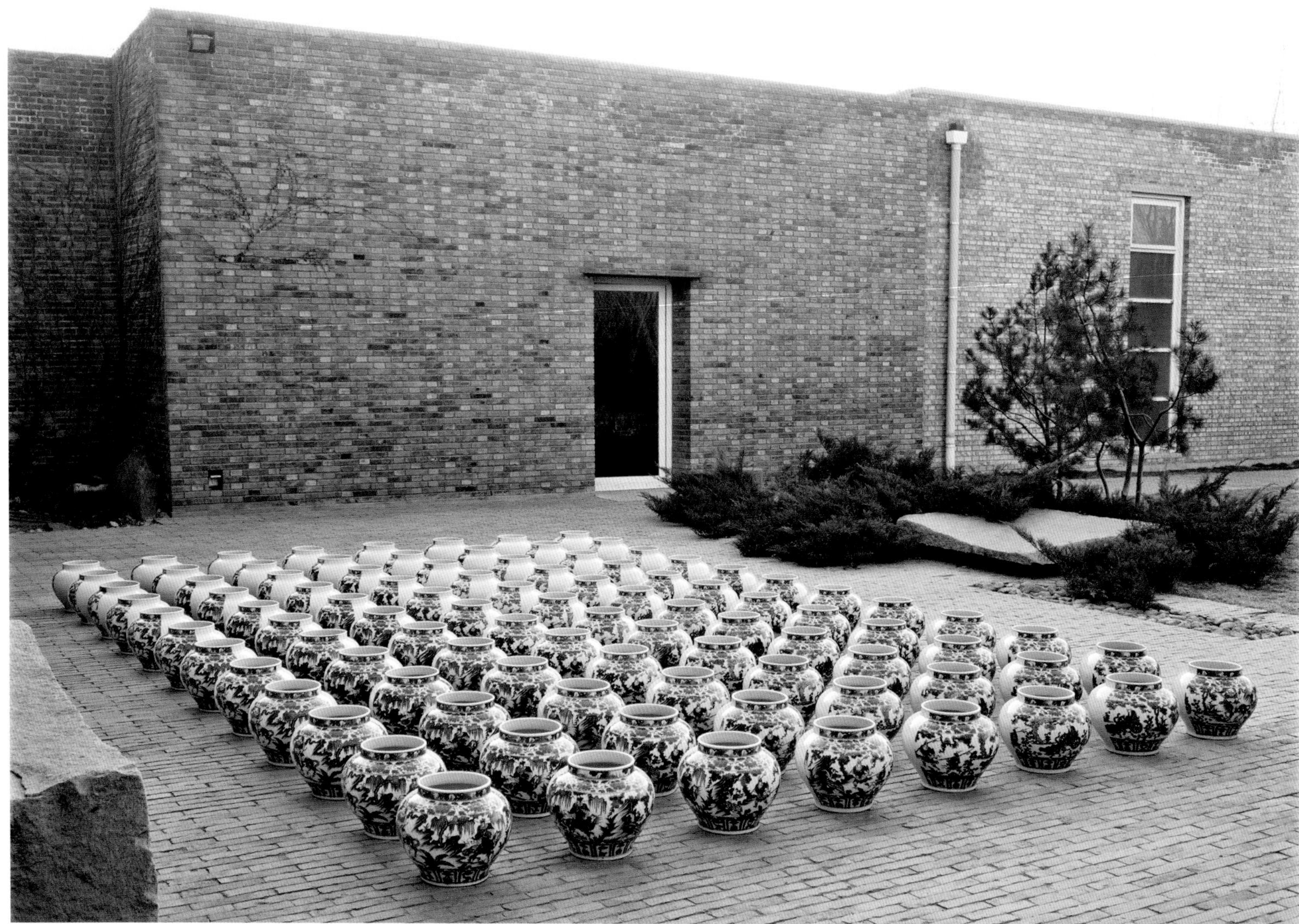

FIG. 43 Ai Weiwei with Serge Spitzer, *Ghost Gu Coming Down the Mountain 1/3*, 2005. Ninety-six blue-and-white porcelain vases, 11 x 14 in. (27 x 36 in.) each. Museum für Moderne Kunst, Frankfurt

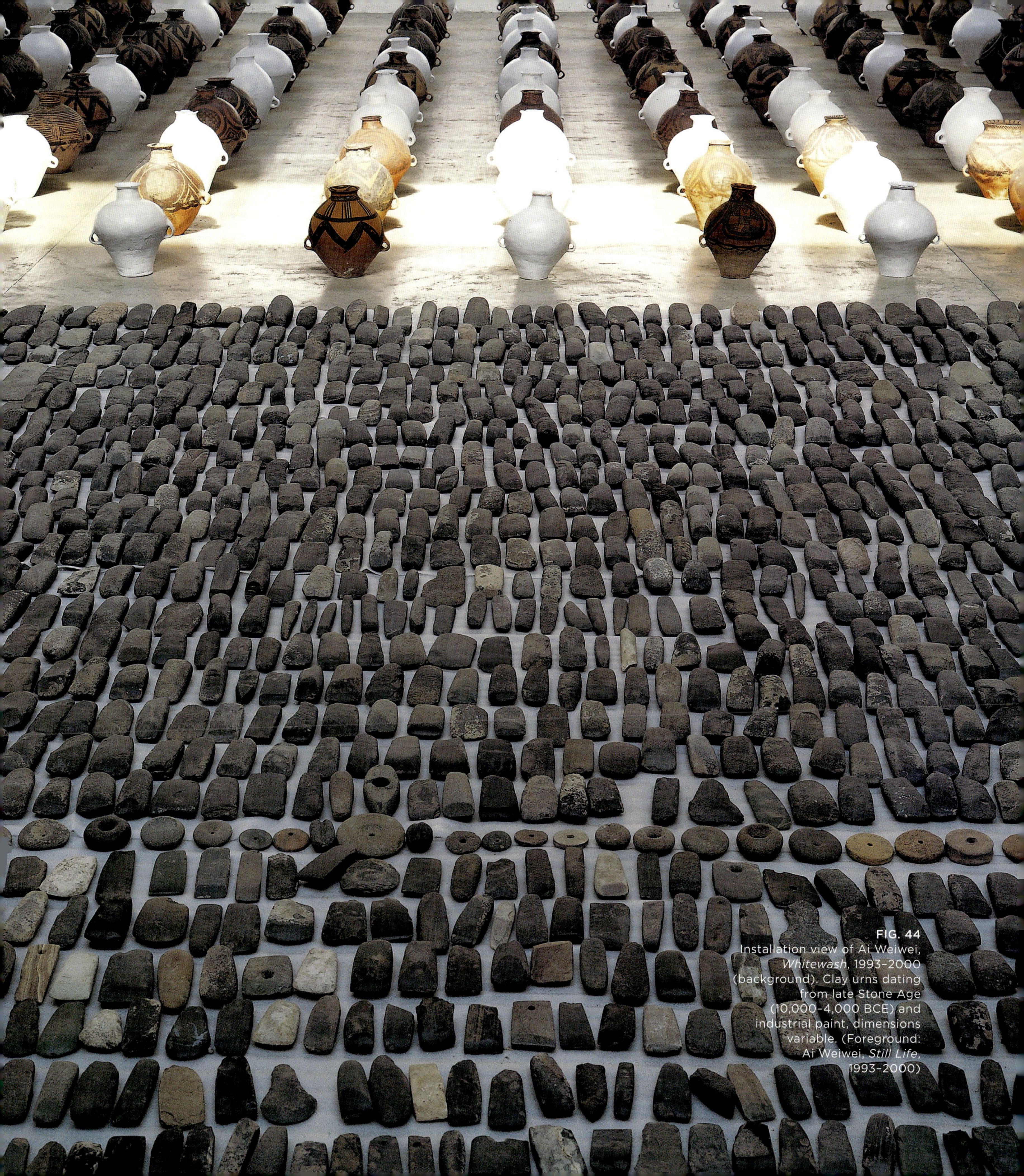

FIG. 44
Installation view of Ai Weiwei,
Whitewash, 1993–2000
(background). Clay urns dating
from late Stone Age
(10,000–4,000 BCE) and
industrial paint, dimensions
variable. (Foreground:
Ai Weiwei, *Still Life*,
1993–2000)

(1986, fig. 42) are both fine examples of his engagement with the concept of the readymade, in which the original and copy collapse into one another as one and the same thing: a new work. Ai Weiwei himself links this body of work to the impact on him of Duchamp, Warhol, and Jasper Johns following his arrival in the United States.[9] We might add the simple fact of living in an environment where he could ill-afford to spend money on art materials, and the overwhelming receptivity that the market had fostered for painting as distinct from conceptual practices, far exceeding that which had been prevalent in the preceding decade.

In many respects, the idea of the copy was little more than an acculturated concept, having greater significance in the West than in Eastern cultures, where the copy had gained equal significance to that of the original. In Thailand, for example, religious temples are periodically replaced by new ones built in exactly the same method and form. Moreover, one may ask, why bother to make copies when the originals were so devalued or at least reasonably obtainable in the marketplace? Why not buy and recycle them in much the same way as was implicated in the notion of the readymade? After all, the quality of the craft would most probably be much higher, and would carry a historical specificity that the copy would not have, especially in ceramics or porcelain ware. Yet, as the time has passed, the disappearance, and hence increasing scarcity, of originals has imbued them with greater value.

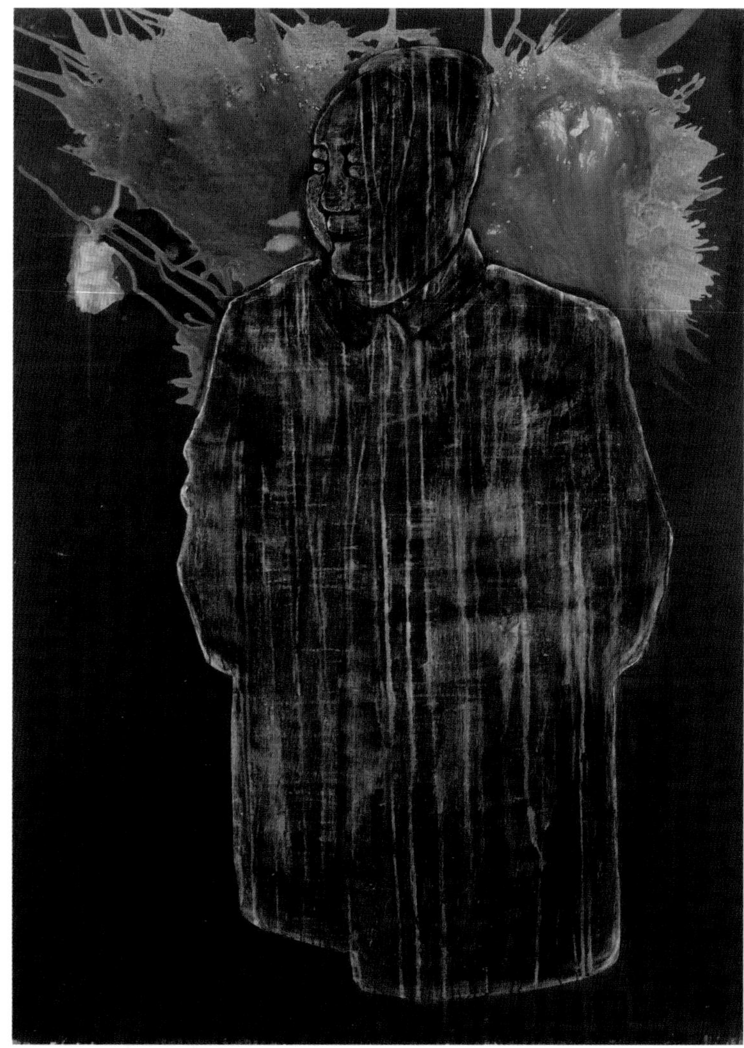

FIG. 45
Ai Weiwei, *Mao 1–3 (triptych)*, 1985. Acrylic on canvas, each 71 x 53 in. (180 x 135 cm). Private collection

The Future of the Past

Ai Weiwei came back to an environment in China in which the emergence of a market economy signified a transformation of the system of aesthetic production, reproduction, and circulation. Traditionally, there had been patronage, commissions, masters, studios, and workshops, while under Communism there had been academies, master artists and craftsmen, and great works that one aspired to copy. The introduction of a market-oriented economy in the early 1990s entailed many shifts, if not the introduction of new laws governing copyright, property, and ownership, or a legal system through which to redefine the concept of authorship and thereby the standardized notions of the original and the copy.

Having been adapted from English, the word "copy" in Chinese is more commonly used to refer to the manufacture or making of something. The practice of copying had been central to Chinese painting traditions, up to and including the Communist era. A young artist would follow the masters with variants, interpretations, or misreadings of the original from which the copy was drawn. This approach makes best sense outside the framework of a Western-based market system. Hence, when Ai Weiwei returned, he found a fundamental shift occurring: a market system that revalidated the original as distinct from the copy. This is nowhere better seen than in the painting associated with one of the most famous blue-and-white porcelain *guans* (jars), from the fourteenth century, and Ai Weiwei's response to it (done in collaboration with Serge

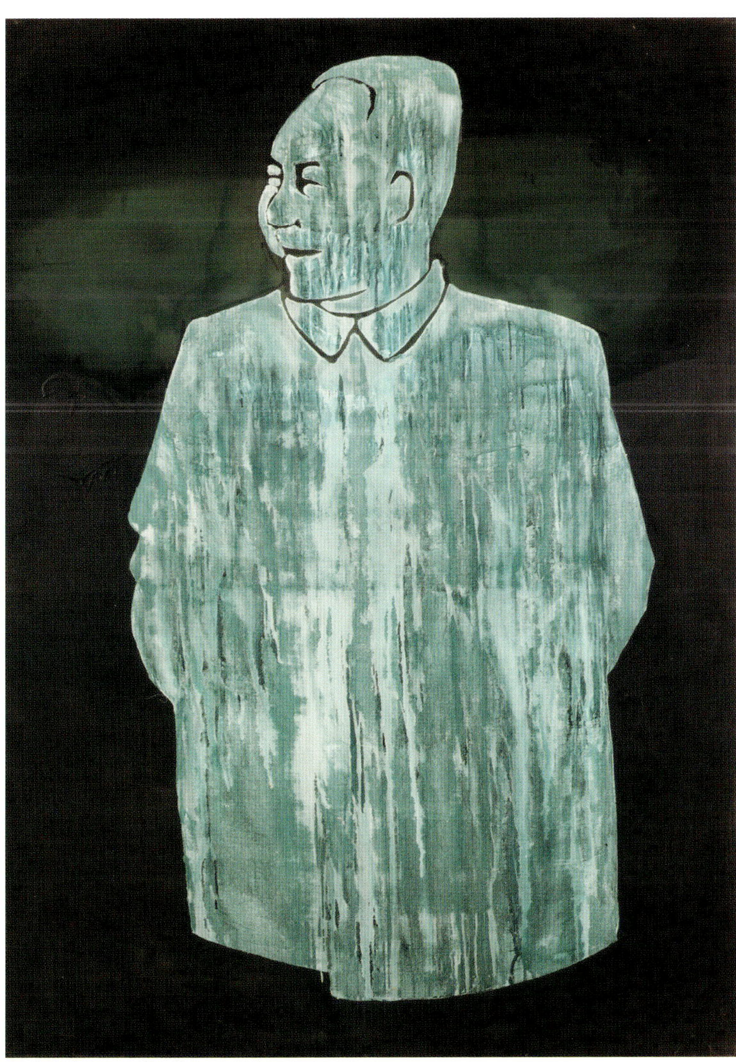

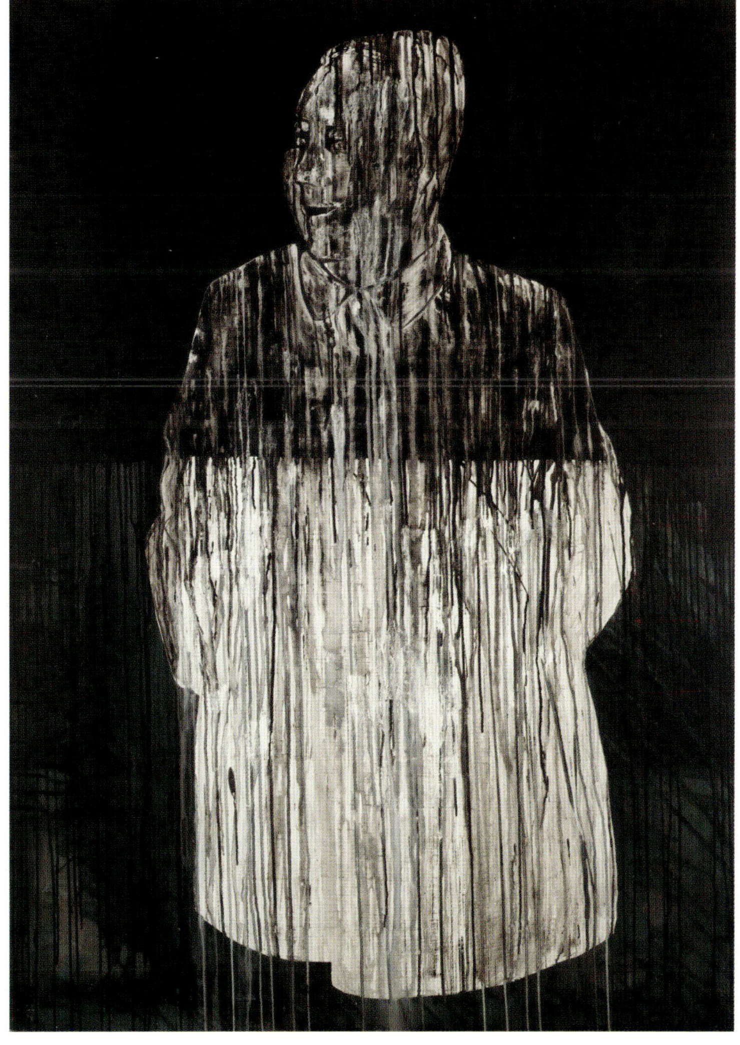

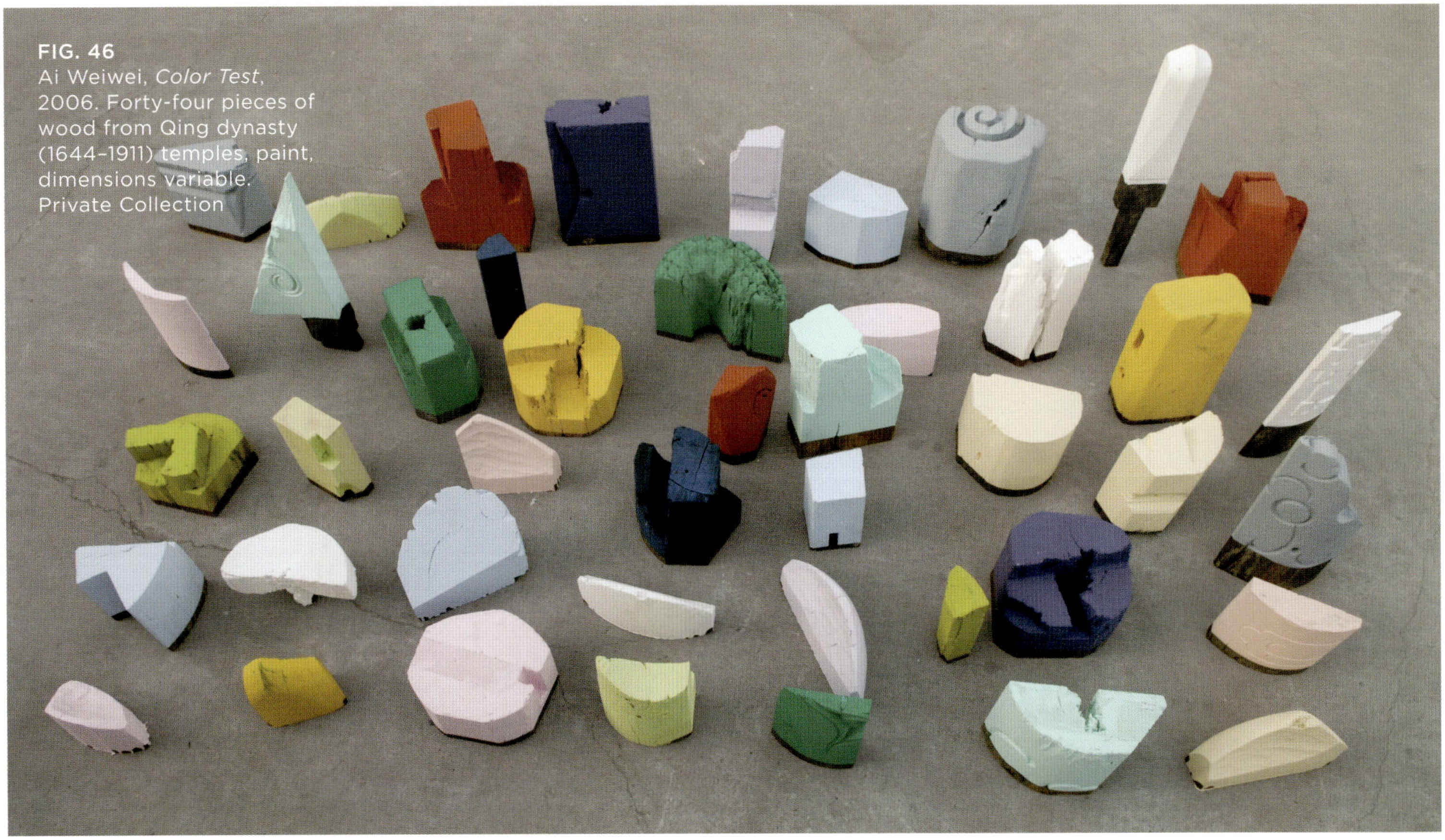

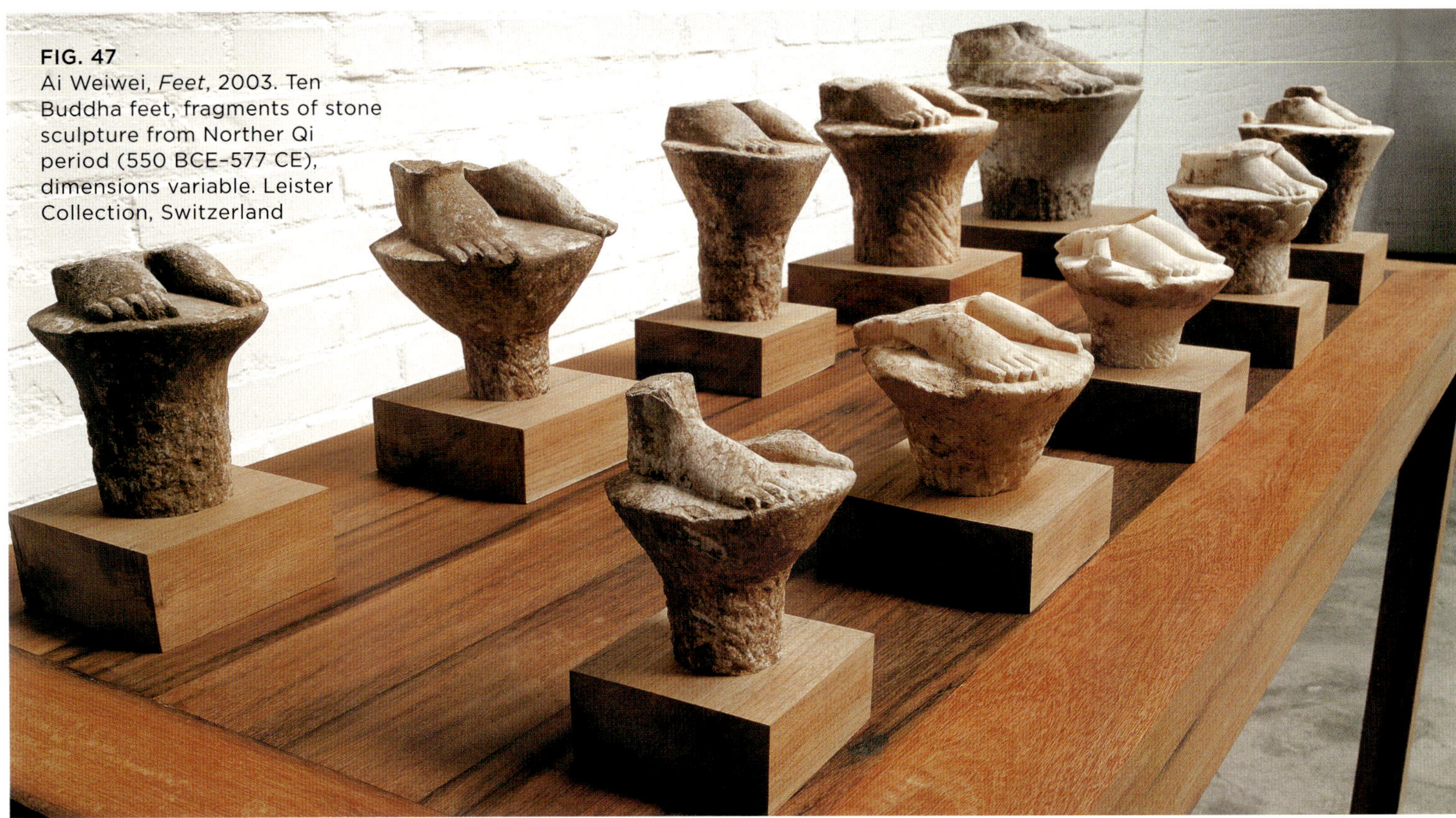

FIG. 46
Ai Weiwei, *Color Test*,
2006. Forty-four pieces of
wood from Qing dynasty
(1644–1911) temples, paint,
dimensions variable.
Private Collection

FIG. 47
Ai Weiwei, *Feet*, 2003. Ten
Buddha feet, fragments of stone
sculpture from Norther Qi
period (550 BCE–577 CE),
dimensions variable. Leister
Collection, Switzerland

Spitzer): *Ghost Gu Coming Down the Mountain* (2005, fig. 43).[10] Going to Jingdezhen, where the medieval guan had first been made, Ai Weiwei and Spitzer requested ninety-six copies of it. They requested, however, that none of the jars be fully painted or include the complete scene as shown in the original. Rather, they instructed that only one-half of each jar was to be painted, with a partial view, while the other half was to be left blank. When the ninety-six jars were placed in a grid, depending upon the vantage point, the viewer would see nothing but a collection of unpainted vases, or various moments of the epic narrative constituting the elements of the story as a whole.[11]

This work, however, should be seen also as a continuation of other explorations of erasure and the copy. Shortly after his return to China, Ai Weiwei began to conceive *Whitewash* (1993–2000) (fig. 44). The work is composed of 132 clay urns dating from the late Stone Age (10,000–4,000 BCE) that literally have been whitewashed. To a degree, the idea of whitewashing already had been explored within the bounds of a received Western modernist aesthetic, in particular instanced by Robert Rauschenberg's famous erasure of a work by Willem de Kooning (*Erased de Kooning Drawing*, 1953), but Ai Weiwei himself had explored this concept in his own New York paintings, in which he tampered with the iconic figure of Mao in a manner that would have been impossible if done and displayed in China (fig. 45).

The colloquial meaning of the term "whitewashed," however, is dramatically changed and recharged by Ai Weiwei once it becomes the subject of address within the context of China. In the first place, we may say the urns have survived only to find themselves subjected to an apparently arbitrary gesture of denial or, perhaps more accurately, they have survived precisely by force of this denial. That is, the work can be viewed as making evident the erasure of differentiation, the leveling of the many to one. Whatever difference they may have had has been simply glossed over. What, then, could be more scandalous than the act of whitewashing these ancient pots? They have been in part destroyed, but the urns themselves remain as evidence of the act. Further, by naming the work *Whitewash*, the artist opens up a potential relay of meanings that is not purely an aesthetic negation, but a reference to the act of covering over or hiding certain facts, evidence, or errors. In short, the use of the word in this instance suggests that the cultural and economic investment given such objects provides a cover for the large-scale destruction happening in China.

We may be reminded of the complex contemporary history of the Three Gorges Dam, if not more broadly of a time when what appears to matter is the cultural artifact as opposed to its people. While material culture is salvaged, if only to be sold off, the cultural fabric of a people and of their inherited traditions and skills disappears.

In the object-based installations that followed, such as *Colored Vases* (1993, ongoing) or *Color Test* (2006, fig. 46), Ai Weiwei seeks to shift perspective and to make visible what remains invisible. Both antique vases and fragments of temple structures have been covered in gaudy paint, invoking once again modern Western painting in general and Color-Field painting in particular, one of the most aestheticized movements of the postwar period. Cultural heritage, we might say, has been reduced to kitsch. Moreover, by throwing a coat of industrial paint over these pre-existent objects so that they assume a uniformity, we may also see this succession of works, predominantly produced in serial form, as mirroring the mass production of ceramics and in turn luxury goods, recalling the early history of the modular production of art in China and its impact on the West.[12]

Ai Weiwei returned to explore yet another dimension of the subject of antique objects in both *Feet* (2003, fig. 47) and *Hands* (2003). In each work, he displays on wooden tables and stone or wooden plinths the discarded fragments of statues found in antiquities markets or still remaining as evidential remains at sacred sites. We know well the looting of famous civilizational sites throughout China and the Asian world, such as Angkor Wat in Cambodia, where, for instance, heads of the Buddha have been sawn off and sold. Without a unified body and head, the sacred function of these statues is rendered inoperative and their identities reduced to a form of apparent anonymity. The museological production of Chinese history attests not only to the fetishization of these objects, but also, as part of an overall shift, to the appropriation and secular commodification of culture under the sign of a national patrimony.

Gathering and grouping together these found fragments, Ai Weiwei proceeds to construct a faux museum display. By so doing, the fragments or remnants come alive again and, while gaining a metonymic power as parts of the missing body, impart value to the image of the hands and feet. Mounted on pedestals, his act of salvaging provides a means of seeing the refined beauty of their detailed sculpting and what may be viewed as a tacit recognition of their profound humanness: the manual dexterity of both feet and hands that shape their earthbound destiny.

Ai Weiwei's recovery of the zodiac heads through the exercise of making copies raises a number of issues that until now have remained shrouded by the events of 1860. In many respects, *Circle of Animals/Zodiac Heads* marks yet another expression of his interest in copying works of minor aesthetic significance alongside major works. In fact, the decision to pursue this project itself invalidates the aesthetic value that may have been assigned to the originals. These works are all by Ai Weiwei and therefore accrue a certain value for reasons of new authorship. But do they accrue any more value for reasons related to the originals? Yes and no. Historical, not aesthetic, value in effect foreshadows the original. To this end we might ask why were copies of the originals not made by the Chinese government? It would have been cheaper and more reliable. The difference is that a well-known artist has made contemporary works that are copies of old objects that are now historically valued; the new works gain their own value insofar as they are, in fact, works by the artist.

Conclusion

Through his work, Ai Weiwei raises a series of questions about cultural violence and history. He explores the relation between the two, a relationship he often re-enacts through his practice. In this regard, his art engages with the concept of a country that oscillates between iconic production and mass manufacture, ruin and production, patrimony and erasure. His work mirrors the dynamics of an unraveling movement forward by which he critically reflects on China's cultural history and its relation to itself. By recalling the original through a copy that declares itself to be nothing less or more than a new work, the artist re-stages the past by virtue of re-signifying the concept of value in terms of the present. This is most true of *Circle of Animals/Zodiac Heads*, insofar as it embodies the transformative conditions for change. These conditions allow for the realization of an imaginative realm of freedom, not by means of a violent overthrow of the past but to the contrary, its embrace as part of the present. The past is therefore lived contemporaneously as opposed to being consigned to the museum as a belated object of memorialization. This latter approach comes too late, insofar as the object becomes a relic whose value is shaped and controlled by a privileged few. This process of memorialization functions in a broader social sphere in regard to sanctifying party leaders to convey a sacred value.

The value of *Circle of Animals/Zodiac Heads* rests with its ability to embody the past in the present, to act as a conduit of historical change. We see the zodiac heads not as looted objects, but more so as new work that has shed its historicity in the process. And yet they still appear as anachronistic, monumental in scale or gilded bright gold, reminiscent of an antique style yet without the patina of the past. To what do they refer, we may ask. Seen inside museums whose collections hold antique and historical objects, they raise the question of what value the original holds that makes it more precious than the copy. The question of loot appears then as neither a moral issue, nor as linked to the conditions of the original heads' production, but rather concerns their subjugation to a life of circulation. Perhaps the contemporary fate of the zodiac bronzes is that they can be read as signs of the past only within the light of the future.

1. For a marvelous exploration of this history, see Marcia Reed and Paola Demattè, eds., *China on Paper: European and Chinese Works from the Late Sixteenth to the Early Nineteenth Century* (Los Angeles: Getty Research Institute, 2007).

2. Richard Strassberg, "War and Peace: Four Intercultural Landscapes," in ibid., 104.

3. See Cécile Beurdeley and Michel Beurdeley, *Giuseppe Castiglione: A Jesuit Painter at the Court of the Chinese Emperors*, trans. Michael Bullock (Rutland, VT: C. E. Tuttle Co., 1971).

4. See Rosemary Scott, "Les têtes en bronzes du Palais d'été de l'empereur Qianlong," in *Collection Yves Saint Laurent et Pierre Bergé*, vol. 5, *Sculptures, objets d'art, art d'Asie, archéologie et mobilier* (Paris: Christie's, 2009), 455–62. This book was the catalogue for the Christie's auction held on February 25, 2009.

5. See Strassberg, "War and Peace," 109ff.

6. Blue-and-white Kangxi porcelain was extremely popular among English and American collectors, notably the painter James McNeill Whistler and the tycoons John Pierpont Morgan, Henry Clay Frick, and John D. Rockefeller, Jr. Frick's Chinese porcelain collection may be seen at the Frick Collection in New York.

7. For a discussion, see my introduction in Charles Merewether, ed., *The Archive* (London: Whitechapel Gallery and Cambridge, MA: MIT Press, 2006).

8. See Charles Merewether, "Looting and Empire," *Grand Street*, no. 72 (Fall 2003): 82–94.

9. See my interview with the artist, "Changing Perspective: Interview with Ai Weiwei," in *Ai Weiwei: Works Beijing 1993–2003* (Beijing: Timezone 8 Books, 2003).

10. For a full account of the work and the original *guan*, see Philip Tinari, "The Leopard and the Tiger: Circular Narratives in Blue and

White," in Waling Boers, Pi Li, Michael Ammann, et al., *Touching the Stones: China Art Now* (Beijing: Timezone 8 Books, 2006), 134–39. The essay was originally published in English, with a German translation by Museum für Moderne Kunst, Frankfurt, on the occasion of the exhibition *Serge Spitzer / Ai Weiwei: Territorial* (May–August 2006), which featured the installation *Ghost Gu Coming Down the Mountain* (2005–6). The subsequent history of the jar also underscores the degree to which Chinese antiquities have become objects of intense market speculation and competing national and international interests.

11. Following this principle, Ai Weiwei mounted a collaborative exhibition with two artist friends, Ding Yi and Wang Xingwei, at the China Art Archives and Warehouse in 2004. The exhibition was dedicated to the organization's first director, Hans van Dijk, who "never stopped looking at things." The three artists could not have been more different in terms of the character of their work. The conceit of the exhibition, however, was that each artist produced photographs, paintings, or sculptures in the name of the other without disclosing who did what. In this manner, the concept of the exhibition, as so often throughout Ai Weiwei's work, raised the question of authorship and, by default, of subjectivity, authenticity, and value. That is, the artwork gathers its authority only as an object invested with value through the conventions of art practice: authorship, display, and so on. What if one of these exhibited works were as good as that ascribed to Ai Weiwei or to Ding Yi or Wang Xingwei? Should or would we value it less? Is it purely the signature that matters?

12. Peter Pakesch makes this point in "A Bowl of Pearls," in Urs Meile, Peter Pakesch, and Ai Weiwei, eds., *Ai Weiwei: Works 2004–2007* (Lucerne: Urs Meile Gallery, 2007). See also Lothar Ledderose, *Ten Thousand Things: Module and Mass Production in Chinese Art* (Princeton, NJ: Princeton University Press, 1998). In this book, Leddcrose shows how the demand for luxury goods in the West contributed both to the development of modern industrial production in the West and to Chinese art.

Circle of Animals/

Zodiac Heads

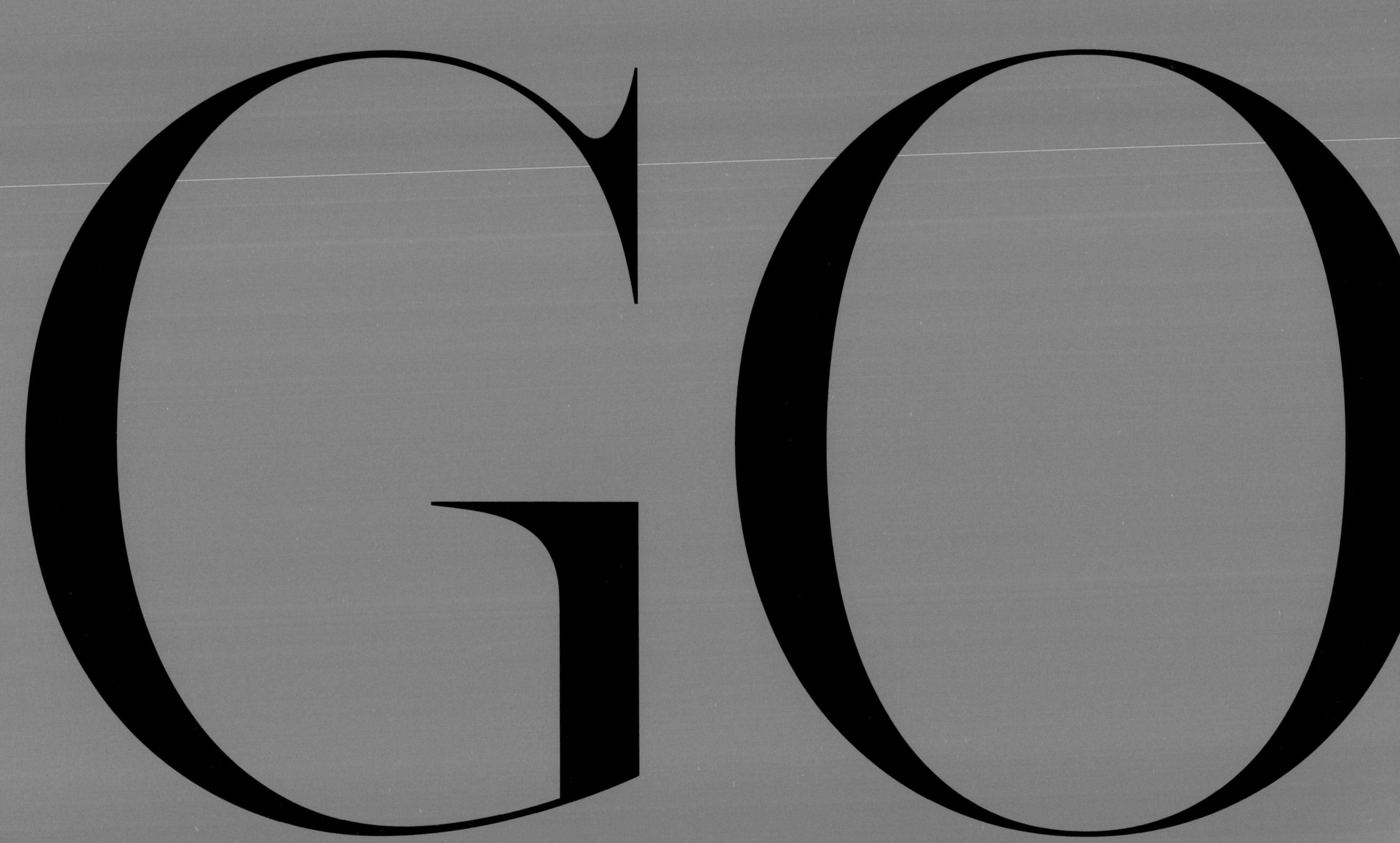

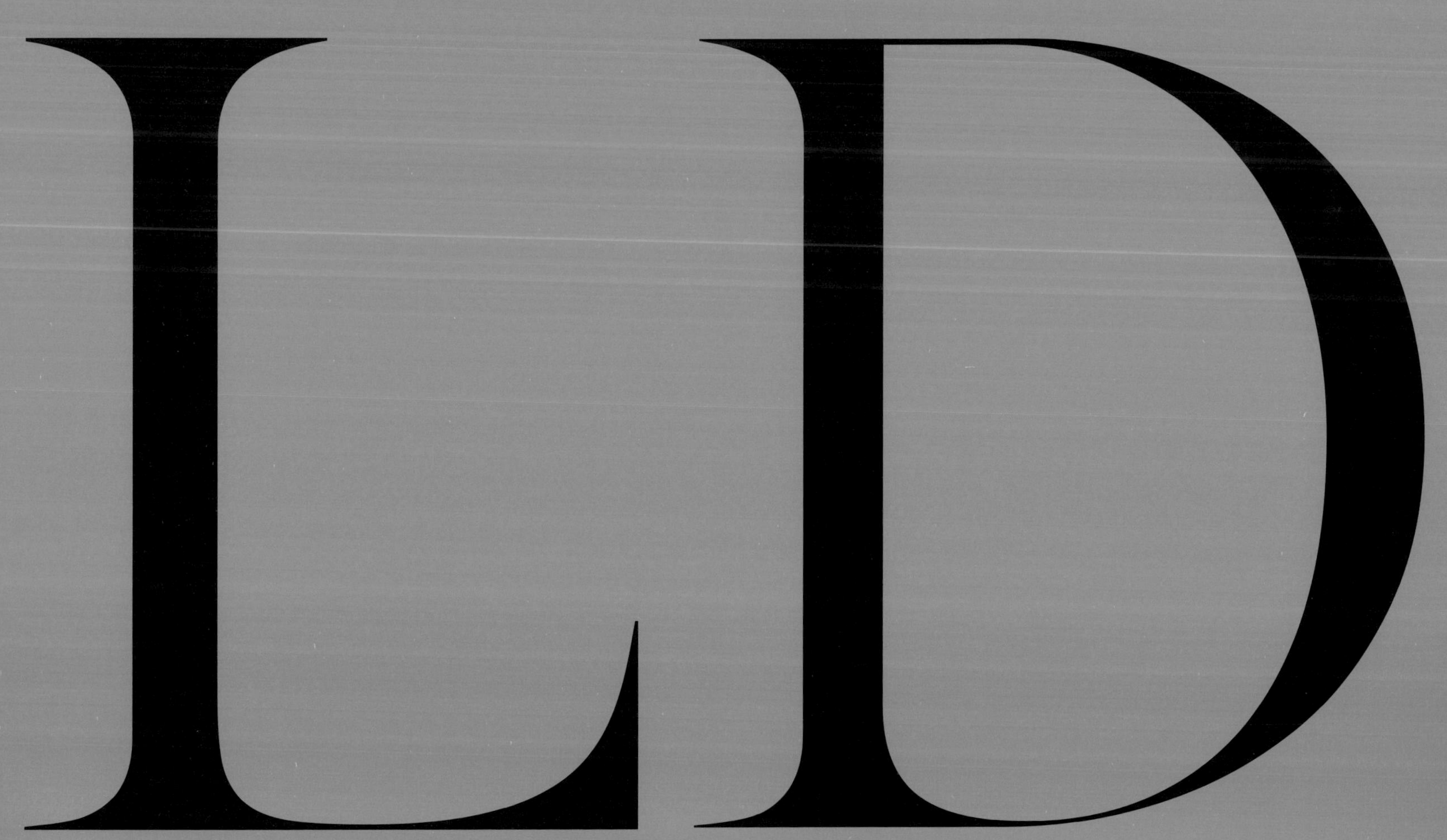

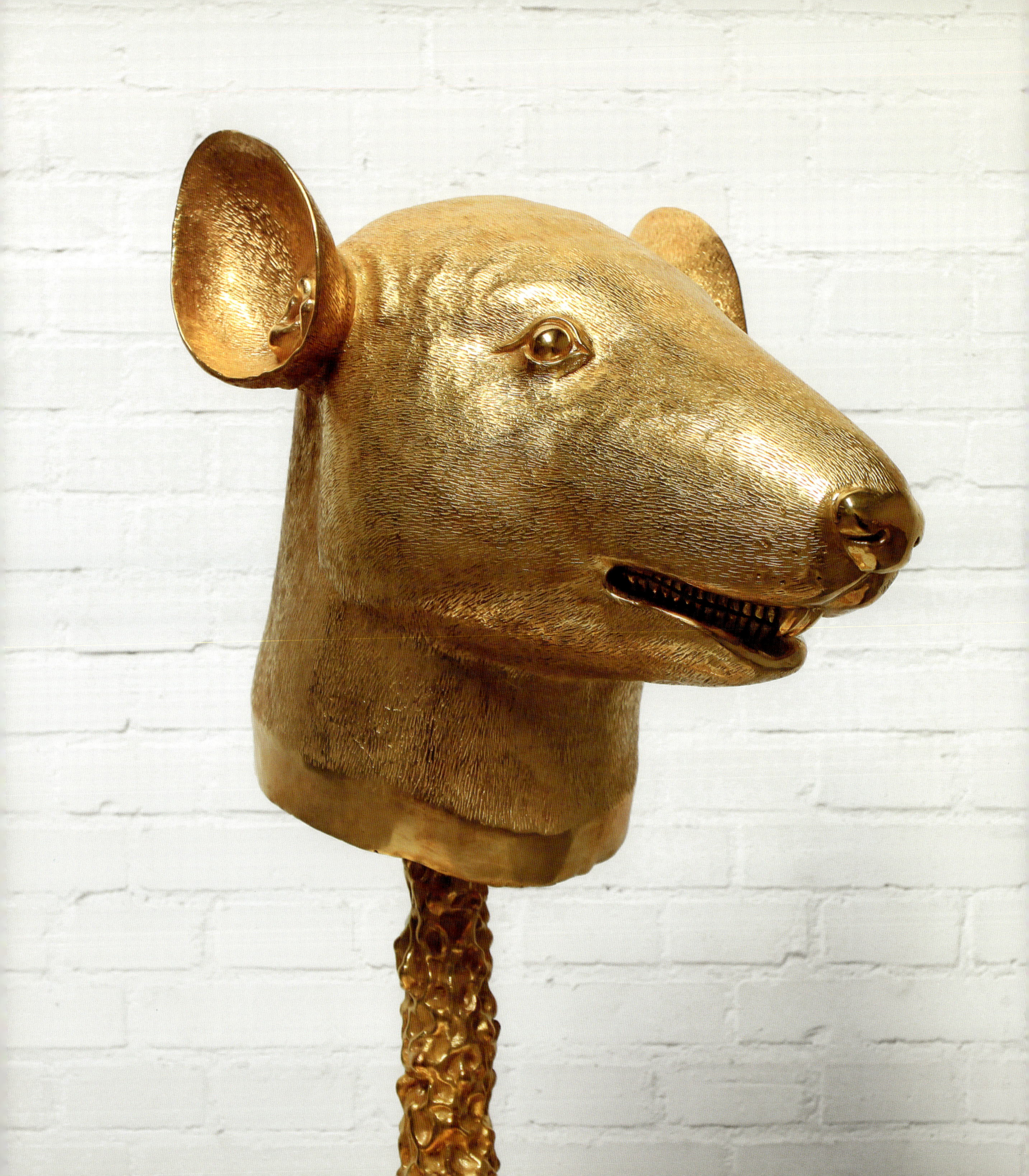

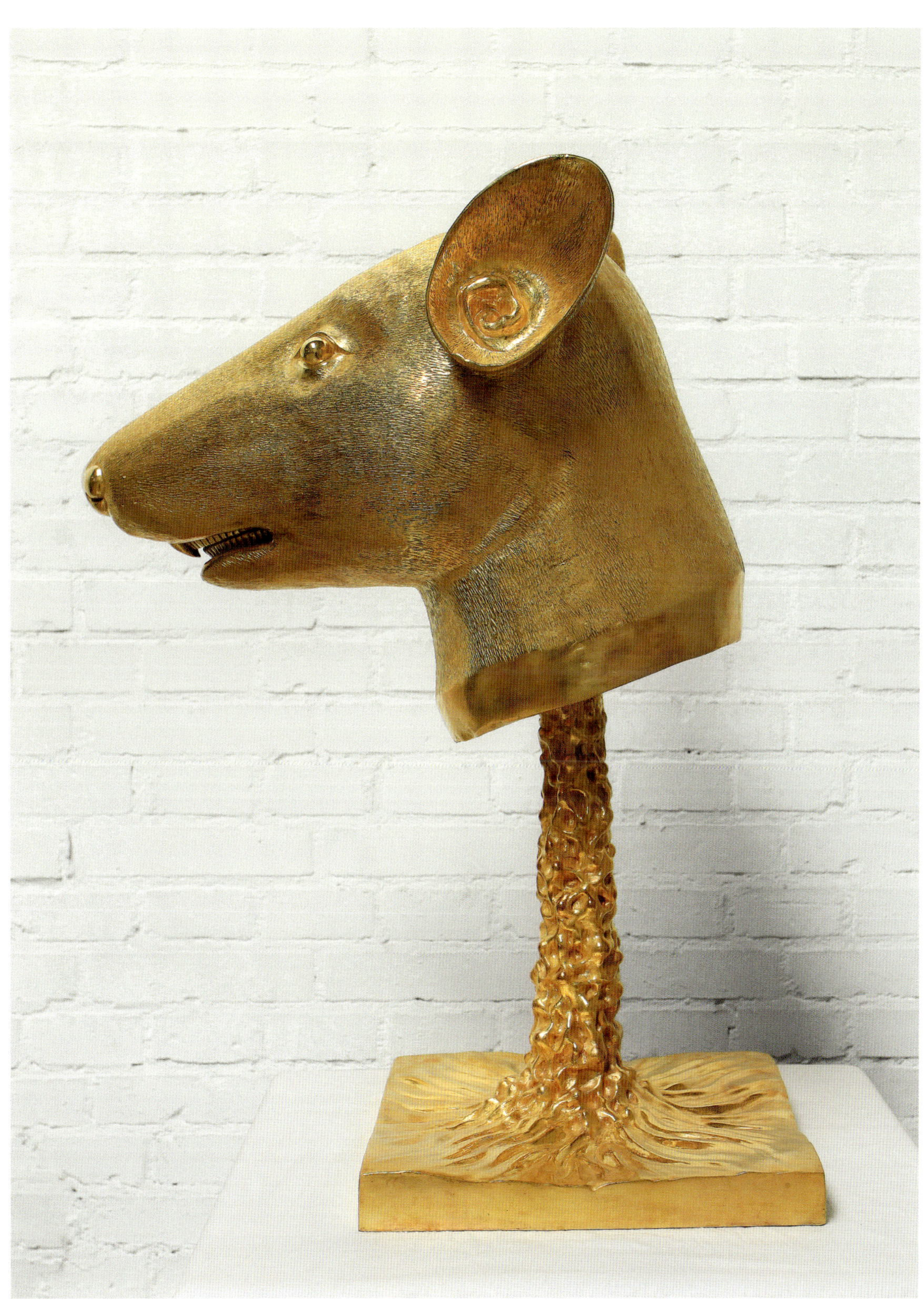

Rat

2010
Bronze with gold patina
28 x 13 x 21 in.
(71 x 33 x 53 cm)

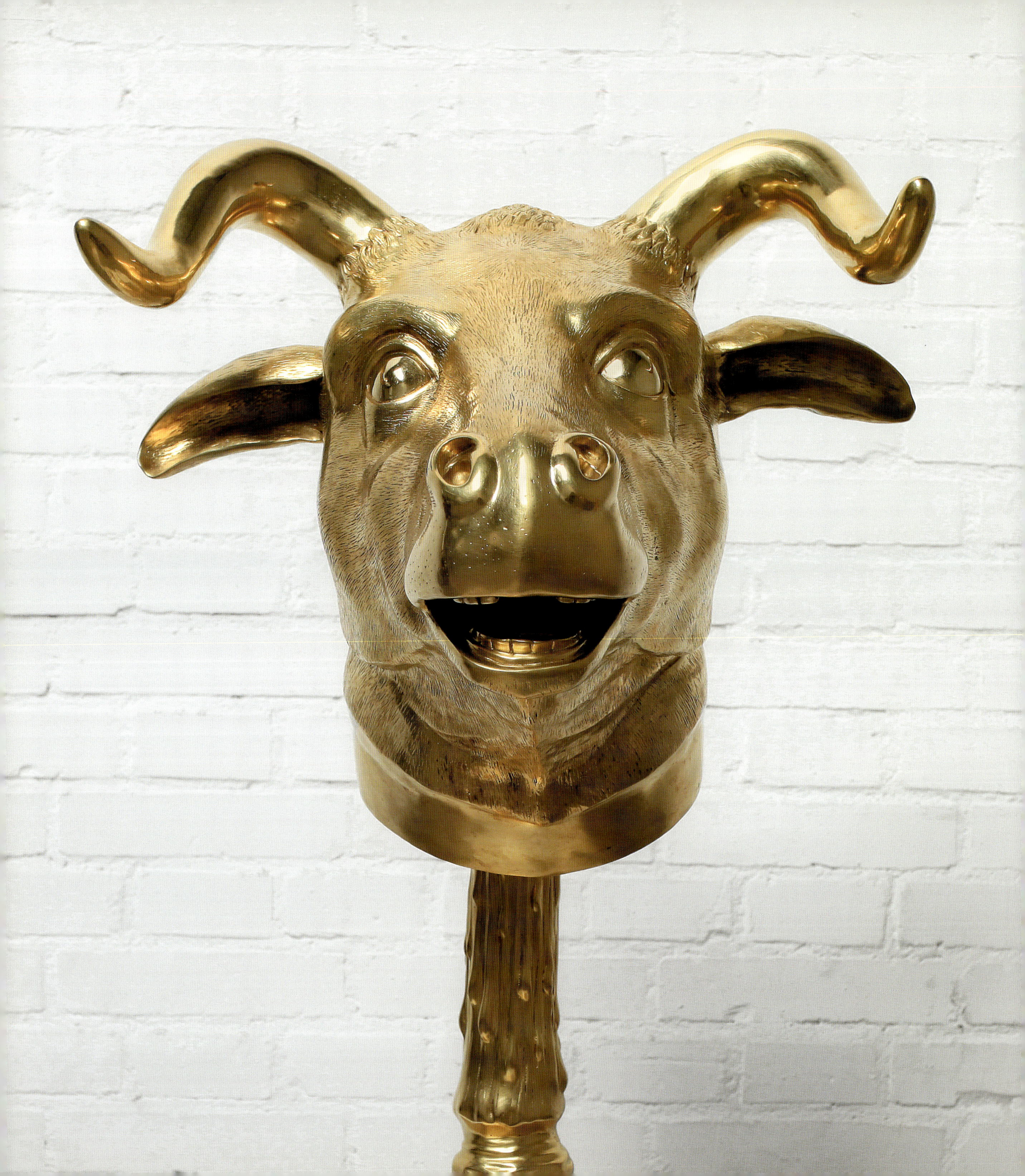

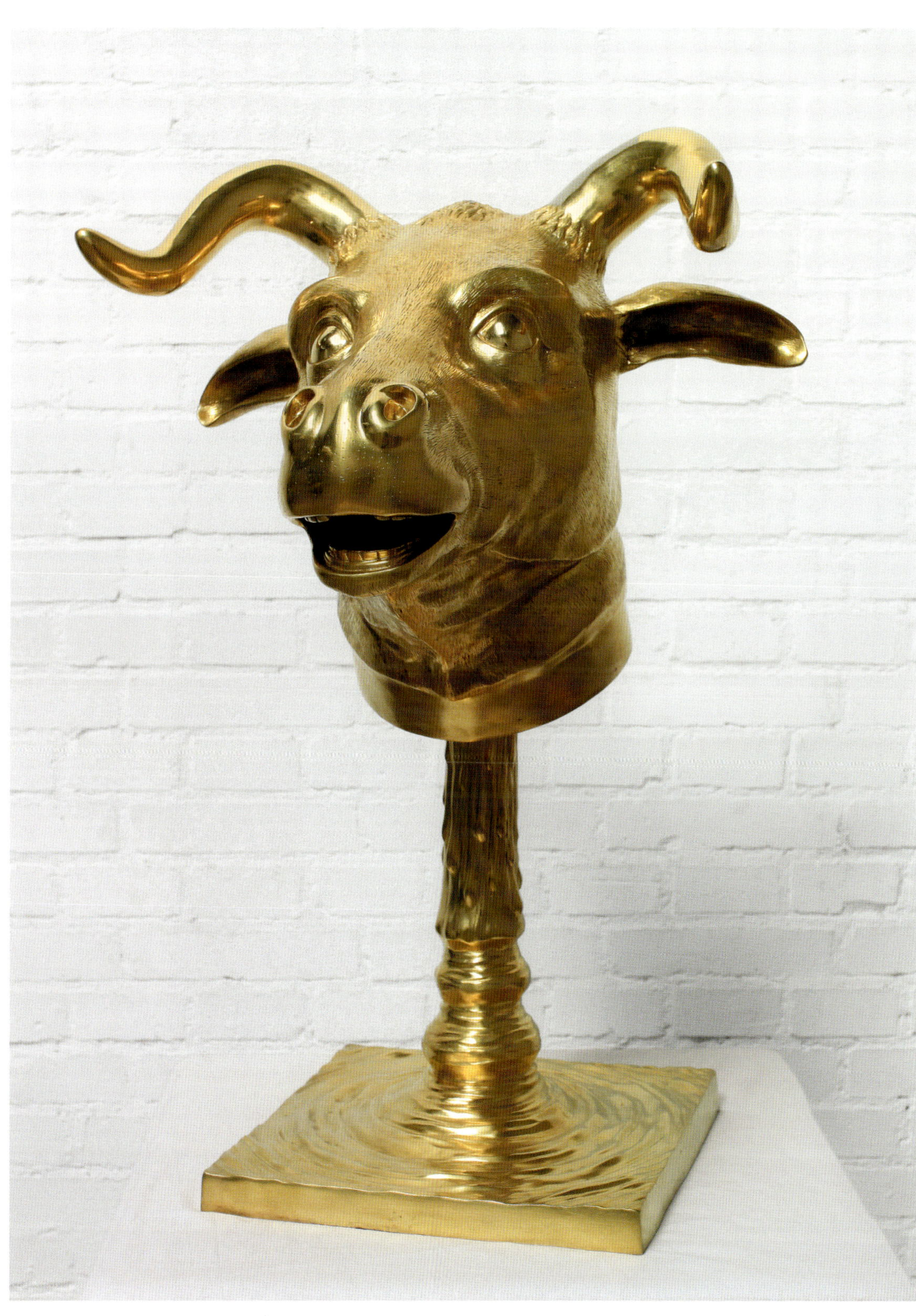

Ox

2010
Bronze with gold patina
29 x 20 x 17 in.
(74 x 51 x 43 cm)

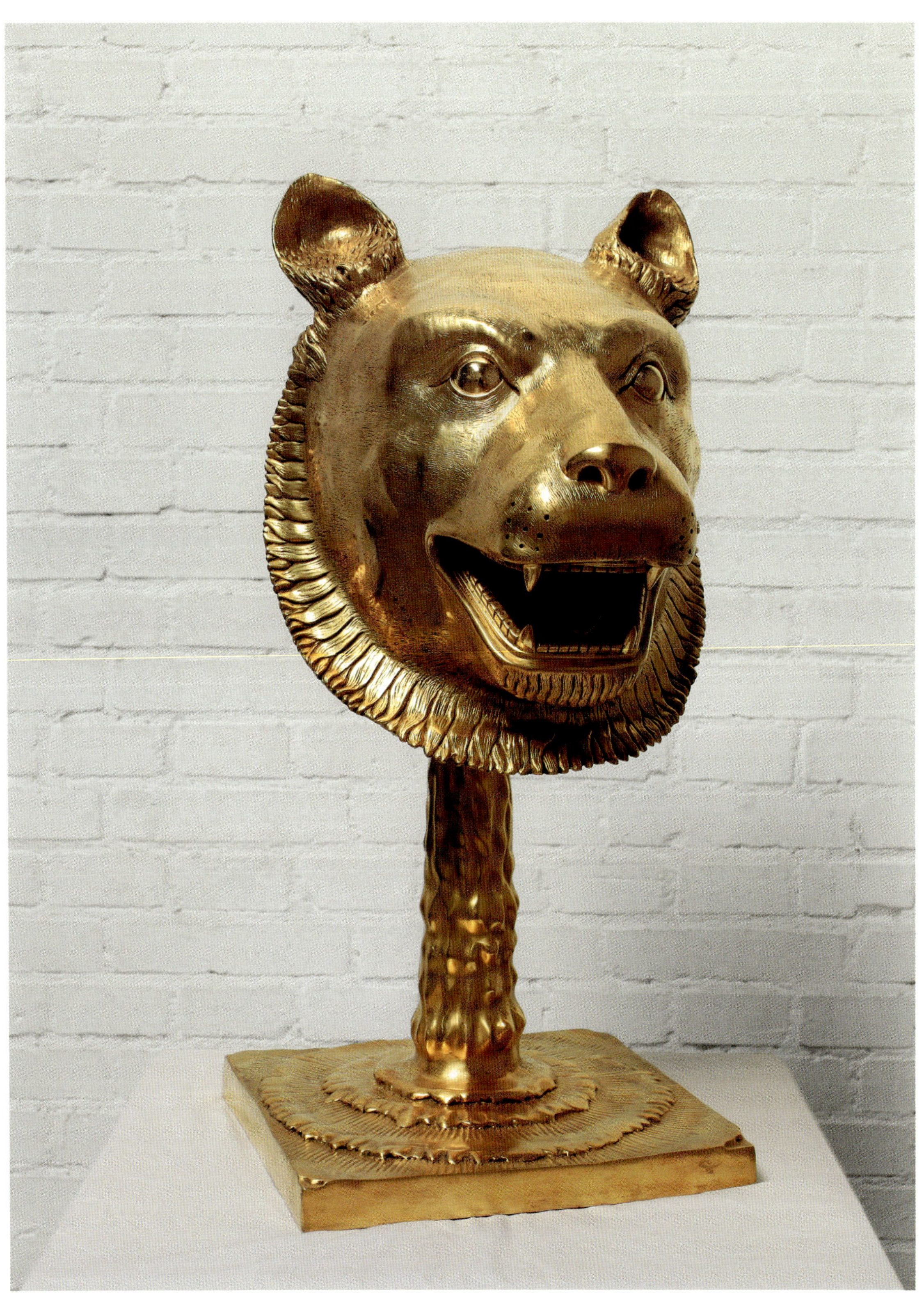

Tiger

2010
Bronze with gold patina
26 x 15 x 17 in.
(66 x 38 x 43 cm)

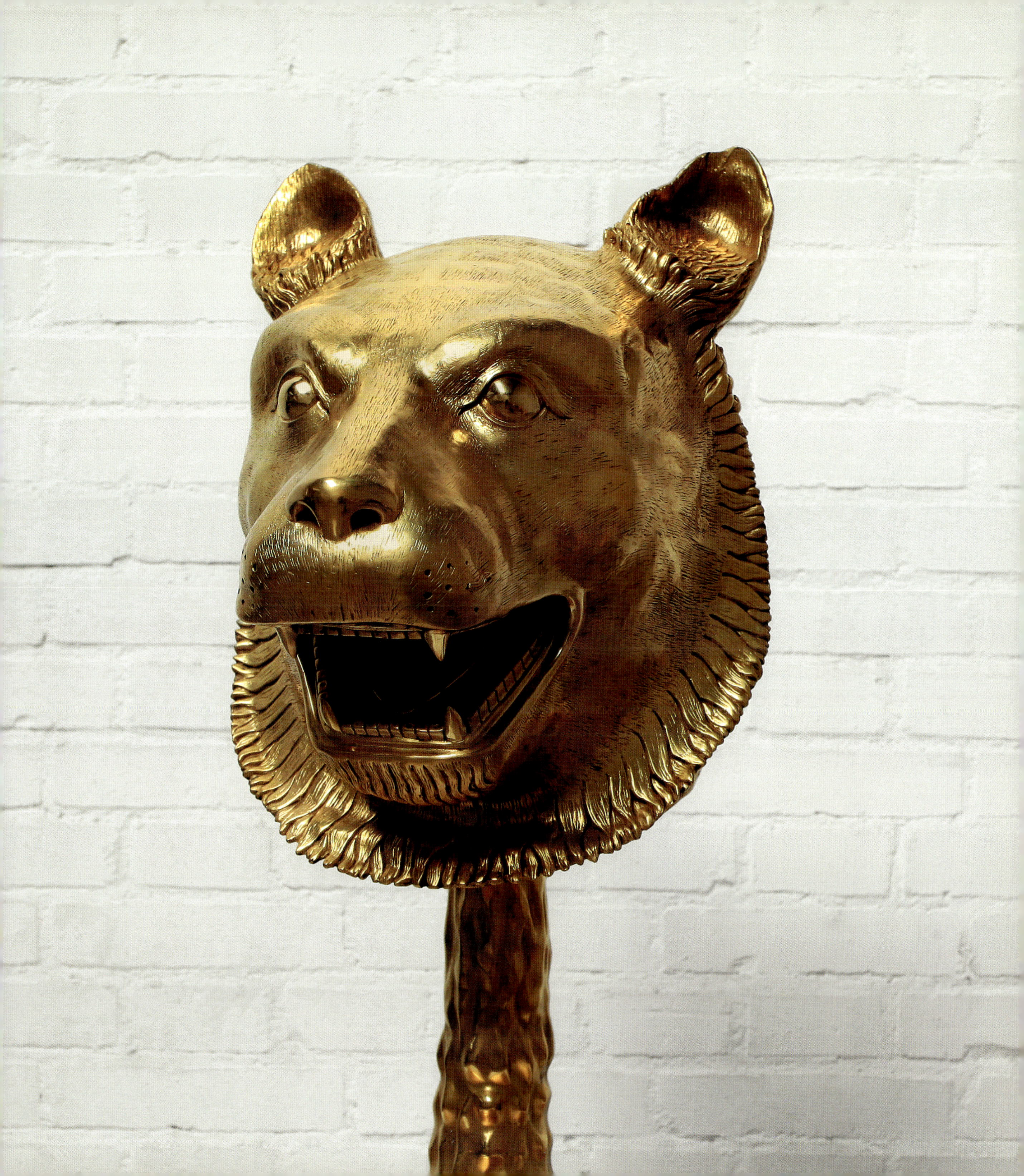

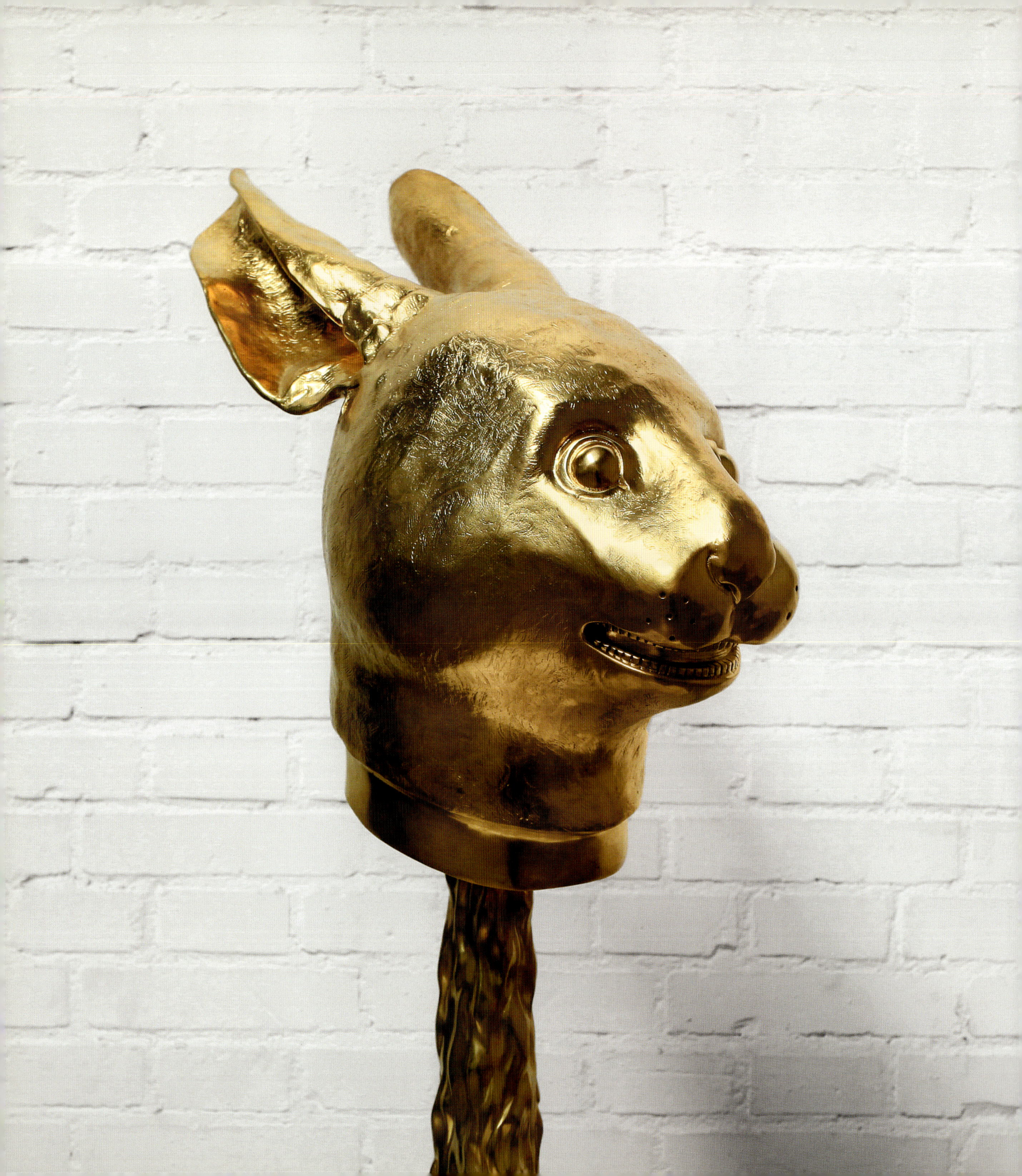

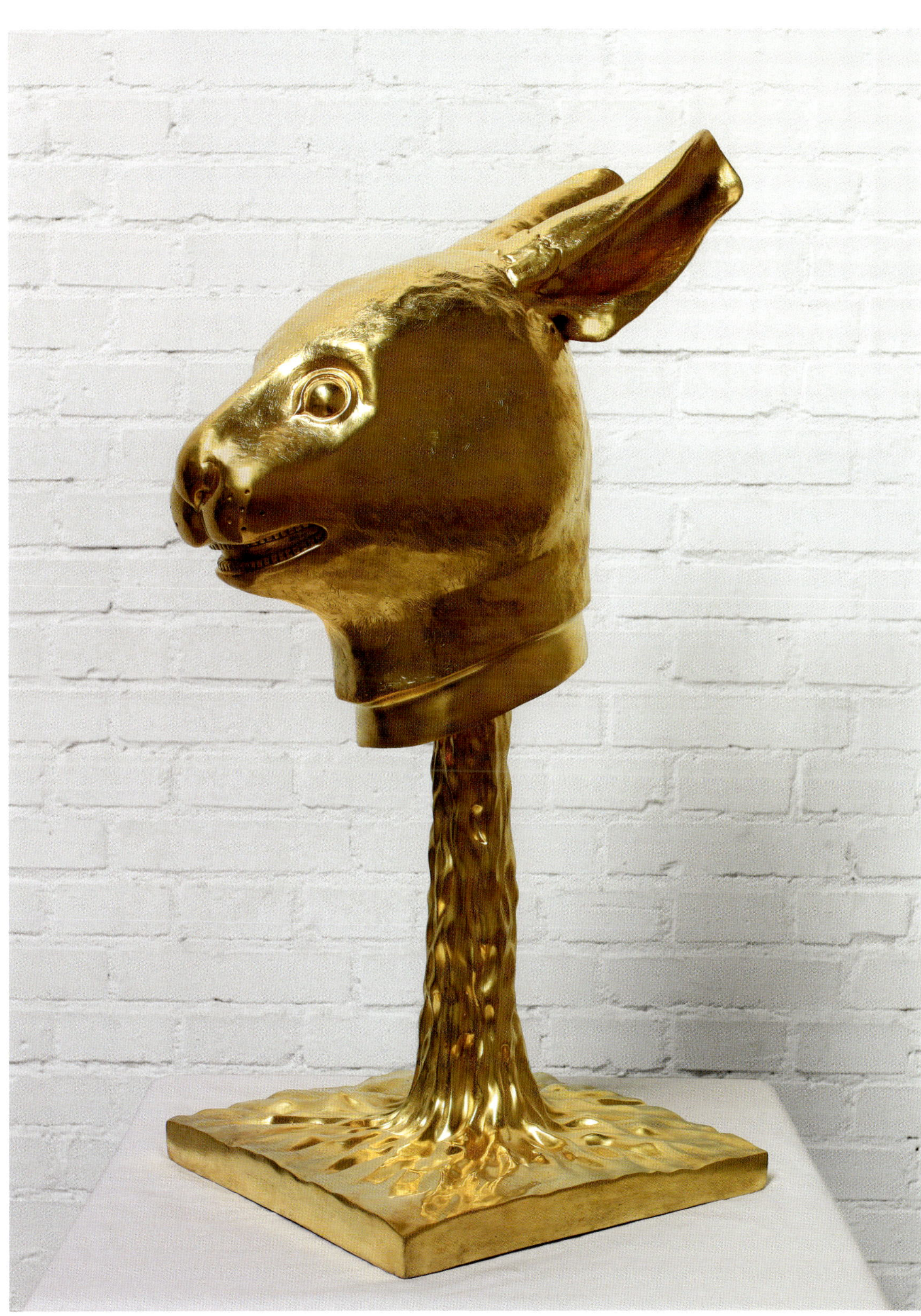

Rabbit

2010
Bronze with gold patina
28 x 10 x 17 in.
(71 x 25 x 48 cm)

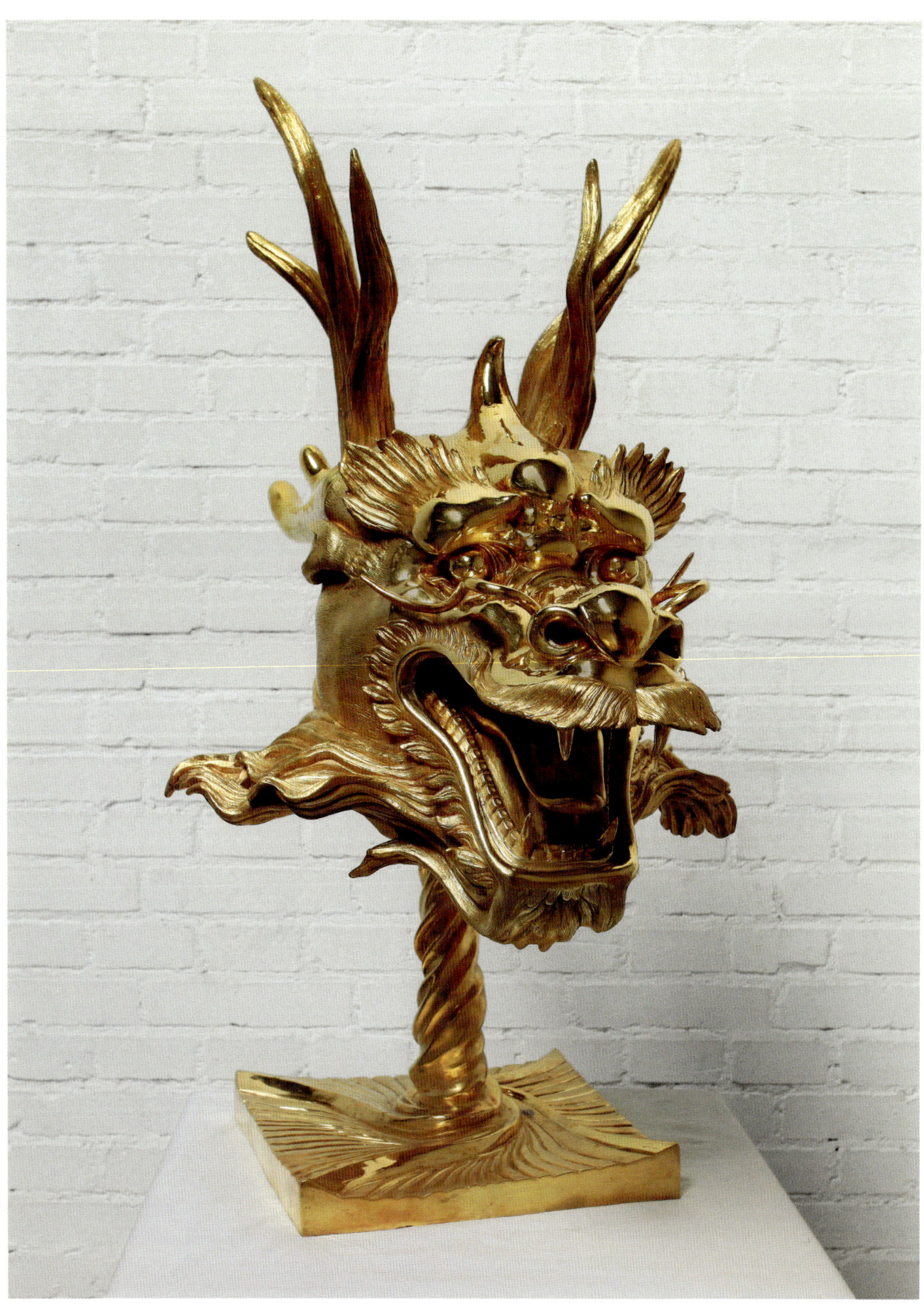

Dragon

2010
Bronze with gold patina
36 x 18 x 26 in.
(91 x 46 x 66 cm)

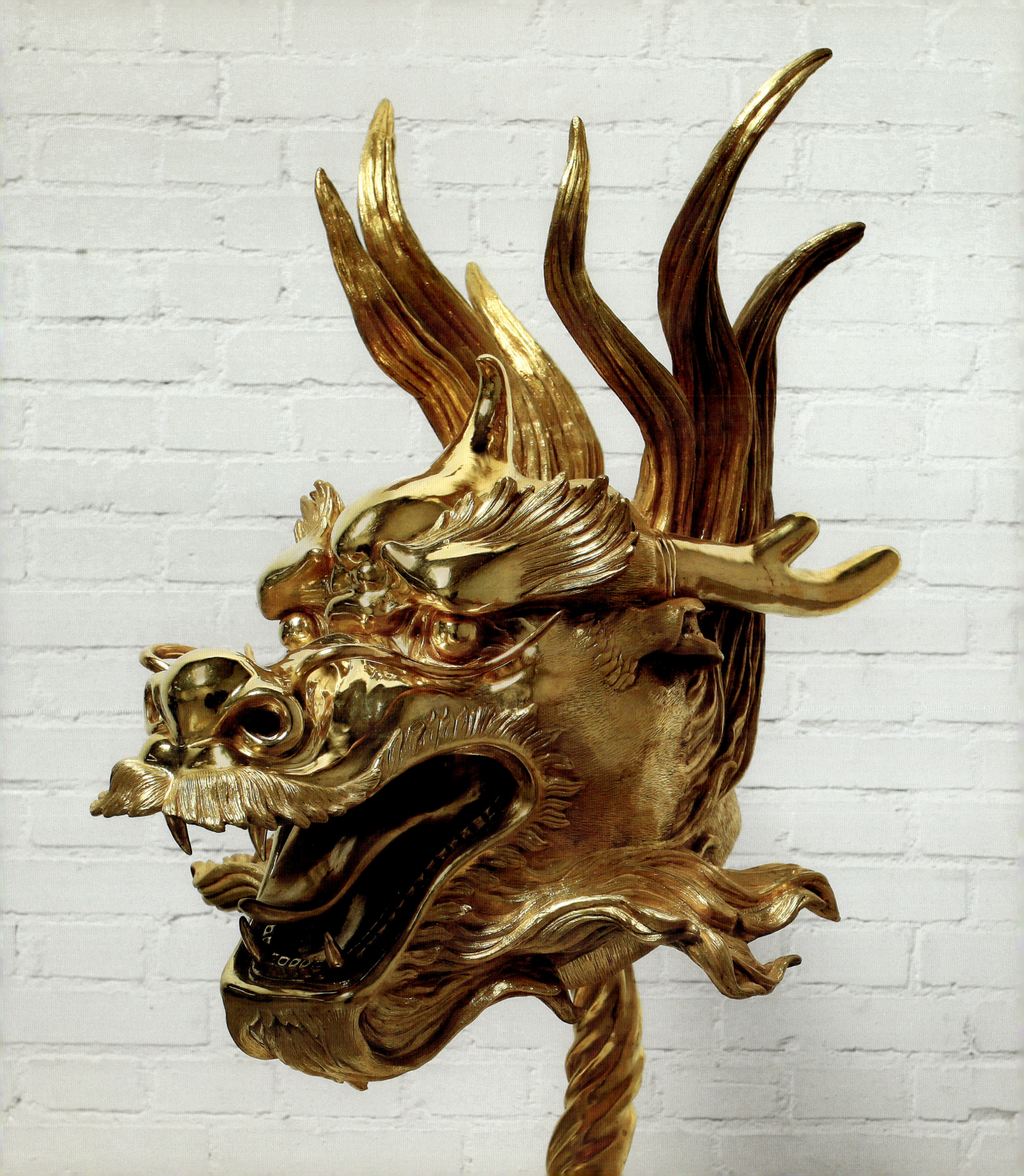

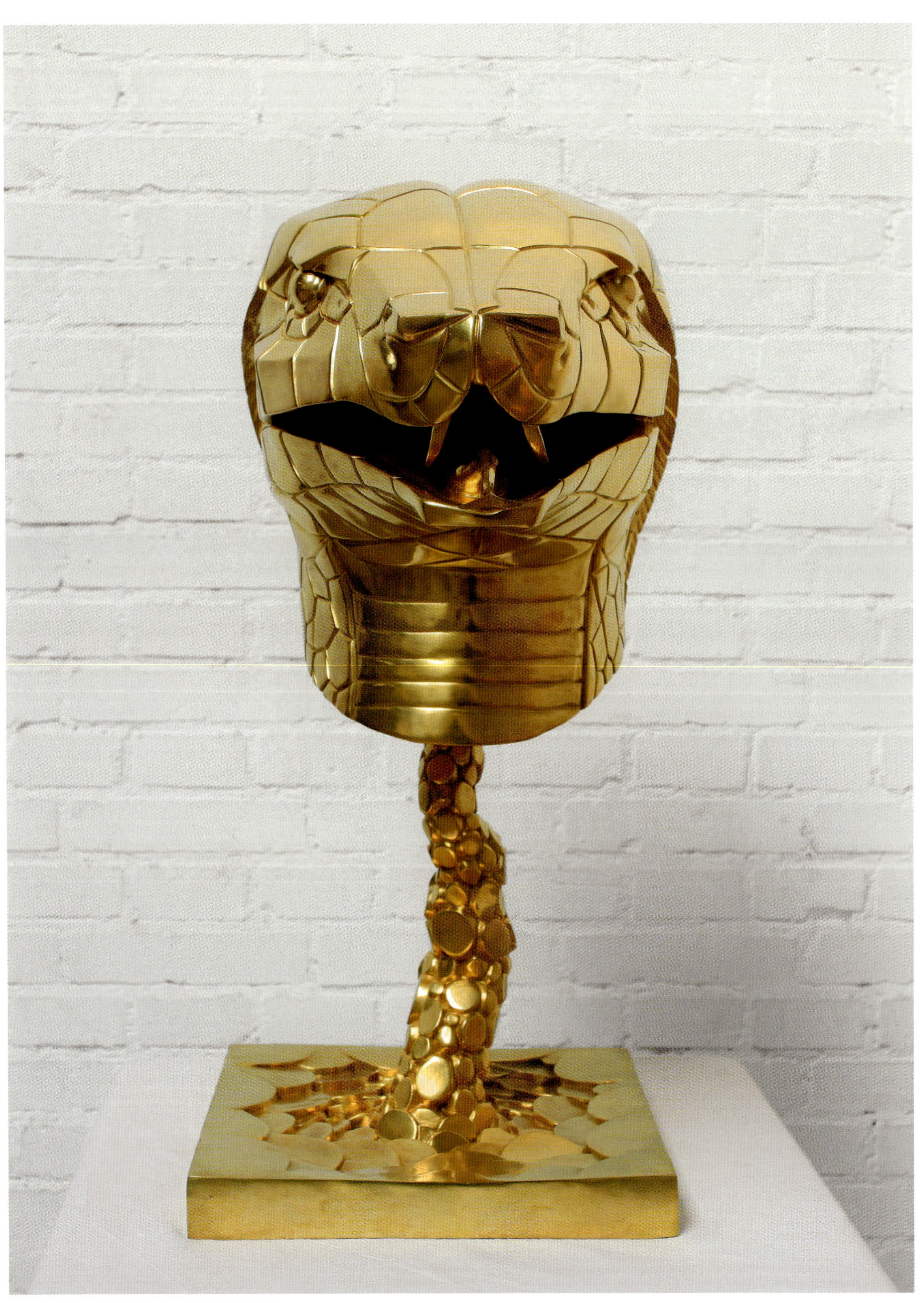

Snake

2010
Bronze with gold patina
28 x 14 x 17 in.
(71 x 36 x 43 cm)

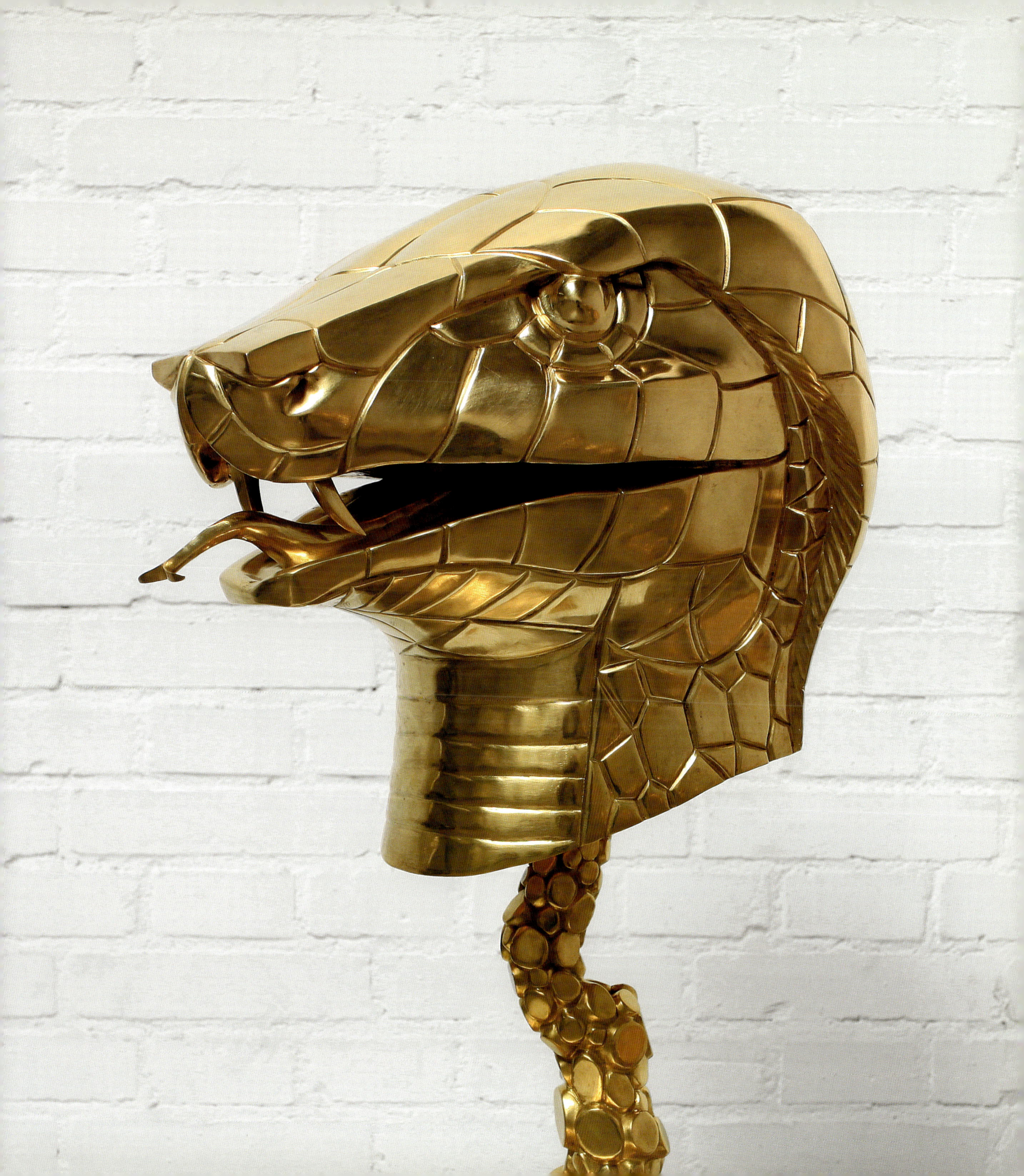

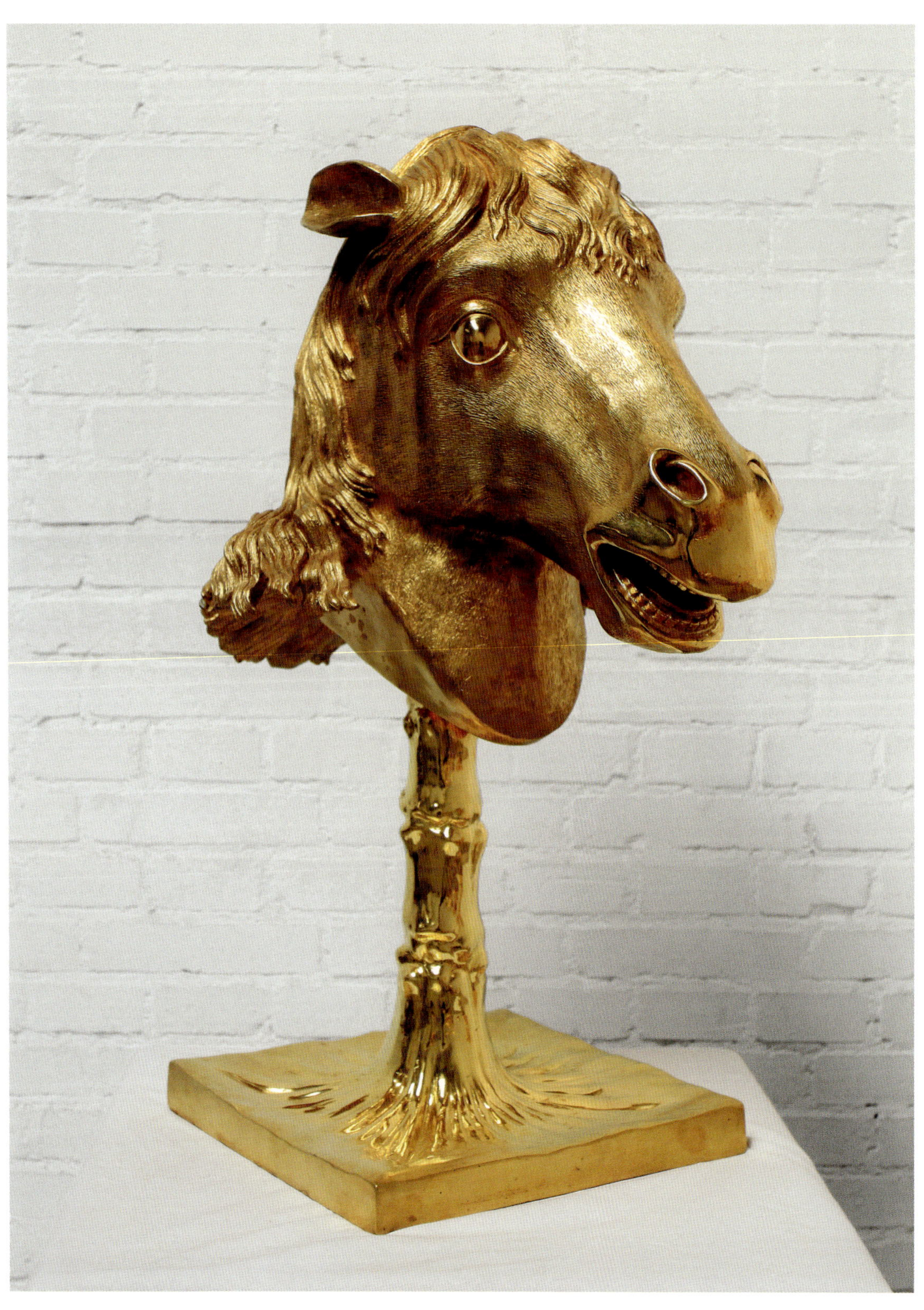

Horse

2010
Bronze with gold patina
29 x 12 x 22 in.
(74 x 31 x 56 cm)

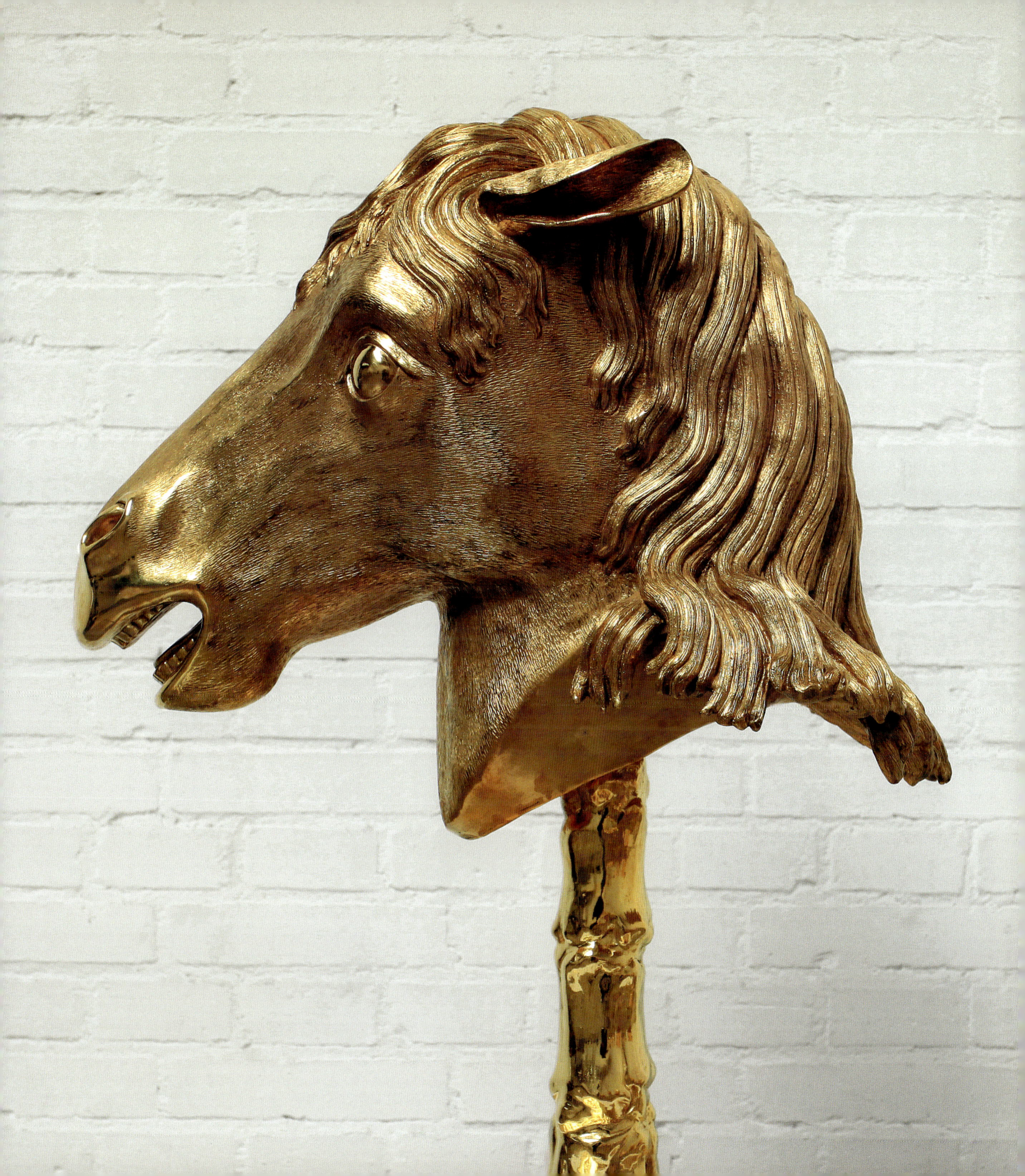

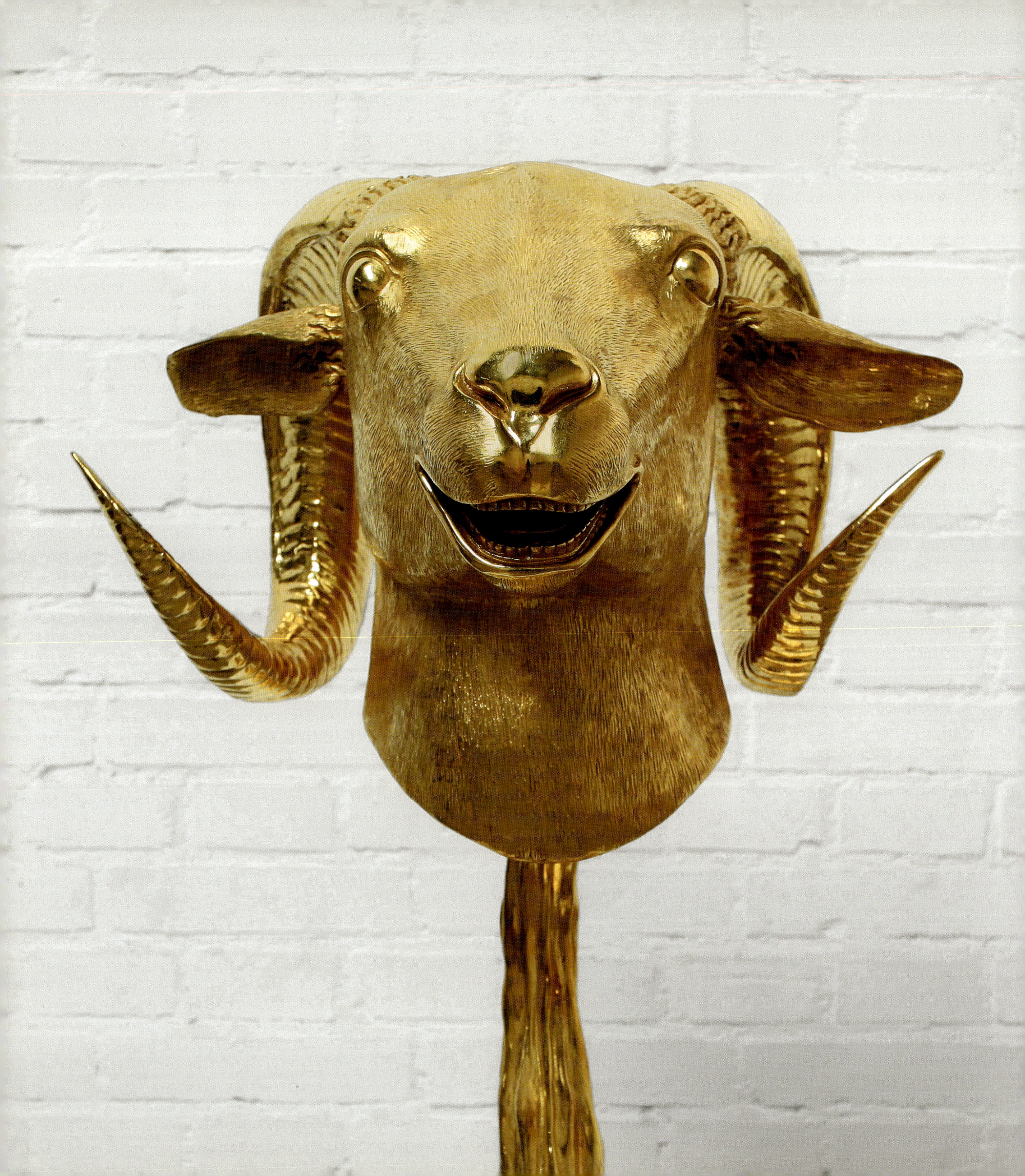

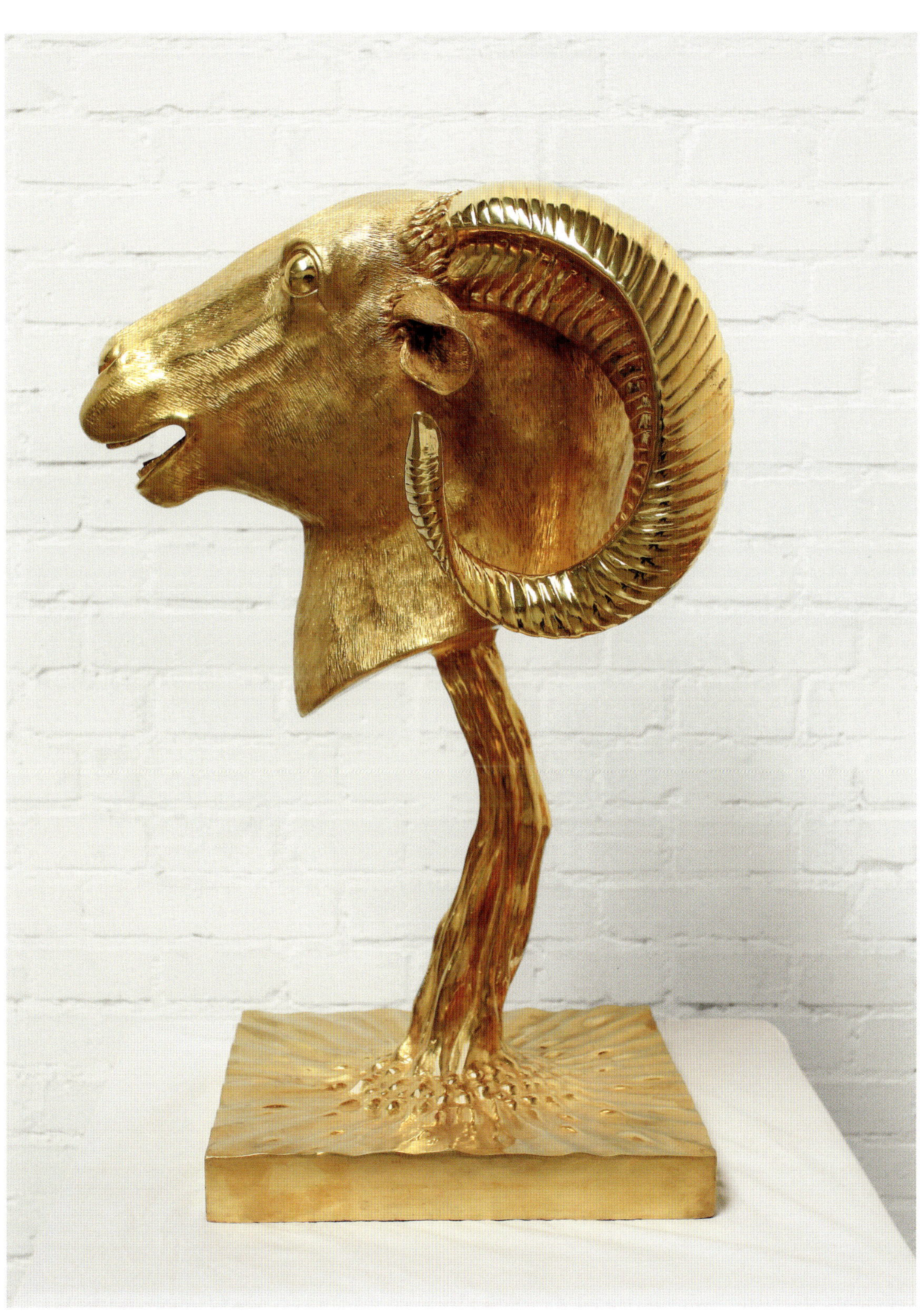

Ram

2010
Bronze with gold patina
25 x 21 x 16 in.
(64 x 53 x 41 cm)

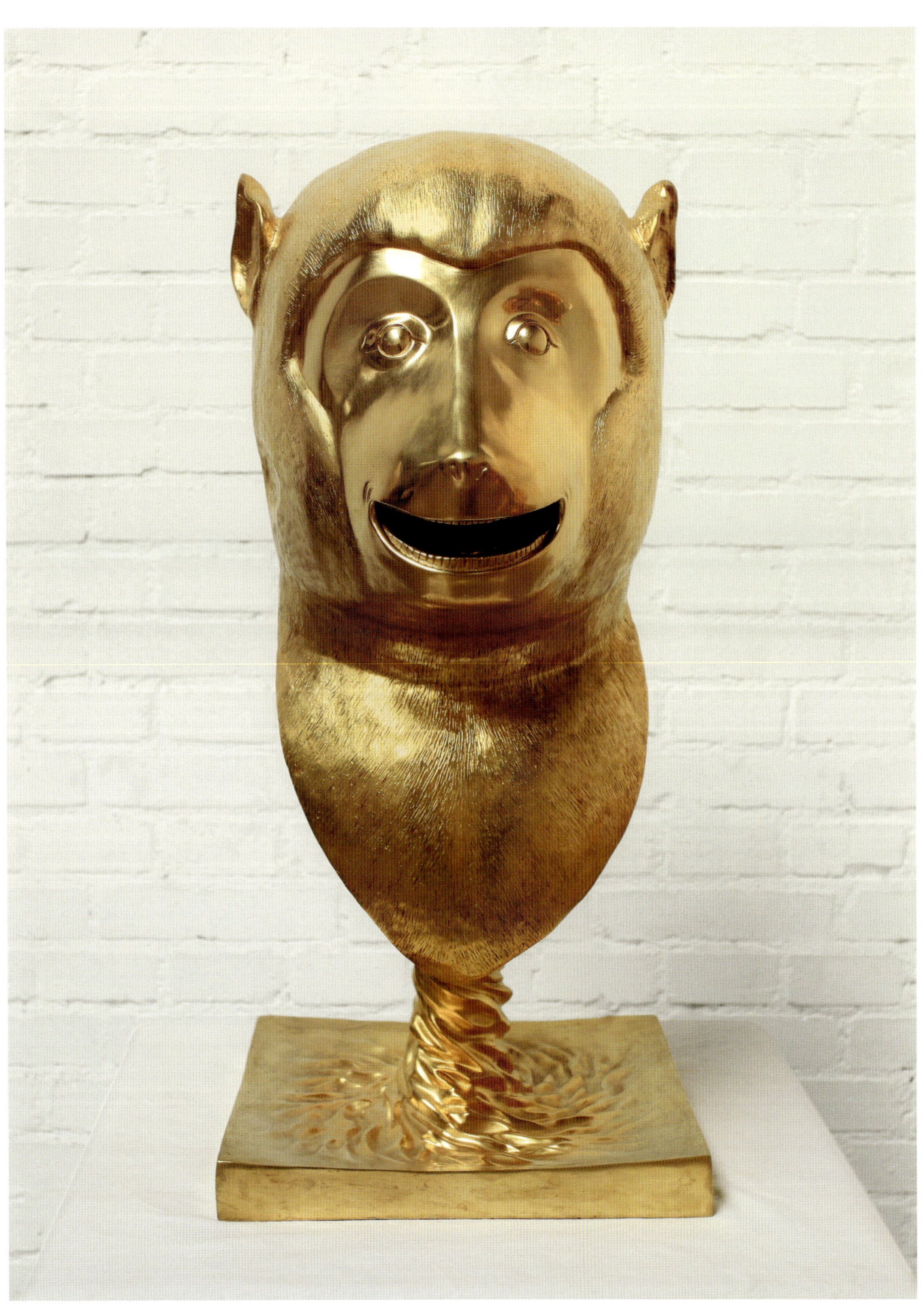

Monkey

2010
Bronze with gold patina
27 x 13 x 15 in.
(69 x 33 x 38 cm)

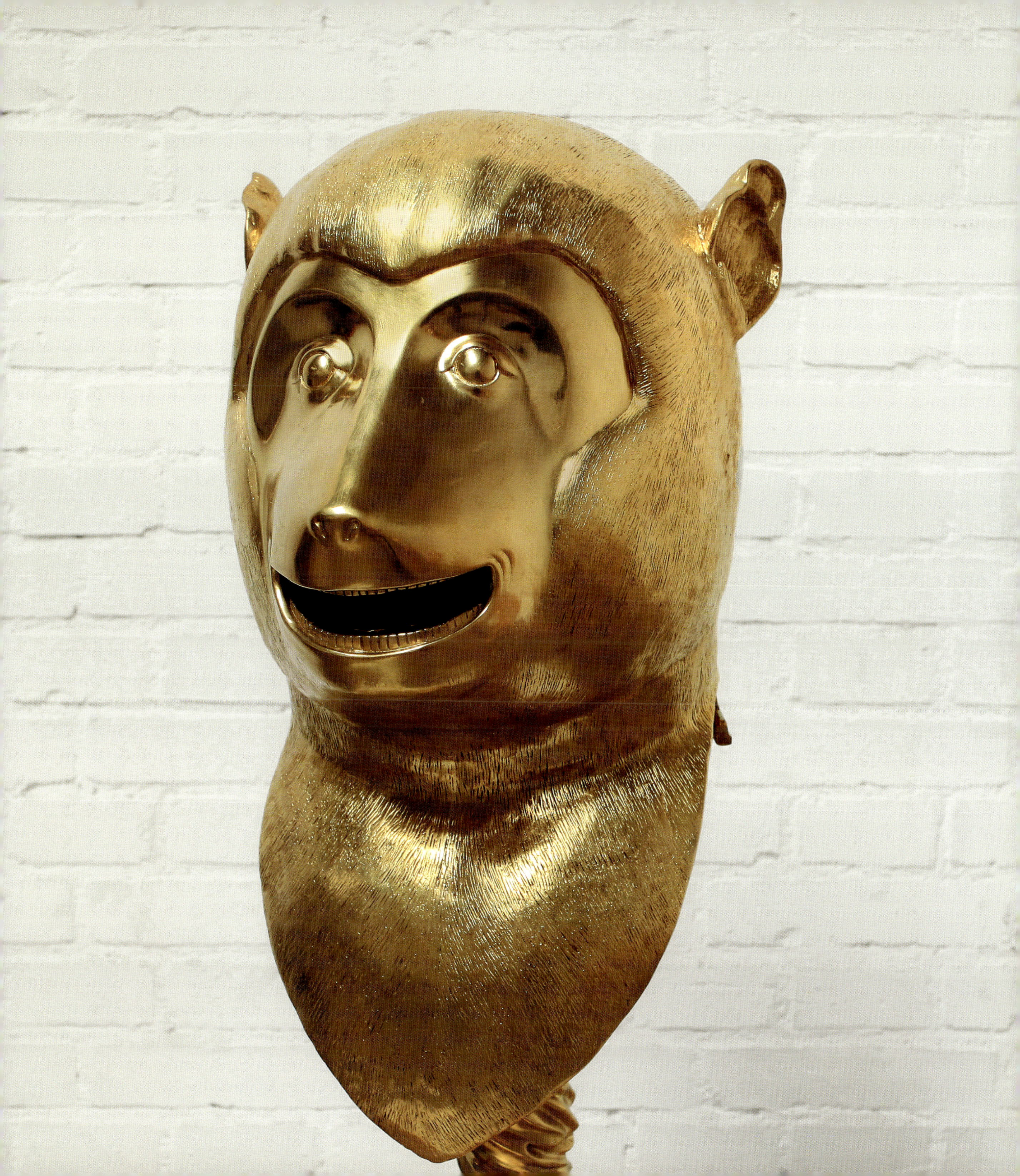

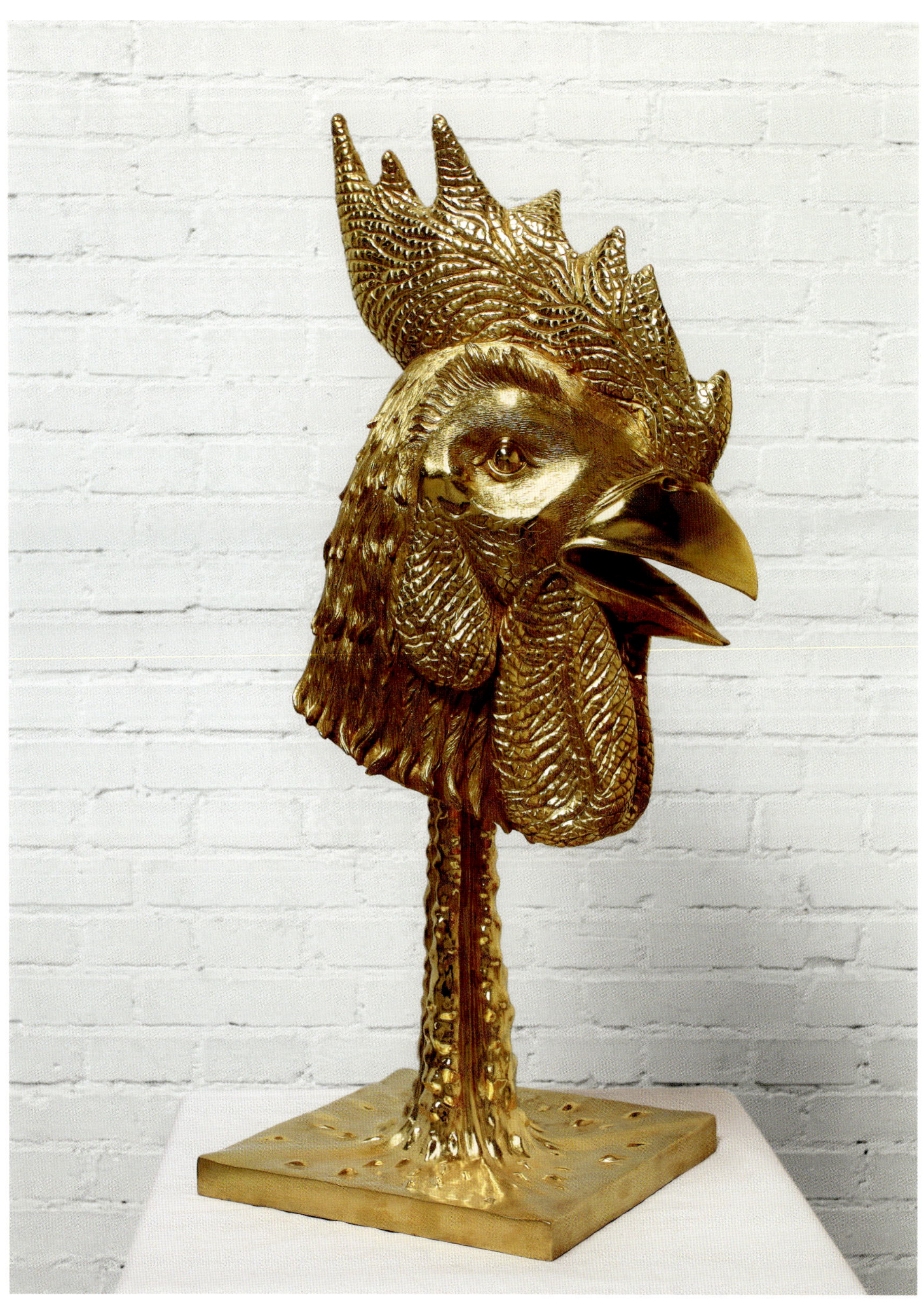

Rooster

2010
Bronze with gold patina
24 x 9 x 17 in.
(61 x 23 x 43 cm)

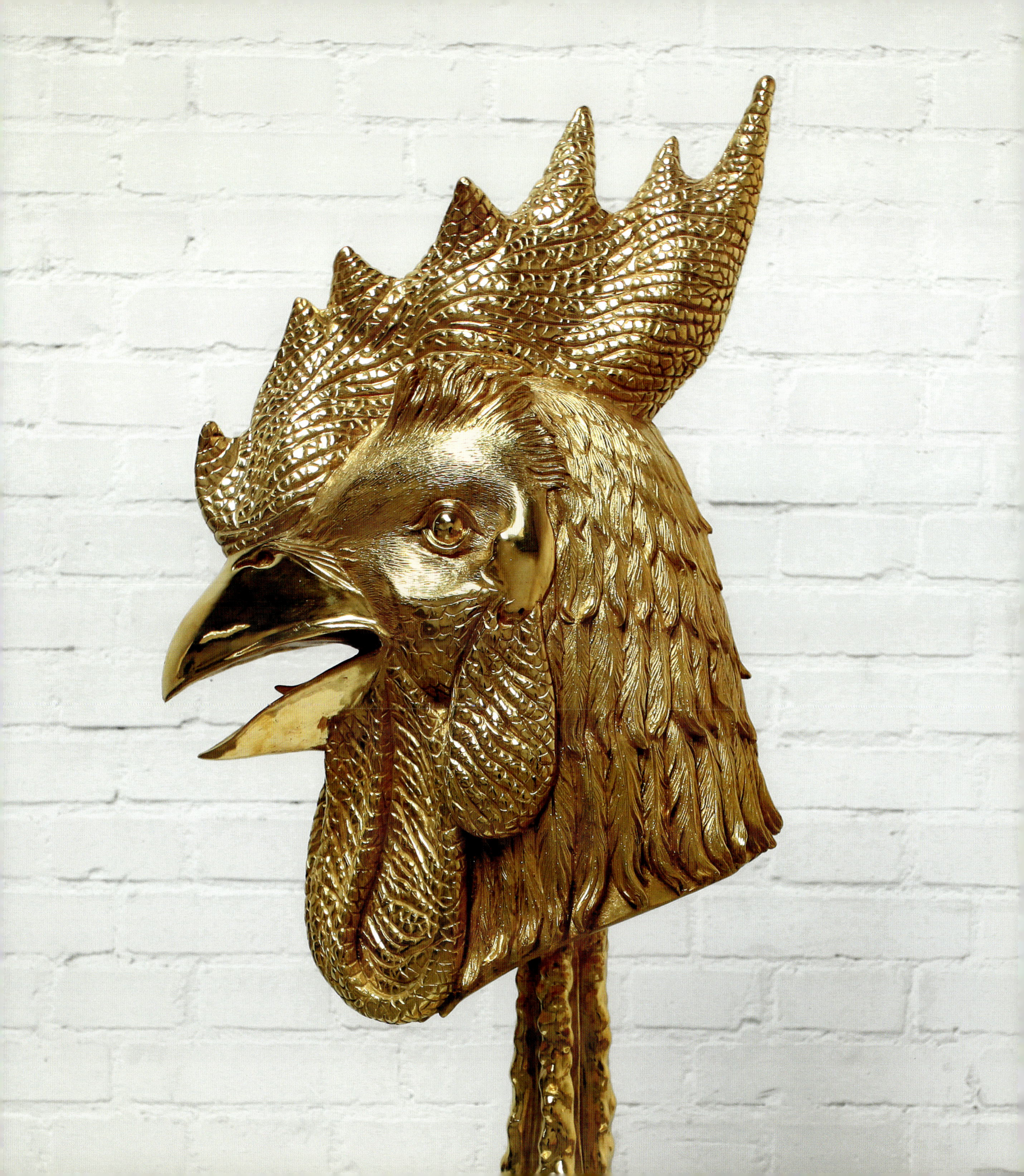

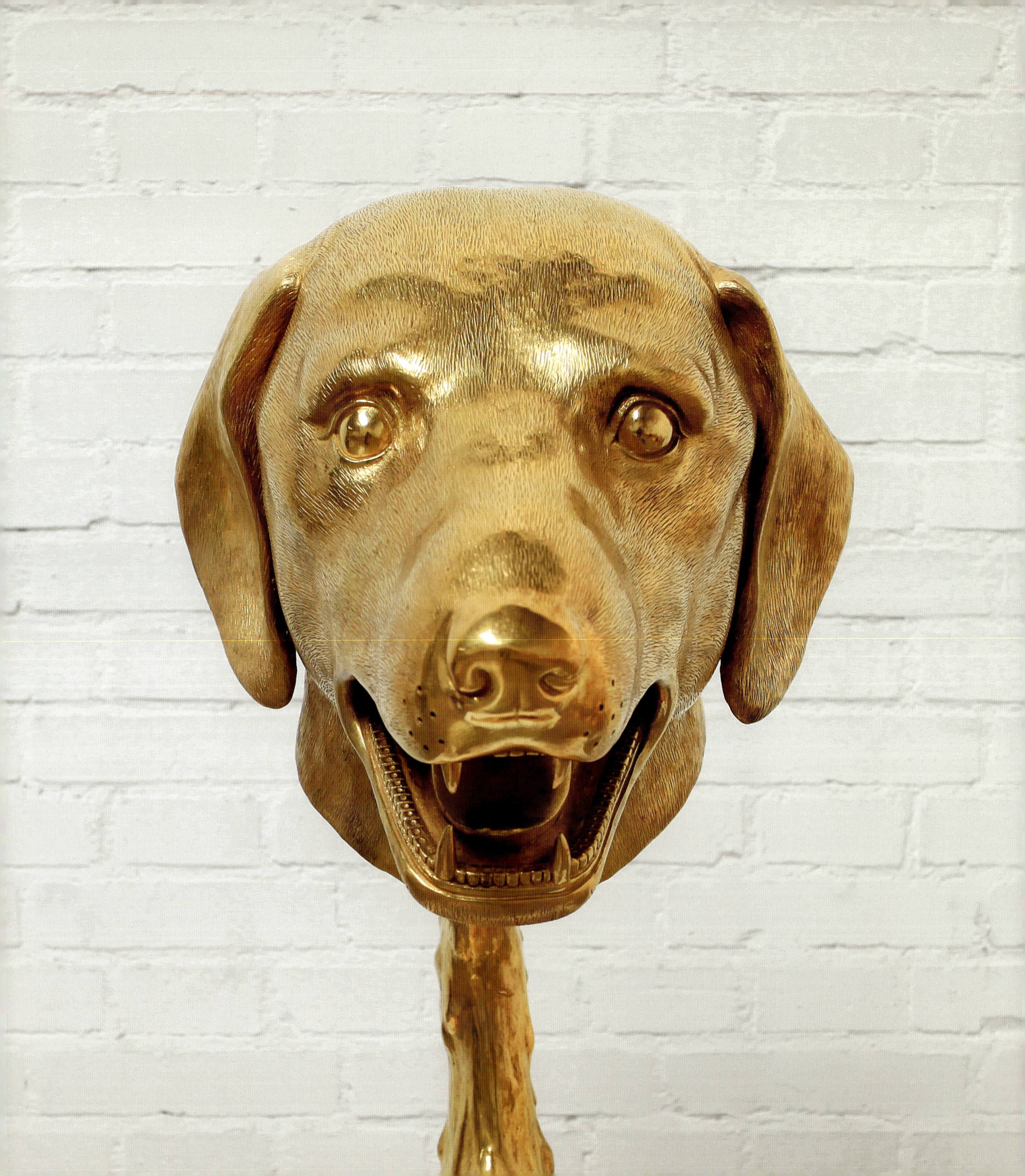

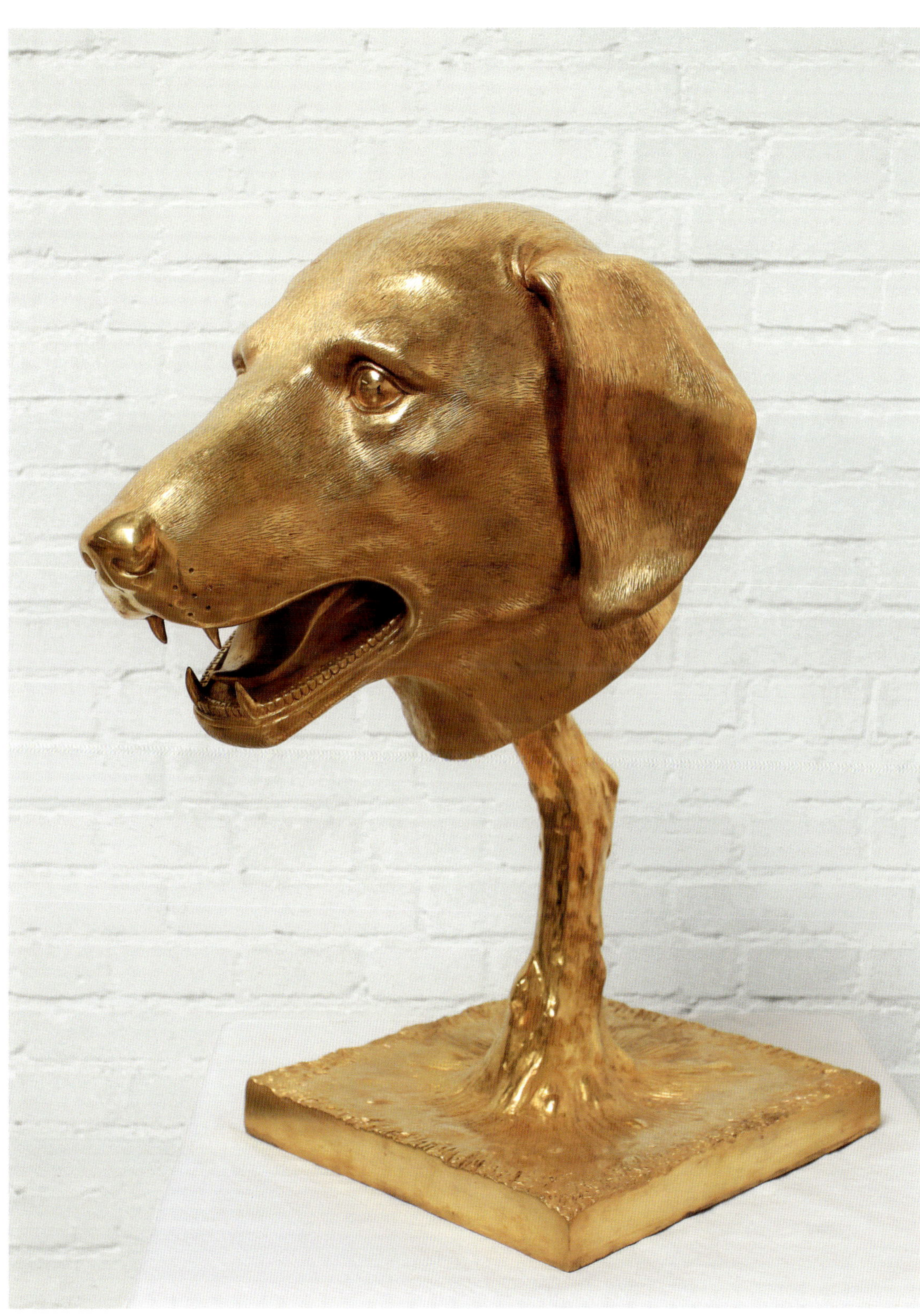

Dog

2010
Bronze with gold patina
25 x 15 x 19 in.
(64 x 38 x 48 cm)

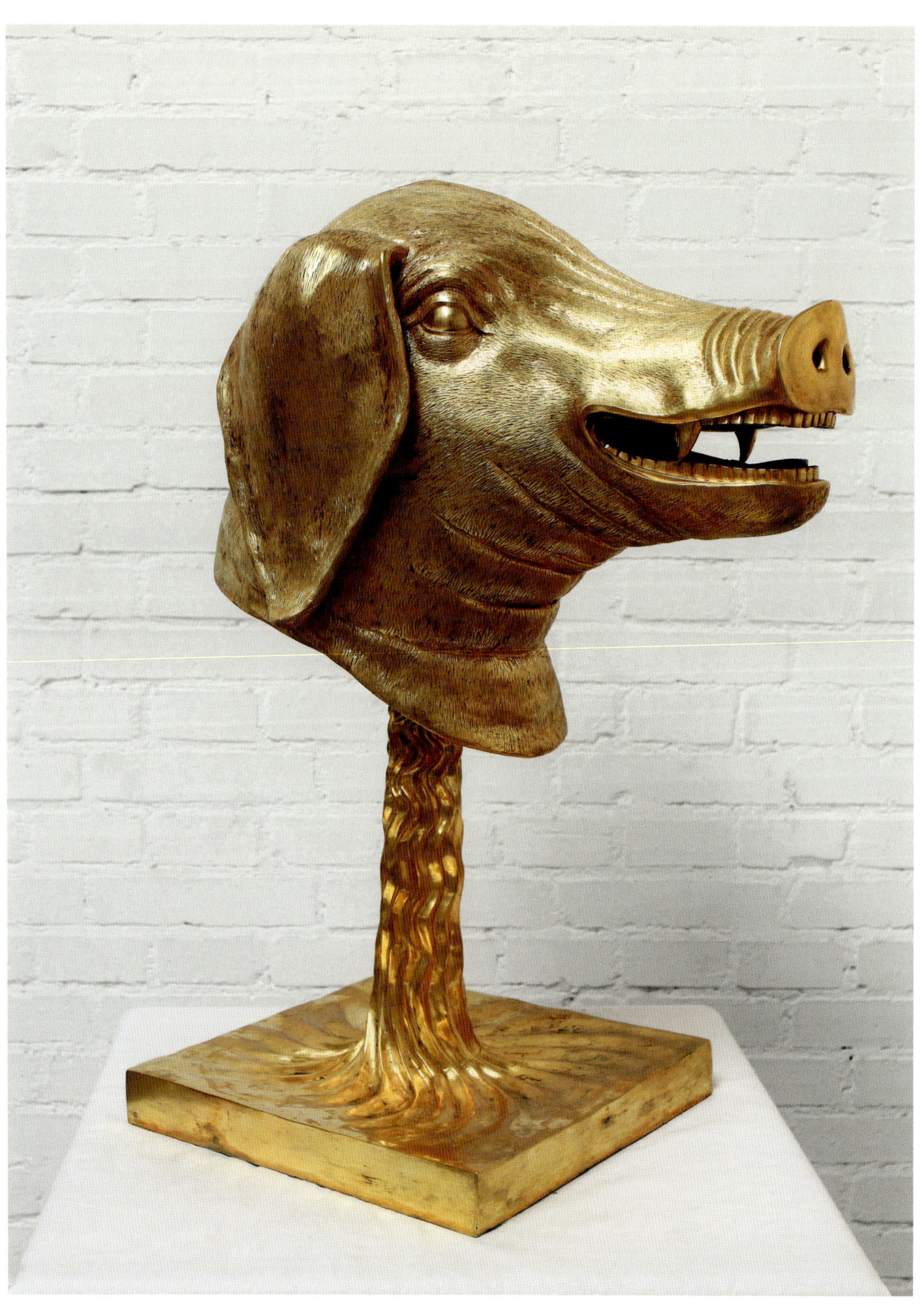

Boar

2010
Bronze with gold patina
27 x 16 x 21 in.
(69 x 41 x 53 cm)

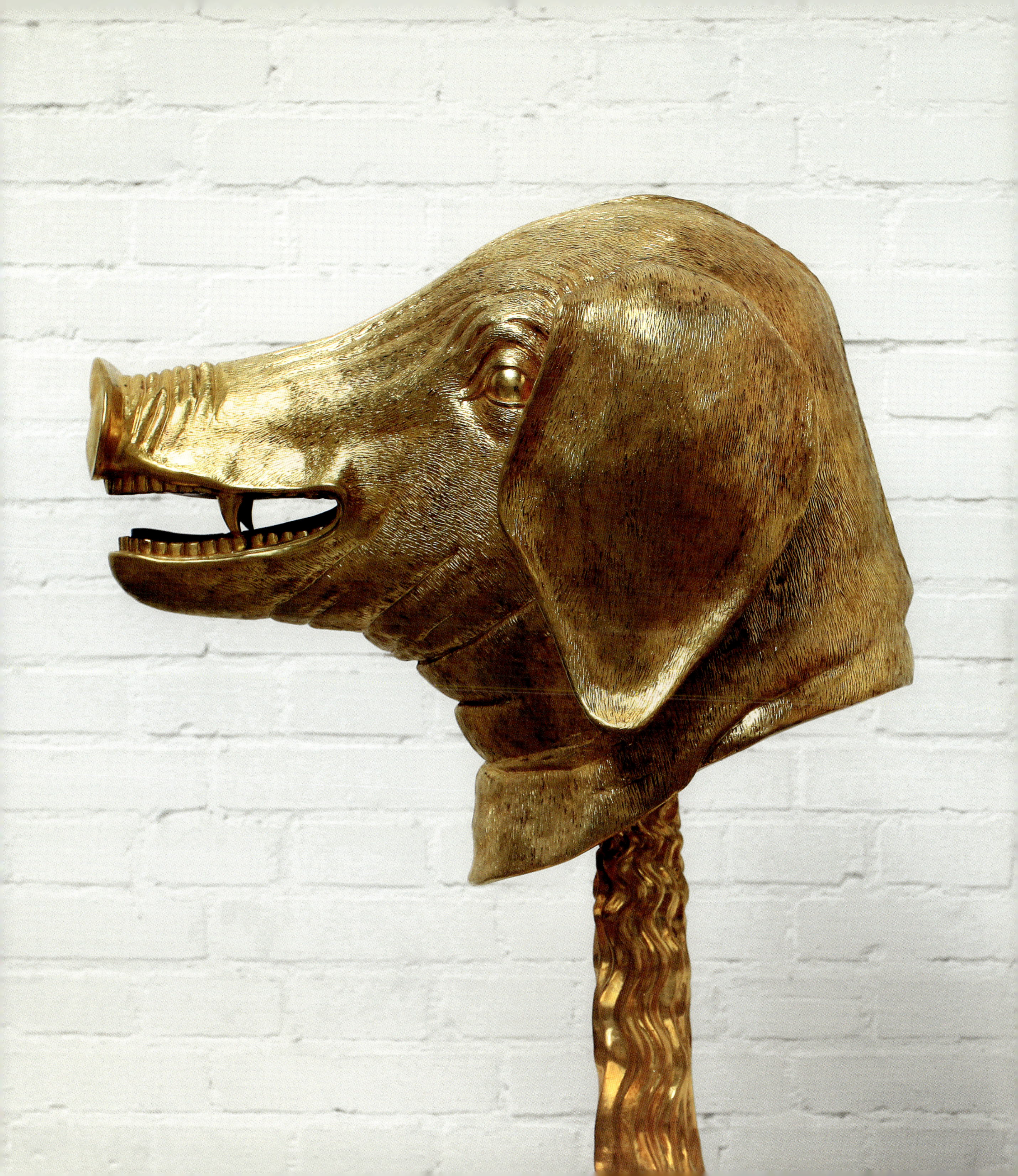

II

Part Two

Circle of Animals/Zodiac Heads and the Twelve-Animal Cycle in China

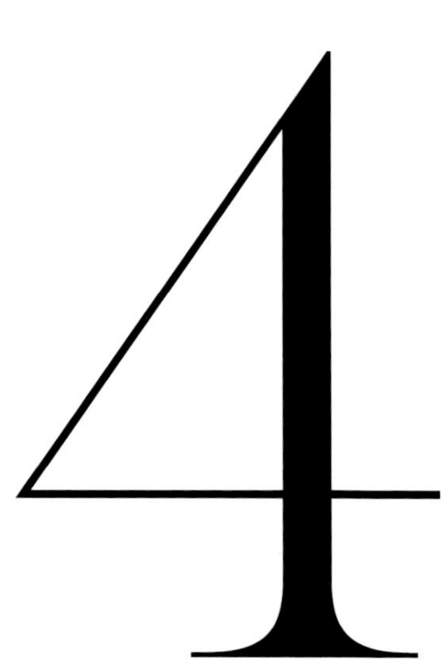

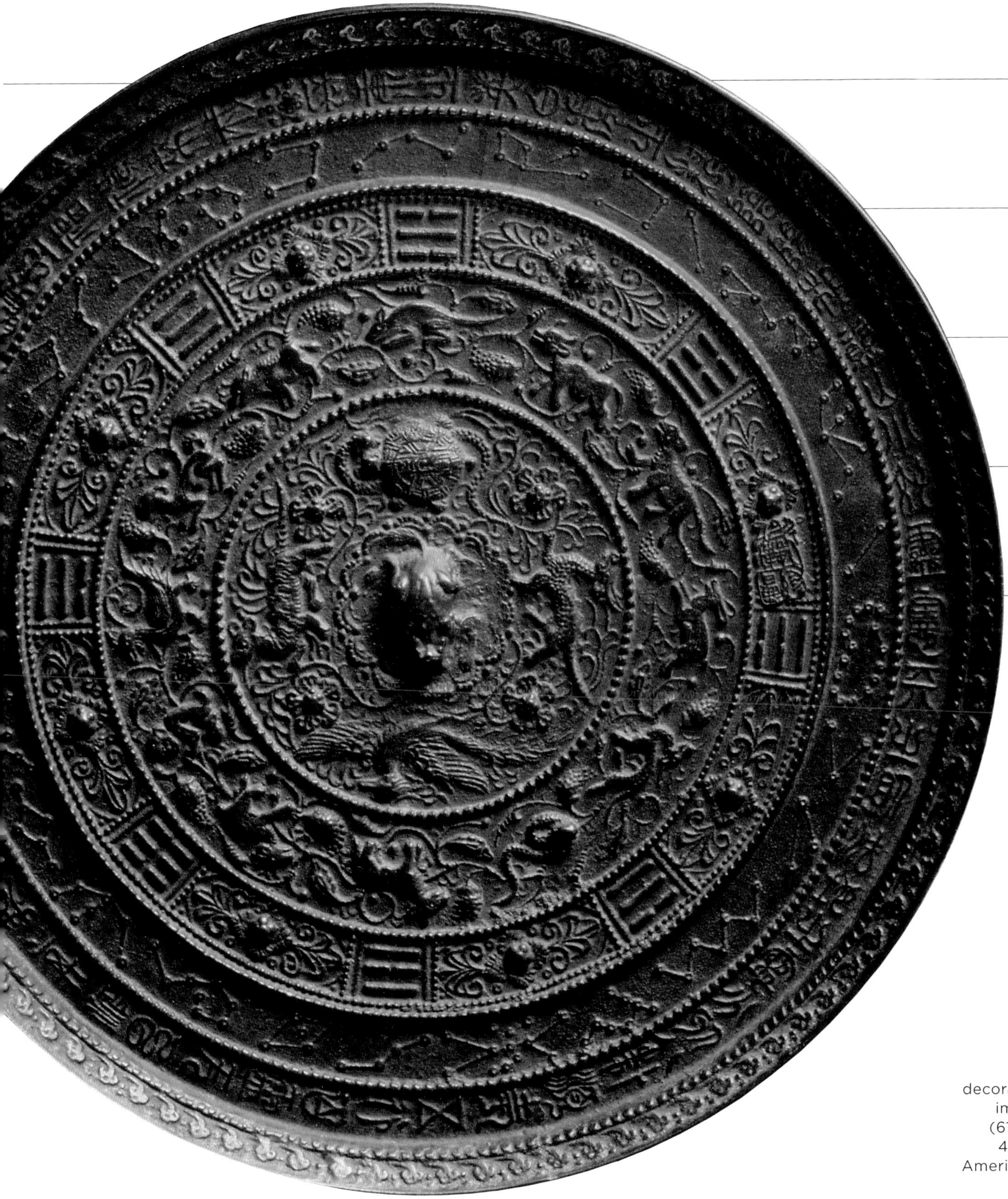

FIG. 48
Circular bronze mirror
decorated with cosmological
imagery, c. Tang dynasty
(618–907). Mirror, bronze,
4 x 5 in. (10.2 x 12.7 cm).
American Museum of Natural
History, New York

AI WEIWEI HAS SAID THAT THE ZODIAC FOUNTAIN OF the Haiyan Tang, in the heart of the European Palaces area of the Yuanming Yuan, was the inspiration for his recent work, *Circle of Animals/Zodiac Heads*. But what was the inspiration behind the original work? As other essays in this volume demonstrate, an understanding of history is fundamental to grasping the multiple reverberations that Ai Weiwei sets in motion in this work. But perhaps equally essential is an understanding of Chinese science and cosmology, the structuring of daily existence and thinking about time. Ai Weiwei's choice of these animals relates not only to the events of 1860, or even to the building of the Yuanming Yuan, but to the foundations of Chinese thought.

The twelve animals represented in the Haiyan Tang zodiac fountain are popularly known in the West as the "Chinese zodiac" of the lunar-year cycle. With the worldwide spread of Chinese culture and the effects of globalization, the twelve animals have entered the Western imagination as emblems of Chinese culture and have been recognized as important elements of a new global astrology, alongside the classic Western zodiac and the Maya calendar cycle. However, the twelve animals of the series—rat, ox, tiger, rabbit, dragon, snake, horse, ram, monkey, rooster, dog, and boar—are neither the equivalents of the twelve signs of the Western zodiac, nor representations of actual zodiac (ecliptic) constellations.[1] In addition, though they are quite significant in the annual cycle, the twelve animals do not symbolize only years. They also mark three other series of twelve: months, days, and the twelve double-hours that comprised the traditional Chinese day.

In the eighteenth-century Haiyan Tang fountain, it was the twelve two-hour periods that were represented. The first animal, the rat, corresponded to the period from eleven p.m. to one a.m., and the ox from one to three a.m. Thereafter came the tiger, rabbit, dragon, snake, horse, ram, monkey, rooster, dog, and lastly the boar, which closed the cycle with the nine-to-eleven p.m. span. When the zodiac fountain was in operation, each animal would spew water from its mouth during its allotted two-hour period. Though the fountain (like the entire palace) no longer exists, an eighteenth-century copperplate engraving by the Manchu artist Yi Lantai (fl. 1749–86) reproduces the front view of the Haiyan Tang, showing how the zodiac fountain was organized.[2] The animal figures were fashioned in two parts: an anthropomorphic stone body and a zoomorphic bronze head (the section

re-created by Ai Weiwei in *Circle of Animals/Zodiac Heads*). The figures were arranged along two sides of the pool, separated by a large, carved, stone scallop shell. Rather than following a linear progression from one end of the pool to the other, the animal sequence alternated sides. The series begins with the rat, nearest the scallop shell on the viewer's right, continues with the ox on the viewer's left next to the shell, then the tiger on the right, and so on until it ends with the boar at the far right. The print depicts the fountain in operation: the horse-headed figure (fig. 49) is ejecting a stream of water into the central pool, indicating the time as *wu*, the double-hour of eleven a.m. to one p.m.[3]

The Twelve Earthly Branches

As noted, the animals symbolized not only the hours of the day, but a total of four time-related series: hours, days, months, and years, each based on a cycle of twelve. These four series are the building blocks of the traditional Chinese lunar-solar calendar— the system that regulated official life in China from high antiquity through the end of the last dynasty, the Qing, in 1911. (With the establishment of the Republic of China, the Gregorian calendar was adopted.[4]) The origin of the twelve animals is obscure, but their association with the traditional calendar ties them to the symbolism of twelve and to ancient astronomy. According to early Chinese texts such as the Zuozhuan and Zhouli,[5] twelve was considered the number of heaven, the perfect measure for calendrical calculations.[6] Known in Chinese as the *shi'er shengxiao* (十二生肖, or twelve birth likenesses), the twelve animals are the symbolic equivalents of the twelve earthly branches (*dizhi* 地支), a duodecimal counting series documented in the earliest known Chinese texts, the Shang dynasty (seventeenth century BCE to 1045) oracle bone inscriptions.

The earthly branches (*zi* 子, *chou* 丑, *yin* 寅, *mao* 卯, *chen* 辰, *si* 巳, *wu* 午, *wei* 未, *shen* 申, *you* 酉, *xu* 戌, *hai* 亥) were devised in the early historic period (second millennium BCE) to track the passing of time in the context of a developing calendar. These twelve signs symbolically rotated clockwise on the celestial equator, indicating compass positions and, by extension, seasons and hours. Thus, for example, *zi* pointed to the north and signaled both midnight and the winter solstice. *Wu* pointed south, indicating noon and the summer solstice; *mao* east, sunrise and spring equinox; and *you* west, sunset and autumnal equinox. The twelve *dizhi* probably originated as symbols to indicate the approximately twelve moons of the solar year, or specifically the twelve times the sun and the moon meet in the skies during a *sui* (岁 year), which were known as the twelve *chen* (辰). Though they do not seem to refer to specific ecliptic or zodiac constellations, as the Western zodiac does, the earthly branches may have indicated the monthly position of the sun in the sky with reference to either circumpolar or equatorial stars or asterisms.[7] Western and Chinese traditional astronomy, and therefore astrology, differed on a fundamental point: the former was primarily based on the ecliptic (the path of the sun in the sky), whereas the latter was equatorial and polar. In the Chinese system, the location of the sun on the celestial equator was deduced by opposition, by observing the monthly position of the full moon in relation to the circumpolar stars, which were linked to the equator by a system of meridians.[8]

In Shang oracular inscriptions, the earthly branches appear to have been used only in the context of the ritual day count. Though the *dizhi* in themselves did not denote days, they did so when combined one-on-one with the ten heavenly stems (*tiangan* 天干), the decimal series that marked the ten-day week (*xun* 旬). Together, earthly branches and heavenly stems formed the *ganzhi* (干支), a sexagesimal (sixty-based) cycle that was at the core of the traditional calendar.[9] In the *ganzhi* system, the ten *tiangan* are coupled with the *dizhi* from one to ten; thereafter the *tiangan* restart at one, whereas the *dizhi* continue to twelve. An entire *ganzhi* cycle is completed on reaching the sixtieth combination; thereafter, both *tiangan* and *dizhi* restart at one for the next cycle.

The *ganzhi* signs eventually came to mark hours, months, and even years. Like the Babylonians and Mayans, the ancient Chinese employed a sexagesimal system for timekeeping, because sixty is a convenient number for calendrical calculations (as is apparent from our retention of sixty-based systems for our own timekeeping). In addition to being a multiple of twelve, sixty approximates two lunar months and holds six ten-day weeks. Six sixty-day cycles gives 360, a number close to the 365 days of the solar year.[10] If the usefulness of the duodecimal series is easy to understand in relation to the hours and months, its association with a cycle of years is not as intuitive. Nonetheless, the twelve-year series has likewise an astronomical rationale. The yearly cycle is in fact based on Jupiter's sidereal period—the time the planet takes to orbit around the sun and return to the same position in the sky—which at 11.86 years is very close to twelve. To mark this twelve-year cycle, the ancient Chinese devised the twelve *ci* (次 Jupiter stations), sections of the celestial vault that helped to track the yearly progression of the planet in the skies.[11] For this characteristic, Jupiter was known in China, and elsewhere in the ancient world, as the "year star" (in Chinese *suixing* 岁星).[12]

From the Twelve Earthly Branches to the Twelve Animals

By the early imperial period, the time of the Qin (221–206 BCE) and Han (206 BCE–220) dynasties, the twelve earthly branches came to correspond to the twelve animals, and the two series were used interchangeably. Thus, the first branch, *zi*, was linked to the rat, the second, *chou*, to the ox, *yin* to the tiger, *mao* to the rabbit, *chen* to the dragon, *si* to the snake, *wu* to the horse, *wei* to the ram, *shen* to the monkey, *you* to the rooster, *xu* to the dog, and *hai* to the boar. Though its origin has not been established with certainty, given the importance of each of the twelve animals in traditional Chinese culture, it is to be assumed that the cycle developed locally, and not in inner Asia, India, or Mesopotamia, as has sometimes been suggested.[13]

The first mention of the twelve animals alongside the earthly branches is found in almanacs unearthed from third-century BCE tombs such as those of Fangmatang and Shuihudi, near Yunmeng in Hubei province.[14] Concerned mainly with the identification of lucky and unlucky days for activities such as travel or war, the Shuihudi day-book highlights the progressive acquisition of divinatory significance by the twelve earthly branches.[15] This transformation, and even the appearance of the twelve animals, may be attributed to the influence of the School of Yin Yang and the Five Elements (*Yin Yang wuxing jia*), a natural philosophy that emerged around the fourth century BCE. This school of thought held that events are governed by the relationship between *yin* and *yang* (the passive and active forces that constitute the universe) and the interactions of five elements or phases (wood, fire, earth, metal, water).[16] According to these theories, each of the ten heavenly stems (*tiangan*), which are coupled with the twelve earthly branches to form the sixty *ganzhi* combinations, are either *yin* or *yang* and are linked with one of the five elements. As a result, in a complete *ganzhi* cycle, the twelve earthly branches and their animals would become sequentially associated with either *yin* or *yang*, and with one of the five elements.

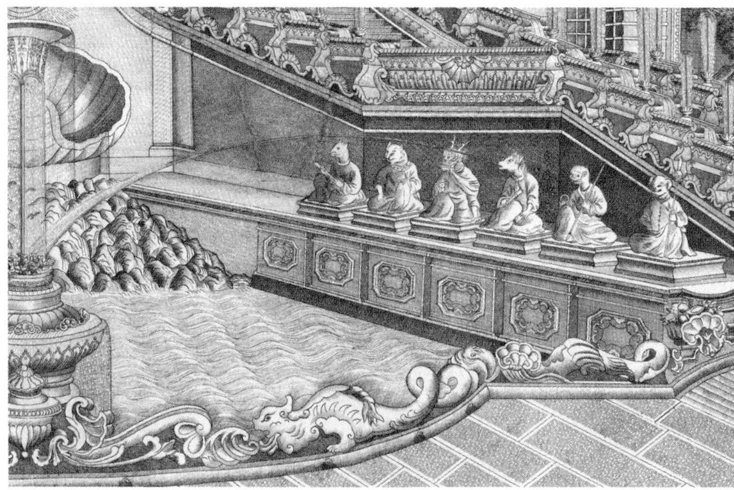

FIG. 49
Detail of engraving by Yi Lantai
showing several figures on the
right side of the Yuanming
Yuan fountain clock. The horse-
headed figure is shown spewing
water, indicating the two-hour
period from 11 a.m. to 1 p.m.

Divination and Prognostication

The sexagesimal *ganzhi* cycle gave rise to a complex
calendrical and prognostication system, whereby predictions
could be made by analyzing different *ganzhi*, animal, and
five-elements combinations for specific dates and times.[17] This
fortune-telling system played a very important part in the life
of the Chinese population up to recent times, so much so
that it caught the attention of foreign visitors. Writing in the
1860s in a series of insightful letters to the *China Mail* that
were eventually published as *Social Life of the Chinese*,
the American missionary Justus Doolittle (1824–1880) gave an
account of the fortune-telling practices of the contemporary
Chinese. In particular, he highlighted how, among the six
common mantic practices, the most popular system was the
one that used "the eight horary characters which denote the
year, month, day and hour of one's birth." The "eight horary
characters" are a reference to the four two-character *ganzhi*
combinations that identified the year, month, day, and hour
of birth. He added that in this system, "There is constant
reference to the 'five elements' and certain 'twelve animals,'"
and that the latter play an important part in fate prognostication, so that "every Chinaman is said to be born under a
certain animal, or to 'belong' to a certain animal."[18] Divination
by the *ganzhi* system was meant not simply to establish
the future of specific individuals (which was thought to be
fixed at birth), but more significantly to find suitable spouses
and to determine dates for rituals, ceremonies, travel, or
business transactions.[19]

Today, this ancient system is much simplified, but the
beliefs persist, both within China and among overseas Chinese
communities. Interest has shifted to the most literal aspects
of the tradition, such as the quality of a year based on
association with a specific animal and element. The focus is
on the birth year of an individual, arising from the belief that
people are influenced by the qualities, and display the
character, of the animal that dominates the year of their birth.
Following tradition, those born in the year of the ox are
believed to be patient, tigers are thought to be courageous,
dogs loyal, and rabbits timid. The tiger, ram, and horse are
deemed inappropriate for women, as these animals are
especially aggressive or mobile—qualities that evidently may
worry a husband. The characteristic of the birth animal can be
attenuated or strengthened based on the association of the
birth year with one of the five elements. Thus, the strong
character of the tiger can be attenuated by an association with
water (a *yin* element, passive and female), but exacerbated
by an association with fire (a *yang* element, active and male).[20]

Sociological studies of birthing trends within Chinese
communities have shown that childbearing can vary
considerably from year to year based on the desirability, or lack
thereof, of some animals. For instance, in mainland China,
2007—the year of the golden (metal) boar—was very popular for
childbirth, as this once-every-sixty-years combination
supposedly brings children riches and success. Similar trends
are observed in countries with large Chinese populations. In
Singapore, the year of the dragon is routinely characterized by
an upsurge in births, because the dragon is the most auspicious
among the twelve animals. On the other hand, the year of the
tiger frequently triggers a drop in births because the animal
is considered inappropriate for girls. Far from being innocuous,
these animal-induced fluctuations in birth rates have caused

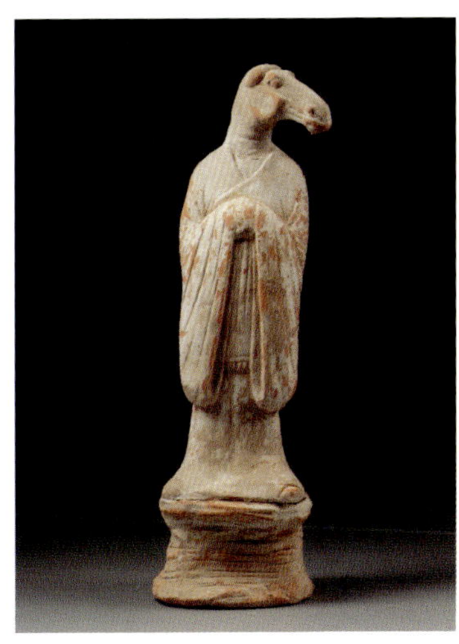

some social problems, particularly in schools, which have to deal with yearly swelling and shrinking of the student body.[21]

It is worth noting that, notwithstanding the great influence of this system on Chinese culture, already in antiquity several thinkers, such as the later Han skeptical philosopher Wang Chong (c. 27–97), were quite critical of the Yin Yang Five Elements philosophy and considered twelve-animals astrology a mass of absurdities.[22]

The Twelve Animals: Visual Representation

The earliest image of the twelve animals may be a rock engraving discovered on the Wulanchabu grassland in Inner Mongolia, which has been tentatively dated to the beginning of the Common Era.[23] Archaeological evidence indicates that visual representation of the twelve animals became common in the fourth and fifth centuries, and even more widespread during the Sui (581–618) and Tang (618–907) dynasties. At that time, the twelve animals were often represented on articles for the living, such as mirrors and coins, and in funerary paraphernalia like tomb paintings, tiles, and statuettes.

With their round forms, ancient Chinese mirrors were thought to mimic the shape of the circular heaven. Their backs were frequently decorated with symbols of cosmological significance, including the twelve animals. This imagery made reference to the perfect structure of the skies, implicitly conferring stability and protection to the mirrors' owners. The symbols were commonly arranged in concentric circular registers, starting at the center with the four animals that represent the four quadrants of the celestial vault. These were followed by the twelve animals, the eight trigrams, and the

twenty-eight lunar stations (fig. 48).[24] Several mirrors carry poetic inscriptions on their outermost registers that explain the symbolism of the decoration.

In the period between the sixth and the eleventh centuries, the twelve animals often appeared as burial paraphernalia in tombs of the elite. There, they functioned as auspicious but also apotropaic symbols, providing a cosmological structure for the burial as well as imparting protection to, and conferring high status on, the deceased.[25] This practice is documented on an epitaph box retrieved from the entranceway to an elite tomb excavated in 1995 in Wanrong county (Shaanxi province). The square stone case, which identifies the deceased as Xue Jing, a member of the extended Tang royal family who died in 720, is decorated with engraved floral designs interspersed with the symbols of the four directions and the twelve animals.[26]

Similar in function are several sets of figures symbolizing the twelve animals that have been excavated from upper-class Sui, Tang, Five Dynasties, and Song burial sites. Made of painted earthenware, the statuettes represent the twelve emblems in different guises: as human figures carrying the animals, as full-bodied animals, and most often as human figures with animal heads. In the latter case, the twelve are customarily dressed as Chinese court officials, a style that resembles the figures of the Haiyan Tang zodiac fountain. Two sets of twelve animals were found in the mid-1950s in Tang tombs unearthed in the suburbs of Xi'an, the site of the ancient dynastic capital Chang'an. Though different in size (the smaller has statuettes ranging between 20 and 28 centimeters tall, the other has figures 36 to 42 centimeters tall), the two sets are comparable in iconography (fig. 50).[27] Similar figures were also excavated from other parts of northern China, such as Shandong and Xinjiang, as well as from the southern provinces of Hunan, Jiangsu, and Fujian (fig. 51). A few sets are in the collection of the Shanghai Museum.[28] Some coins, specially made for talismanic use and with no value as currency, also carried the twelve animals for similar auspicious purposes. Though the tradition of auspicious coins began in the Han dynasty, it was largely in the Song period that the images of the animals appeared as standard decoration.[29]

In the later imperial period, from roughly the mid-fourteenth to the early twentieth centuries, representations of the twelve animals were used primarily outside funerary art. For instance, images of the twelve animals occasionally appeared on the circular diagrams of portable sundials, which became popular after the fourteenth century, though most often these instruments employed the twelve earthly branches as time marks.[30]

During the Ming and Qing dynasties, the animals appeared as propitious decorative objects and elements on banners, paintings, temple architecture, and garden ornamentation (fig. 52). Since the Taoists are particularly fond of cosmological and astronomical symbols, the images of the twelve animals, which are minor gods of Taoism, sometimes also appeared in Taoist paintings and temple décor.[31] Their importance in Taoist iconography continues to the present day: at the Baiyun Guan (白云观 White Clouds Monastery), headquarters of the Taoist

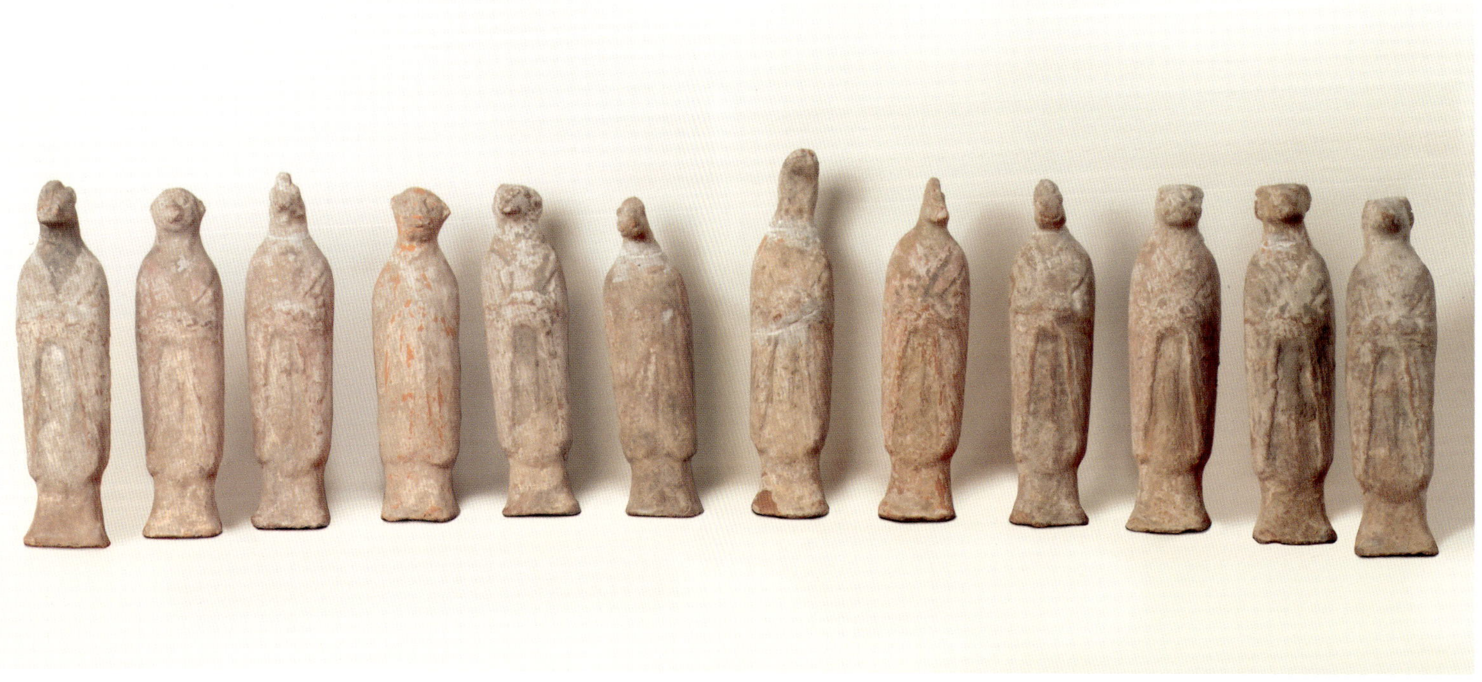

FIG. 51 Set of twelve animal-headed earthenware figures of the calendrical cycle, Tang dynasty (618–907). Dimensions variable. Philadelphia Museum of Art

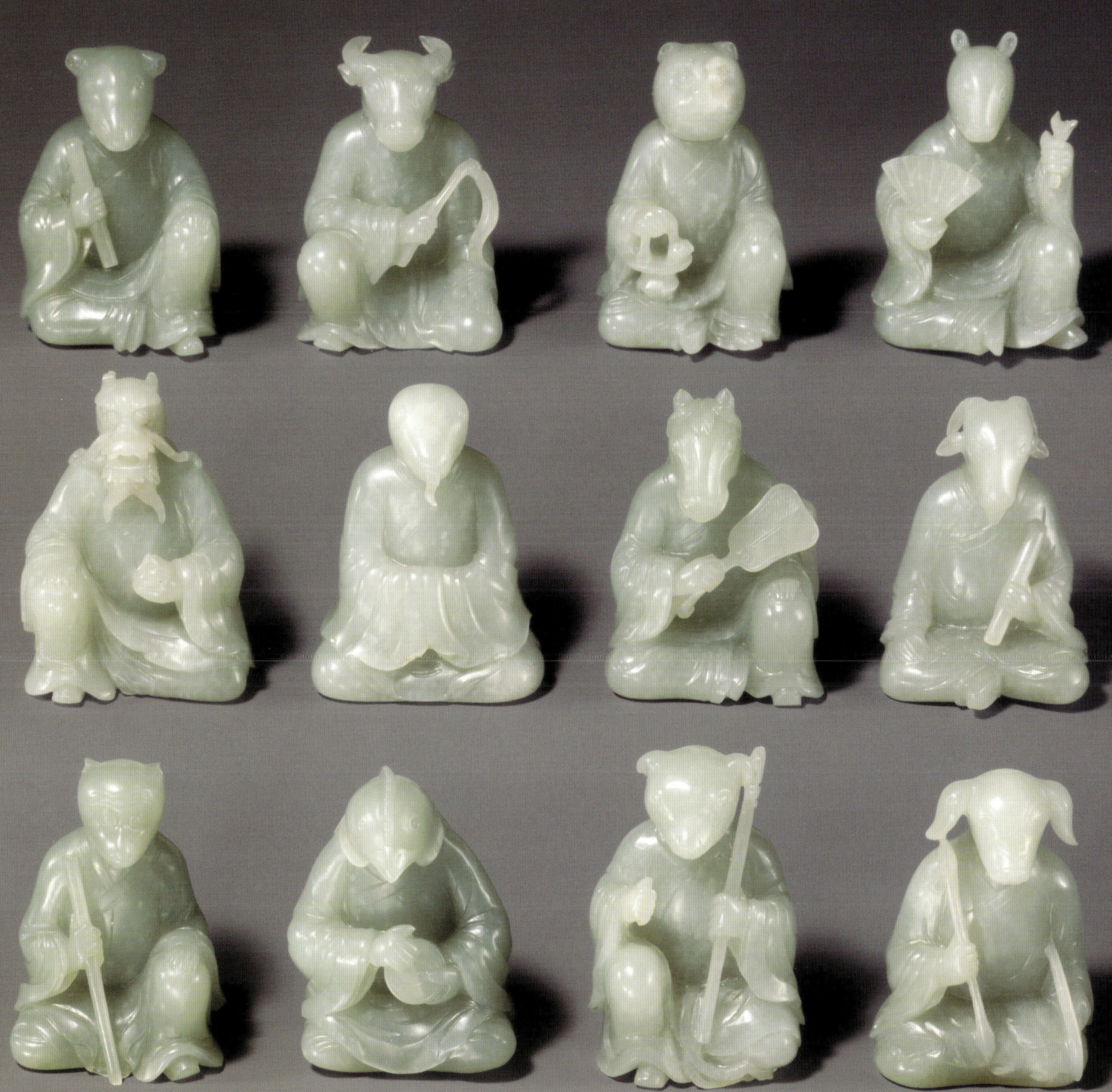

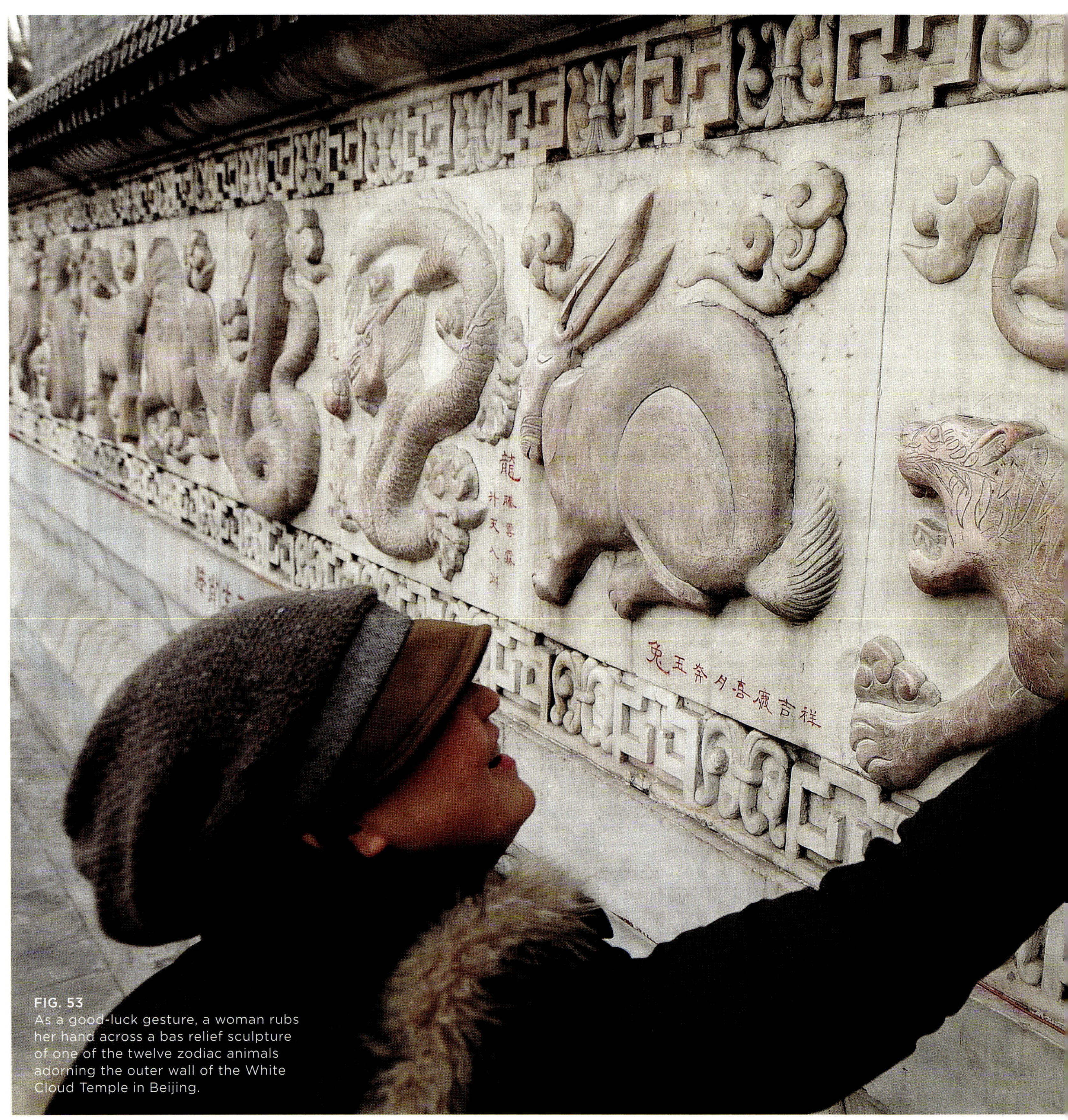

FIG. 53
As a good-luck gesture, a woman rubs her hand across a bas relief sculpture of one of the twelve zodiac animals adorning the outer wall of the White Cloud Temple in Beijing.

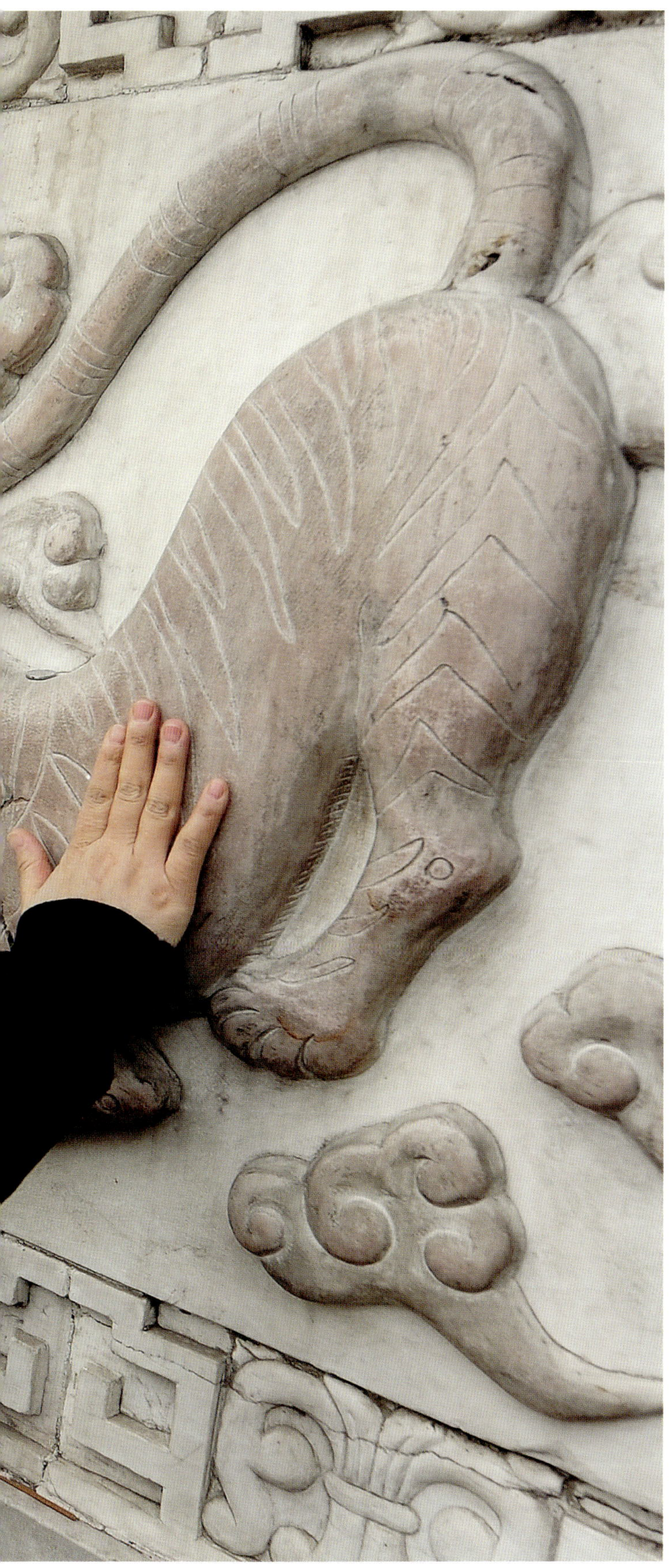

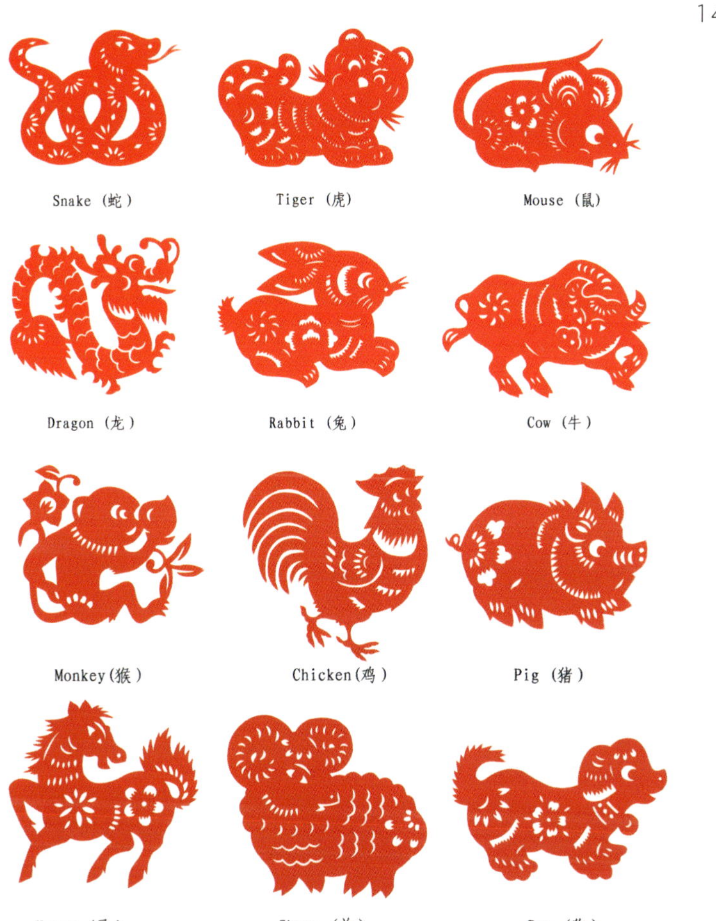

FIG. 54 Contemporary folk-art paper cuts of the zodiac animals

Quanzhen sect in Beijing, the twelve animals are represented in a series of stone tiles made in 1993, which are attached to a long wall associated with the temple (fig. 53).

The twelve animals were also imagined, or read into, natural stones or stone installations set up in the gardens of aristocratic or imperial residences. For instance, in the Yuhua Yuan, a Ming-era imperial garden within the Forbidden City that was redesigned in the early Qing era, the installations of Lake Tai rocks supposedly enclosed the likenesses of the twelve animals. Similarly, at the Yihe Yuan—an imperial retreat built in the late nineteenth century on the western outskirts of Beijing and known in the West as the Summer Palace—Lake Tai stones installed on the south side of Longevity Hill are supposed to resemble the twelve animals.[32] In contemporary times, the tradition of the twelve animals continues. They appear in folk art, such as New Year's prints, paper cutouts, and children's clothing, as well as in official imagery such as postage stamps (fig. 54).[33]

The Twelve Animals and the European Palaces of the Yuanming Yuan

The auspicious uses of the twelve animals documented in Ming and Qing garden and architectural settings may have prompted the adoption of this symbolism for the Haiyan Tang fountain of the European Palaces of the Yuanming Yuan. Still, it is also obvious that this fountain, like the rest of the European Palaces section, was a unique work that combined traditional Chinese symbolism with European iconography and technology. It is also important to consider that as whole, the Yuanming Yuan was a metaphor for the geographic spread of Qing imperial power, and further, that the Qing rulers were not Chinese but Manchu—invaders who had taken over China at the fall of the Ming dynasty in 1644.

Created between the seventeenth and eighteenth centuries on the orders of the early Qing emperors, the Yuanming Yuan recapitulates and reiterates the complex history of the modern relations between China and the world.[34] In the late seventeenth century, the Kangxi Emperor set up an imperial retreat, the Changchun Yuan, or Garden of Joyful Spring, in an area northwest of Beijing. The emperor then gave a nearby estate to his son, the future Yongzheng Emperor, naming it Yuanming Yuan. Yongzheng, who disliked the Forbidden City, chose the Yuanming Yuan as his preferred residence and seat of governance (fig. 55). His successor, the Qianlong Emperor, added more land to the original Yuanming Yuan, creating within its now greatly enlarged confines a series of palaces and views modeled after the most famous gardens of China.[35] Once these were completed in 1744, the Qianlong Emperor decided to create within the Yuanming Yuan a small section featuring European-style buildings and gardens. In this exotic project he was inspired by prints illustrating royal and aristocratic gardens in France and Italy, which Jesuit missionaries, employed as artists and scientists at the Chinese court, had presented to him.[36] The Xiyanglou, or European Palaces, of the Yuanming Yuan were constructed between 1747 and 1783 under the leadership of the Jesuit missionaries. The architecture was mainly conceived by the Milanese Giuseppe Castiglione (1688–1766), whereas the waterworks, such as the one in the Haiyan Tang zodiac fountain, were designed by the French Michel Benoist (1715–1774).[37]

The global collaboration which was brought to bear on the construction of the Yuanming Yuan and the European Palaces ended with the change in international power dynamics that emerged in the nineteenth century. In 1860, the Yuanming Yuan was devastated and pillaged by Anglo-French troops in retaliation for the killing of a number European diplomats who had been sent to negotiate with the Chinese emperor.[38] As a result of this pillaging, some heads of the twelve animals from the Haiyan Tang fountain were taken out of China, eventually entering foreign collections. (Others were presumably lost or melted down for their metal.) Thereafter the European Palaces and the entire Yuanming Yuan suffered years of pillaging and neglect. Indifference toward the gardens ended only in the post-Mao era.

In recent times, the Chinese government, with the help of wealthy "patriotic" collectors, has been trying to repatriate all the heads that remain abroad, mounting a public-relations campaign that presents these objects as symbols of the suffering of China at foreign hands. This is ironic, because, like the European Palaces of the Yuanming Yuan, the Haiyan Tang zodiac fountain and its animals are a quintessentially hybrid project: ordered by a Manchu emperor, designed by European missionaries, built by Chinese artisans, and featuring a mélange of European and Chinese design and technology. In *Circle of Animals/Zodiac Heads*, Ai Weiwei aptly employs the traditional Chinese symbolism of the twelve animals and the history of the Yuanming Yuan to expose the contradictions of this contemporary government-sponsored patriotism in the People's Republic of China. Contrary to a rhetoric that presents the twelve bronze heads of the Haiyan Tang zodiac fountain as paramount emblems of Chinese national identity, the twelve animals reinterpreted by Ai Weiwei are symbols of an early globalization.

---

1. See Shigeru Nakayama, "Characteristics of Chinese Astrology," *Isis* 57, no. 4 (1966): 442–54.

2. Various set of the twenty prints by Yi Lantai published in Beijing in 1786 are held in collections in China, Europe, and the United States, where they are referred to under different titles. An early Chinese title was *Xieqiqu tu* (Pictures of the Harmony of Surprise and Delight Pavilion); another was *Changchun Yuan shuifatu* (Images of the Fountains in the Garden of Eternal Spring). In anglophone countries, they are generally known by the English title, *The European Pavilions in the Garden of Perfect Brightness*. For information about the whereabouts of different sets and details on the Getty Research Institute copy, see Marcia Reed and Paola Demattè, eds., *China on Paper: European and Chinese Works from the Late Sixteenth to the Early Nineteenth Century* (Los Angeles: Getty Research Institute, 2007), cat. no. 30, 204; Richard E. Strassberg, "War and Peace: Four

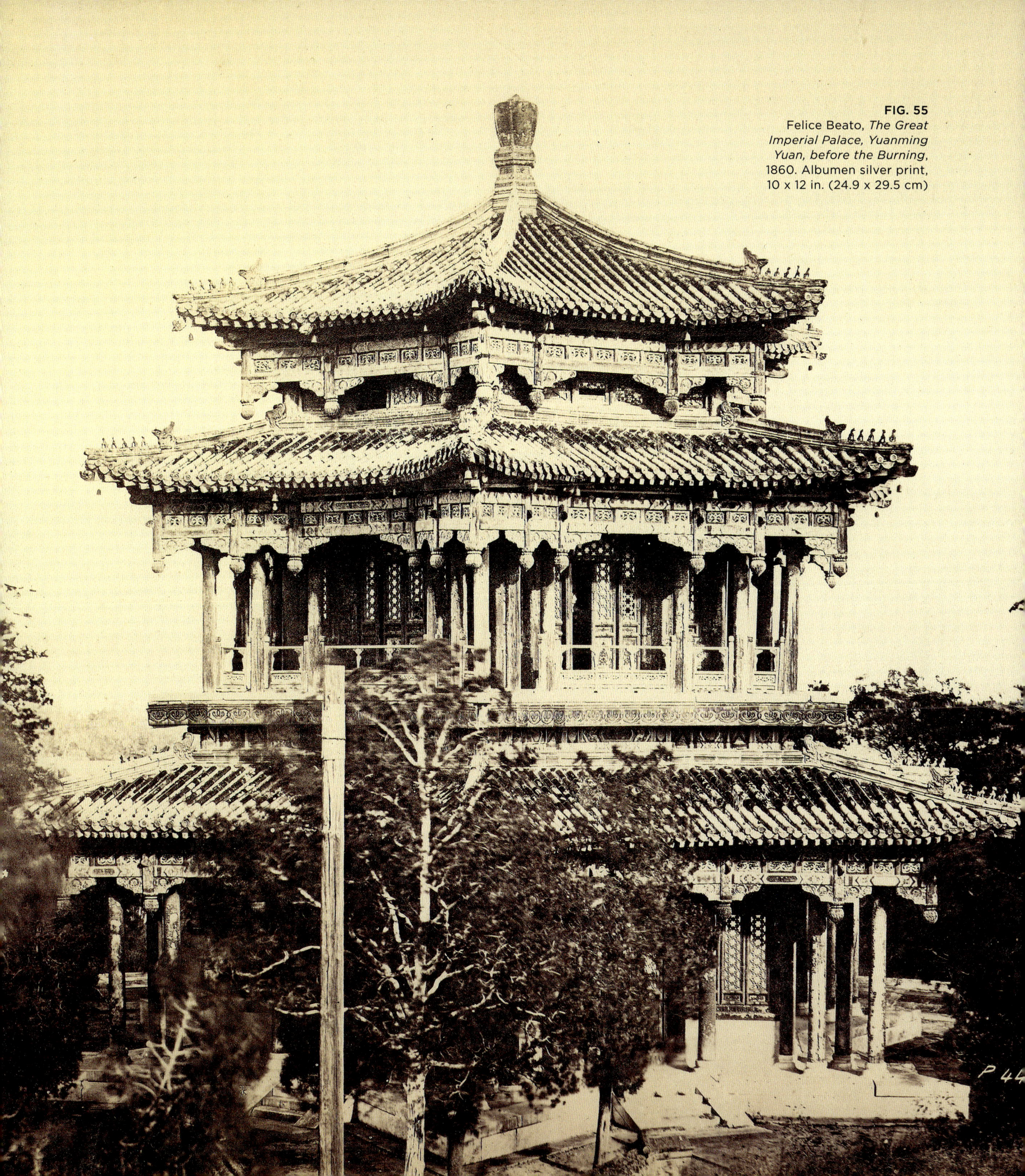

FIG. 55
Felice Beato, *The Great Imperial Palace, Yuanming Yuan, before the Burning,* 1860. Albumen silver print, 10 x 12 in. (24.9 x 29.5 cm)

Intercultural Landscapes," in Reed and Paola Demattè, eds., *China on Paper*, 104–20; cat. no. 10, 114, 138–39. See also Antoine Durand and Régine Thiriez, "Engraving of the Emperor of China's European Palaces," *Biblion: The Bulletin of the New York Public Library* 1, no. 2 (1993): 81–107.

3. According to some reports, at noon the twelve animals would collectively spew water from their mouths. Yucheng Wu, *Sheng xiao yu Zhongguo wen hua* (The Twelve Animals and Chinese Culture) (Beijing: Renmin Press, 2003), 861.

4. Richard J. Smith, *Chinese Almanacs* (Oxford: Oxford University Press, 1992), 1, 40.

5. The *Zuozhuan* (Zuo Commentary) and the *Zhouli* (Rites of Zhou) are Confucian classics which were likely composed in the fourth century BCE. The first is a historical commentary on the chronicle *Chunqiu* (Spring and Autumn) of the period between 722 and 463 BCE; the second, a description of Zhou state administration and its ritual organization. Michael Loewe, ed., *Early Chinese Texts: A Bibliographical Guide* (Berkeley: Society for the Study of Early China & Institute of Asian Studies, University of California, 1993) 24–32, 67–76.

6. Wu, *Sheng xiao yu Zhongguo wen hua*, 10–11.

7. Though no twelve constellations are attached to the twelve earthly branches, they are associated with the twenty-eight lunar mansions, sections of the sky that marked the movement of the moon by associations with asterisms (clusters of stars smaller than constellations). See Steven Little with Shawn Eichman, *Taoism and the Arts of China* (Chicago: Art Institute of Chicago and Berkeley: University of California Press, 2000), 143; and Edward H. Schafer, *Pacing the Void: Tang Approaches to the Stars* (Berkeley: University of California Press, 1977), 76.

8. Joseph Needham, *Science and Civilisation in China*, vol. 3, *Mathematics and the Sciences of Heaven and Earth* (Cambridge: Cambridge University Press, 1959), 396–406.

9. Though the coupling of a series of ten with one of twelve gives 120 different combinations, by combining the two series sequentially, the range of combinations is reduced by half.

10. Needham, *Science and Civilisation in China*, vol. 3, 396–98; Donald Harper, "Warring States: Natural Philosophy and Occult Thought," in M. Lowe and E. Shaughnessy, eds., *The Cambridge History of Ancient China: From the Origins of Civilization to 221 B.C.* (Cambridge: Cambridge University Press, 1999), 833.

11. The twelve Jupiter stations are supposed to correspond to the twelve earthly branches. See Little, *Taoism and the Arts of China*, 143; Schafer, *Pacing the Void*, 76.

12. Needham, *Science and Civilisation in China*, vol. 3, 402–6.

13. Édouard Chavannes, "Le cycle Turc des douze animaux," *T'oung Pao* 7, no. 1 (1906): 117. On the animal cycles in ancient civilizations, see David H. Kelley, "Calendar Animals and Deities," *Southwestern Journal of Anthropology* 16, no. 3 (1960): 317–37.

14. Roel Sterckx, *The Animal and the Daemon in Early China* (New York: SUNY Press, 2002), 67. Los Angeles County Museum of Art, ed.,

The Quest for Eternity: Chinese Ceramic Sculptures from the People's Republic of China (Los Angeles: Los Angeles County Museum of Art and San Francisco: Chronicle Books, 1987), 142.

15. On the Shuihudi burial (Qin tomb 11), see Lexian Liu, *Shuihudi Qinjian Rishu yanjiu* (Research on the Qin Tablet Almanac from Shuihudi), (Taibei: Wenjin, 1993), 118–19.

16. Harper, "Warring States," 832–34.

17. Needham, *Science and Civilisation in China*, vol. 2, *History of Scientific Thought* (Cambridge: Cambridge University Press, 1956), 232, 357; Smith, *Chinese Almanacs*.

18. Justus Doolittle, *Social Life of the Chinese, with Some Account of Their Religious, Governmental, Educational, and Business Customs and Opinions, with Special but Not Exclusive Reference to Fuhchau* (New York: Harper, 1876), 574–83.

19. Richard J. Smith, *China's Cultural Heritage: The Qing Dynasty, 1644–1912* (Boulder, CO: Westview Press, 1994), 246–47; Nakayama, "Characteristics of Chinese Astrology."

20. Richard J. Smith, *Fortune Tellers and Philosophers: Divination in Traditional Chinese Society* (Boulder, CO: Westview Press, 1991), 189. See also Smith, *Chinese Almanacs*.

21. See Daniel Goodkind, "Chinese Lunar Year Birth Timing in Singapore: New Concerns for Child Quality Amidst Multicultural Modernity," *Journal of Marriage and Family* 58, no. 3 (1995): 784–95.

22. Needham, *Science and Civilisation in China*, vol. 2, 265–66.

23. Wu, *Shengxiao yu Zhongguo wenhua*, 861; Shanlin Gai, *Zhongguo yanhua xue* (Chinese Rock Art) (Beijing: Shu mu wen xian chu ban she, 2003), 158.

24. The four animals (dragon, bird, tiger, turtle-snake) represent the eastern, southern, western, and northern quadrants of the sky and are not related to the twelve animals.

25. Mary H. Fong, "Antecedents of Sui-Tang Burial Practices in Shaanxi," *Artibus Asiae* 51, no. 3–4 (1991): 158 and fig. 11.

26. Shaanxi Institute of Archaeology, *Tang dai Xue Jing mu fajue baogao* (Beijing: Kexue, 2000), 52–63, figs. 78–89, pl. 94–100.

27. See Museo di Storia Cinese di Pechino et al., *Cina a Venezia* (Milano: Electa, 1986); Los Angeles County Museum, *Quest for Eternity*, 76, 141–42.

28. Angela Falco Howard et al., *Chinese Sculpture* (New Haven: Yale University Press, 2006), 148–54; Pu An'guo, *Zhongguo sh er sheng xiao tu ji* (Patterns of the Twelve Animals) (Xianggang: Wan li shu dian, 1987), 36–41.

29. Wu, *Shengxiao yu Zhongguo wen hua*, 833–38.

30. Needham, *Science and Civilisation in China*, vol. 3, 310–11.

31. Little, *Taoism and the Arts of China*, 227.

32. Wu, *Shengxiao yu Zhongguo wen hua*, 845–46; see also Maggie Keswick and Alison Hardie, *The Chinese Garden* (Cambridge: Harvard University Press, 2003), 137.

33. See Pu An'guo, *Zhongguo sh er sheng xiao tu ji* (Patterns of the Twelve Animals).

34. See Young-tsu Wong, *A Paradise Lost: The Imperial Garden Yuanming Yuan* (Honolulu: University of Hawai'i Press, 2001).

35. The Jesuit artist and missionary Jean-Denis Attiret described in great detail the Yuanming Yuan in one of his letters from China. See Jean-Denis Attiret, "Lettre à M. de Assaut, 1er novembre 1743," *Lettres édificantes et curieuses écrits des missions étrangères*, vol. 28 (Paris: Les Frères Jésuites, 1749): 1–49.

36. Vincent Droguet, "Les Palais Européens de l'emperor Qianlong et leurs sources italiennes," *Histoire de l'art* 25/26 (1994): 15–28.

37. Strassberg, "War and Peace," 104–20.

38. Geremie R. Barmé, "The Garden of Perfect Brightness, A Life in Ruins," *East Asian History*, no. 11 (1996): 111–58.

Mid-Qing Arts and Jesuit Visions: Visual Encounters and Exchanges in 18th-Century Beijing

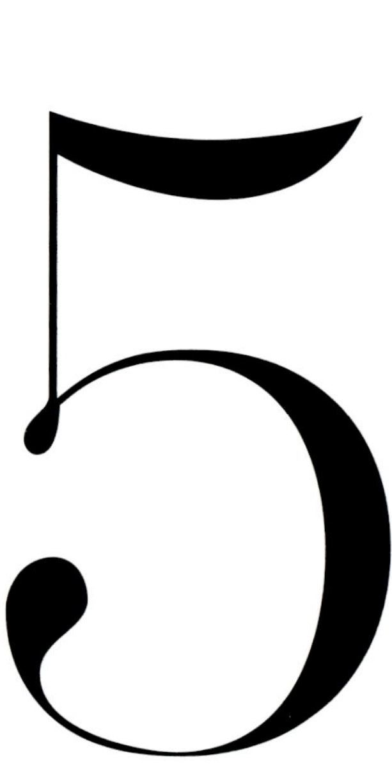

5

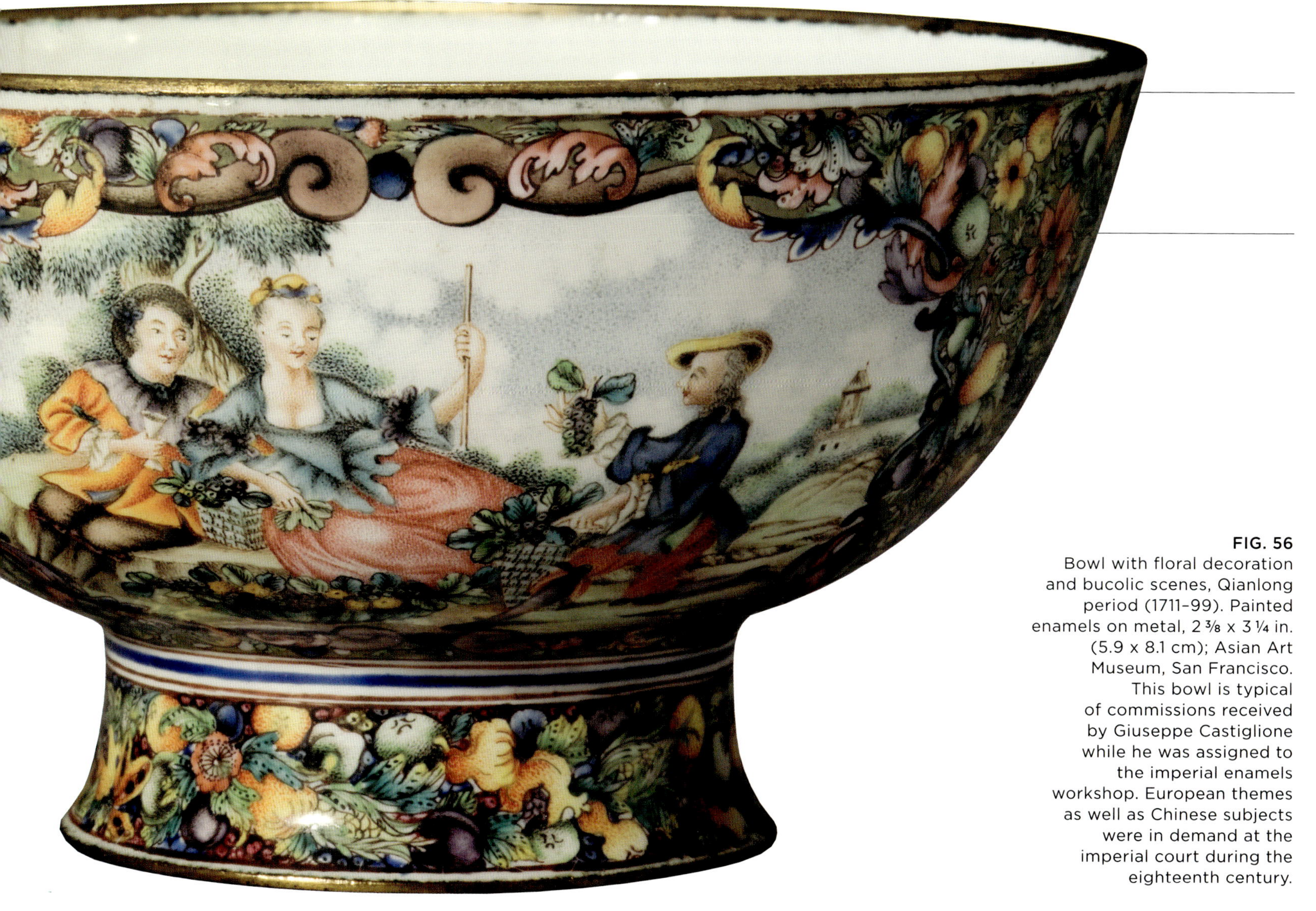

FIG. 56
Bowl with floral decoration and bucolic scenes, Qianlong period (1711–99). Painted enamels on metal, 2 ⅜ x 3 ¼ in. (5.9 x 8.1 cm); Asian Art Museum, San Francisco. This bowl is typical of commissions received by Giuseppe Castiglione while he was assigned to the imperial enamels workshop. European themes as well as Chinese subjects were in demand at the imperial court during the eighteenth century.

ESTABLISHED IN 1540 BY IGNATIUS OF LOYOLA, THE Society of Jesus quickly became one of the most active early modern religious institutions, and the only Catholic order that set up its missionary work through a worldwide communication system. At the beginning of the seventeenth century, with the open support of the Holy See, the Jesuits entered China through European trade routes to Asia. In 1601 the Jesuit Father Matteo Ricci (1552–1610) obtained permission to reach Beijing, and consequently secured a Jesuit post in the capital of the Ming empire. The richness and vastness of the empire, coupled with an intellectual culture that the Jesuits found comparable to Europe in terms of its antiquity, "morality," and literary knowledge, made China a promising ground for Catholic evangelization. The first missionaries like Ricci, however, soon realized that their work could be realized only by means of a broad cultural adaptation that encompassed learning the Chinese language and in turn the local literary culture. Adaptation was indeed part of the Society's missionary strategy: first, the Christian message had to penetrate the ruling elites in order to spread to the entire society.[1] For this reason, the Jesuit order cultivated the interchange with the Chinese imperial house by offering to the Qing rulers the services of various individuals from Europe. These individuals, mostly members of the Jesuit order, were equipped with theoretical and practical knowledge in different fields, from astronomy to painting, from the production of firearms to medicine. By the early 1700s, the Jesuits had already acquired a century of experience in China and had been embedded at the Qing court since the fall of the previous Ming dynasty in 1644. In practical terms, the Jesuits—together with the few clerics from other missionary orders present in eighteenth-century China—became the protagonists of a unique intercultural exchange, which was primarily performed and negotiated within the walls of the imperial palaces in Beijing.

The Imperial Store of Knowledge

At the end of the seventeenth century, the global fortunes of the Jesuits in the Chinese capital coincided with the interests of the mid-Qing emperors in the fields of astronomy, calendric studies, and mathematics. Such a dialogue, made viable by the appointment of Jesuit members to imperial administrative

FIG. 57 The Beijing Ancient Observatory, completed in 1442, as seen today. At the end of seventeenth century, the instruments used for astronomical observations were reconstructed under the supervision of the Flemish Jesuit Ferdinand Verbiest.

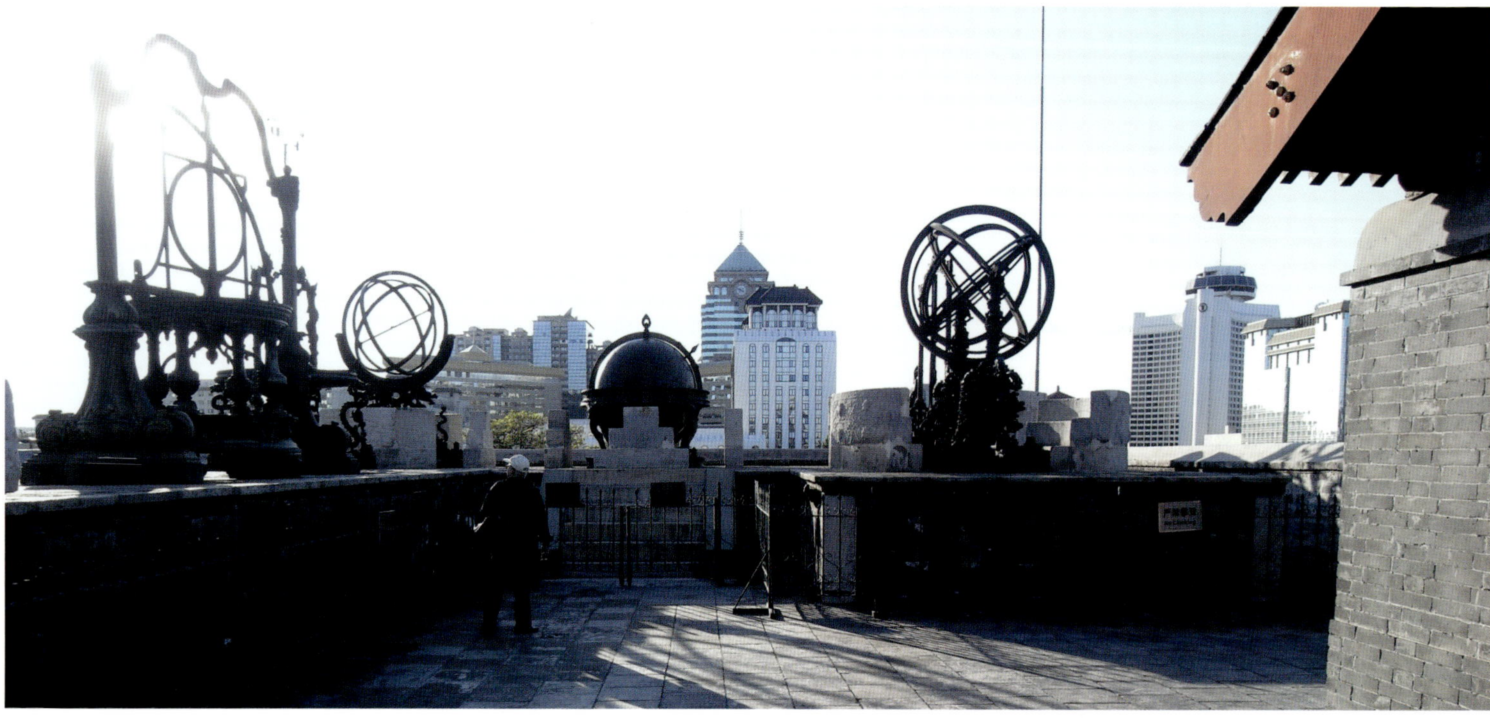

positions in Beijing, had commenced during the Shunqi era (1644–1661) with the employment of Adam Schall (1591–1666), a German Jesuit, on the imperial Board of Astronomy (fig. 57). His successor in the same board, the Flemish Ferdinand Verbiest (1623–1688), explicitly addressed the Jesuit order about the unique opportunity of exploiting the Kangxi Emperor's request for highly specialized experts from Europe, as a means of embedding a group of Jesuits in the core of the imperial household in Beijing.[2] Verbiest specifically stated that members of the order sent to China had to be capable of comprehending courtly language and serving in the imperial workshops.

Throughout his life, Kangxi (康熙, r. 1661–1722) expressed a great curiosity about Western science, art, and technology, including mathematics and its applications. He was also involved in commissions of enamels and clocks, and fascinated by European medicine. Therefore, it was no surprise to the Jesuits when, at the beginning of the eighteenth century, the emperor and his retinue honored them with a visit to the French mission's compound to enjoy a peculiar visual display. The show had been organized by Filippo Maria Grimaldi (1638–1712), who, from 1688 was—as the successor to Verbiest—director of the Board of Astronomy and Mathematics and thus an imperial official himself. As a mathematician and astronomer, Grimaldi was comfortable with the geometrical delineation of optical wonders. On this occasion, he planned to amaze his imperial audience by deceiving the sight through anamorphosis, peep shows, and magic lanterns. The Jesuits invited the emperor and his entourage into the garden: on every wall was a painted landscape fifteen meters long, filled with mountains, forests, and wild animals. It was an homage to one of the most valued activities of the Manchu elite: hunting as a metaphor for warfare and authority. The walls were irregular, with doors and windows breaking their surfaces, further stimulating the eye to wander, looking for consistency, patterns, and interesting details. However, there was more. The Jesuit fathers invited their guests to stand close to one side of each wall. There, if viewed from a certain angle, the painted landscape morphed into a human figure; thus, two different images were contained in one depiction. On the walls of the French mission, Grimaldi had created anamorphic pictures: optically deformed images that accelerate the optical perspective and can be perceived only if viewed from a specific angle. Anamorphosis can also be viewed by deploying "conical, cylindrical, or pyramidal mirrors to rectify the vision."[3] The Jesuits provided such an optical set to the emperor and

his officials, and as a finale to the gathering, the visit ended with the viewing of architectural drawings in books taken from the shelves of the French mission's bountiful library. If the anamorphic images were intended to amuse, the architectural drawings were meant to display the culture that lay behind the drawn lines: geometry, mathematics, and their applications, such as perspective, architecture, astronomy, and cartography. The Jesuits reasoned that if they could convince the Kangxi Emperor that all of this represented the ultimate means to describe the world, then it would not be difficult to bring the Manchu elites to a comprehension and love of God—the source of these mathematical wonders.

Kangxi, however, did not follow the monotheistic cultural view from Europe. He was sufficiently well informed to develop a comprehensive opinion about the potential uses of geometry and mathematics, without being bound to metaphysical explanations that had no foundation in Chinese thought. As a Qing emperor, his role was to mediate and control, not revolutionize. Moreover, his duty was to make it possible for the Jesuits' visual and textual knowledge to be stored by means of local languages—Manchu and Chinese—without suppressing local traditions. From this perspective, the teaching of European knowledge systems was what Kangxi primarily supported. When men like Grimaldi arrived at court, the emperor's first concern was to assign them apprentices whose task was to study and document the foreign erudition. The emperor's goal was to transform alien expertise into local competences in order to create a shared store of knowledge.

In the first decade of the eighteenth century, the emperor was looking for a skillful painter from Europe. Certainly, Europeans like Grimaldi at the Board of Astronomy could successfully deceive the eye with anamorphosis—but in the end they were mathematicians, not professionally trained painters. Kangxi was interested in hiring someone who could display, explain, and transmit all aspects of the Western canon of painting. By 1705, the well-informed Jesuits at the Qing court, always aware of the emperor's wishes, had identified a promising candidate in Europe: Giuseppe Castiglione (1688–1766), a young professional painter from Milan.[4] After accepting the position, he was taken into the Jesuit order as a lay brother and dispatched to China as quickly as possible—a process that, though expedited, still required several years.[5] In 1712, Grimaldi, author of the anamorphic display, died. In the Jesuits' subsequent audiences with the emperor, Kangxi insistently asked for the famous Castiglione, promised by the

Fathers. The Jesuits in turn guaranteed that he was on his way and would arrive soon, but the arduous journey and other obstacles slowed his arrival. It was a difficult situation for the missionaries at court. The emperor would have to wait another three years for a professional painter from Europe, and his impatience would only increase.[6]

Finally, in 1715, Castiglione crossed through the heavy doors of the Forbidden City. The newly arrived Milanese artist had come to answer questions and perhaps demonstrate some of his painting skills. Kangxi was eager to test him personally. Castiglione presented the emperor with a painting of a dog, and in response to Kangxi's request, painted the picture of a bird on the spot. We do not know what the emperor thought of these two pictures. Jesuit sources, however, affirmed that the emperor was impressed by the realism of the bird, and that he promptly assigned Castiglione a few disciples. The emperor's questioning was very detailed: Kangxi asked Castiglione if he could paint portraits and produce perspective paintings. Castiglione humbly replied that he "can depict human figures and for the rest he knows a little."[7]

It is not clear if Kangxi liked Castiglione's paintings or not. Of the known surviving works dating to his reign, only a fan painted in collaboration with a local court artist is likely to display traces of Castiglione's own hand.[8] One can be sure, however, that Castiglione's expertise in the arts of Europe was not wasted; the support received from the emperors who succeeded Kangxi demonstrated that, from the very beginning, Castiglione's knowledge successfully merged with the experience of the local artists.

Controlling Visual Diversity

After the death of Kangxi in 1722, Castiglione's career took a new turn. The transition of power revealed that the new Yongzheng Emperor (雍正, r. 1722-35)—and in turn the Qing imperial household—considered Castiglione's versatility and artistic knowledge particularly precious. This was evident in the remarkable fact that in the mourning period after Kangxi's death—a time when the Jesuits employed by the past emperor, as well as the majority of the officials, were forbidden to enter the court—the new emperor authorized Castiglione's access to the Forbidden City to work on his painting commissions. Along with Castiglione, the only other European receiving such authorization was Father Angelo di Borgo S.Siro, an Italian clockmaker.[9] It is this pair, whose skills—clock-making and

painting—at first glance seem unrelated, who represent the seed of what would later become the architectural commission for the Yuanming Yuan, the Garden of Perfect Brightness.

At this point, however, Castiglione was still occupied with strengthening his position at court. During Kangxi's reign, he was employed as an enamel painter—surely a less prominent role than executing painting commissions received from the emperor in person. Castiglione, however, was in Beijing to stay; eventually enamels came into fashion at court, and his firm hand in painting minuscule pictures on enameled pieces was highly valued (figs. 56, 58). As a professional artist, he knew perfectly well what he had to learn in his first years in China: the language of Chinese court painting, what pleased the emperor, the organization of the painting workshops, and the procedures for submitting paintings to the throne. This was indeed a time-consuming task, especially when coupled with the duties of instructing imperial household apprentices, and with evenings perhaps devoted to Jesuit commissions. In his paintings for the throne, no Christian images or themes from European political and literary culture were permitted. Castiglione was obliged to learn the aesthetic language of the Qing.

Things turned out well for him. After an initial tenure in the enamels workshop, Castiglione began to have serious problems with his sight, and he convinced the Yongzheng Emperor that the saturated environment of the workshop might well ruin his eyes forever.[10] Castiglione was at that point already working on several commissions for the emperor, including murals and scroll paintings using a variety of techniques, mediums, and materials. Slowly, the Milanese artist began to understand the emperor's taste, and in turn his paintings were rewarded with gifts. In November 1723, Yongzheng demonstrated his approval for a mural painting—at present unknown—by giving Castiglione silk, meals from the imperial table, and one of his own hats.[11] As such gestures indicate, the Italian painter quickly became a favored individual at court, a status that soon earned him the rank of civil official.

Like other painters in the imperial household workshops, Castiglione entered the service of the emperor on recommendation—though a very particular sort of recommendation, coming from the Jesuits. As a European, Castiglione did not receive a formal salary but, as with the mentioned fortunate commission for Yongzheng, successful achievements meant gifts and special benefits. On the other

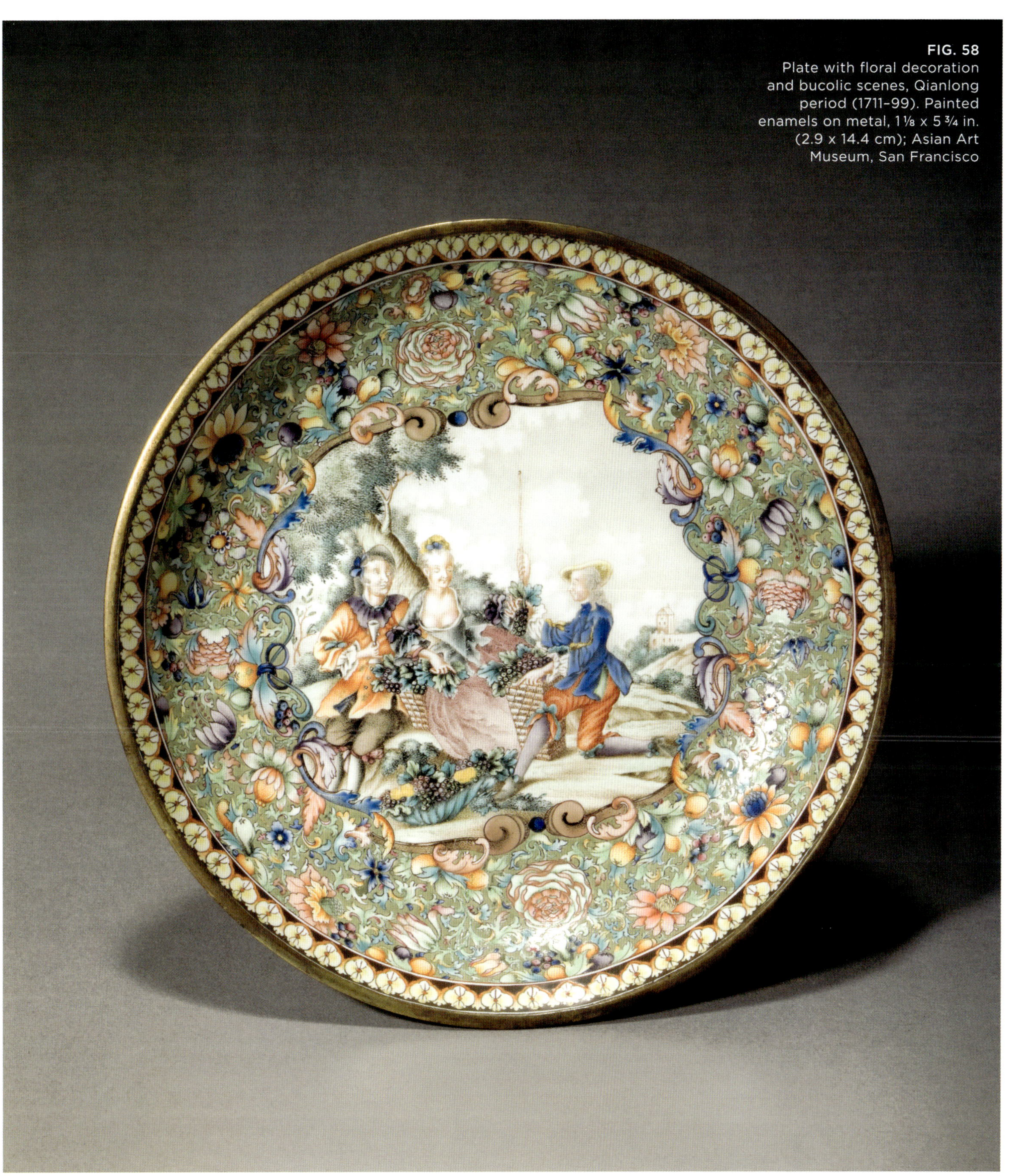

FIG. 58
Plate with floral decoration
and bucolic scenes, Qianlong
period (1711–99). Painted
enamels on metal, 1 ⅛ x 5 ¾ in.
(2.9 x 14.4 cm); Asian Art
Museum, San Francisco

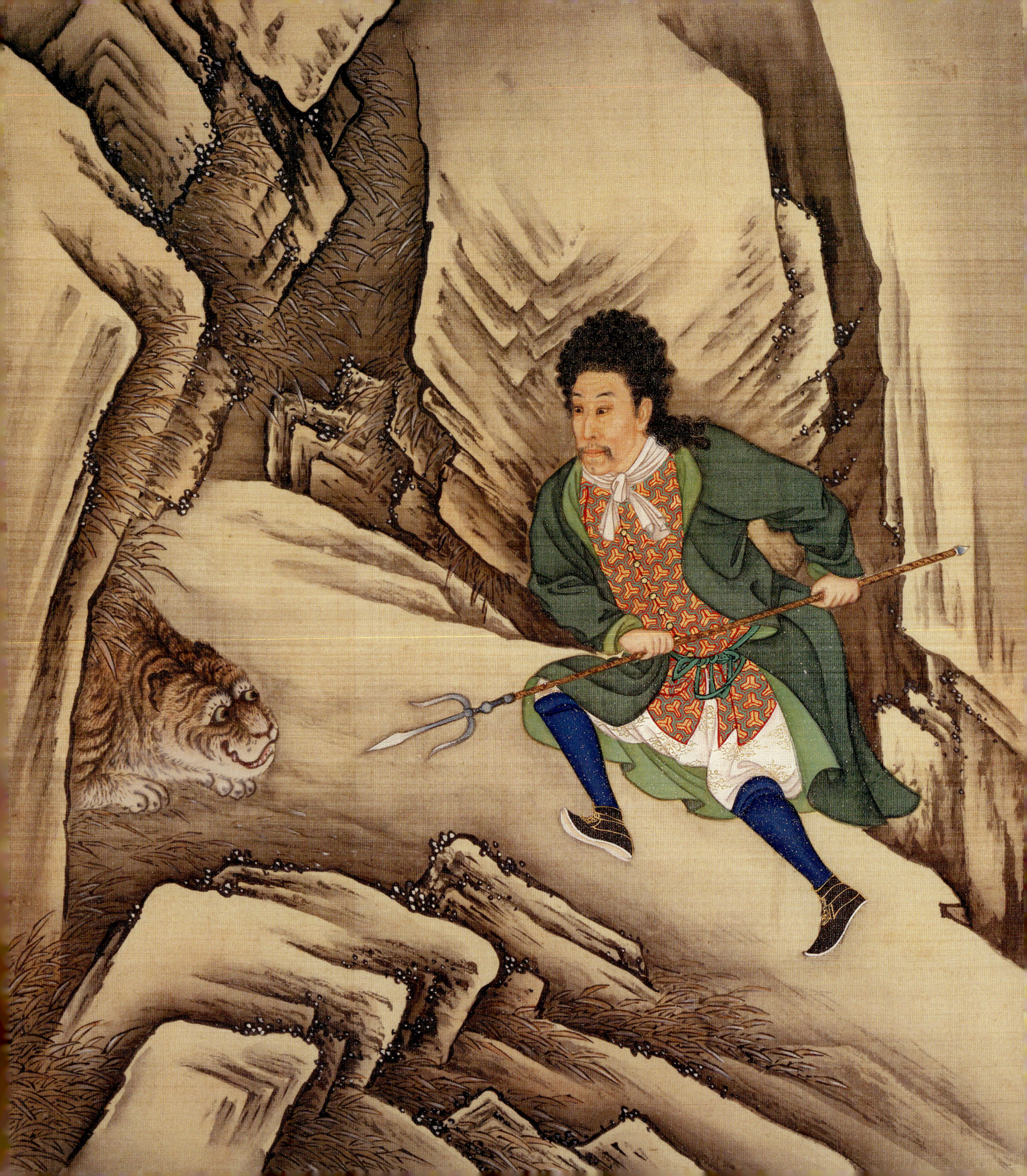

FIG. 59
Yongzheng as European Killing a Tiger, from "Life Portraits of the Yongzheng Emperor in Costumes," 13 portraits, Qing dynasty (1644–1911), Yongzheng period (1711–99). Ink and color on silk, 14 x 12 in. (34.9 x 31 cm). Palace Museum, Beijing

hand, irritating the imperial patron with inadequate works or an unproductive pace could mean penalties or even dismissal.[12] Castiglione thus became a professional court painter, working from seven in the morning to five in the evening, his spare time devoted to fulfilling Jesuit commissions, obligations, and routines.

In the Yongzheng era, the cultural diversity embodied at court by Castiglione and other Europeans began to be indirectly represented, at the emperor's behest, not merely as the mute storing of foreign knowledge, but as a visually controlled diversity. Ruling over a multi-ethnic empire required maintaining equilibrium among ethnic differences while defending the Manchu ethnicity and its right to rule. One of the reasons for the mid-Qing emperors' success was the containment of the empire's substantial cultural differences through the act of storing foreign knowledge. The emperors also commissioned pictures that drew on imagery representative of the various religious and cultural traditions present within China (Buddhism, Taoism, Confucianism, Islam), and the ethnic groups defined as Mongolian, Chinese, Manchu, Uyghur, and Tibetan. In keeping with this strategy, the Jesuits in Beijing appeared to the emperor as useful agents of one of many cultural entities—European—to be contained and controlled within the Qing Empire. Such practices of acquisition and incorporation—which were seen as required acts of government—might reach the very image of the emperor himself.[13] In fact, the emperor could be pictured in the guise of different cultural, ethnic, and religious identities without ridicule to his imperial persona. In an album by an anonymous court artist, for instance, Yongzheng enjoys thirteen such transformations: in one image, for example, he is a Taoist priest awakening a dragon from hibernation; in another, he is a bewigged European chasing a tiger (fig. 59). If Kangxi's dialogue with the Europeans in Beijing was centered on the control of knowledge and acquisition of data, the image of his son in a European wig displayed the control of images by means of paintings or texts. The Yongzheng Emperor used his own image to display the Qing supremacy over cultural, political, and religious diversity.

Such a performance was partly mirrored by Castiglione's professional life at court: by this point, the Milanese was both a European painter and a Qing artist. In Castiglione's case, however, the control of his own image was the product of a forced adaptation requiring a real transformation: he had to answer to a Chinese name, Lang Shining (郎世宁); wear Manchu silk robes; and speak Chinese. His understanding of the language was of primary importance. Thus equipped, already in the first years of his engagement at court under Yongzheng, Castiglione met his forthcoming imperial patron, Prince Hungli, the future Qianlong Emperor. The young prince knew the artist very well, having been a four-year-old boy when the Italian entered the service of his grandfather, the Kangxi Emperor. Hungli had been accustomed to roam the imperial painting workshops, and it is not difficult to imagine the young prince becoming familiar with Castiglione's work. When, in 1735, he ascended the throne with the name of Qianlong, he was twenty-four years old, and he knew perfectly what the status of the Italian artist within the imperial painting workshops should be. In the first year of his reign, he commissioned two very important pictures from Castiglione: the accession portrait depicting the emperor in formal robe with the symbols of imperial power (fig. 7, page 56), and a hand scroll that portrays the young emperor flanked by his noble consorts.[14] The Italian painter had become the creator and guardian of the image of the imperial persona.

The patronage of Qianlong, however, extended beyond the trust conferred on Castiglione in portraiture. The emperor wanted to demonstrate that he could traverse, undamaged, the cultural boundaries represented by foreign painting techniques. Unlike his father, who required stylistic consistency in his commissioned artworks, Qianlong gave Castiglione the freedom to incorporate Italian painting fundamentals in Qing scrolls. This occurred especially in commissions that required teams of painters to complete. For example, when Castiglione and other imperial artists worked on a portrait of the emperor reviewing the troops—an oversized painting intended to be glued to the wall of the imperial palace—he was free to paint part of the composition in an Italian style.[15] In fact, two sections of the landscape, the sky and lower left corner of the foreground, are completely disjointed from the space depicted in the rest of the work, which is painted by local artists, in the Chinese manner, with

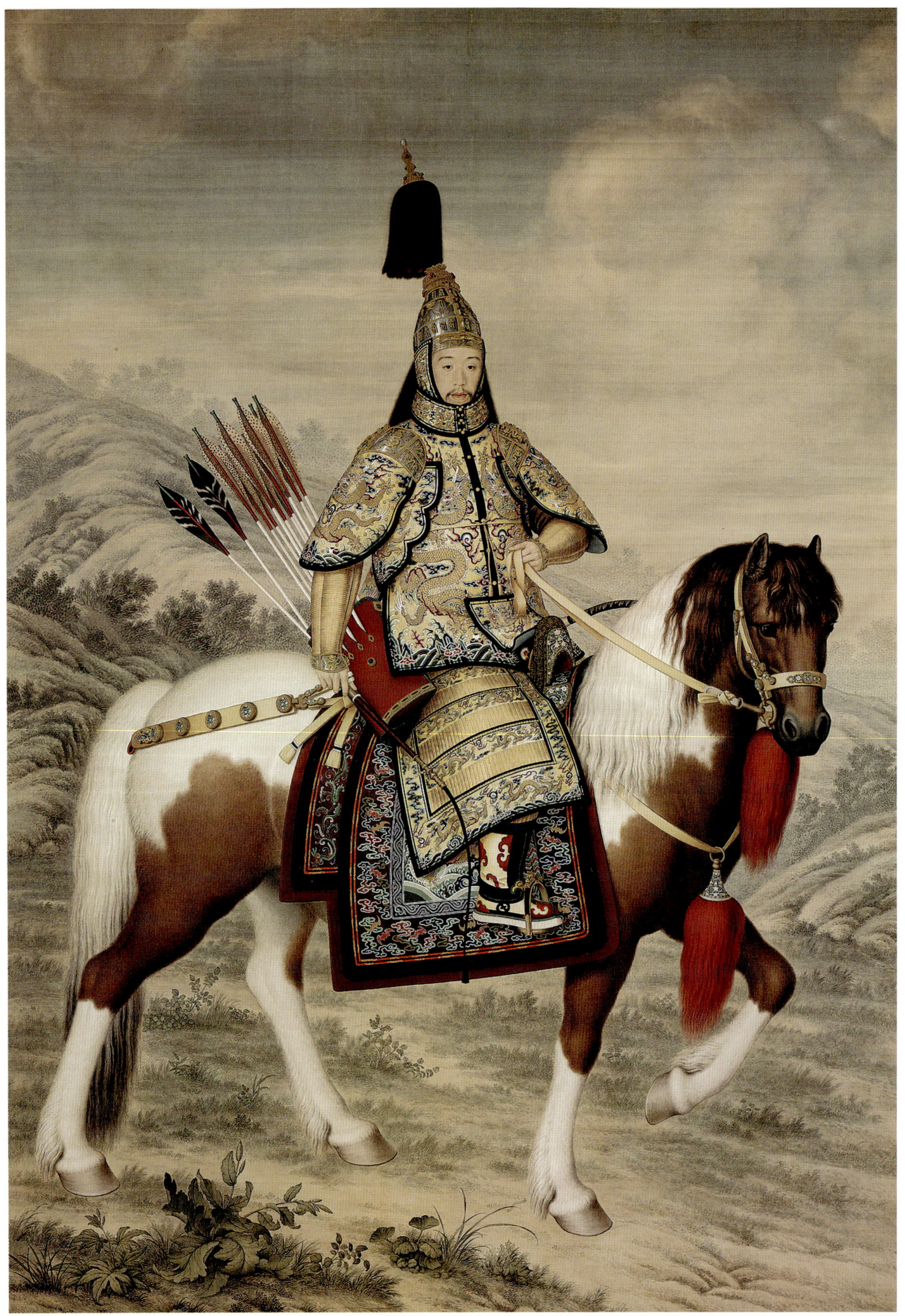

FIG. 60
Giuseppe Castiglione with others, *The Qianlong Emperor in Ceremonial Armor on Horseback*, 1758. Ink and color on silk, 127 x 91 in. (322.5 x 232 cm). Palace Museum, Beijing

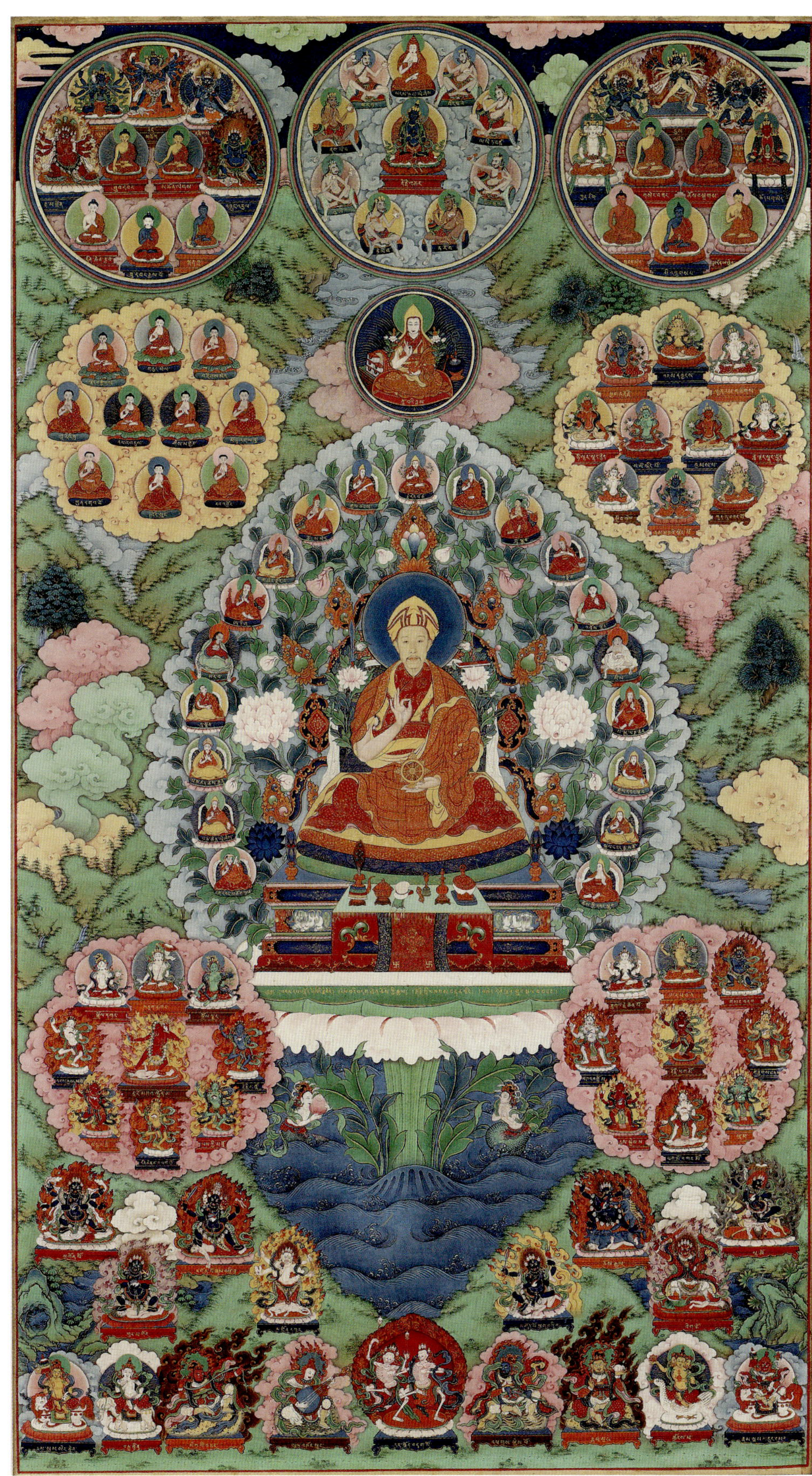

FIG. 61
Giuseppe Castiglione with others, *Qianlong as a Manifestation of Manjushri, the Bodhisattva of Wisdom*, c. Qing dynasty (1644–1911), Qianlong period (1711–99). Ink, color, and gold on silk, 44 ¾ x 25 ⅜ in. (113.6 x 64.3 cm). Freer Gallery of Art, Smithsonian Institution, Washington, D.C.

small touches of the brush (fig. 60). By contrast, the sky is painted in the European style, with blended colors and delicate clouds, and the plants in the foreground corner are meticulously delineated in chiaroscuro. The figure of the emperor on horseback is painted by Castiglione in soft shades to render the texture of Western realism, and it floats over this landscape, having no shadow to anchor it to the ground. Even today, this spatial and pictorial variety within a single work offers a challenge to Western viewers. When looking, for instance, at the *thangka* depicting Qianlong as the Manjugosha Emperor—the emanation of Manjushri, the bodhisattva of wisdom and an important founding symbol of the Manchu tribes—the eye is drawn to the center of the composition, where the emperor's face, painted by Castiglione, emerges from the colored surface (fig. 61). Only the face is shaded in the European style: all around it sprouts the cosmic vision of a pantheon of Buddhist figures, delineated in the style and colors of the Tibetan tradition. Some have maintained that Castiglione was the victim of a subterfuge—that he was asked to reproduce Qianlong's face on an empty surface, with the rest of the painting added later. This assumes that as a Jesuit, he would have refused to paint a non-Catholic religious image.[16] We cannot, however, be completely sure that Castiglione did not in fact collaborate with others to produce a work of Buddhist art: at the Qing court, not even a Jesuit could ignore the visual syncretism advanced by Qianlong.

Moving the Flow of Time

In the eighteenth century, Western clocks collected by the mid-Qing emperors and those assembled in a dedicated imperial workshop in Beijing were described using various terms. They were named with reference to their acoustic and mechanical qualities—for instance, *zimingzhong* (自鸣钟, self-sounding bell)—or their origins: *xiwu* (西物, Western things) or *yangwu* (洋物, foreign things). Also, clocks displaying automata, such as moving scenery and figures, were called *qiqi* (奇器, strange things) or *wanyi*, (玩仪, playthings).[17] Under the Kangxi Emperor, clocks had already become one of the official items that could be given as diplomatic gifts or bestowed upon deserving members of the imperial apparatus, and the Qing household had organized a specific storeroom for them. Imperial clockmakers were charged with the important task of repairing and maintaining the clocks' mechanisms in good working order. It is perhaps for this reason that

Yongzheng had allowed Angelo di Borgo S.Siro, along with Castiglione, to continue working during the transitional period when he assumed the throne: the clockmaker had to ensure that the perpetual movements of the precious clocks did not stop. Automata were not seen as different from clocks. According to an eighteenth-century dictionary, both were machines that "contain the source of their motion." More precisely, clocks were considered "ordinary" automata, while automata themselves were considered "extraordinary" and thus more complex mechanisms.[18] Clocks with automata are real "playthings"; they may in fact be considered theatrical stages where, along with the measurement of time, mechanical movements are on display in the form of automata shaped as animals and figures.

Within this miniaturized space, the painting skills of Castiglione and the knowledge of mechanics based on clock-making technology came together. The two practices could finally provide Qianlong with both a real, three-dimensional space and the forms to fill it. The potential of this development far surpassed the illusion of depth achieved by applying paint to flat surfaces by means of convergent perspective, which the Jesuits had been promoting without success at court. In 1752, for the sixtieth birthday of Qianlong's mother, Dowager Empress Chongqing (崇庆皇太后), they prepared a beautiful clock-automata as a gift.[19] The object was a clock with a semicircular mechanical theater composed of three scenes with paintings by Castiglione.[20] The stage was filled with moving sculptures, but most interestingly with a basin and a waterfall emptying into it. The basin was a mirror; the waterfall, glass threads so fine that, seen from a distance, they "imitated well" the flow of water. The time was pointed out by a duck in the basin, which moved its beak to indicate the hour.[21] The clock-theater celebrated not only the dowager empress's birthday, but also the emperor's patronage of an architectural project that had started a few years previously, in 1747, and which by 1752 was still underway: the construction of European-style palaces and landscapes, designed in a hybrid rococo manner, in a section of the Yuanming Yuan.[22] The term "Yuanming Yuan" first described a portion of imperial land in the northwest part of the capital, which had gardens and pavilions used by the Kangxi Emperor. In 1709, he commissioned the construction of a pleasure palace for his son Yongzheng.[23] When Qianlong assumed the throne, the garden had already been serving as a long-term residence for Yongzheng.

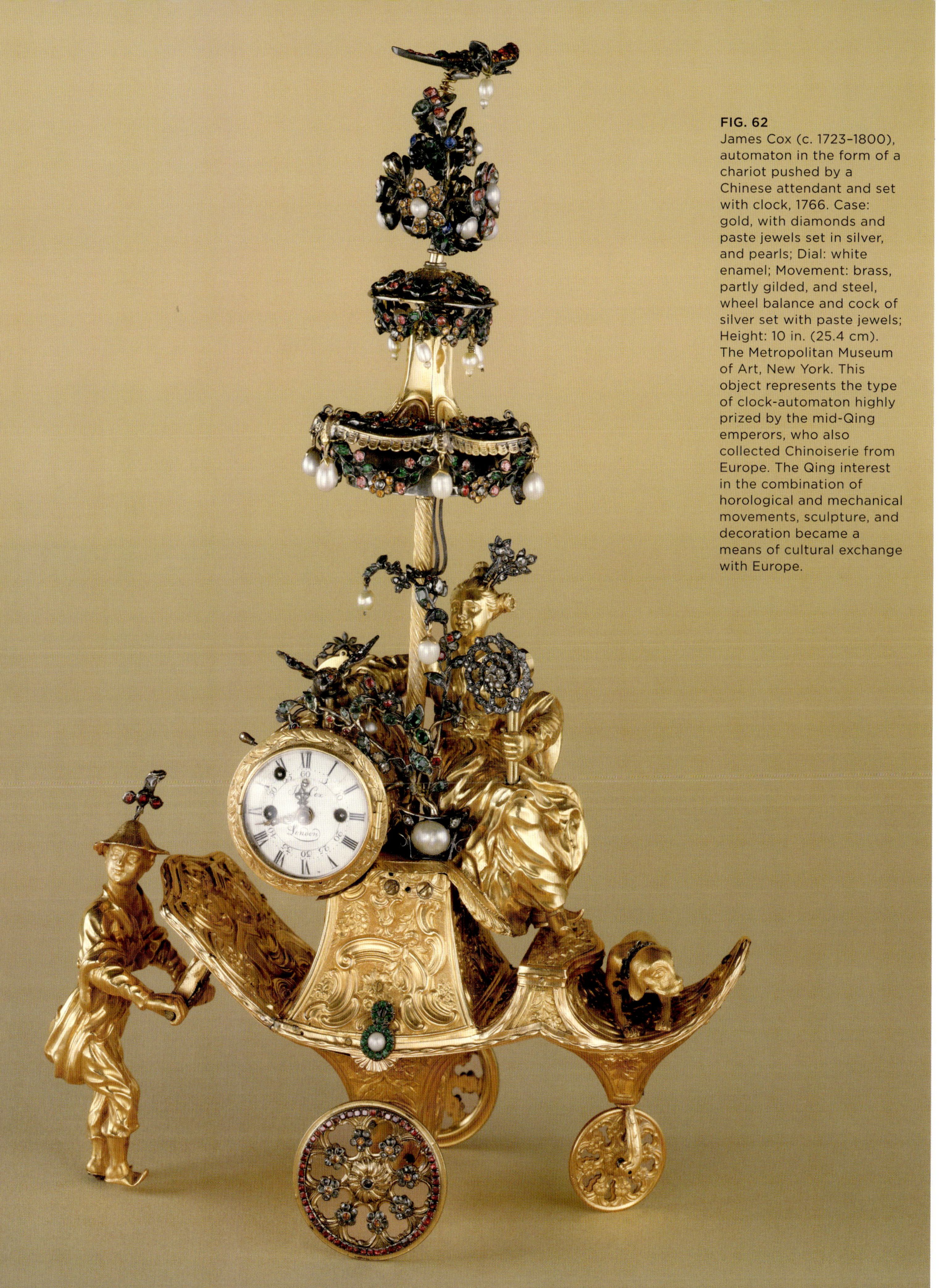

FIG. 62
James Cox (c. 1723–1800), automaton in the form of a chariot pushed by a Chinese attendant and set with clock, 1766. Case: gold, with diamonds and paste jewels set in silver, and pearls; Dial: white enamel; Movement: brass, partly gilded, and steel, wheel balance and cock of silver set with paste jewels; Height: 10 in. (25.4 cm). The Metropolitan Museum of Art, New York. This object represents the type of clock-automaton highly prized by the mid-Qing emperors, who also collected Chinoiserie from Europe. The Qing interest in the combination of horological and mechanical movements, sculpture, and decoration became a means of cultural exchange with Europe.

The area of the European Palaces consisted of several buildings with their enclosed gardens and pavilions, featuring basins, fountains, waterworks and their machinery, as well as aviaries, a maze, and a section with perspective paintings organized as an outdoor theatrical stage.[24] The infrastructure of the European buildings was Chinese: wooden columns embedded in brick walls covered by red plaster. The roofs were composed of Chinese glazed tiles of different colors.[25] Inside the palaces were trompe-l'oeil paintings made by Castiglione and his assistants; European furniture and Western objects were also on display. The project was in Castiglione's hands, but Michel Benoist, S.J. (1715–1774), a French Jesuit mathematician and cartographer, also had a crucial role in the enterprise: it was he who planned the engineering and construction of the fountains and complex waterworks. The Western fountains were not secondary elements in the commission of the European section of the Yuanming Yuan: they were the main feature, around which the entire space was constructed. According to a Jesuit source, it was after looking at the engraved image of a European fountain that Qianlong became interested in commissioning a series of Western-style waterworks and architectural projects. The name of Father Benoist came to light at that moment as the one most capable of coordinating the construction of the complex machinery for pumping the water from a reservoir and distributing its flow to the various elaborate fountains.[26] Benoist was the "clockmaker" of the Yuanming Yuan, and Castiglione its scenographer.

From the time of Kangxi, the mid-Qing emperors had been accustomed to European fountains, ephemeral architecture, and paintings that used European-style convergent perspective.[27] The Yuanming Yuan therefore was not commissioned simply for the display of intriguing Western novelties, and only to a certain degree should it be considered a theme park where a version of Europe was on display. More than this, the garden was a site where the Qianlong Emperor displayed and controlled the movements of foreign mechanisms—the hydraulic apparatus—and Western architectonic views in a space that was in scale with Chinese garden architecture. When the work on the rococo-style buildings was completed in 1759, in front of the western façade of the largest palace, the Haiyan Tang (海晏堂),

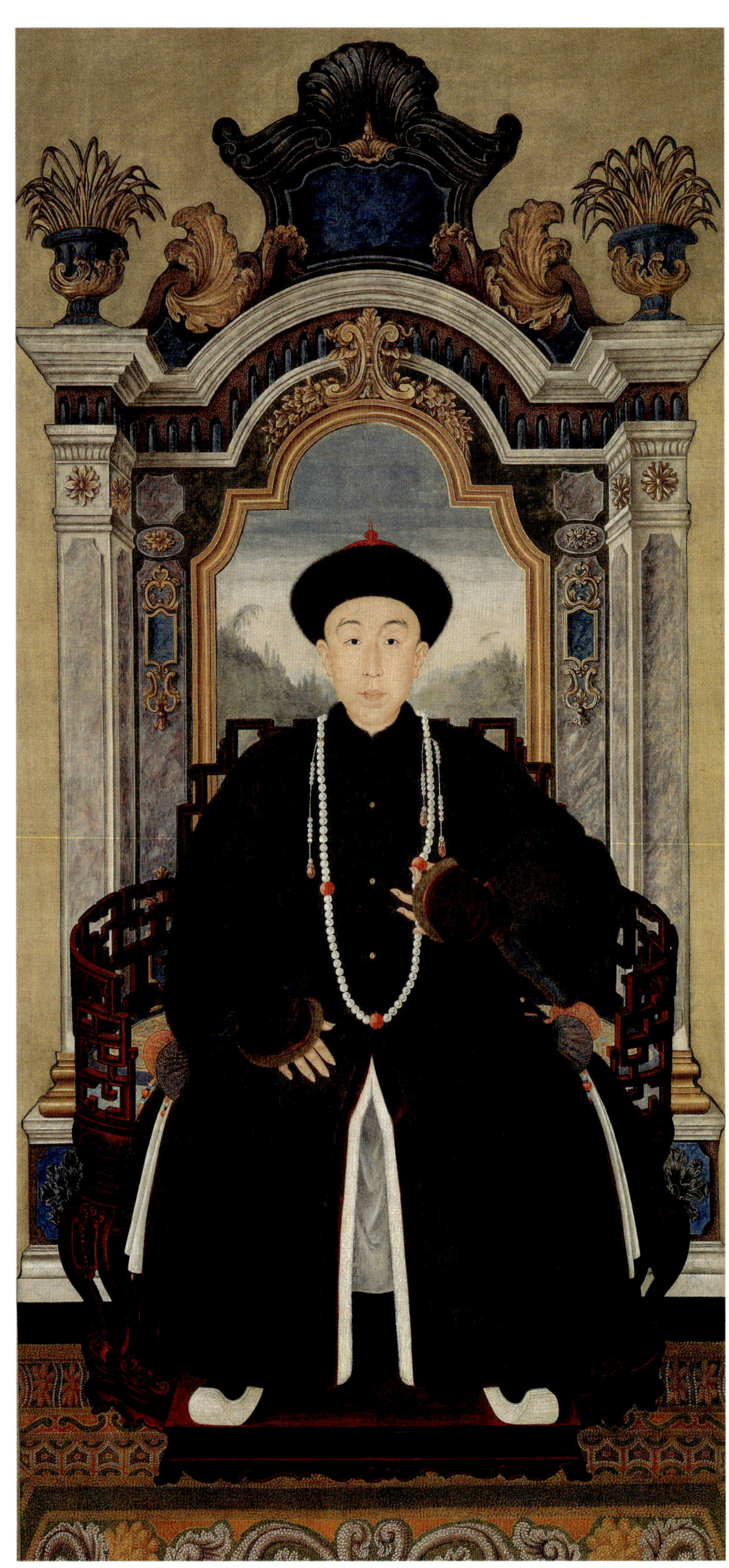

FIG. 63 *Portrait of Hongyan, Prince Guo (1733–1765)*, Qing dynasty (1644–1911), Qianlong period (1711–99). Ink and color on silk, 87 ½ x 40 ⅞ in. (222.1 x 103.7 cm). Arthur M. Sackler Gallery, Smithsonian Institution, Washington, D.C.

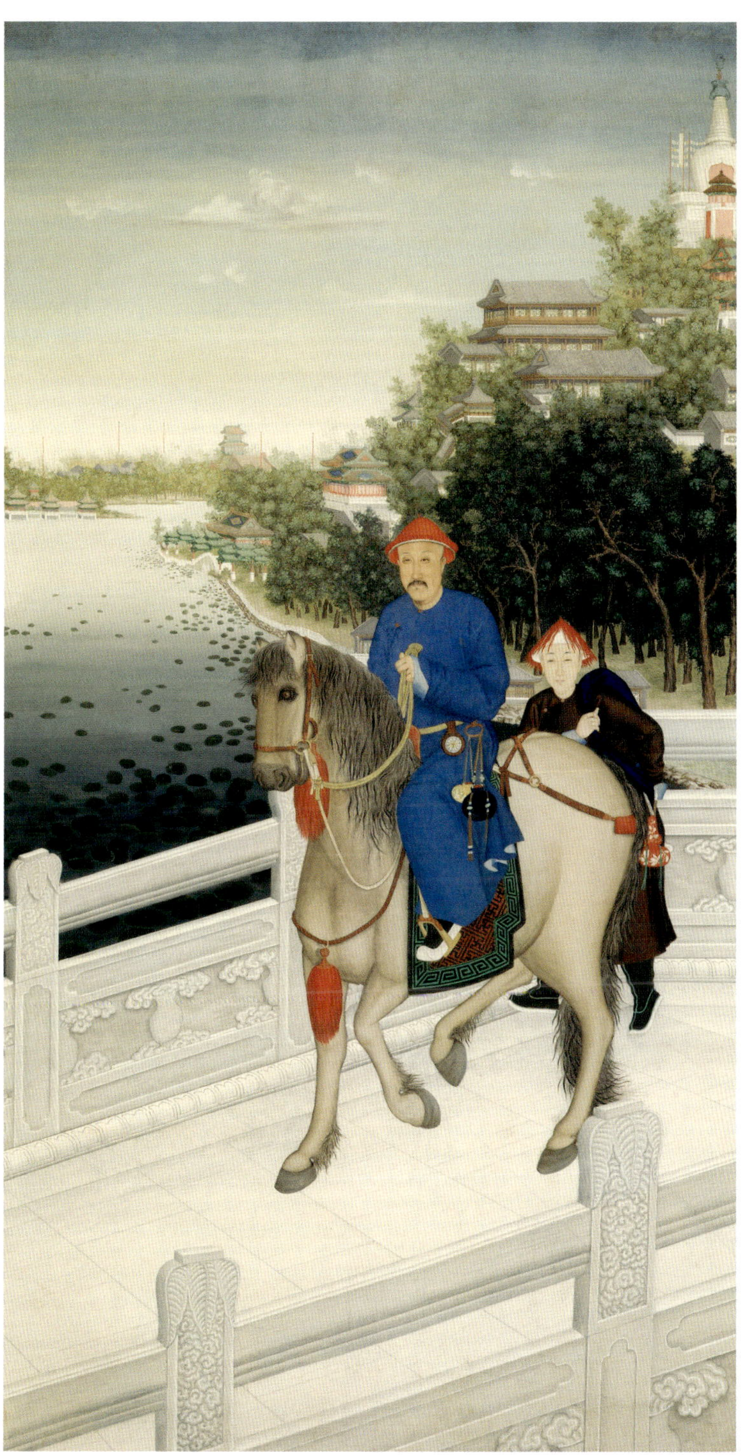

FIG. 64 *Portrait of the Qianlong Emperor in front of the White Pagoda*, Qing dynasty (1644–1911), twentieth century or possibly late eighteenth century. Ink and color on paper, 100 ¾ x 53 ¼ in. (255.9 x 135.3 cm). Arthur M. Sackler Gallery, Smithsonian Institution, Washington, D.C.

was a striking zodiac fountain clock designed by Castiglione and engineered by Benoist (pp. 14–15). In this instance, the water was not made of glass and mirrors, as in the miniature clock-theater given to the dowager empress in 1752. Instead, it was a real stream of water filling the basin of the fountain. In addition, along either side of the basin was a line of animals in human garb, sculpted in stone with cast-bronze heads. The animals represented the twelve signs of the Chinese zodiac, as well as the twelve divisions of the day, and together they functioned as a clock. Every two hours, a different animal spouted water, and at noon they all spouted in concert. It was in such a movement that the Qing command of Western knowledge found its synthesis: imperial time articulated by the twelve animals of Chinese tradition, powered by a European hydraulic machine within a rococo architectonic frame filled with imperial symbols. Moreover, the hydraulic knowledge coming from Europe was not seen by Qianlong as a good alternative power source for local chronological instruments: the Chinese and Manchu already possessed highly functional water-clocks, or clepsydras, which worked by means of an out- or in-flowing stream of water that measured time or drove the movement of astronomical instruments. The Haiyan Tang zodiac fountain celebrated and represented the striking combination of natural and mechanically induced motions: cradling the twelve animals was the stone balustrade of the stairway, used as the river-bed for a controlled flow of water that, from step to step, was collected in the main basin. Water, here, was the visible means of understanding how the collected, regulated flow that represented China met the pumped, forced stream symbolizing Europe.

In Qianlong's reign, the cultural exchange that began with Kangxi's interest in learning Western mathematics and passed through Yongzheng's visual interpretation of diversity assumed its ultimate shape: the control of a hybrid Chinese-European space, exerted by ruling over the intangible movements of water, time, fountains, and architecture. No longer was control a matter of interpreting the passage from two-dimensional pictures to three-dimensional space, but rather the display of three-dimensional life within the enclosed space of the Yuanming Yuan. Consider a painting of Prince Guo (1733–1765), sixth son of the Yongzheng Emperor and half-brother to Qianlong, portraying him in front of a European-style architectonic stage (fig. 63). As the image indicates, the ruling Manchus were comfortable standing, as Manchus, in the imaginary space delineated by foreign pictures. Wigs were no longer needed.[28]

Evidently, the three mid-Qing emperors and the Jesuits in China were all protagonists in this unique dialogue. In a pre-industrial age, however, the quasi-perpetual movement of such an incredible exchange had little chance of survival. After Benoist's death in 1774, the hydraulic machinery became inoperative, and no one at court could repair it: the knowledge was as ephemeral as flowing water.[29] Castiglione, designer of the European section of the garden, had died in 1766, eight years before. Today, of the Yuanming Yuan, only ruins remain: the principal destruction was suffered in 1860 during the Second Opium War, when Anglo-French troops plundered and burned the buildings. After that convulsive episode, the Yuanming Yuan descended, like its authors and patrons, into a controlled oblivion.

But the ruins of the exchange between the mid-Qing emperors and Europe were destined to be rearranged. During the period extending from the foundation of the Chinese republic in 1912 to the foundation of the People's Republic of China in 1949, works of art from the imperial collection stored inside the Forbidden City were studied and copied for the first time. In the third decade of the twentieth century, the idea of a national museum took shape, together with the publication of catalogues and inventories of the works of imperial painters of the Qing dynasty. In this same period, Qianlong re-appeared like a ghost: in a portrait signed "Lang Shining" by an anonymous painter who forged the style of the Milanese, the Qing emperor is shown riding across a bridge in the imperial park of Beihai, with the White Pagoda in the background (fig. 64). Qianlong, probably followed by one of his sons, is wearing a casual robe and a European pocket-watch with two silk pouches at the waist. The convergent perspective used for the background does not seem to relate to the portraits in the foreground, and no shadows anchor the group to the ground. It is an image fluctuating in all directions, but with very old attributes: clocks from the West, greatly prized by the mid-Qing emperors, and the pouches which, in larger sizes, were traditionally used for carrying food for long rides. As remnants of the nomadic Manchu past, they stand for a journey that never ends, perhaps toward an indistinct modernity.

In the second half of the twentieth century, the same nomadic and symbolic path surfaced in the shape of the looted bronze heads of the zodiac fountain of the Yuanming Yuan, which had been dispersed to various private collections around the world and more recently sold at auction. They quickly became visual tags of a new Chinese identity, formed by the memories of the last dynasty, suppressed and then reformulated by means of a new national cultural consciousness developed by different artistic movements in the post-Mao period, in particular during the 1980s. Today, the heads are the subject of interconnected debates on looted art, Western imperialism, Chinese nationalism, and the commodification of cultures. Strikingly, significant voices in such debates have originated from the actual space occupied by the remains of Yuanming Yuan. For instance, in the early 1980s, members of the unofficial art group The Stars, including Ai Weiwei, were accustomed to meeting secretly in the garden to read poems amid the rococo ruins.[30] In a way, the Yuanming Yuan and the bronze heads designed by Castiglione did not lose their original ability to move the waters of exchange and estrangement. The twelve zodiac heads of Ai Weiwei's *Circle of Animals/Zodiac Heads* are in fact part of the same history of dialogue and rupture. Their long pedestals suggest a violent eradication but also a fountain-like spouting, producing a new interpretation of the contested past, and at the same time, a response to the current exploitation of the artistic inheritance of China.

---

1. This research was conducted with the aid of a post-doctoral fellowship from the Ricci Institute for Chinese-Western Cultural History, University of San Francisco, which I thankfully acknowledge. For an interesting overview on the Jesuit missionary enterprise, see Luke Clossey, *Salvation and Globalization in the Early Jesuit Missions* (Cambridge: Cambridge University Press, 2008).

2. Henry Josson and Leopold Willaert, *Correspondance de Ferdinand Verbiest de la Compagnie de Jésus* (1623–1688), *Directeur de l'Observatoire de Pékin* (Brussels: Palais des Académies, 1938); for Verbiest's observations, see 230–53, 234, 238.

3. The optical reception in the French garden is described by Jean Baptiste Du Halde in his *Description géographique, historique, chronologique, politique, et physique de l'Empire de la Chine et de la Tartarie chinoise*, vol. 3 (Paris: P. G. Le Mercier, 1736), 332–36 (for the quotation, see 335).

4. On Castiglione's life and oeuvre, see the author's "La famille de Giuseppe Castiglione (1688–1766)" and "Les peintures génoises de Giuseppe Castiglione," in *Michèle Pirazzoli-t'Serstevens, Giuseppe Castiglione 1688–1766: Peintre et architecte à la cour de Chine* (Paris: Thalia, 2007), 18–25.

5. On Castiglione's mission, see the author's "Reconciling Two Careers: The Jesuit Memoir of Giuseppe Castiglione, Lay Brother and Qing Imperial Painter," *Eighteenth-Century Studies* 42, no. 1 (2008): 45–59.

6. Evidence on the delayed transfer of Castiglione to China may be

found in the Jesuit Archive (Archivum Romanum Societatis Iesu, ARSI), Rome; see Goa 9, vol. 2, 500–1 r./v., April 6, 1713 and April 18, 1713.

7. The episode is recounted in Castiglione's posthumous memoir, *Memoria postuma*, ARSI, Bras. 28, 92 r.- 93 v, 92.

8. The painting depicts the training of a horse on the northern borders. Castiglione probably painted the horse and Jiao Bingzhen, the landscape; see Wai-kam Ho, ed., *Eight Dynasties of Chinese Painting: The Collections of the Nelson Gallery-Atkins Museum, Kansas City, and the Cleveland Museum of Art* (Cleveland: Cleveland Museum of Art and Bloomington: Indiana University Press, 1980), 354.

9. See *Catalogus Missionariorum, qui actu existent in Imperio Sinarum*, Scritture riferite nei congressi—Indie Orientali, Cina, 1723, 559 v., in the Archivio Propaganda Fide (APF), Rome.

10. This information is given by Matteo Ripa in a letter written in Naples after his return to Italy. APF, Scritture riferite nei congressi – Indie Orientali, Cina, Miscellanea 17, 633, October 6, 1725, in the APF. Yongzheng's employment of Castiglione as a painter of architecture is also documented in Anita Chung, *Drawing Boundaries: Architectural Images in Qing China* (Honolulu: University of Hawai'i Press, 2004), 52.

11. The list of gifts, along with information about the commission, are in Fondo Gesuitico, Biblioteca Nazionale, Rome, *Nuovi riscontri dalla Cina*, 1723, ms. 1254, n. 31, 315 r.-318 r., 315 v- 316 r.

12. Yang Boda, "The Development of the Ch'ien-lung Painting Academy," in Alfreda Murck and Wen C. Fong, eds., *Words and Images* (New York: Metropolitan Museum of Art; Princeton, NJ: Princeton University Press, 1991), 333–56, 345.

13. In *The Double Screen: Medium and Representation in Chinese Painting* (London: Reaktion Books, 1996), 200, Wu Hung, discussing important aspects of this Qing policy, pertinently states that "efforts, which ensured the cultural and artistic continuity, were themselves carefully calculated political acts."

14. For the Castiglione accession portrait, today in the Palace Museum in Beijing, see Zhang Hongxing, ed., *The Qianlong Emperor: Treasures from the Forbidden City* (Edinburgh: National Museum of Scotland, 2002), 36. On the handscroll of Qianlong with the noble consorts, now in the collection of the Cleveland Museum of Art, see Wai-kam Ho, ed., *Eight Dynasties of Chinese Painting*, 355.

15. On this commission, see Zhu Jiajin, "Castiglione's *Tieluo* Paintings," *Orientations* 19, no. 11 (1988): 80–83; and Pamela Kyle Crossley, *A Translucent Mirror: History and Identity in Qing Imperial Ideology* (Berkeley: University of California Press, 1999), 275–78.

16. Patricia Berger, *Empire of Emptiness: Buddhist Art and Political Authority in Qing China* (Honolulu: University of Hawaii Press, 2003), 55.

17. Catherine Pagani, "*Eastern Magnificence and European Ingenuity*": *Clocks of Late Imperial China* (Ann Arbor: University of Michigan Press, 2004), 18–19.

18. Henri Paulian Aimé, *Dizionario Portatile di Fisica*, vol. 1 (Venice: Silvestro Gatti, 1794), 81.

19. On the European arts and the celebration for the dowager empress, see Ellen Uitzinger, "For the Man Who Had Everything: Western-Style Exotica in Birthday Celebrations at the Court of Ch'ien-lung," in Leonard Blussé and Harriet T. Zurndorfer, eds., *Conflict and Accommodation in Early Modern East Asia: Essays in Honour of Erik Zürcher* (Leiden: E.J. Brill, 1993), 216–39.

20. George Robert Loehr, *Giuseppe Castiglione (1688–1766): Pittore di corte di Ch'ien-Lung, imperatore della Cina* (Rome: ISMEO, 1940), 24.

21. The clock-automata is described by Amiot; see *Choix des lettres édifiantes*, vol. 3 (Paris: Imprimerie de Casimir, 1835), 59–68, 67–68.

22. The complex was built in two stages, 1747–51 and 1751/53–59; see Michèle Pirazzoli t'Serstevens, "The Emperor Qianlong's European Palaces," *Orientations* 19, no. 11 (1988): 61–71.

23. Carroll Brown Malone, *History of the Peking Summer Palaces Under the Ch'ing Dynasty* (Urbana: University of Illinois, 1934), 43.

24. See the fascinating study of the garden and its cultural context by John R. Finlay, "The Qianlong Emperor's Western Vistas: Linear Perspective and Trompe l'Oeil Illusion in the European Palaces of the Yuanming Yuan," *Bulletin de l'École française d'Extrême-Orient* 94 (2007): 159–93.

25. Michel Pirazzoli-t'Serstevens, "Europeomania at the Chinese Court: The Palace of the Delights of Harmony (1747–1751), Architecture and Interior Decoration," *Transactions of the Oriental Ceramic Society* 65 (2000–1): 47–60, 51.

26. Finlay, "Qianlong Emperor's Western Vistas," 161–62.

27. Pirazzoli, "Europeomania," 48.

28. The portrait, owned by the Smithsonian Collections (Freer Gallery of Art and Arthur M. Sackler Gallery, Smithsonian Institution) in Washington, DC, is discussed in Finlay, "Qianlong Emperor's Western Vistas," 182–83.

29. Malone, *History of the Peking Summer Palaces*, 154.

30. Emerging in the late 1970s, The Stars anticipated the New Wave art movement of 1985.

Heads of State:
Looting, Nationalism,
and Repatriation
of the Zodiac Bronzes

6

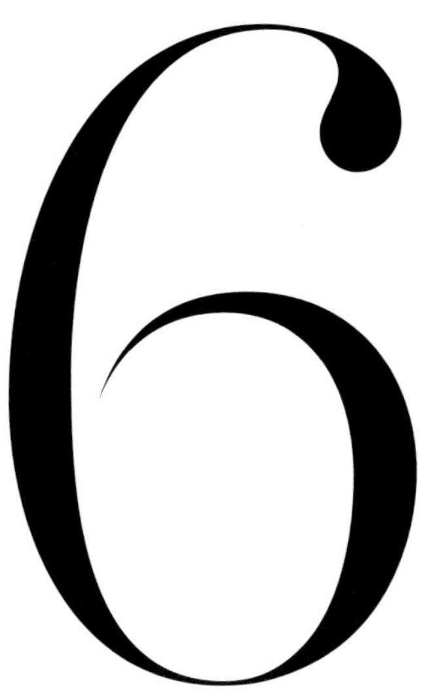

FIG. 65
Illustration of a French soldier
leading a Chinese porter with
loot, in Armand Lucy, *Souvenirs
de voyage: Lettres intimes sur
la campagne de Chine en 1860*
(Marseille, Jules Barile, 1861),
p. 113. Wood engraving

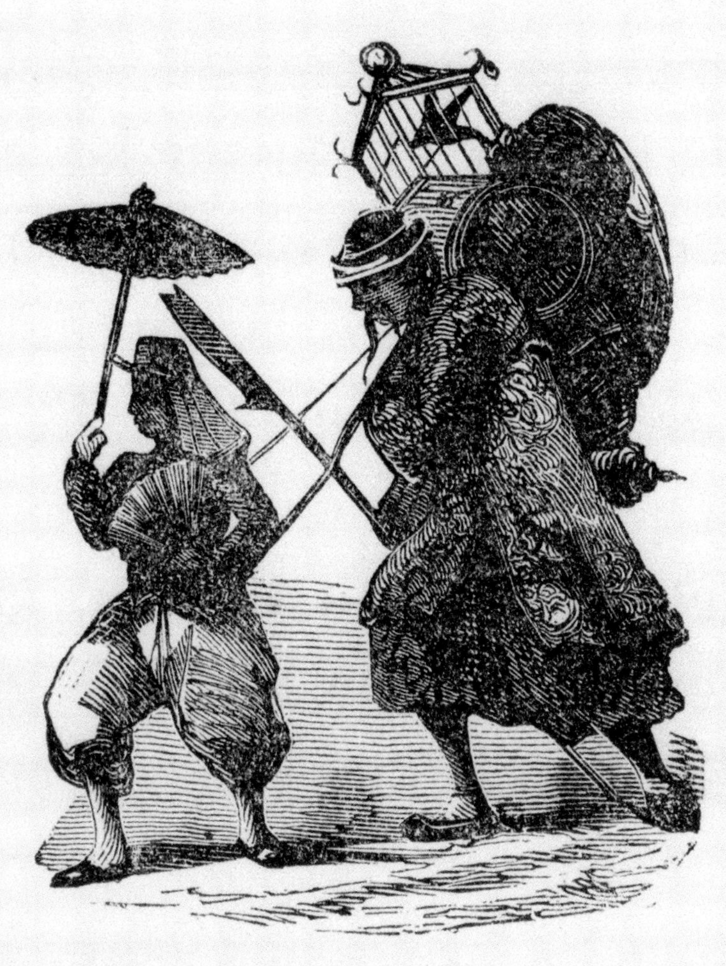

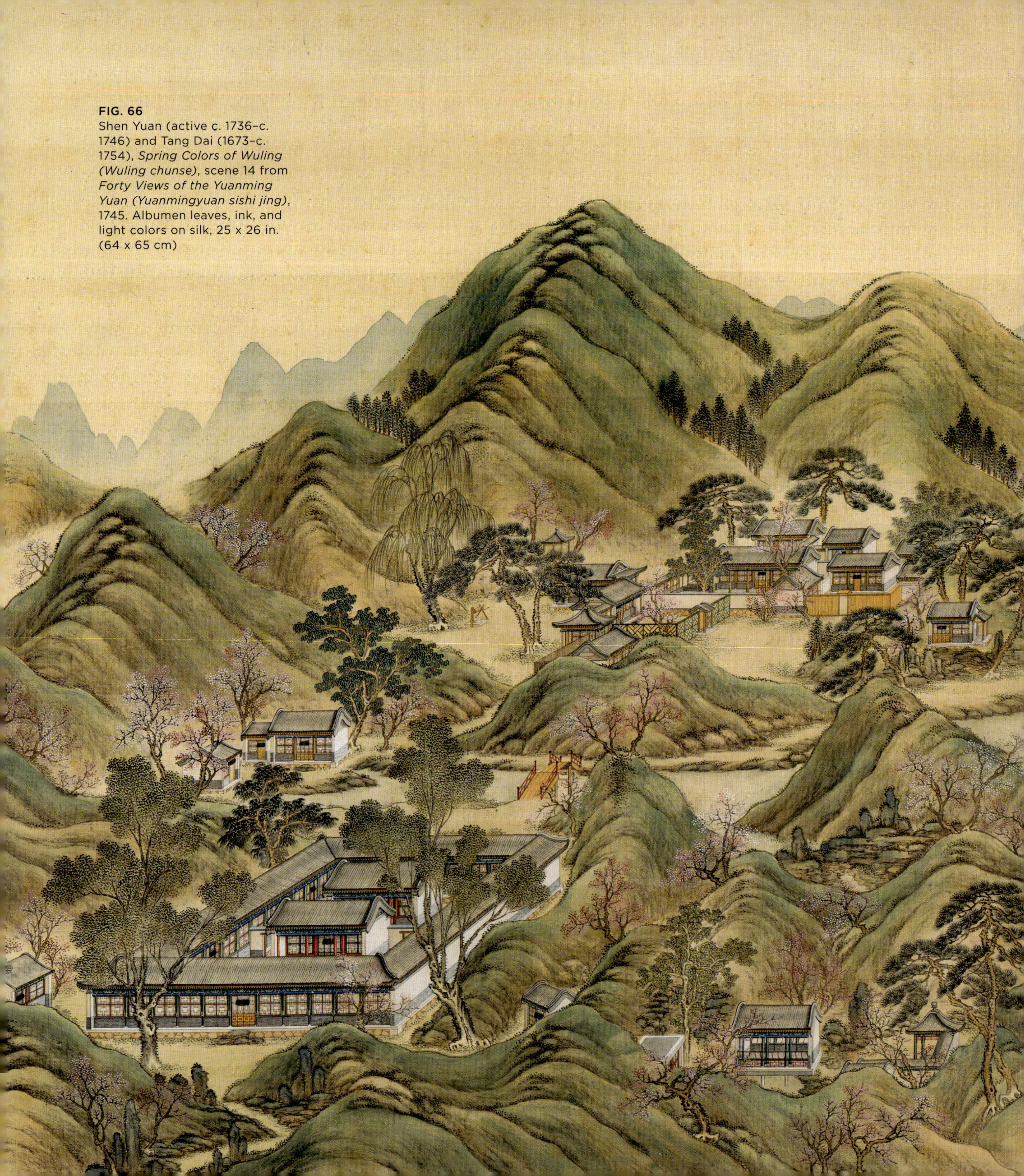

FIG. 66
Shen Yuan (active c. 1736–c. 1746) and Tang Dai (1673–c. 1754), *Spring Colors of Wuling (Wuling chunse)*, scene 14 from *Forty Views of the Yuanming Yuan (Yuanmingyuan sishi jing)*, 1745. Albumen leaves, ink, and light colors on silk, 25 x 26 in. (64 x 65 cm)

IN THE EARLY MILLENNIA OF IMPERIAL CHINA, STORIES circulated about a group of nine bronze tripod vessels cast during the semi-mythical Xia dynasty (c. 2100–1600 BCE). Endowed with magical properties, the bronzes were passed from one dynasty to another, their transfer conferring political legitimacy on the new dynasty even as it articulated the previous dynasty's loss of divine mandate to rule. According to stories told much later, when the Zhou dynasty (c. 1050–256 BCE) lost its mandate, the tripods sank into a river but reappeared there with the establishment of the Qin dynasty (221–206 BCE). The euphoric First Emperor of Qin—leader of the famed Terracotta Army—organized a retrieval effort. But just as the tripods were hauled above the river, birds appeared to snip the ropes with their beaks and the tripods were lost again. The Qin's failure to regain these tangible symbols of political legitimacy signified divine rejection of its right to rule. Lasting less than two decades, the dynasty became one of the shortest in Chinese history.

Two thousand years later during the Qing dynasty (1644–1911), one of the last emperors lost a different set of bronzes, this time depicting the heads of the twelve Chinese zodiac animals. These rat, ox, tiger, rabbit, dragon, snake, horse, ram, monkey, rooster, dog, and boar heads originally topped the spouts of an ingenious zodiac fountain in the Yuanming Yuan (圆明园). Set in front of the stone Palace of the Calm Seas (*Haiyan Tang* 海宴堂) within the Yuanming Yuan's "European Palaces" (*Xiyanglou* 西洋楼) area, the animals spouted together at noon and individually on each sign's two-hour period of the day. But at the end of the Second Opium War (1856–60), they were looted from the garden, along with innumerable other treasures, just before the entire 350 hectares of the Yuanming Yuan were burned.

Although the European Palaces' surviving white stone ruins occupy only a fiftieth of the entire Yuanming Yuan, they have long symbolized China's "century of national humiliation" (*bainian guochi* 百年国耻) and the losses inflicted by imperialist foreign powers between 1840 and 1945. But in the past decade, China has become the world's second largest economy behind the United States, and the new purchasing power of Chinese art collectors has strengthened the international art market's attentions toward the People's Republic. Along with its increasingly international outlook, China's iconography of national humiliation has expanded correspondingly, from the domestic icons of the Yuanming Yuan's ruins to its looted—and recoverable—treasures still in foreign hands.

Although an unknown number of objects were either looted or destroyed in 1860, today China focuses most emphatically on the zodiac bronzes. When compared with the masterworks of China's ancient bronze-casting tradition that inspired political legend, the zodiac bronzes have prompted some critics to characterize them as merely "eighteenth-century lawn ornaments" for their straightforward cosmological symbolism and uncomplicated aesthetics.[1] Although the zodiac bronzes are little known beyond Chinese and China-watchers, their imperial origins and history as imperialistic plunder imbue the heads with intense political and economic value in the twenty-first century. China's commitment to repatriating its lost and looted "national treasures" (*guobao* 国宝) from foreign collectors and museums is encapsulated in these twelve pieces, as is the profound political symbolism of their return. The zodiac bronzes have become not only the global icons of Chinese nationalism, but a critical benchmark against which China measures its redemption from national humiliation and political legitimacy on the international stage.

Innovation and Decay

In 1707, the Manchu Kangxi Emperor (康熙, r. 1661–1722) began building the Yuanming Yuan in the Beijing suburbs six miles northwest of the Forbidden City (fig. 66).[2] Although his successor Yongzheng (雍正, r. 1722–35) also added to the garden, it expanded most significantly under the Qianlong Emperor (乾隆, r. 1735–96). This powerful conquest ruler, equally enamored of statecraft and aesthetics, commissioned the European Jesuits serving his court to design the European Palaces and their fountains. The European Palaces are most heavily indebted to Italian painter and lay brother Giuseppe Castiglione (Lang Shining 郎世宁, 1688–1766). The hydraulics that supported its fountains are credited to mathematician and astronomer Michel Benoist, S.J. (Jiang Youren 蒋友仁, 1715–1774).[3] Chinese artisans executed their designs.

These stone-built pleasure palaces were never residential sites. Instead, they served as luxurious leisure spaces providing elegant storage and display for Qianlong's many European and Sino-European treasures. Interspersed among the buildings were gardens manifesting a unique hybrid of Chinese and European landscape design, and a number of themed fountains depicting scenes populated by bronze animal spouts. These included a water scene with birds and crustaceans, small individual fountains with monkeys sheltering from the "rain" under trees and umbrellas, and a magnificent hunt scene with dogs chasing a stag.[4] The zodiac fountain was a highlight of the European Palaces, located in its very center. Although the white stone ruins today seem visually analogous to Greco-Roman ruins, colorful tile shards scattered around the site provide evidence of the Palaces' original varied palette.

But even during their heyday of the eighteenth century, the European Palaces began to decay as the knowledge needed to repair them died with the Jesuits. Benoist died in 1774, and at least as early as the 1780s, the hydraulic systems were failing. In advance of scheduled imperial visits, hundreds of eunuchs hauled water into the fountains' reservoirs with ropes and buckets. "You cannot imagine the artificial means employed here to make [the fountains] play,"[5] wrote Jean Joseph Marie Amiot, S.J. (Qian Deming 钱德明, 1718–1793), an imperial translator and head of the French Jesuit mission to China. As imperial purse strings tightened, the European Palaces became a source of raw materials: in 1795, the copper pipes that provided the zodiac fountain with its waterworks were dismantled and repurposed.[6] Between changing imperial tastes and continually dwindling wealth, in the first half of the nineteenth century the European Palaces suffered from benign neglect. No longer did the imperial coffers fund lavish gardens: money was now directed against the dual threats of domestic rebellion and international encroachment.

Commoditizing the Yuanming Yuan

After China's defeat in the First Opium War (1839–42), treaties signed with Great Britain, France, and other countries granted foreign nations dramatically increased trade privileges and other enviable commercial concessions in China. But when these unequal treaties expired in 1856, the Qing government refused to ratify new treaties that further limited its power. The goal of the Second Opium War was, simply put, to ensure the treaties' ratification and achieve their trade concessions for Britain and France. General Charles Cousin Montauban (1796–1878) and diplomat Baron Jean-Baptiste Louis Gros (1793–1870) led the French troops, while the British were led by Sir James Hope Grant (1808–1875) and James Bruce, eighth Earl of Elgin and Her Majesty's High Commissioner and Plenipotentiary in China. Lord Elgin (fig. 67) was the son of Thomas Bruce, seventh Earl of Elgin, best known for removing the "Elgin Marbles" from the Parthenon and spawning the

world's most well-known debate for and against the repatriation of looted objects.

The 17,000 troops of the allied forces, plus naval units and a Chinese coolie corps of 2,500 men, advanced toward Beijing by sea and land during the summer and early autumn of 1860. Arriving outside Beijing's city walls on October 5, a contingent continued marching north and west of the city in search of Qing troops. On October 7, French troops arrived at the Yuanming Yuan, which was left largely unguarded as the Xianfeng Emperor (咸丰, r. 1850–61) and his family fled Beijing for a "hunting excursion" at the imperial summer retreat 250 kilometers away. Although none of the allied soldiers had ever visited the Yuanming Yuan before, it was easily recognized: the gardens had been renowned in Europe for over a century. French Jesuit letters describing the site had stimulated the sweeping eighteenth-century European trend of Chinese-inspired garden design.[7] The British embassy to China during the period 1792–94, which sought unsuccessfully to attain concessions similar to those gained in the Opium Wars, was also housed in the Yuanming Yuan.[8] This familiarity, combined with the visible richness of the Yuanming Yuan's treasures and their intimate association with the Chinese emperor, unquestionably increased the troops' interest in retaining objects from the garden. Irresistibly valuable jades, silks, porcelains, bronzes, furs, lacquerware, clocks, watches, silver, gold, and more were freely available for the taking. The looting began.

Contradictions abound among the many firsthand accounts of what took place in the Yuanming Yuan during October 1860. British and French troops accused each other of beginning the plunder. General Montauban denied that looting took place at all, even as his soldiers began selling their wares in camp. Maurice d'Herrison, General Montauban's secretary and interpreter, wrote that the Chinese instigated the looting.[9] But sources agree that the looters themselves were not solely white Europeans. Indian Army troops constituted approximately one-third of the total British forces, and Qing subjects not only availed themselves of the objects at hand but also served as porters for the allied looters.[10] The French command simply allowed their soldiers' looting to run its course, believing that the men would eventually tire of the game and cease. In the meantime, what a game it was: enameled vases were used for bowling,[11] while chandeliers and mirrors became objects of target practice.[12] British looting, as James L. Hevia has demonstrated, was governed by British Prize Law.[13] All loot (except, interestingly, objects purchased

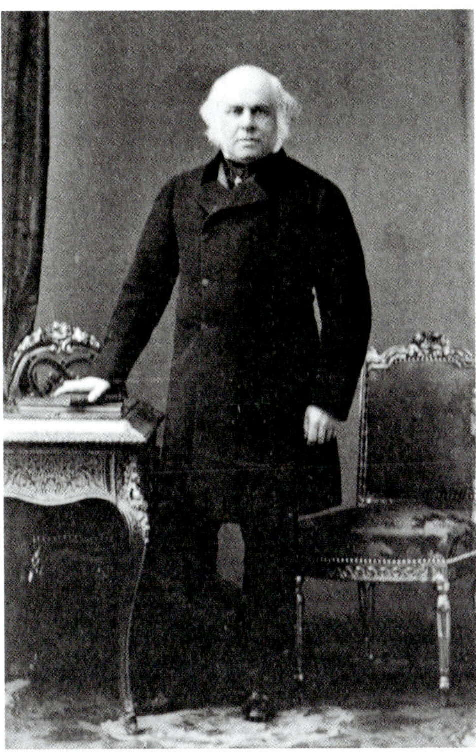

FIG. 67
Portrait of James Bruce, Lord Elgin (1811–1863). Black-and-white photograph, 5 x 4 in. (13 x 10 cm). Library and Archives Canada, Ottawa

FIG. 68
William Bambridge (1819–1879), photograph of "Looty, the first Pekingese dog in Britain, brought by Captain Dunne, 99th Regiment, from Yuanmingyuan, the Summer Palace near Beijing, as a gift for Queen Victoria in April 1861"

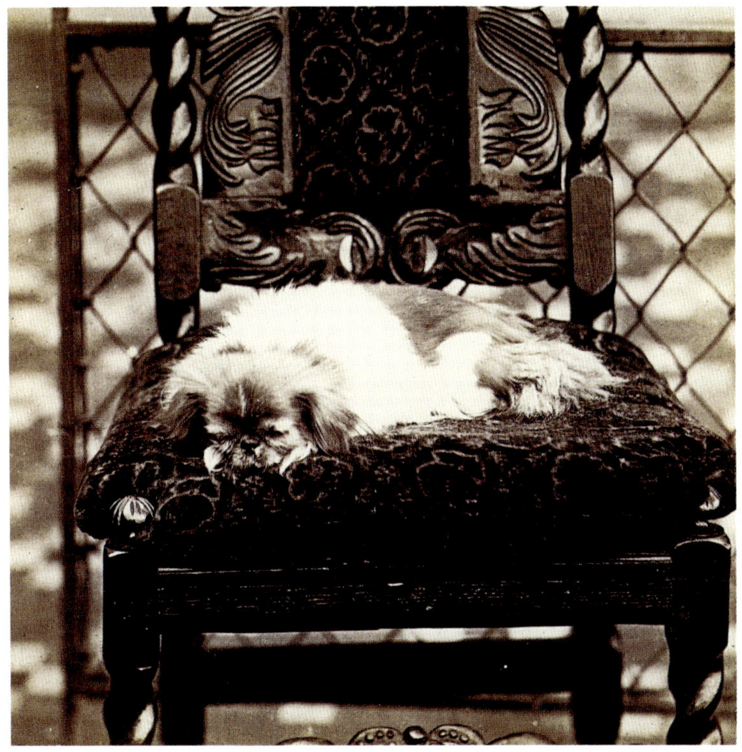

from the French) was submitted to the army's prize agents for inventory and general auction. The sale's proceeds were then distributed among the officers and men, all to maintain military order while converting plunder into private property.[14] The money was distributed relative to rank, with first-class field officers receiving £60 and privates receiving £5, a handsome sum considering that a British soldier's monthly salary was approximately £1.[15]

This first sale of Yuanming Yuan goods took place at allied headquarters, on the grounds of the Yellow Temple (*Huang Si* 黄寺) just outside Beijing's Anding Gate (*Anding Men* 安定门) in the north city wall. Reverend R. J. L. M'Ghee, chaplain to the British forces, reported that although smallish jades went for £10–30 and furs for £10–50, competition for the objects was energized by the rumor that one soldier had an unlimited commission from Baron Rothschild.[16] General Grant himself bought "a necklace of the finest green jade, with rubies, which, by a label attached to it, we ascertained had been presented to the Emperor by a famous Tartar chief."[17] Robert Swinhoe, staff interpreter to General Grant, records that even the "most trivial article" sold for £2–3, while a court robe sold for £120.[18] Such auctions were usually conducted back in England well after the end of a campaign: the sale and immediate

distribution of its £26,000 of prize money in the field might have been unprecedented.[19] Were it not for the distribution, the soldiers would have been unable to purchase the objects.

While the troops chose objects both for their monetary value and as gifts for loved ones, Lord Elgin and General Montauban chose special objects for Queen Victoria (r. 1837–1901) and Emperor Napoléon III (r. 1852–70). Among Queen Victoria's few gifts[20] were a pair of 1.2-meter-high cloisonné enamel vases from the Yuanming Yuan's main audience hall, a jeweled imperial cap, and "Looty," a small Pekingese dog found wandering the garden (fig. 68).[21] Objects taken for Napoléon III included imperial clothing and armor, a gilt bronze Tibetan Buddhist stupa, large enamel vases in various colors, two gilt bronze dragons from a marble bridge on the palace grounds, jewelry, goblets, lacquerware, porcelain, and a large number of varied "curios."[22]

Few firsthand accounts discuss the European Palaces, but this area of the Yuanming Yuan resonated deeply with the French. Press correspondent Antoine Fauchery, attached to the French troops, called the Yuanming Yuan the "Chinese Versailles or Saint-Cloud," and compared the European Palaces with "Trianon, Luciennes, or Marly—take your pick!"[23] Lieutenant-Colonel Charles Dupin wrote of the Palaces'

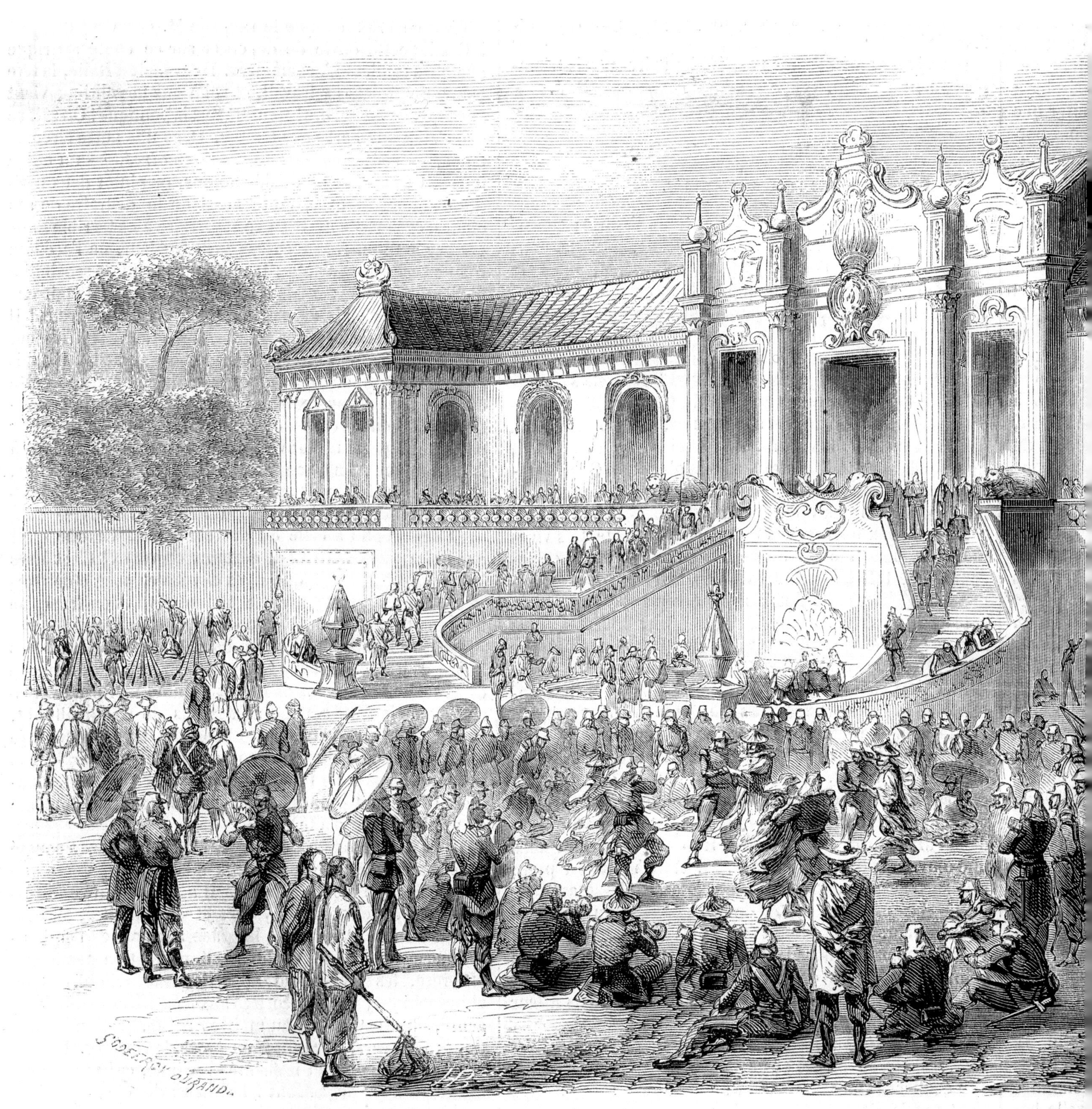

Occupation du palais de Yuan-nineg-yuan par les troupes françaises. — D'après les croquis de M. B. J., officier d

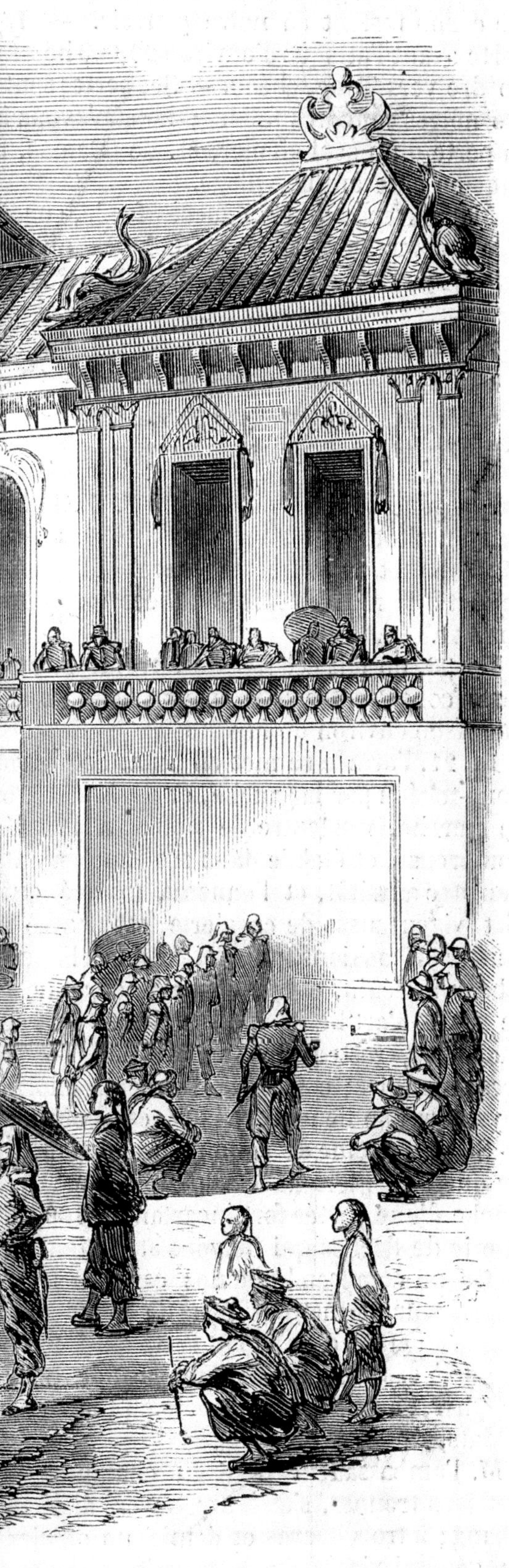

FIG. 69
"Occupation of the Yuanming Yuan Palace by French Troops," from *L'Illustration*, Paris, 22 December 1860

OVERLEAF:
FIG. 70
M. Moullin, "The new Chinese museum of Her Majesty the Empress, installed in the palace at Fontainebleau," from *Le Monde illustré*, Paris, 4 July 1863

disrepair both inside and out, commenting on what was obviously long-term neglect.[24] While no known account specifically mentions the zodiac bronzes, the Palace of the Calm Seas and its zodiac fountain seem to have made a deep impression on the French. On December 22, 1860, the Parisian weekly *L'Illustration* published a sketch titled "Occupation of the Yuanming Yuan Palace by French Troops" (fig. 69) that depicted the palace and its zodiac fountain surrounded by Europeans and Chinese. A rare image of the undestroyed site, it is ironic that this particular vista was chosen from hundreds in the Yuanming Yuan to best illustrate the famed gardens: soon enough, the zodiac bronzes that are mere shadowy suggestions in the sketch would come to represent the looting in its entirety.

Looting and breakage might have been the worst suffered by the Yuanming Yuan were it not for the allied prisoners. Qing troops had imprisoned a group of thirty-six French and British soldiers, diplomats, translators, and press correspondents. Upon their release, it was discovered that nineteen men died, and the seventeen survivors were horribly disfigured by the same exposure, starvation, torture, and excruciating hog-tying that killed their companions. An enraged desire for vengeance pushed the allied leaders to debate the appropriate punishment for Beijing. Although destroying the Forbidden City was considered, Elgin argued that destroying the Yuanming Yuan was the only choice. It was the emperor's favorite residence, a site used by imperial elite rather than the innocent populace, the place where some of the prisoners had been briefly held and tortured, and he wrongly believed it had already been divested of its treasures through plunder.[25]

The French refused to participate in the burning, as General Montauban declared it "an unnecessary retaliation" (*une représaille inutile*).[26] So on October 18–19, 1860, more than four thousand British troops of the 1st Infantry Division set fire to the gardens and surrounding villages. In advance of the burning, a second wave of looting took place that was largely ignored by both commanders and later commentators. Reverend M'Ghee describes opening doors into buildings not yet reached by the flames, with many precious items still inside: "take them all, they will be burned in half-an-hour if you don't; this is a case of 'salvage,' not plunder. More [jades], more books, carpets, pictures, enamels, everything you can imagine."[27] Although it was only the final incident of the Second Opium War, the scope of the Yuanming Yuan's looting and destruction led directly to Anglo-French victory and Chinese defeat.

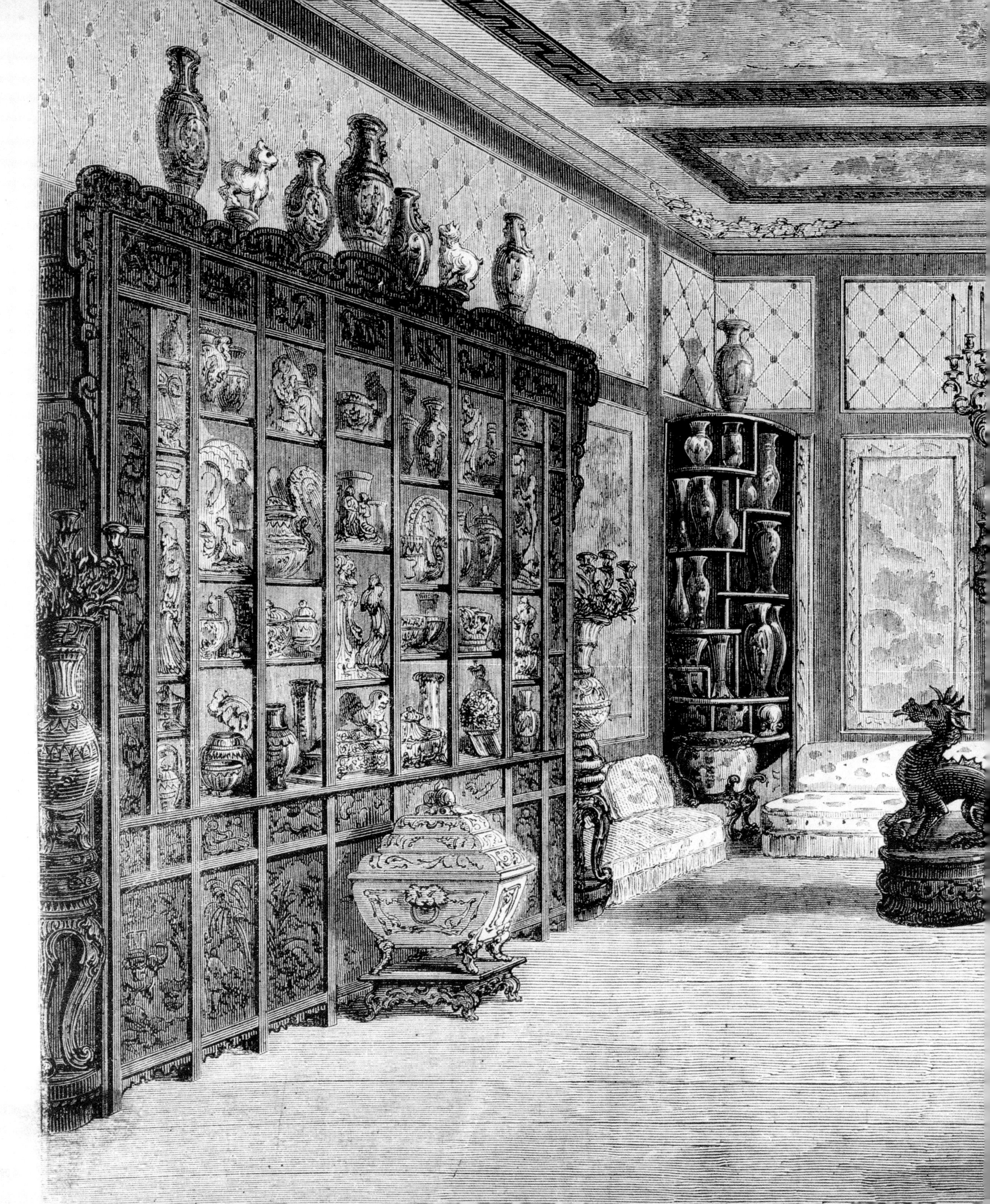

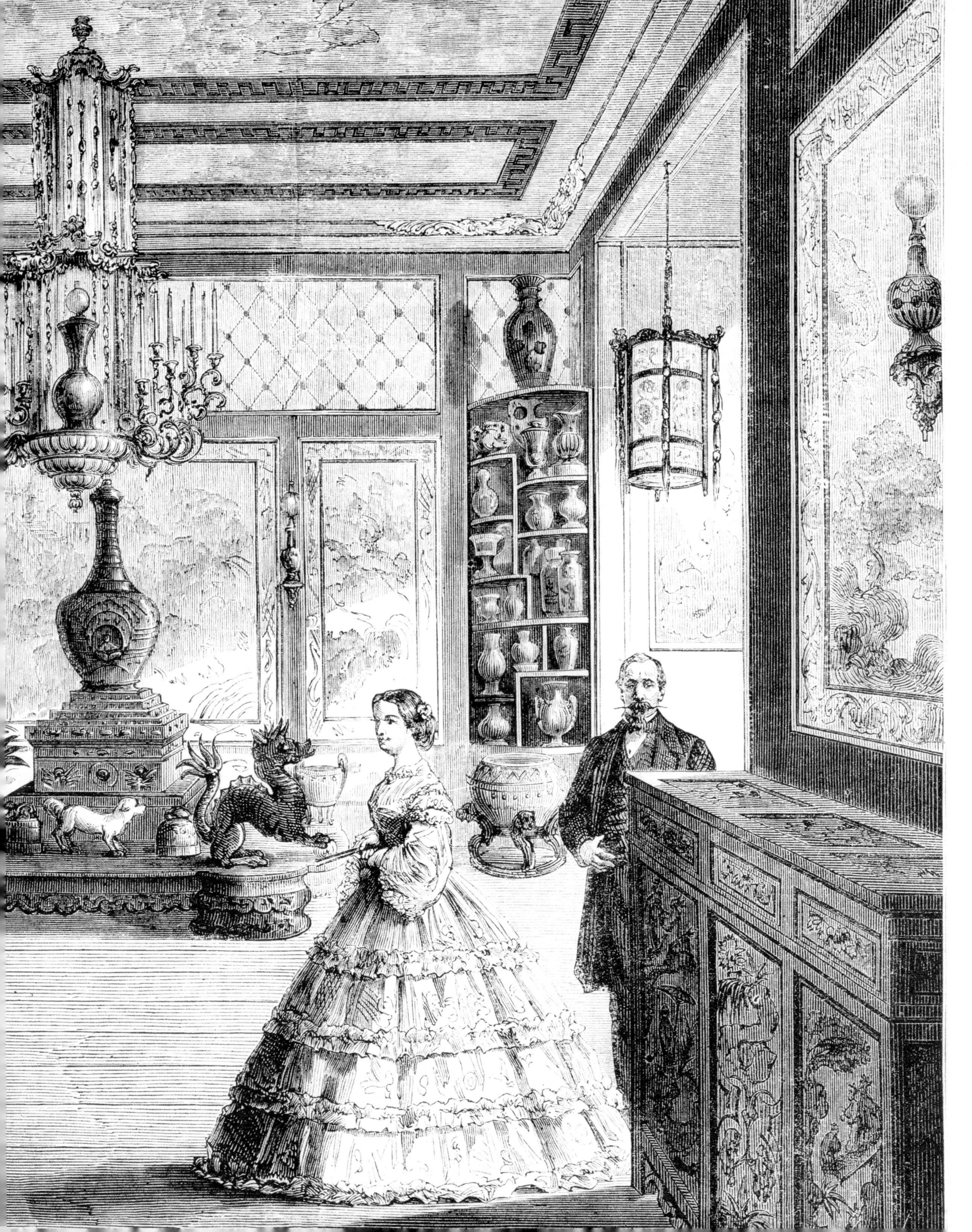

LE MONDE ILLUSTRÉ

As the troops returned home, they introduced objects previously reserved for the Chinese throne into the Western public sphere. Only the eighteenth-century missionaries and embassies had previously encountered works of such high quality: most Europeans were familiar with "Chinese" objects only through the *Chinoiserie* porcelains and enamels produced for Western markets, of mercantile quality with export-only formats and decorations. In contrast, the Yuanming Yuan treasures were created exclusively for the imperial court, with the requisite unsurpassed quality and richness. Naturally, the economic and political value of the Yuanming Yuan's treasures increased dramatically in European museums and salesrooms. France publicly displayed the full array of items selected for Napoléon III at his primary residence in Paris, the Tuileries Palace, in April 1861. Both Paris's *Le Monde Illustré* and the *Illustrated London News* covered the exhibition for their readers; the *News* suggested that the Tuileries exhibition ameliorated the indignity of the objects' removal from China because they remained in imperial possession.[28] China scholar Guillaume Pauthier positively reviewed the show for France's first professional art-history journal, *Gazette des beaux-arts*, but decried the destruction that had brought the treasures to France.[29] After the exhibition, the military objects were sent to what is now the Museé de l'Armée in Paris, while the remainder joined Empress Eugénie's private collection in the specially created Musée Chinois de l'Impératrice at Fontainebleau (fig. 70), which can still be visited today.

Soon after, Yuanming Yuan items began to appear on the auction block. For nothing more than mere money, Europeans could possess both shards of Chinese imperial aura and souvenirs of Anglo-French victory over the Eastern emperor. Between 1861 and 1866, at least thirteen sales that included objects from the "Summer Palace" were held in London at Phillips (now Phillips, De Pury and Company) and Christie, Manson, & Woods (now Christie's). In Paris, twenty-one "Palais d'Été" auctions were held at Hôtel Drouot between 1861 and 1863.[30] Five of the zodiac bronzes are said to have sold in a Paris auction in 1861.[31] The objects were subtly transformed when they entered the art market, evolving from exclusive works of Chinese art and craft to collectible commodities with both imperial and imperialist overtones. Those overtones remain today, but their nuances have changed with the development of a national humiliation discourse specifically linked to the stone ruins of the Yuanming Yuan's European Palaces and the garden's many looted treasures.

The Iconography of National Humiliation

China's concept of "national humiliation" (*guochi* 国耻), which refers to its military defeats, unequal treaties, and geographic losses sustained during the hundred-or-so years of imperialistic interest in the Middle Kingdom, developed only in the early twentieth century. William A. Callahan has traced the trajectory of this discourse, from National Humiliation Maps published during the Republican Era (1911–49), to Mao Zedong's speech founding the People's Republic in 1949, which liberated the new Communist state from its past humiliations.[32] After the 1989 events in Tian'anmen Square, searching for ways to unify public attention and refocus public energies toward a common (foreign) enemy, the government actively relaunched the discourse and visual culture of national humiliation as a mass patriotic education campaign. Beginning early in the life of a Chinese citizen, the Yuanming Yuan ruins are now at the core of patriotic education in national humiliation—or what might be more aptly termed "nationalistic humiliation" for the strong patriotic feelings it is designed to incite.

In summer 2010, in the leadup to the one hundred fiftieth commemoration of the Yuanming Yuan's destruction, children's live-action puppet shows were staged among the garden's ruins. Dwarf actors combined puppetry, martial arts, and slapstick comedy to demonstrate to China's youngest citizens that utterly idiotic French and British troops destroyed the gardens and stole its treasures. A spokeswoman for the production argued that the play was "very good patriotic education" for the children and accurately presented the facts of 1860, although she acknowledged that foreigners might well find the portrayals offensive.[33] Watching the play with their children, the parents in the audience might have remembered a different popular-culture use of the Yuanming Yuan as the *mise-en-scène* for youthful patriotic education. In 1981, the narrative turning point of Zhang Nuanxin's (张暖忻) well-known and important film *Drive to Win* (*Sha'ou* 沙鸥, Youth Studio) was set among the ruins of the European Palace. The despairing protagonist, a volleyball player for China's national team, has lost her fiancé, her health, and most important, a sporting victory over Japan that has sent her to the ruins to grieve. As the camera lingers on broken stones and fragmented decorations, she correlates her painful personal losses to China's national humiliation, renewing her life's purpose in the name of national service. At the cost of her own mobility, she coaches the national team to victory over Japan in the Asian Championships, symbolically diminishing the national humiliation embodied by the ruins—even though Japan was not a participant in the events of 1860.

Although the West's cult of ruins began centuries before, Chinese art and visual culture largely avoided portraying ruins until the late nineteenth century. In the premodern era, ruins were typically evoked only in poetry: Chinese art historian and critic Wu Hung has noted that classical painting, China's fine art *par excellence*, almost never depicted ruins because such images were inauspicious.[34] Western photographers arrived during the late-nineteenth and early-twentieth centuries to take pictures of the decaying European Palaces, simultaneously introducing the Western aestheticization of ruins and producing modern images that literally pictured the ruins of China's glorious past. No photographs exist of the European Palaces before 1860: it is through images that measure the site's inexorable decay over time that the ruins of the European Palaces became the domestic icons of China's humiliation at imperialist hands.[35]

The domestic discourse and visual culture of national humiliation embodied in the ruins began to be extended to its looted objects quite early in the twentieth century. A lexicon of "collective shame and personal grief" was employed by influential reformist writers to describe their humiliating experiences encountering Yuanming Yuan loot on display in Western museums.[36] But as China closed in on itself during the middle decades of the twentieth century, it is only in the last ten years that Yuanming Yuan loot in foreign hands has regained its potent symbolism through its sale in the world's auction houses. As the most easily recognized and understood of the looted objects, the zodiac bronzes quickly became the international icons of China's national humiliation. With China's new global economic and political power, their commercial repatriation has also become both intensely controversial and symbolic.

Politics for Sale

In the late 1980s, five zodiac bronzes suddenly appeared for sale at Sotheby's. In October 1987, the monkey and the boar were sold in New York after being on loan to the Metropolitan Museum of Art,[37] while the ox, horse, and tiger were sold in London in June 1989. Neither of these sales raised even mild opposition: certainly in June 1989, Beijing's attention—along with the world's—was turned toward the controversial events in Tian'anmen Square. More than a decade later, in April 2000, the ox and monkey heads were featured in "The Imperial Sale" at Christie's Hong Kong. Each was estimated at approximately $500,000, but sold for almost twice that at a total of $2 million. At Sotheby's two days later, the tiger head alone sold for $2 million, more than three times its sales estimate. Both Sotheby's and Christie's included catalogue entries and essays that explicitly discussed the heads' Yuanming Yuan provenance and the events of 1860. Despite protests by Chinese politicians and citizens, the sales went forward, prompting *New York Times* arts writer Souren Melikian to presciently predict that the sale would have "incalculable repercussions in the international approach to cultural monuments."[38]

All three bronzes were purchased by the Poly Group, a Beijing-based corporation affiliated with the People's Liberation Army (PLA), for the Poly Art Museum (*Baoli yishu bowuguan* 保利艺术博物馆).[39] A tiny space hidden inside the massive Poly Theater, the Poly Art Museum is the first in China to be operated by a state-owned enterprise. Its self-stated aim is "to develop and display traditional national culture and art, and to rescue and protect Chinese cultural relics lost abroad."[40] Exhibiting ancient bronze vessels and medieval Buddhist stone carvings in a few dimly lit rooms dedicated to repatriation, the Poly Museum charges an admission fee nearly equal to that of the Forbidden City, although the former imperial palace spans tens of hectares while the Poly occupies only tens of square meters. Although the Poly Group officially separated from the PLA in 1999 (due to a national policy ending military involvement in business), a whiff of military retribution hovers over the Group's quest to repatriate Yuanming Yuan objects.

At the time of their acquisition, a Poly Group representative labeled the zodiac bronzes "invaluable 'national treasures'" and expressed the hope that their purchase would encourage more of the heads to come to light.[41] That wish was soon rewarded in the person of Macanese casino tycoon Dr. Stanley Ho (何鸿燊). Ho purchased the boar head from a private Taiwanese collector in 2003 and donated it to the Poly Museum; helped sponsor a national touring exhibition of the four repatriated heads; and in 2007 privately purchased the horse head (fig. 71) for China from Sotheby's Hong Kong for a record-breaking sum of $8.9 million. Both the auction house and China's State Administration of Cultural Heritage (*Guojia wenwu ju* 国家文物局) publicly commended Dr. Ho for his indisputable patriotism.[42]

In February 2009, Christie's Paris included the heads of the rat and rabbit in a sale of works from the collection of the late French fashion designer Yves Saint Laurent and his partner Pierre Bergé. Sino-French relations were already strained by the Dalai Lama's 2008 visit to France, and the bronzes' sale intensified the conflict. The Chinese government formally complained to France, netizens made angry online accusations of continued imperialism, and a group of Chinese lawyers attempted unsuccessfully to block the sale in the French courts. Bergé further incensed the Chinese by announcing that he would return both heads to China on the condition that the government restore human rights and political and religious freedom to Tibet. But the controversial sale went forward, the zodiac bronzes selling for a combined total of $40.4 million to Xiamen art dealer Cai Mingchao (蔡铭超).

But Cai refused to pay, stating that he bid falsely on behalf of the entire Chinese people in order to stop the sale.[43] As an unpaid advisor to the National Treasures Fund affiliated with the Ministry of Culture, Cai was immediately suspected of acting with official blessing, but the government was quick to distance itself. Then a story surfaced that Cai outbid a legitimate offer by a Chinese executive in London who intended to repatriate the bronzes.[44] Reactions to Cai's stunt were roundly mixed: while some applauded the dealer as a patriot, critics argued that he prevented the bronzes' legitimate return, damaged China's reputation as a trustworthy actor on the world stage, and doubly exploited nationalistic fervor to generate increased publicity and inflated sale prices for the auction. The zodiac bronzes were subsequently withdrawn from the sale after the fact, and sources say that the heads were quietly returned to Bergé.

The whereabouts of the final five heads—dragon, snake, rooster, ram, and dog—remain unknown.

Repatriating the Heads of State

In the one hundred fifty years since the Yuanming Yuan was first looted, its objects have retained the prestige of their imperial provenance, which appeals to both Western and Chinese collectors. But for the Chinese, these objects have also gained a galvanizing *frisson* of nationalism that confirms a collector's patriotism as well as his or her wealth and taste. As might be expected, with China's recent metamorphosis into the world's third-largest art market behind the United States and Britain[45] comes "natural repatriation"—a term coined by Patti Wong, chairman of Sotheby's China and Southeast Asia, for the phenomenon of mainlanders building their Chinese art collections with top-quality and imperial objects.[46]

But to the delight of its citizens, the Chinese government has recently begun taking active repatriation measures. Soon after the rat and rabbit incident, Vice Minister of Culture Ouyang Jian (欧阳坚) stated that

> China will never consent to illegal possession of stolen cultural relics. How we retrieve them is another matter. We will never stop questioning the legitimacy of such possession, and will continue to seek the return of all relics stolen and illegally exported in the past by all necessary means in accordance with related international conventions and Chinese laws.[47]

In December 2009, an eight-member delegation of Chinese cultural experts, accompanied by a television crew from state-owned China Central Television, visited a dozen major U.S. museums to identify and begin reclaiming looted Yuanming Yuan items around the world. Sponsored by a Chinese liquor company, the nationalistic quest to institutions such as the

Horse head made for the zodiac fountain of the Yuanming Yuan, Qing dynasty (1644–1911), Qianlong period (1711–99). In 2007, this head was privately purchased for China by Macanese casino tycoon Dr. Stanley Ho at a record-breaking price of $8.9 million.

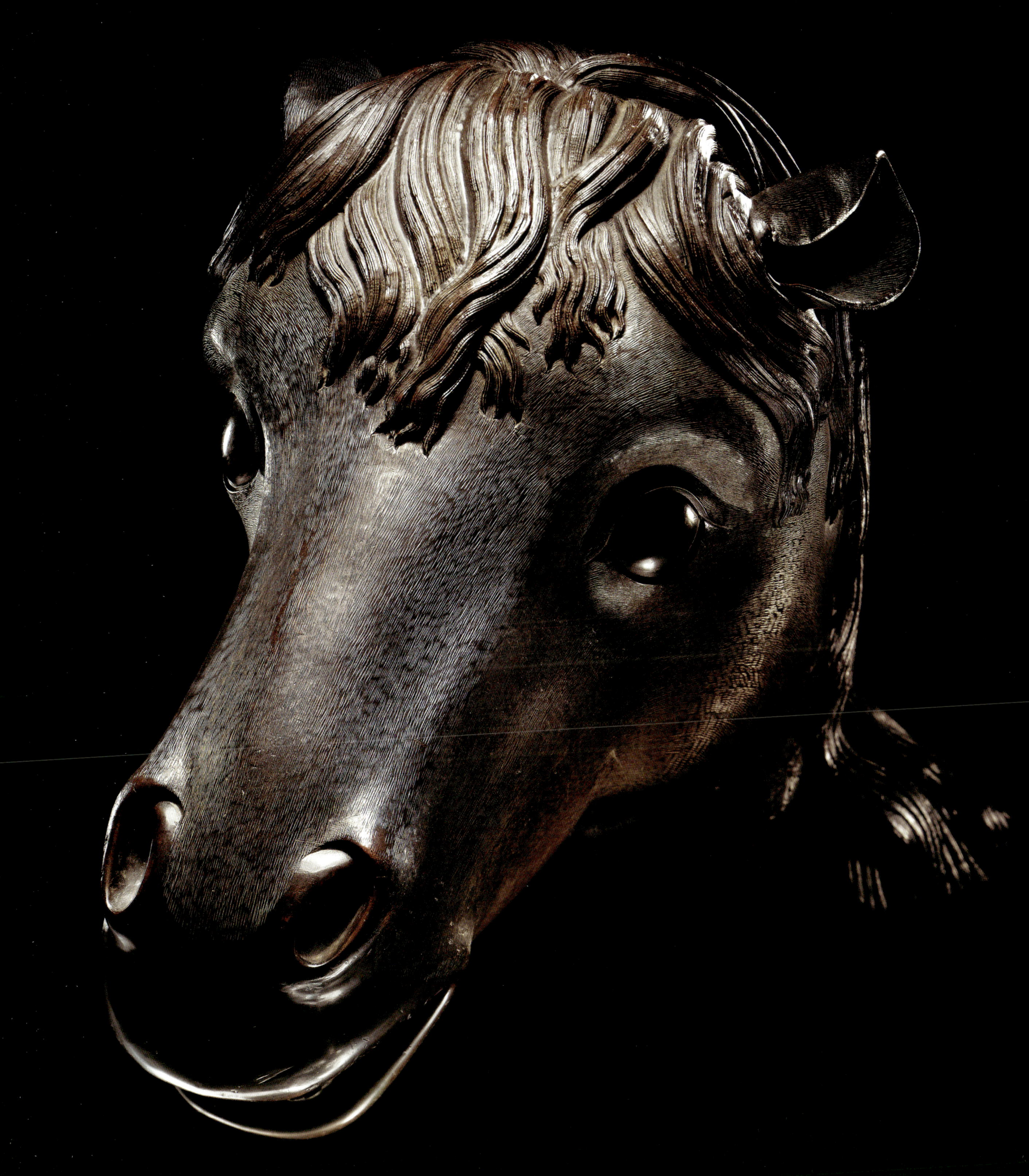

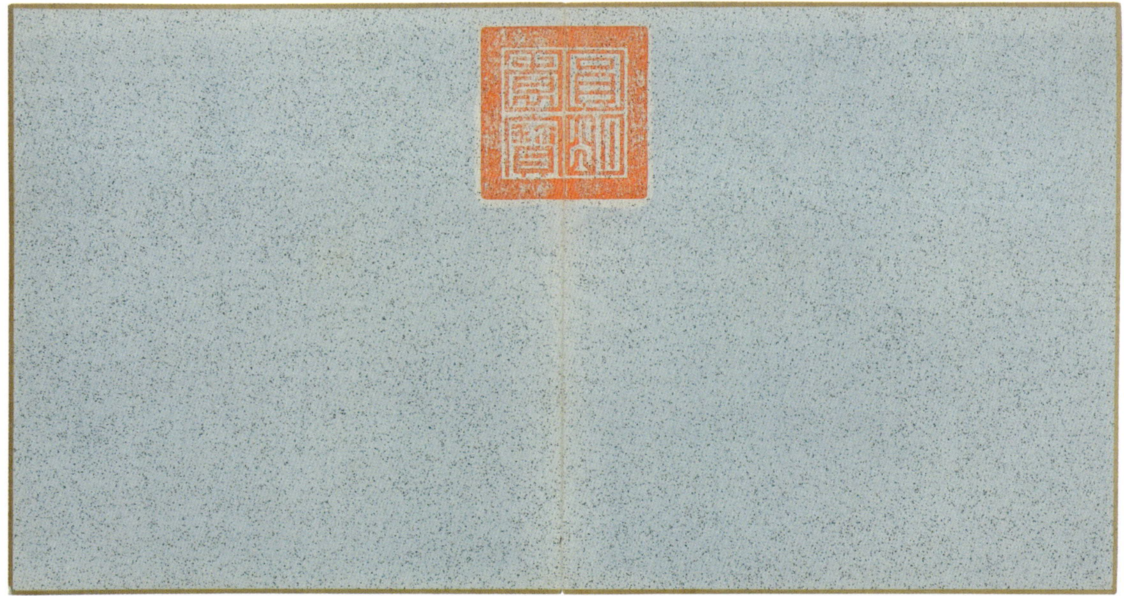

FIG. 72
Huang Dao (active
c. 1736–1795); Jiang Renshu
(active c. 1736–1795);
Men Yingzhao (active
c. 1736–1795); album leaf
from *Illustrations of
Costumes from the Qianlong
Court*, c. 1785. Ink, silk,
and paper, 16 ⅝ x 32 in.
(42.2 x 81.7 cm).
The Mactaggart Art
Collection, University of
Alberta Museums, Edmonton,
Canada. The album
leaf is stamped with the
Yuanming Yuan seal.

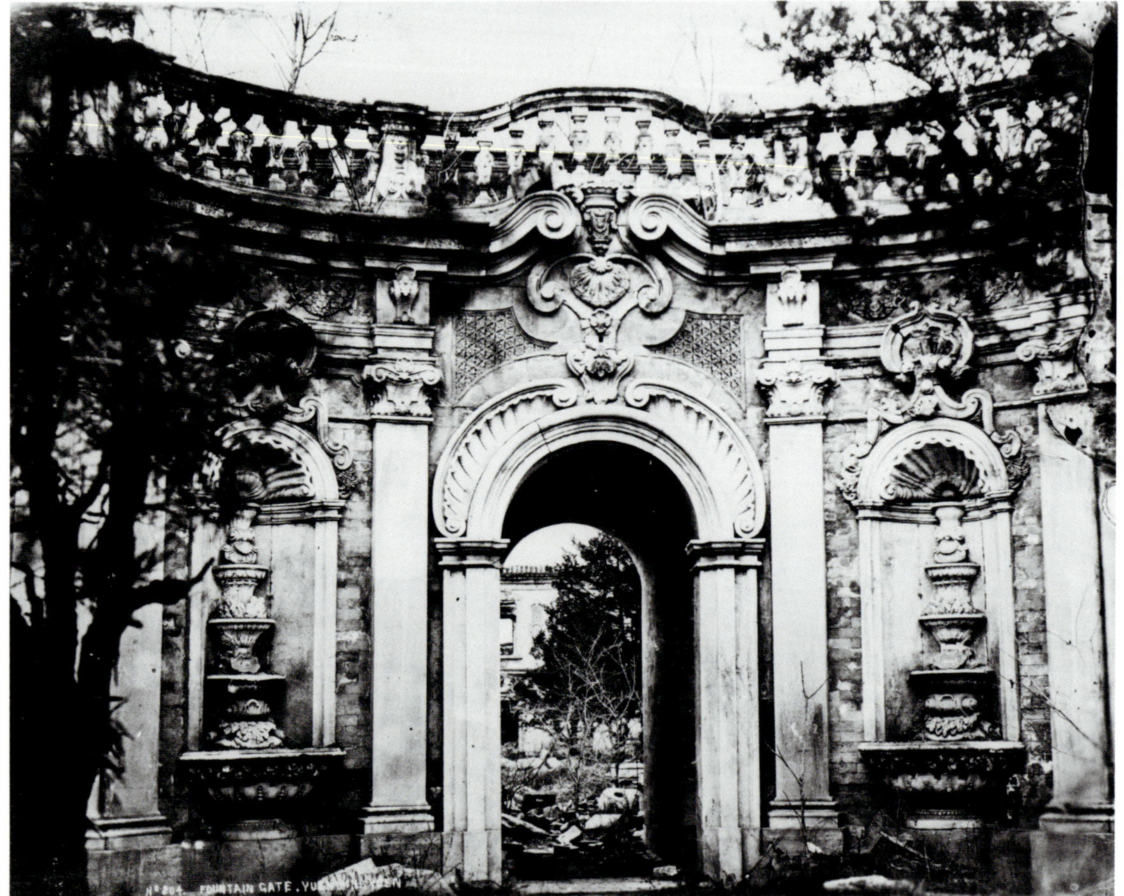

FIG. 73
Thomas Child (1841–1898),
albumen print of the East
Gate to the Aviary, 1877

FIG. 74
Ernst Ohlmer (1847–1927),
photograph of the Palace of
the Calm Seas (*Haiyan Tang*),
c. 1870–78. Wet collodion
glass negative, 6 ½ x 10 in.
(16.6 x 25.6 cm).
The ruins of the zodiac
fountain are visible in the
foreground, including a few
of the platforms on which
the animal-headed figures
were placed.

Metropolitan Museum of Art and the Smithsonian's Arthur M. Sackler Gallery and Freer Gallery of Art has thus far been successful only as a public-relations opportunity.[48] But one wonders what would have happened had the delegation arrived at the Metropolitan Museum in the 1980s, when the monkey and boar heads were on loan there. Or what might occur if the delegation should visit other museums holding objects with Yuanming Yuan origins, such as Oxford's Ashmolean Museum, which displays a tapestry that its text panel proclaims was "looted" from the Yuanming Yuan, or the Mactaggart Art Collection at the University of Alberta, which includes a court costume album (fig. 72) stamped with the Yuanming Yuan seal that "[distinguishes the collection] from other public and private holdings of Chinese costume."[49] This clear evidence of Yuanming Yuan *elginisme*—a French term referring to the act of removing cultural property from its original site[50] that alludes to the Parthenon's Elgin but is more than applicable to the Yuanming Yuan's Elgin as well—could begin to concern museum curators.

That the Yuanming Yuan's Elgin was a "second-generation cultural criminal"[51] is oddly absent from Chinese discourse on the zodiac bronzes. The Elgin Marbles not only metonymize the worldwide corpus of unrepatriated cultural property, but are also the eponymous examples of *elginisme* in action. If the

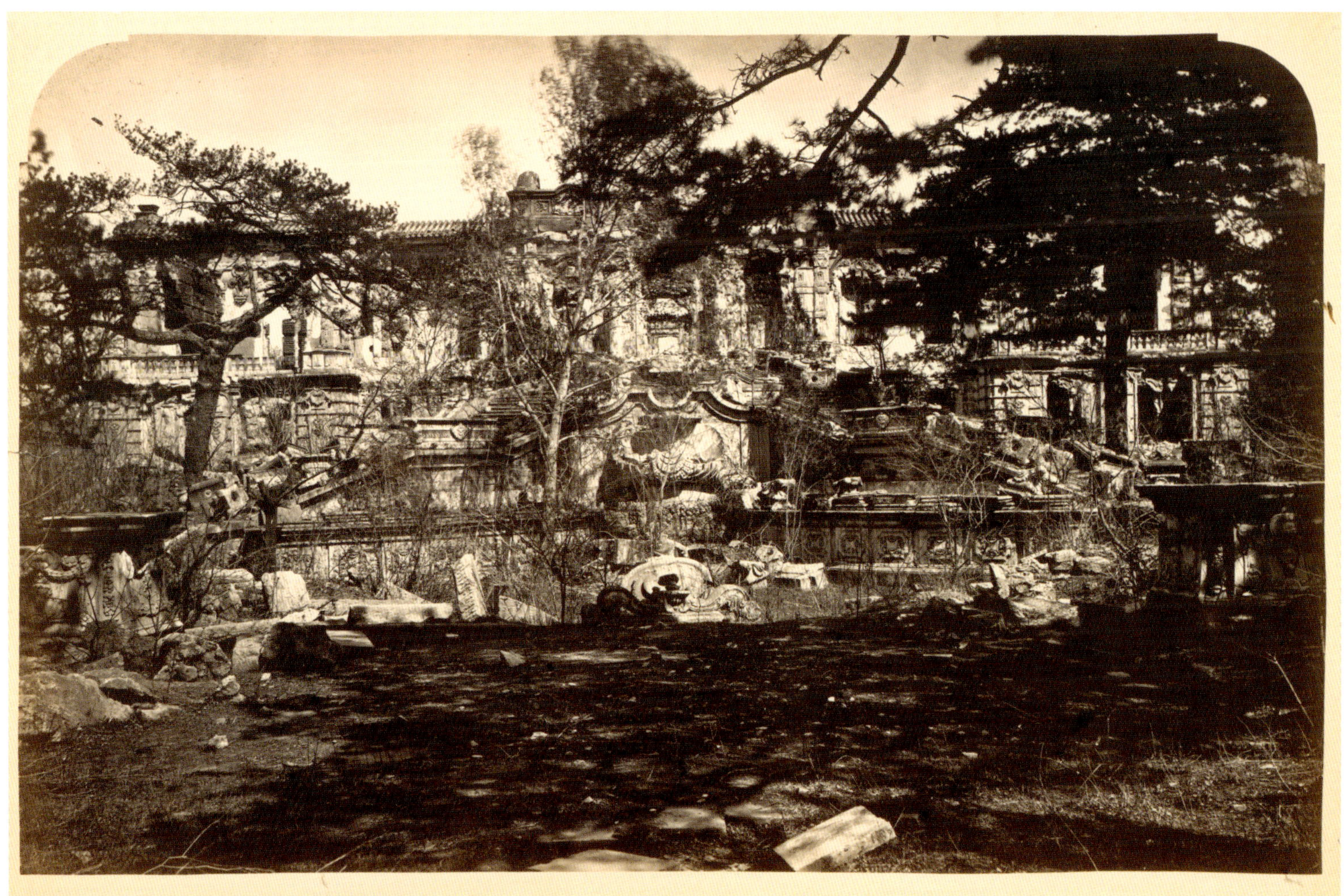

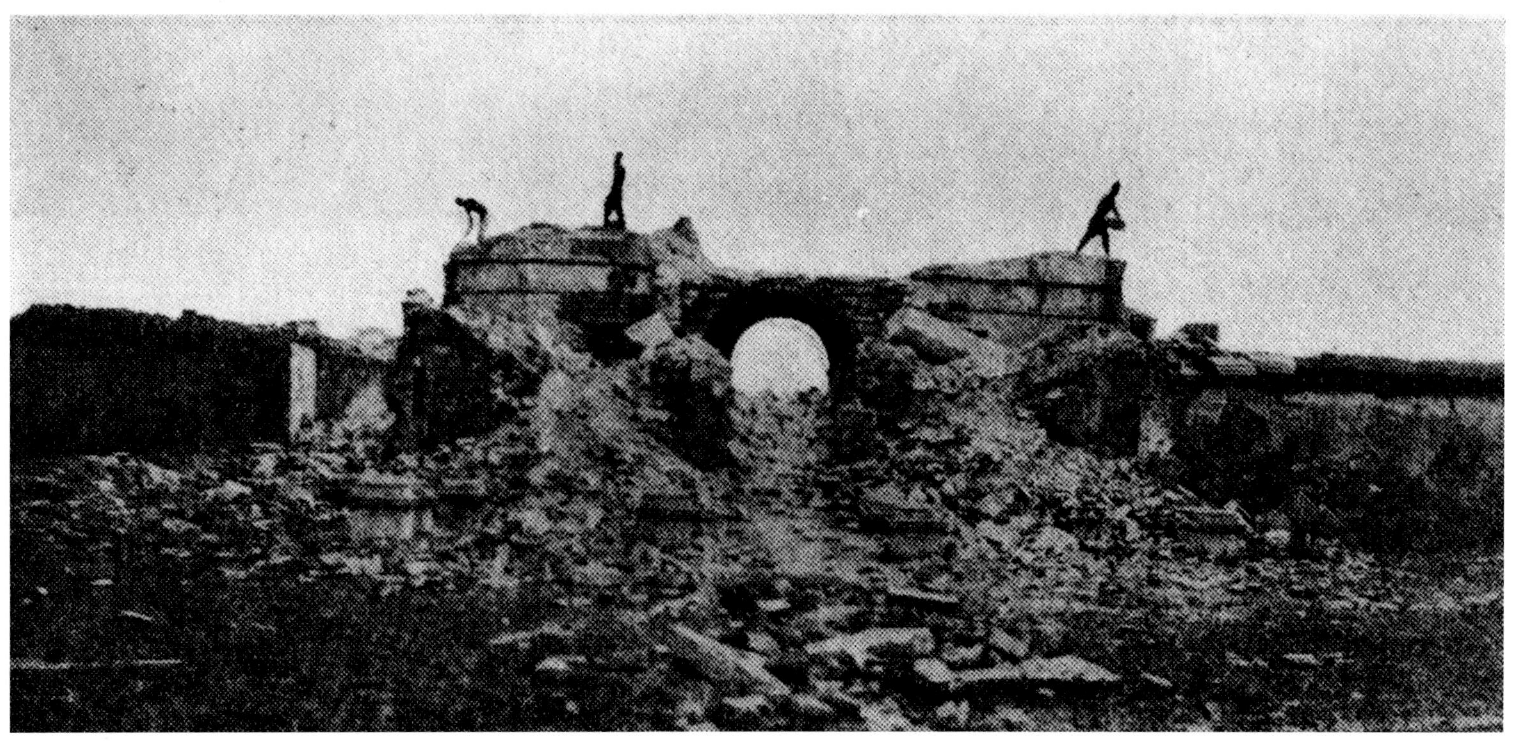

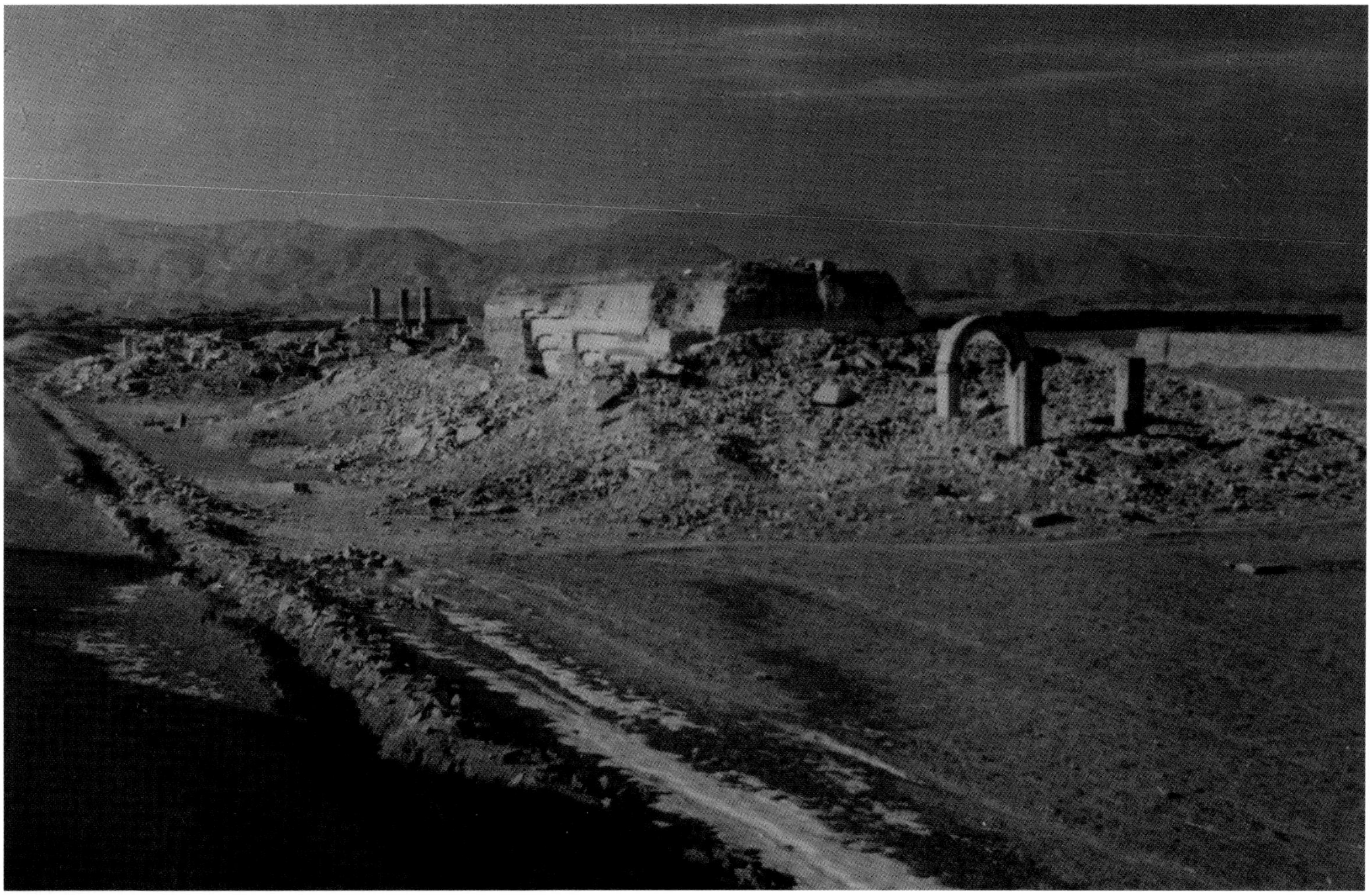

zodiac bronzes were known as the "Elgin Bronzes"—a name as wildly evocative and equally inaccurate as "Old Summer Palace"—it is not unlikely that the world would pay more attention to the issue of repatriating Yuanming Yuan loot to China. While both the seventh and eighth Earls of Elgin have been vilified for their actions, however, the same late-nineteenth- and early-twentieth century photographs that motivated China's cult of the Yuanming Yuan ruins reveal that the European Palaces remained remarkably intact after the conflagration (figs. 73, 74). Photographs taken over the remainder of the "century of national humiliation" reveal that the buildings were reduced to rubble only after 1860. The natural ravages of time were aided by the widespread dismantling of the buildings for building materials (fig. 75), so that only decades later could the site truly be considered a ruin (fig. 76).

As developers repeatedly try to transform the Yuanming Yuan into a theme park,[52] scholars and officials alike grow increasingly and publicly critical about the thousands of cultural sites that are destroyed daily in the name of urban development.[53] Some argue that China lacks both the infrastructure and the mentality required to properly care for repatriated objects. Researchers on the 2009 scouting trip indicated that an object in a climate-controlled Western museum might be in better hands there than in the spartan, unheated exhibition spaces that so frequently serve as museums in China—the Yuanming Yuan museum included.[54]

Among all the arguments used to justify the zodiac bronzes' repatriation, cultural nationalism is most consistently applied: the bronzes belong to China because they are Chinese. But because the European Palaces were designed from the beginning as an amalgamation of Chinese and Western culture, China is often accused of artificially constructing this cultural nationalism. The zodiac bronzes were designed by Europeans, cast by Chinese and possibly Manchu artisans, and created for an emperor who was ethnically Manchu. Consequently, they might be seen as what the 1954 Hague Convention for the Protection of Cultural Property in the Event of Armed Conflict calls "the cultural heritage of all mankind." Although China is party to all three primary international repatriation laws—the 1954 Hague Convention, the 1970 UNESCO Convention on the Means of Prohibiting and Preventing the Illicit Import, Export and Transfer of Ownership of Cultural Property, and the 1995 UNIDROIT Convention on Stolen or Illegally Exported Cultural Objects—thus far none have been applicable to the zodiac bronzes' repatriation. In April 2000, China lodged a request at UNESCO's Beijing office to halt the ox, monkey, and tiger head sales in Hong Kong. But citing the 1970 Convention, UNESCO bluntly responded that it could not assist in repatriating any goods looted from the Yuanming Yuan in 1860, especially from Hong Kong:

This property fell outside the prescription period of the 1970 Convention and it should be noted for the future that, when informing UNESCO of Hong Kong's status with regard to UNESCO conventions, China failed to indicate that the 1970 Convention would apply to the territory. The same goes for the 1995 UNIDROIT Convention. UNESCO cannot therefore help China to recover any cultural property, be it stolen, illicitly exported or discovered in clandestine excavations, [which] goes on sale or is found in Hong Kong. Since Hong Kong is fully part of China, the Committee has no competence for cultural property stolen in the past or future.[55]

Redemption in Bronze

The events of 1860 did not mark the end of the Yuanming Yuan's looting. Despite popular belief that the garden was irredeemable wreckage after the British burning, nineteenth-century records indicate that it could have been repaired. After a few feeble restoration attempts by the throne in the 1870s, the gardens became instead a seemingly endless source of loot and building materials for both local citizens and the imperial court.[56] Out of Yuanming Yuan rubble—and contributing to its ruination—grew the *Yihe Yuan* (颐和园 Garden of Nourishing Harmony), the "New Summer Palace" retirement compound for the Empress Dowager Cixi (慈禧, 1835–1908). In the twentieth century, the Yuanming Yuan continued to be scoured for profit and practicality: by foreign troops and defeated Qing soldiers in search of treasures after the Boxer Rebellion of 1900;[57]

FIG. 75
Carroll Brown Malone, "The Peacock Cage Being Torn Down, about 1924"

FIG. 76
Hedda Morrison (1909-1991), photograph of the Palace of the Calm Seas (*Haiyan Tang*) with the Western Hills in the distance, c. 1933-46. Gelatin silver print, 2 3/4 x 4 in. (7 x 10.5 cm)

impoverished former imperial household caretakers seeking objects to sell after the 1911 revolution; warlords and civil officials sourcing building materials during the Republican era; farmers and villagers desperate for cropland during the Japanese occupation and Great Leap Forward (1958–61); intellectuals requiring reeducation through hard labor during the Cultural Revolution (1966–76); artists seeking studio and performance space in the 1980s and 1990s; and developers lusting after the ever-growing domestic tourist economy in the 2000s.

Both aesthetically and academically, far more important works were looted from the Yuanming Yuan than the zodiac bronzes, such as the single album of paintings paired with imperial poems (fig. 49) that picture the garden during its halcyon days. This priceless album has survived only because Charles Dupin, who wrote so disappointedly about the neglect suffered by the European Palaces, looted it in 1860 and sold it in 1862 at Hôtel Drouot in Paris. Drouot initially offered the album at 300,000 francs in February 1862, but the public wanted ceramics and "curios" rather than the flatly two-dimensional Chinese paintings. After the album failed to sell, it was sold for 4,000 francs to a dealer who flipped it a month later at a 5 percent profit, selling it for 4,200 francs to the imperial library that became the Bibliothèque Nationale de France, which has preserved it since.[58]

Would the zodiac bronzes have survived at all if they had not been looted? Had they remained in China, would they have been melted down in the backyard furnaces of the Great Leap Forward, or destroyed during the Cultural Revolution as evidence of China's feudal past? Might they have been shipped to Taiwan in 1949 as the Nationalists fled the mainland ahead of Communist takeover with as many crates of Forbidden City treasures as they could muster? As much as China tries to smooth over the complex cultural politics of its twentieth century, during which many of its treasures were either destroyed or dispersed, a counterfactual consideration raises interesting rebuttals to the questions of repatriation.

China might draw hope for the repatriation of its looted Yuanming Yuan treasures from cases of major Western museums returning illegally or suspiciously obtained objects to their countries of origin, or from works looted by the Nazis during World War II being returned to their rightful owners. But beyond the necessity of locating the remaining bronzes in order for repatriation to occur, Richard Kraus rightly points out that these other cases are primarily intra-Western and not cross-cultural.[59] The major international repatriation laws invoked in the Western cases have been deemed inapplicable to Yuanming Yuan loot. And some Chinese have begun suggesting that the cost of repatriating the zodiac bronzes is far too high relative to the public need, such as for rebuilding housing destroyed by both urban development and natural disasters such as the 2008 Sichuan earthquake.[60]

But the language used by Chinese media to discuss objects looted from the Yuanming Yuan continues to conflate past and present within a personalized discourse of national(istic) humiliation. A 2009 article in *People's Daily* titled "National Treasures Scattered after Several Robberies" discussed not recent thefts, such as China's growing plague of robberies from tombs, archaeological sites, and under-guarded museums, but Yuanming Yuan loot in Euro-American collections.[61] Articles such as these demonstrate that what seems to sting China most deeply is the world's general ignorance of the Yuanming Yuan's history and its lack of interest in the twin issues of the objects' looting and repatriation. With every new Yuanming Yuan object that appears on the market, the fraught historical background is repeated in multiple languages. Yet as angry as China is about the Yuanming Yuan, its press is not generally willing to employ the same inflammatory tactics in Western languages that are used in Chinese. Until only a few years ago, a white stone "national humiliation" wall was set in the Yuanming Yuan, drawing visitors' attention with oversized gold characters that read "Never Forget National Humiliation" (*wu wang guochi* 勿忘国耻). After China won the 2008 Olympic bid, the bellicose anti-foreign language of the explanatory text panels set around the European Palaces was almost completely obliterated in advance of the Olympic audiences' arrival.

During the ancient imperial dynasties, acquiring a divine bronze tripod was considered an auspicious omen confirming political legitimacy and power, and the mythical vessels retained that identity throughout the history of imperial China. The zodiac bronzes have become the divine tripods of contemporary Chinese government, their return heavily burdened with symbolism. As China evolved from a "humiliated" feudal empire in the twentieth century into a formidable international contender in the twenty-first, the twelve zodiac bronzes remain emblems of their possessors' political power: while China lacks them, "the West" retains some intangible and indefinable superiority. But China's possession of the ox, boar, tiger, monkey, and horse heads confirms, at least to the Chinese, that the balance of power is shifting and China is inching toward a perceived victory over "the West" in a long-running battle. While other nations measure China's power by its economic growth and international influence, for China's own citizens it is difficult to imagine anything more symbolically indicative of their nation's might than the full reunification of the zodiac bronzes on their native soil. The bleached bones of the European Palaces may continue to symbolize China's past indignities, but should all twelve zodiac bronzes be repatriated to China, their encoded political legitimacy might just bring forth China's final redemption from all past humiliation.

1. Richard Curt Kraus, "The Repatriation of Plundered Chinese Art," *China Quarterly*, no. 199 (September 2009): 838.

2. The Yuanming Yuan is commonly, but incorrectly, referred to in Western languages by the evocative names "Summer Palace" or "Old Summer Palace." The true summer retreat, "Mountain Retreat for Escaping Heat" (*Bishushan Zhuang* 避暑山庄) was 250 kilometers north of the capital, outside the boundaries of the Great Wall.

3. Michèle Pirazzoli-t'Serstevens, "A Pluridisciplinary Research on Castiglione and the Emperor Ch'ien-lung's European Palaces, Part I," *National Palace Museum Bulletin* 24 no. 4 (September–October 1989): 2. The eighteenth-century European Jesuits' abilities were not lost on the British in 1860: Reverend R. J. L. M'Ghee noted admiringly that "[t]hese missionaries are generally learned in something else besides religion, and thus they beat ours out of the field altogether." R. J. L. M'Ghee, *How We Got Into Pekin: A Narrative of the Campaign in China of 1860* (London: Richard Bentley, 1862), 285.

4. Our knowledge of the European Palaces fountains comes almost entirely from eighteenth-century engravings, rather than from fountain pieces that have surfaced, like the zodiac bronzes.

5. "Extrait d'une lettre de M. Amiot, missionaire," Beijing, January 25, 1787, in *Mémoires concernant l'histoire, les sciences, les arts, les moeurs, les usages, etc., des chinoises; par les missionaires de Pékin*, vol. 14 (Paris: 1789), 527–28.

6. Geremie Barmé, "The Garden of Perfect Brightness, A Life in Ruins," *East Asian History*, no. 11 (1996): 126.

7. In particular, Jean-Denis Attiret, S.J.'s letter to M. d'Assaut in Paris, November 1, 1743, in *Lettres édifiantes et curieuses*, vol. 3 (Paris: 1749), 786–94.

8. Although the men were allowed to roam the gardens, they were not made aware of the European Palaces, perhaps because of the disrepair of the buildings even during that time. See James L. Hevia, *Cherishing Men from Afar: Qing Guest Ritual and the Macartney Embassy of 1793* (Durham: Duke University Press, 1995).

9. Maurice d'Herrison, "The Loot of the Imperial Summer Palace at Pekin," *Annual Report of the Smithsonian Institution* (Washington, DC: US Government Printing Office, 1901), 601–35.

10. M'Ghee, *How We Got into Pekin*, 212, 216; Robert Swinhoe, *Narrative of the North China Campaign of 1860* (London: Smith, Elder, and Co., 1861), 307. The Qing government later executed a few Chinese looters, and although a month's amnesty was announced in which imperial treasures could be turned in without fear of punishment, few objects were actually returned to the imperial collection. See Young-tsu Wong, *A Paradise Lost: The Imperial Garden Yuanming Yuan* (Honolulu: University of Hawai'i Press, 2001), 154–55.

11. Armand Lucy, *Souvenirs de voyage: Lettres intimes sur la campagne de Chine en 1860* (Marseille: Jules Barile, 1861), 107.

12. Swinhoe, *Narrative*, 305–6.

13. James L. Hevia, *English Lessons: The Pedagogy of Imperialism in Nineteenth-Century China* (Durham: Duke University Press, 2003), chap. 4; "Looting Beijing: 1860, 1900," in Lydia H. Liu, ed., *Tokens of Exchange: The Problem of Translation in Global Circulations* (Durham: Duke University Press, 1999), 192–213; "Loot's Fate: The Economy of Plunder and the Moral Life of Objects 'From the Summer Palace of the Emperor of China,'" *History and Anthropology* 6, no. 4 (1994): 319–45.

14. Hevia, *English Lessons*, 83.

15. Ibid., 85–86.

16. M'Ghee, *How We Got into Pekin*, 294.

17. Henry Knollys with Sir James Hope Grant, *Incidents in the China War of 1860, Compiled from the Private Journals of General Sir Hope Grant* (Edinburgh: William Blackwood and Sons, 1875), 194. Grant notes that he paid "fifty dollars" for the item, inexplicably not using British pound sterling notation in his journals, even though all the other prices he records were marked in pounds.

18. Swinhoe, *Narrative*, 311.

19. Knollys and Grant, *Incidents*, 193.

20. Queen Victoria received significantly fewer "gifts" from her soldiers than Napoléon, as the following discussion will demonstrate. I am tempted to speculate that the reasons are somehow connected to the restraining principles of British Prize Law, although the British "restraint" in the looting and willingness to burn the garden marks an intriguing contrast to the unrestrained plunder of the French troops who refused to participate in its destruction. But as the sources below note, the French felt a far closer aesthetic affinity with the European Palaces: it is perhaps unsurprising that they were unwilling to burn buildings that reminded them of French palaces.

21. Hevia, *English Lessons*, 86–87.

22. Charles de Mutrécy, *Journal de la campagne de Chine* (Paris: A Bourdilliatet, 1861), 2–5–26; Greg M. Thomas, "The Looting of Yuanming and the Translation of Chinese Art in Europe," *Nineteenth-Century Art Worldwide* 7, no. 2 (Autumn 2008), n.p., http://www.19thc-artworldwide.org/index.php/autumn08/93-the-looting-of-yuanming-and-the-translation-of-chinese-art-in-europe.

23. Antoine Fauchery, "Lettres de Chine," *Le Moniteur Universel*, no. 362, December 28, 1860, 1533–34, quoted and trans. in Thomas, "Looting of Yuanming," n.p.

24. Paul Varin [Charles Dupin], *Expédition de Chine* (Paris: Michel Lévy Frères, 1862), 240–41.

25. Hevia, *English Lessons*, 107.

26. Mutrécy, *Campagne de Chine*, 28.

27. M'Ghee, *How We Got into Pekin*, 286.

28. Hevia, "Loot's Fate," 327, citing *Illustrated London News*, April 13, 1861, 334, 339.

29. Guillaume Pauthier, "Des curiosités chinoises exposées aux Tuileries," *Gazette des beaux-arts* 9, no. 6 (March 15, 1861), cited in Thomas, "Looting of Yuanming, n.p.

30. Hevia, *English Lessons*, 93–95; Thomas, "Looting of Yuanming," n.p.

31. It should be noted here that the source for this statement did not explicitly note its own source of the information, and that, to my knowledge, no one has examined the French auction catalogues from the period specifically looking for the zodiac bronzes. "Chinese Art: Redeemed," *Economist*, May 4, 2000, http://www.economist.com/node/333230.

32. William A. Callahan, "The Cartography of National Humiliation and the Emergence of China's Geobody," *Public Culture* 21, no. 1 (2009): 141–73; "History, Identity, and Security: Producing and Consuming Nationalism in China," *Critical Asian Studies* 38 (2006): 179–208; "National Insecurities: Humiliation, Salvation, and Chinese Nationalism," *Alternatives* 29 (2004): 199–218.

33. Hao Ying, "Teaching Hatred Amid the Lotus," *Global Times*, July 27, 2010, http://www.globaltimes.cn/www/english/metro-beijing/community/events/2010-07/556386.html.

34. Wu Hung, "Ruins, Fragmentation, and the Chinese Modern/Postmodern," in Gao Minglu, ed., *Inside Out: New Chinese Art* (San Francisco: San Francisco Museum of Modern Art; New York: Asia Society Galleries; Berkeley: University of California Press, 1998), 60.

35. Photographs of the ruined European Palaces still fascinate the public. In the summer of 2010, an exhibition of Ernst Ohlmer's images was held at the Millennium Monument in Beijing.

36. Hevia, *English Lessons*, 333–34.

37. "An Important Imperial Bronze Head of an Ox from the Zodiac Fountain in the *Yuanming Yuan*," cat. entry for Lot 517, Sale 2030 ("The Imperial Sale"), Christie's Hong Kong, April 30, 2000, http://www.christies.com/LotFinder/lot_details.aspx?from=searchresults&intObjectID=1789540&sid=cc28b5b1-ae52-401e-84ee-7e0c74bd606d.

38. Souren Melikian, "Auction Houses Add Insult to Injury," *New York Times*, May 6, 2000, http://www.nytimes.com/2000/05/06/style/06iht-lon.t.html?pagewanted=all.

39. The Chinese name of the Poly Group (*baoli* 保利) roughly translates to "protect profits" or "protect benefits."

40. "Poly Art Museum," http://www.polypm.com.cn/english/bwge.php.

41. Wu Zhong, "China's Renegade Patriot Faces Backlash," *Asia Times*, March 11, 2009, http://www.atimes.com/atimes/China/KC11Ad01.html.

42. "Dr. Stanley Ho Donates to China the Bronze Horse Head of the Summer Palace Purchased at Sotheby's Hong Kong," press release, Sotheby's Hong Kong, September 2007, http://investor.shareholder.com/common/download/download.cfm?CompanyID=BID&FileID=132752&FileKey=5bd96326-5e09-4a09-8117-a73a45db3046&filename=132752.pdf.

43. Wu Zhong, "China's Renegade Patriot."

44. "Yves Saint Laurent Sale: Caveat Venditor," *Economist*, March 5, 2009, http://www.economist.com/node/13226433/.

45. "The Art Market: Made in China," *Economist*, November 27, 2009, http://www.economist.com/node/14996765.

46. "Treasures Reclaimed," *Economist*, November 26, 2009, http://www.economist.com/node/14941165.

47. "Ministry: Christie's Development in China to be Severely Affected," *People's Daily*, March 13, 2009, http://english.peopledaily.com.cn/90001/90776/90883/6613870.html.

48. Andrew Jacobs, "China Hunts for Art Treasures in U.S. Museums," *New York Times*, December 17, 2009, http://www.nytimes.com/2009/12/17/world/asia/17china.html.

49. "The Mactaggart Collection—About the Collection," http://museums.ualberta.ca/mactaggart/About.aspx#.

50. "Forme de vandalisme consistant à arracher les ouevres d'art de leur pays d'origine pour en constituer des collections privées ou publiques," in *Grand Larousse de la langue française* (1972), 1528, quoted in John Henry Merryman, "Thinking about the Elgin Marbles," in Merryman, ed., *Thinking about the Elgin Marbles: Critical Essays on Cultural Property, Art and Law* (The Hague: Kluwer Law International, 2000), 45. Merryman has shrewdly pointed to the Louvre and quipped, "It takes one to know one."

51. Kraus, "Repatriation," 839.

52. Erik Eckholm, "A Glorious Ruin and a Face-Lift Furor," *New York Times*, August 10, 1999, http://www.nytimes.com/1999/08/10/world/beijing-journal-a-glorious-ruin-and-a-face-lift-furor.html; "Facelift for the Old Summer Palace," *Global Times*, June 9, 2010, http://life.globaltimes.cn/travel/2010-06/540226.html.

53. *China Daily* recently reported that between 2007 and 2010, development resulted in the loss of 23,600 registered cultural sites from the SACH's list. Xie Yu, "'Missing' cultural sites number 23,600," *China Daily*, December 1, 2009, http://www.chinadaily.com.cn/china/2009-12/01/content_9081953.htm; Tania Branigan, "China heritage chief says building boom is destroying country's heritage," *Guardian*, August 4, 2010, http://www.guardian.co.uk/world/2010/aug/04/china-culture-cities-heritage.

54. Jacobs, "China Hunts for Art Treasures," http://www.nytimes.com/2009/12/17/world/asia/17china.html.

55. UNESCO Secretariat Report, Intergovernmental Committee for Promoting the Return of Cultural Property to its Countries of Origin or its Restitution in Case of Illicit Appropriation, Eleventh session, Phnom Penh, Cambodia, March 6–9, 2001, art. I.9, unesdoc.unesco.org/images/0012/001212/121239e.pdf.

56. Barmé, "A Life in Ruins," 136–37.

57. Evidence of the 1900 looting is the British Museum's Chinese painting masterpiece, *Admonitions of the Instructress to the Court Ladies* (*Nüshi zhen tu* 女史箴图), a sixth-century copy of a fourth-century painting by Gu Kaizhi (c. 344–406). The British officer who owned it brought the scroll to the museum in 1902 for an appraisal of the jade toggle on its wrapper, and the work was bought for the collection in 1903 at a cost of £25. While the family maintains that a "lady of high birth" gifted the scroll to the officer, this story remains uncorroborated, and the painting's long imperial collection pedigree is extremely well documented; cf. Charles Mason, "The British Museum *Admonitions* Scroll: A Cultural Biography," *Orientations* 32, no. 5 (June 2001): 30–34.

58. Thomas, "Looting of Yuanming," n.p.; Varin (Dupin), *Expédition*, 240–41.

59. Kraus, "Politics of Art Repatriation," 216.

60. Ibid., 206.

61. "National Treasures Scattered after Several Robberies," *People's Daily*, October 23, 2009, http://english.peopledaily. cn/90001/90782/90873/6792520.html#.

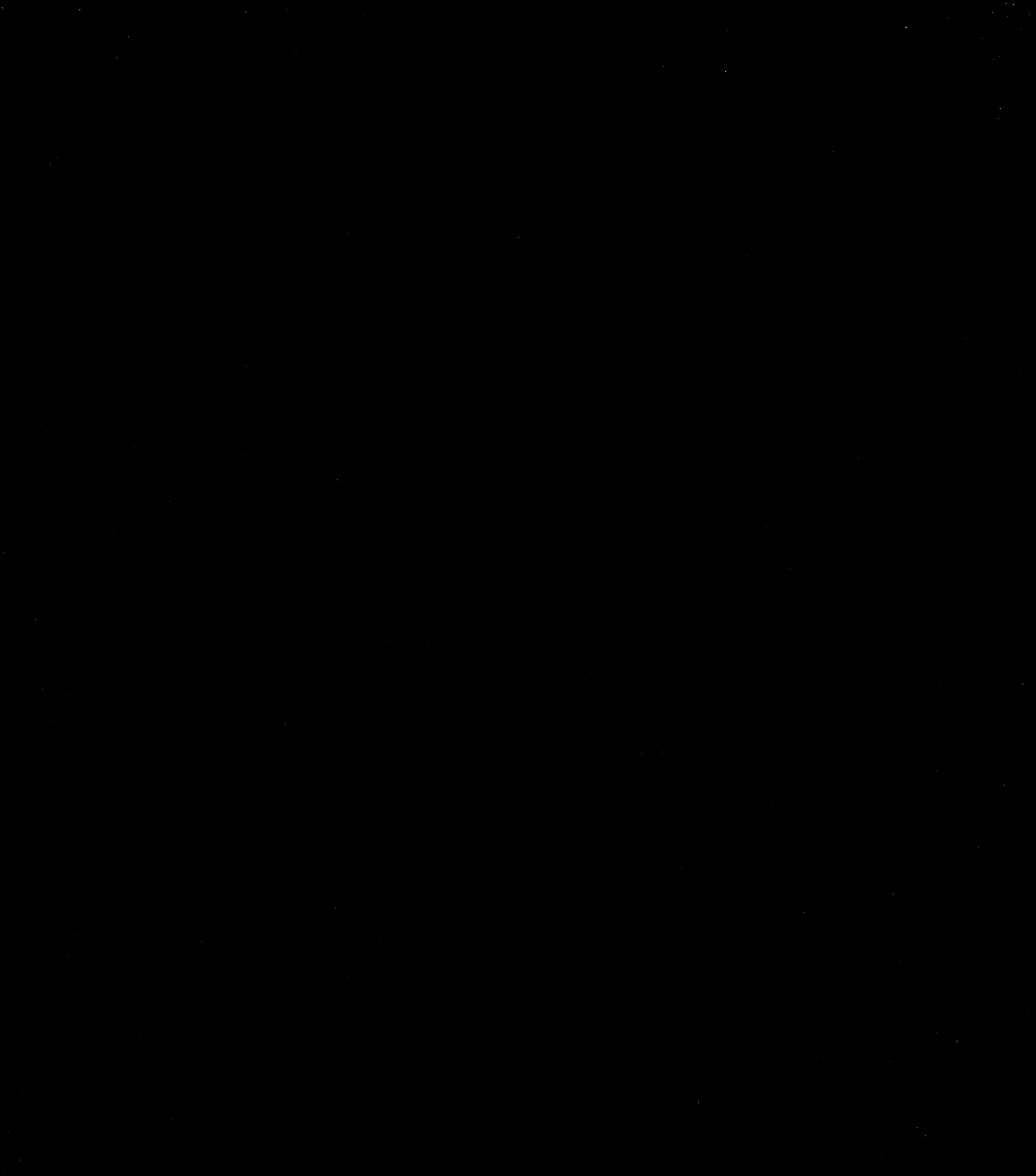

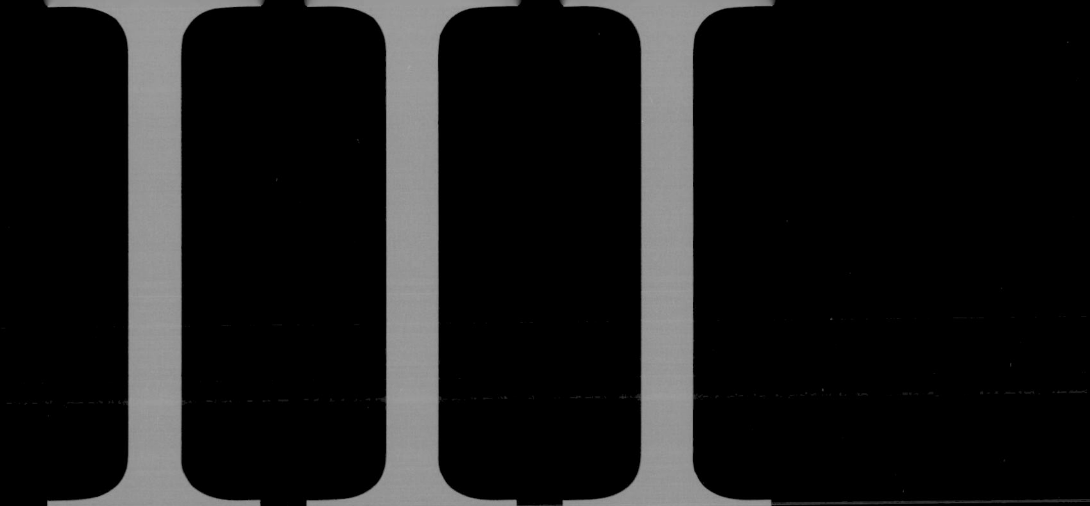

III

Part Three

The Heads at Auction: Two Experts Weigh In

7

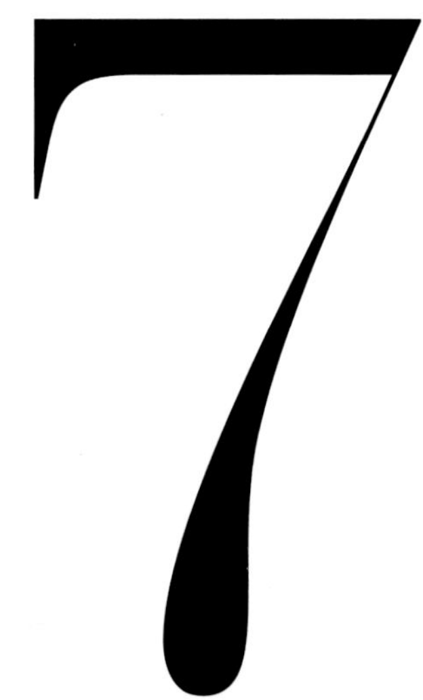

FIG. 77
Bronze rat head made for the
zodiac fountain of the Yuanming
Yuan, Qing dynasty (1644–1911),
Qianlong period (1711–99), on
display prior to Christie's auction
of the Yves Saint Laurent estate
in February 2009

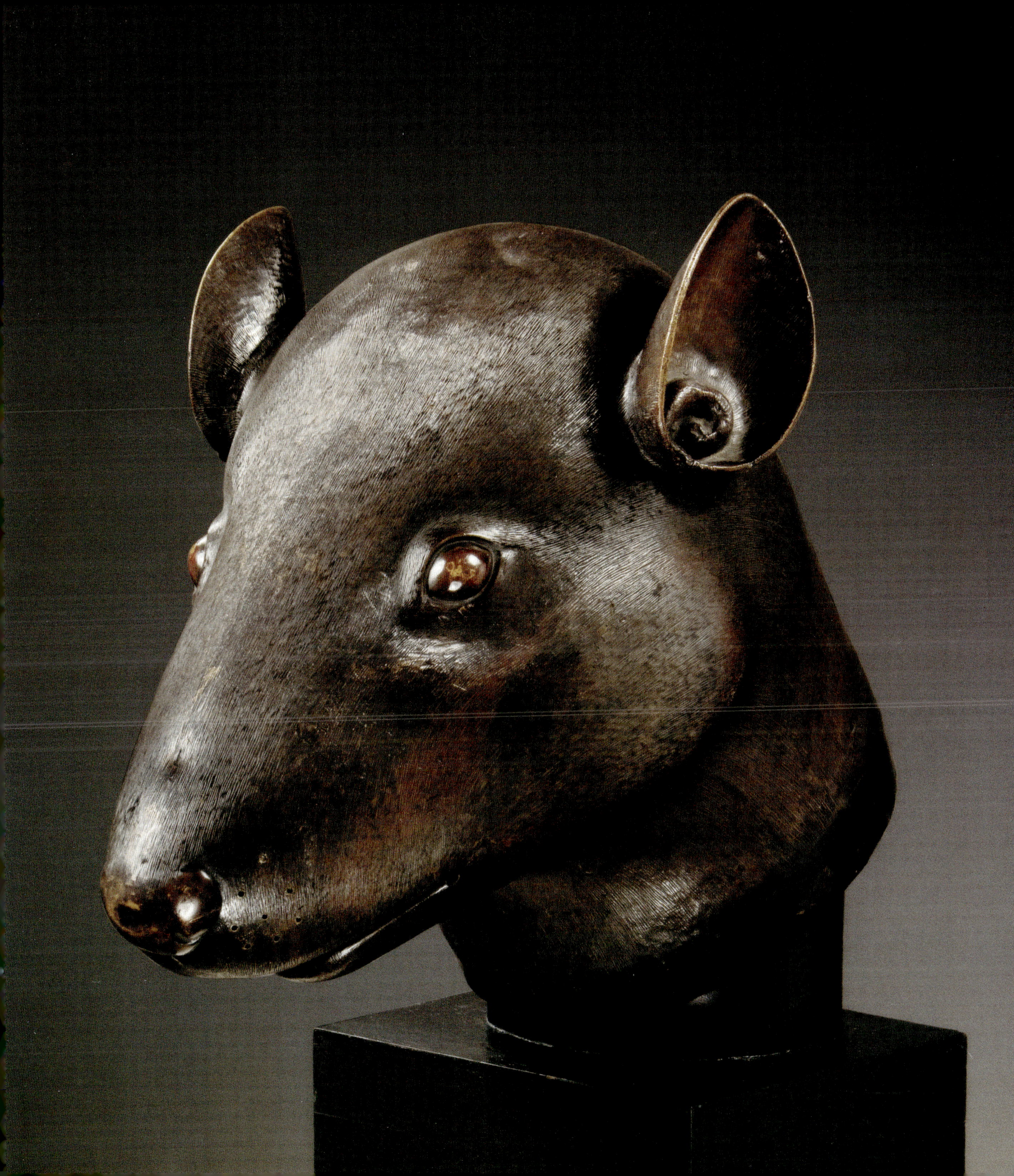

Lark E. Mason and Joe-Hynn Yang, experts in the fields of Chinese art and antiquities, spent substantial portions of their careers at major auction houses—Mason, more than twenty years at Sotheby's, and Yang, over a decade at Sotheby's and Christie's. Each was involved in sales of bronze zodiac heads from the Yuanming Yuan fountain, and they are among the select few to have examined individual heads closely. Here, they talk about the auctions they were involved in, the history of the bronze heads, the zodiac fountain, the Yuanming Yuan, and the significance of the heads today. Their comments are edited from interviews conducted in 2010 by Colin Jones and film director Alison Klayman for a forthcoming documentary about Ai Weiwei and Circle of Animals/Zodiac Heads.

The 1987 Auctions

Lark E. Mason: I had been working at Sotheby's since 1979, in New York. My job at the time was to catalogue and to find things for sale in our auctions, which we held on a regular basis throughout the year. I was called by a gentleman in New York who had what he said were some animal heads. He said they had been on loan to the Metropolitan Museum of Art but not displayed, and finally they had asked him to come pick them up. He had no use for them and wanted to sell them.

And I thought, Why are you calling the Chinese department? He said, Well, I believe these are Chinese. Would you take a look? And what he brought in were the boar and the monkey from what we now know is the zodiac fountain. I believe it was in early 1987 that this happened. So I did some research and called the people at the Metropolitan Museum. They gave me what little information they had, and then I started doing some more research and discovered, in fact, that they were part of the zodiac fountain that had been designed by Giuseppe Castiglione.

When looking at any artwork, there are certain indications of authenticity that one looks for. Obviously, now that these have received so much notoriety, if the missing heads were suddenly to appear and did not have a believable provenance, I think a lot of people would look at them with skepticism, because you'd be expecting that these things might be copied. But at the time, nobody was interested in copying them. There was no reason, and the process to make them would have been fairly complicated. Having looked at a lot of Chinese art, I knew that there was certain evidence of age that you expect to see on metal, which was evident on these. From years of

handling, touching, and working with something, there's always that kind of patina. And the type of workmanship was consistent with eighteenth-century workmanship. So they had all the characteristics that one would expect to see on something that was authentic. And once they passed that test, I was confident that these were what they purported to be.

In 1860, the sacking of the Yuanming Yuan takes place, and then shortly afterward things are brought out of China (fig. 78). Things are also sold at the market places in Beijing. These items that were part of the imperial repository are now out on the open market. They are being bought and sold and traded, and a lot of them were taken out of the country and became curiosities. Great works of art became mementos of this event, and largely disappeared. When these heads surfaced in 1987, what made the difference was that you knew they had been at the Metropolitan Museum, so they weren't hidden in a closet someplace. But what made the difference was bringing them to Sotheby's at auction, which provided a platform where thousands of people who cared about Chinese art and history actually had an opportunity to know what they were—to read the story, to know that these were from the fountain, and they were part of this clashing of Western and Chinese forces during this tumultuous political period.

It was impossible to trace the monkey and the boar directly back further than the current owner—the owner at the time, a Western man, a New Yorker. He had bought them many years ago, I think in a public auction someplace. He did not have any other information. That just disappeared, because I don't think anybody cared. They were thought of as decorations. That's what happens over time. The association that objects have with this turbulent past, or having been something that was prized by the emperor of China—it just receded into such a distant past that no one cared. So for the fellow who owned them, these were just decorations.

There was a mix of bidders at the 1987 auction, Western and Hong Kong Chinese. Ultimately, one of the heads was bought by a Western buyer and the other by a buyer representing a Chinese dealer in Hong Kong.

Bringing the boar and monkey heads to the attention of a large number of people made it possible for other people to re-evaluate their own holdings in this area, particularly when they saw that they sold for far more at the time than had been expected. I don't recollect exactly what the estimates were, but I think they were about $60,000 to $80,000, or $50,000 to $70,000 each, and one of them made $150,000 and the other

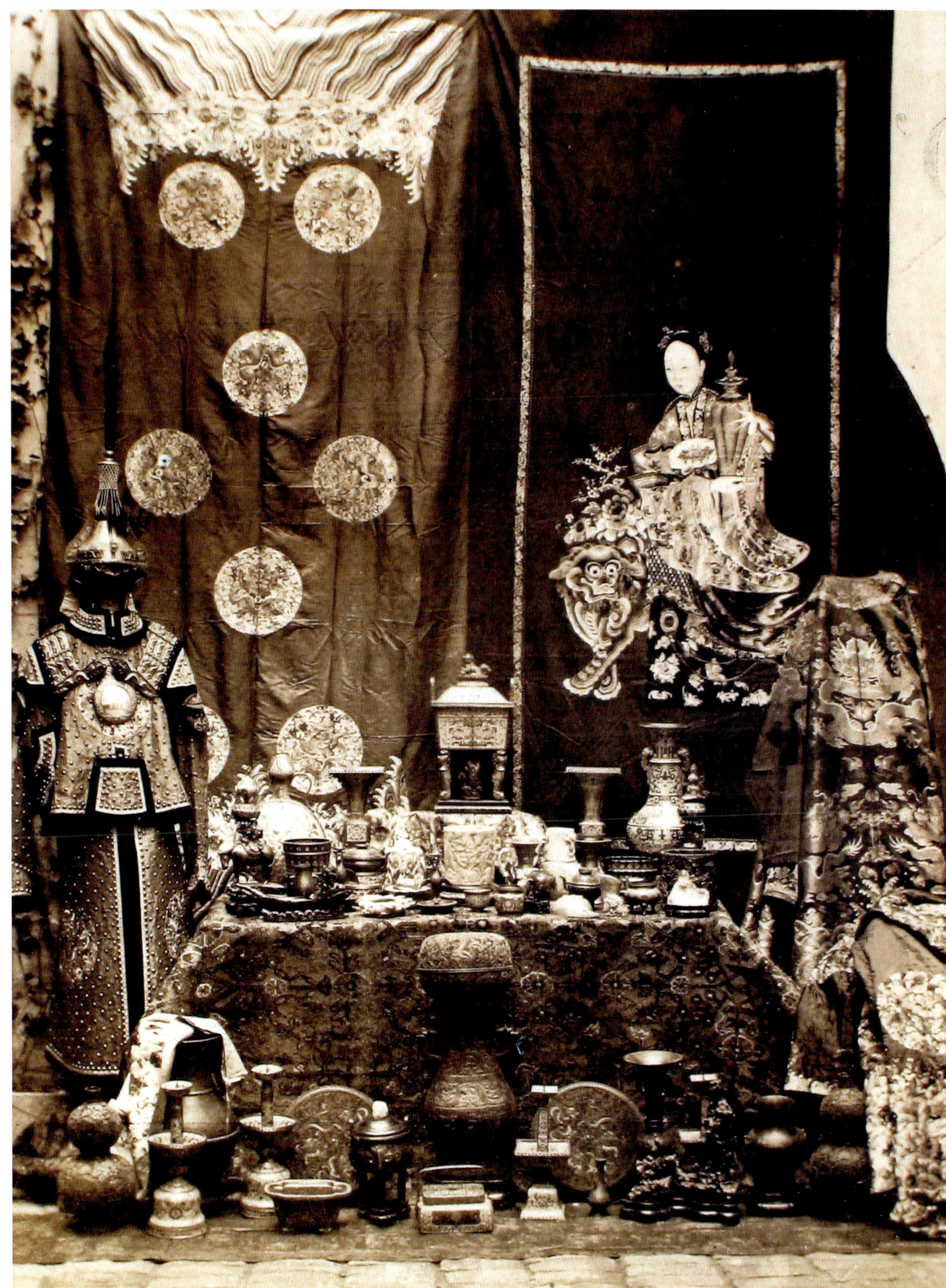

FIG. 78
Image from the catalogue of a sale of objects looted from the Yuanming Yuan, presented by Charles Pillet at the Hôtel Drouot, Paris, 12 December 1861. One of the first auctions of such objects in Europe, the sale was so unusual that it merited prints of this photograph pasted into individual copies of the catalogue.

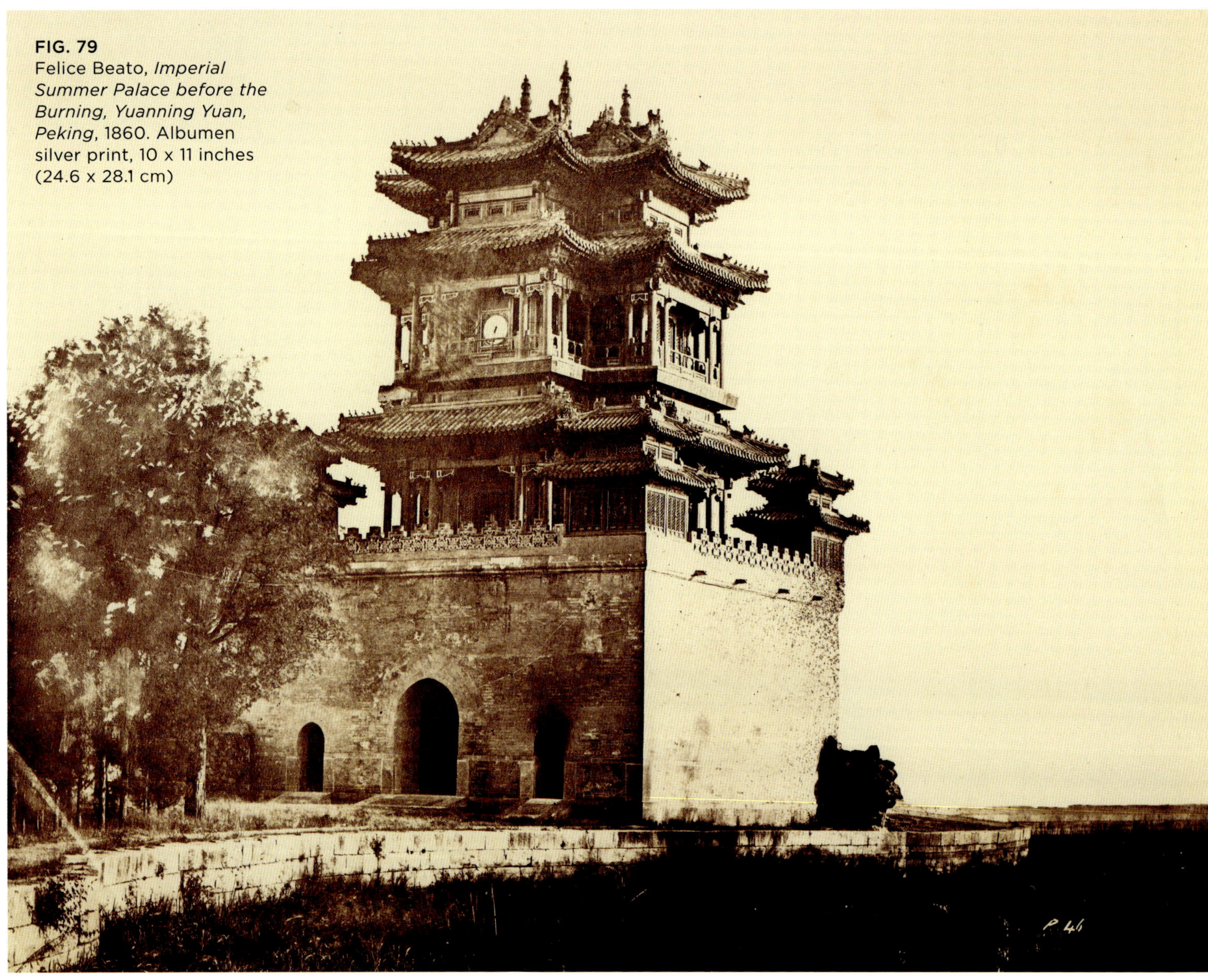

FIG. 79
Felice Beato, *Imperial Summer Palace before the Burning, Yuanning Yuan, Peking*, 1860. Albumen silver print, 10 x 11 inches (24.6 x 28.1 cm)

was about $90,000 or so. They made far more than we had expected, and that put a spotlight on them. Our press department sent the word out: look at these amazing prices for these unusual heads. And when that occurred, people started to pay attention.

At the time, I think we had identified where three other heads were. So with these two, we knew the whereabouts of five. Over a period of time, others started to surface. At this point, several are still missing. I assume that those are probably in somebody's garden somewhere, likely in Europe—someone who has not been paying attention to current events. Or they're in the basement of some small museum, and they've just gone unnoticed.

At the time of the 1987 auction, there was no real interest from China. Most of the people I knew in China at the time were uncertain what to think about the Yuanming Yuan themselves. Here is one of the great sites in the history of the Qing dynasty, which is also the site of an embarrassing political situation where you had Western powers coming in and destroying this monument, which had not been built in a Chinese style.

The 2000, 2008, and 2009 Auctions

Joe-Hynn Yang: Through my role in assisting the presentation of Sotheby's auctions and Chinese works of art worldwide, I was involved with the presentation of the tiger head for sale at Sotheby's Hong Kong in 2000. That really was the watershed moment, because of the galvanization of a community and an outspoken voice to try to win back so-called relics for the nation. It was the first time you could see a groundswell of opinion building online, through online newspapers and blogs. People trying to gather support to meet and protest the offer on the open market. Of course, this wasn't the first time these pieces had been offered—it was just that there had been a hiatus of several years since any of these Yuanming Yuan heads had come onto the market in the late 1980s. So perhaps during that period, people's opinions began to shift. I think the freedom of information within China, and China's own sense of itself on the world stage, started to crystallize in a slightly different way, and that found expression in the events of 2000—the tiger head being offered, and also the ox and monkey heads at Christie's.

The appearance of three Yuanming Yuan heads in the market after such a long hiatus was definitely the highlight of that season. Of course, there was a certain element of notoriety because of the protests—this ongoing build-up of tension, particularly with opinion pages that we could see online, or through the domestic mainland Chinese press. We could see this build-up of tension around April and May of 2000.

Since 2000, when the tiger head was offered, and the ox and the monkey heads, I've been lucky enough to also be involved in supporting the sale of the horse's head in Hong Kong in 2007. And then of course, when I moved to Christie's,

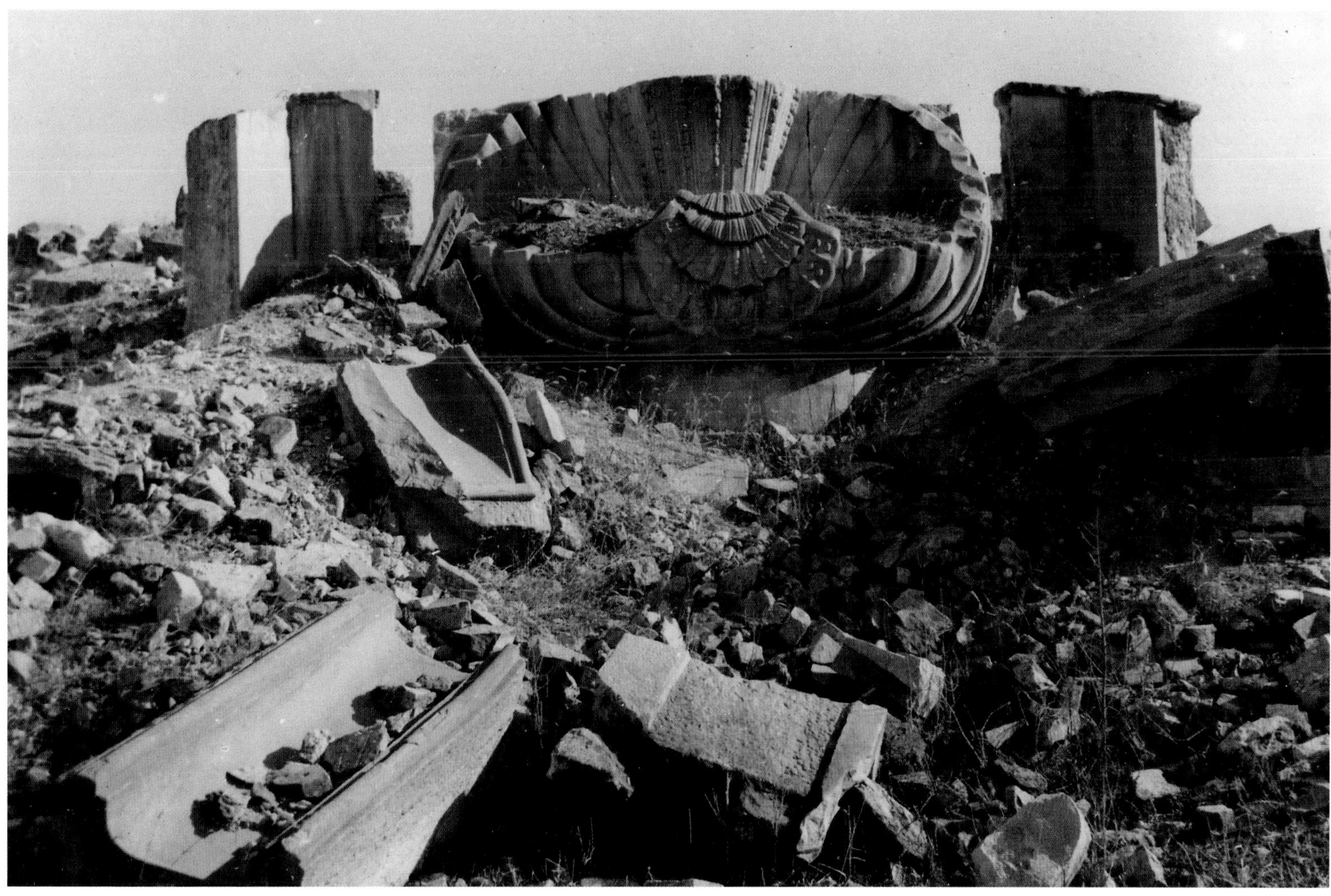

FIG. 80 Hedda Morrison, *Stone fragments with relief work at Yuanming Yuan*, 1933–46. Gelatin silver print, 2 ¾ x 4 in. (7 x 10.5 cm)

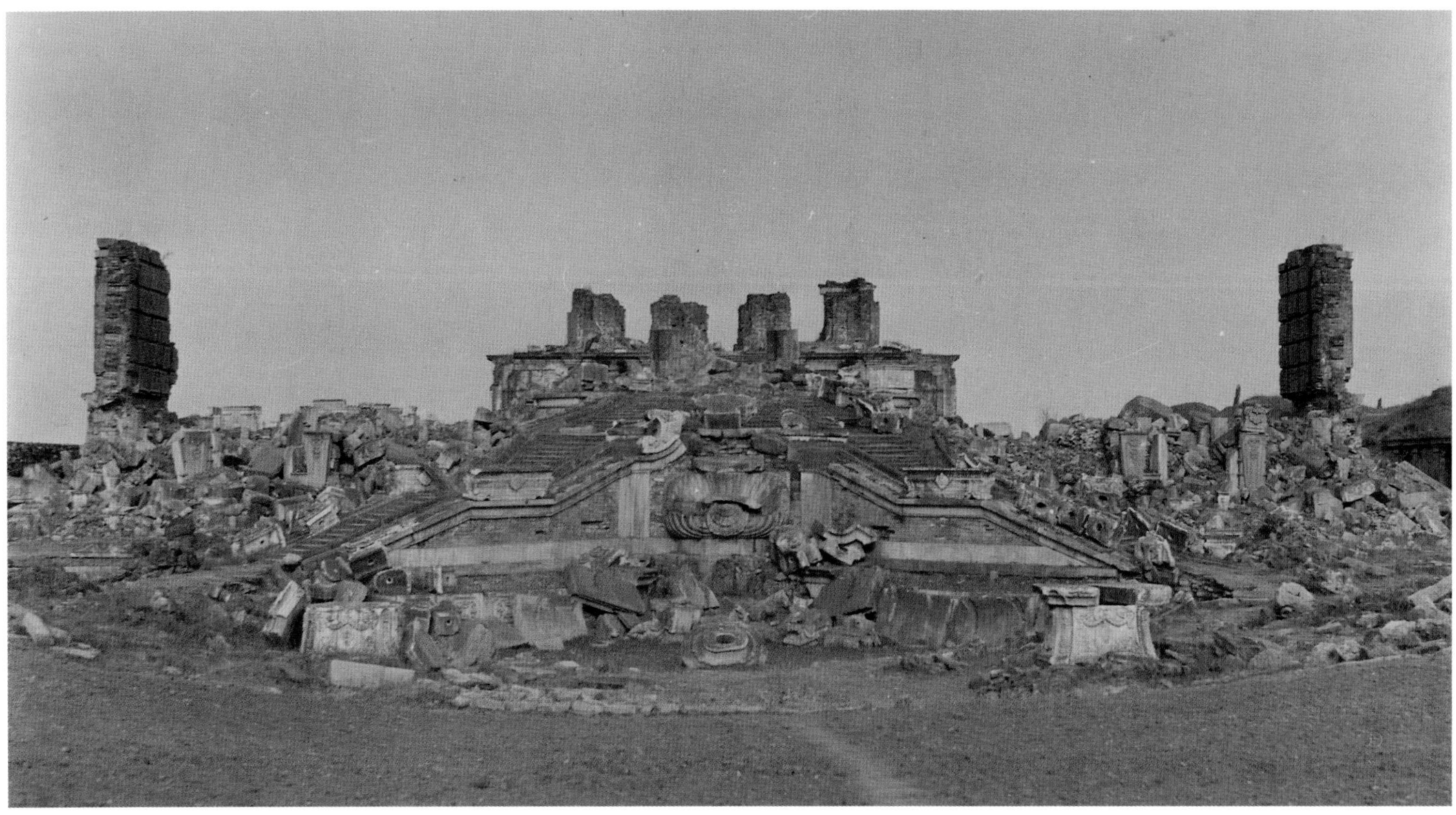

FIG. 81 Sidney D. Gamble, *Old Summer Palace Ruins*. Contact print from nitrate negative, 3 ⅜ x 4 ⅜ in. (8.4 x 10.9 cm) Taken in the early 1920s (c. 1923), this photograph depicts the ruins of the zodiac fountain before the Palace of the Calm Seas (*Haiyan Tang*).

having the opportunity to inspect and handle and review the rabbit and rat heads when they came on their promotional tour from Paris to New York at Rockefeller Center, in advance of the Yves Saint Laurent sale in February 2009.

Of course, now we know that the winning bidders at the 2000 auction of the tiger head were representatives of the corporate consortium the Poly Group, which acquired those heads in the end. But at the time, their faces weren't recognized by the larger collecting community of primarily overseas Chinese—say, people from Hong Kong and Taiwan. So there was a certain element of mystery and intrigue about it. They themselves were very excited, very eager, bidding aggressively and with a good measure of confidence. It was really quite interesting, and I think it marked a new phase in the auction market for Chinese art.

In terms of bidding, the regular progression of auction increments is perhaps 10 percent or so: from 1,000 to 1,100 to 1,200, and then when you get to 100,000 to 110,000, and so on. More aggressive bidding or jumping a bid is to skip those increments quite aggressively—for example, rather than from

100 to 110 or 120, jumping aggressively to 150, 200, or 250. It's almost as if you're trying to shake someone off your tail, as it were. You're leaping ahead of them in increments that are so aggressive, the implication is that you have such deep pockets that nothing will prevent you from acquiring this piece.

You contrast that tiger head sale in 2000 with the 2009 Yves Saint Laurent sale, where there was so much publicity leading up to it. One can see the difference, during that very narrow span of just nine years, in the handling of these heads. The Yves Saint Laurent sale was so much more of a well-managed public-relations process, where the protestors trying to block the sale already knew how to manage the press, and the successful bidder was also trying to manage the public relations in relation to that sale. And both of them doing it separately from the auction house, which was trying to control the message going out in general. Not only do you see an escalation in the dollar value of these heads, but in public-relations sensitivity about them.

I think 2000 was really the cusp. Before that, mainland Chinese buyers represented probably 5 percent of buyers within the worldwide auction market. The last decade has seen that shift from 5 percent to now 55 or 65 percent, which is a huge growth in the amount of buying potential that any one country has gained over any field in the art market worldwide. For one country to gain such a great dominance within a market, as China has within the Chinese art market, is really remarkable.

The Qianlong Emperor and the Yuanming Yuan

Yang: When the Yuanming Yuan was built in the eighteenth century, it had a huge impact on the imperial court. At the time, the Qianlong court was really looking to the West, so that most of the objects with Yuanming Yuan provenance seemed to have a slightly European flavor to them—in the gilding, the decorative motifs, the shapes. You're getting elaborate clocks, you're getting paintings with some three-dimensional perspective, works of art such as porcelain or cloisonné that follow European-style shapes and with European-style decoration.

When the fountain was made, it was already part of this architectural complex that was very much seen as non-Chinese. The Yuanming Yuan and that particular complex of palaces were seen as Chinese versions of what baroque and rococo European palaces might have looked like. It was very much a whimsical interpretation—like the reverse of the Sanssouci Palace in Potsdam, Germany, where you have a pavilion done in the rococo equivalent of chinoiserie, a Chinese pavilion but in a European style. Here you have in China, probably within the same fifty-year span, European palaces that are essentially the Chinese interpretation of what a European palace might look like, but set in Beijing and using Chinese craftsmen to build these pillars and baroque-rococo shells. So for the fountain to have been set in this context, although having a Chinese subject, it was very much seen as an embellishment of a Western decorative scheme (fig. 81).

Mason: They're Western animal heads for an amusing fountain that had complicated clockwork mechanical features. But aside from being a marvel of engineering at the time, I think they were largely considered to be just amusing. These were not imbued with any great importance by Qianlong. He would have just thought that they were amusing and attractive and would rival anything that the king of France would have had, which is probably what he was more concerned about.

The heads have changed from something that was just an amusing curiosity, sitting on someone's mantelpiece, to something of great nationalistic importance and fervor. Again, these were created by Westerners working in China under the direction of the court for the Chinese emperor. So there was tremendous collaboration and an internationalism that existed at the time that surrounded these and the other items in the entire Yuanming Yuan complex. It's not the objects that are filled with any particular meaning, it's the symbolism that the Yuanming Yuan has for a lot of people—as a scene of a great travesty, an incursion of Western powers making China submit to their will.

The heads are extremely interesting because they are this mix of Western and Eastern design, and it bespeaks of the commerce that was so important, then and now, between China and the West. And the tension that's created as these two cultures are mutually dependent upon each other. They were then, and they are now—that hasn't changed. It's that kind of tension that has been placed in these heads, at least in China. Here in the West, I don't think people understand it.

The Heads as Objects

Mason: The heads are bronze, but with a high copper content. Each has a sort of a little collar, an area around the base which was undecorated, where it would fit onto the rest of the body. Which presumably must have been marble or some other material—we don't know really, because all we have are the heads.

The surface on both the boar and the monkey heads was finely engraved and incised to simulate fur. You could see the little hairs on the fur, quite well done. They had this rich, coppery reddish color that had accrued over many years of handling, which was very attractive. They weren't particularly damaged in any way, as you would have expected if they were pulled roughly off the bases. But it's my understanding that they had been disassembled before the troops came in and had been put into storage. That would make sense, because a number of soldiers going in might not have been very careful in taking the heads off these things. But these showed no evidence of any kind of rough handling, for any of the ones that I have seen. There are no big dents, bangs, splits, cracks, or anything like that. And they are fairly thinly man-ufactured—the metal is quite thin, so it wouldn't take much to damage them. So they were well cared for.

Yang: Interestingly, when you look inside the heads, you can see sharp foundry marks—points from which, when the mold was being made, the bronze channels flowed, so you could get an even coverage of bronze all the way around a three-dimensional piece. So when you look inside the head, you see the remnants of lots of little spikes that have been cut down in a distinctive fashion. Some have been cut down to a greater extent than the others, and some are just left with tiny vestigial bumps. The interior finishing of these heads is in its own way very distinctive, and only the same person or workshop would have done them in the same kind of way.

Entering the Marketplace

Mason: The question is how many Yuanming Yuan artworks and artifacts were taken directly by the military officers and soldiers. We don't really know. Sometimes these items come up for sale, and they'll actually say that Colonel So-and-So or Captain So-and-So retrieved this from the Yuanming Yuan. There were a large number of items that were not taken by the Western soldiers, but were taken by the Chinese in and around the area—merchants who were buying and selling these things themselves. And they entered into the market there. So whether the heads came to Paris or not, we don't know.

Why would anybody be particularly interested in something that is an element from a fountain? It's not like this was a magnificent gilt bronze statue of Qianlong astride his favorite horse. You could understand somebody making a to-do about that, but this is a bronze fountain head of an animal. That's not something I could imagine a soldier being very excited about. It would hardly spell money. And they're big, so how many of these could you carry? Could you carry two of them? You certainly couldn't carry a number of them in a duffle bag, because they are going to get bashed about. And why would you do that if you had a choice of picking things of infinitely more value that are small? Why would you pick these bulky fountain heads? It doesn't make sense. I have a hard time imagining that you're some British corporal who's decided that he wants to take a pig's head home. I think his wife would have hit him in the head with it and been very upset.

Yang: There's an additional complicating factor as to why it's hard for us to really determine for certain whether any one piece really did come from the Yuanming Yuan, beyond the lack of records. During the dispersal of objects from Beijing and the fall of Qing government in the early part of the twentieth century, a lot of pieces were offered on the open market, and it became a selling point if the provenance were embellished by saying it came from the sacking of the Summer Palace.

So you're getting old invoices from Spink & Son, or you're getting old invoices from various English dealers at the time who were supplying collectors in Europe and in England. And also in America, where you would get invoices that would say, Came from the sacking of the Summer Palace. But you know some of it could have just been hearsay, could have been the source in Beijing, or the representative who was buying it from Beijing at that time. It was partly because Chinese art was seen perhaps as a little exotic in the West, and people collected these things without actually noting the record for every particular item. People used to buy things in bulk and trade them in bulk, and there's very, very little paperwork and documentation. That's just the nature of the Chinese art market.

I don't think any of the heads have much documentation. It's interesting that through most of the twentieth century, the heads have lain completely dormant. There's a huge break in what we understand to be the chains of ownership.

The Zodiac Heads Today

Mason: The twenty engravings by Yi Lantai that were done in the mid-eighteenth century were made in limited quantities and depict the architectural elements of the Yuanming Yuan European complex (pp. 14–15). In all those engravings, as far as I am aware, the only works of art that are separate, have survived, and are traded as commodities are these animal heads. The only things. The rest of it is rubble that is part of the Yuanming Yuan park. We don't have depictions of the interiors showing the Western tapestries and the great Western works of art that Qianlong received, the great Chinese works of art that were there, the Chinese artworks inside the palace that were made in a Western style—the jades, the bronzes, the paintings, all types of things that were there. We don't have pictures of those. We have a picture of the fountain, and it's easy to see the heads. That is why these have been singled out.

We had this Yi Lantai engraving at Sotheby's. Qianlong had them made as if to say: "I'm very proud of this complex. I'm proud that I am an internationalist, that I have artwork that is Chinese and European and Italian and English and everything in here because I am a man of world. I am on the world stage standing astride everything." That's what he was trying to communicate. He had a Western, European-designed palace with Chinese elements for that reason. He was proud in proclaiming that to the world, because he wanted to dominate in commerce and in art and whatever. He wanted to be recognized for his achievements and influence. There was this great struggle over who was going to be the dominant trading country power at the time. It sounds familiar, doesn't it? Two hundred and something years later, it's not very different.

I think nothing would be better than to assemble all twelve bronze heads and have them back in China. I think that would be fantastic, and I would love to see the day. But pulling them back together is a tough thing to do. In a way, it's great that they've been dispersed, because it helps tell the story of the internationalism of the Chinese court, the Chinese government in the late eighteenth century, to the rest of the world—that it was not, as has been so often depicted, just an insular little inward-looking place. Although there certainly were those elements. But there were also the elements of people who wanted to trade and expand and reach out to other cultures and have an understanding of those cultures.

Yang: At the time it was built, the Yuanming Yuan was very influential in general popular culture, which was the culture of the imperial court. Then, when the Yuanming Yuan heads were sacked, that also had a huge impact on the general culture at the time. As these key objects were trickling out through the art market, China's vision of itself and its sense of self-importance were cut to the quick, really beaten down.

And of course now, in the early decades of the twenty-first century, we're seeing a resurgent China—China in a completely different position from where it was in the nineteenth century. So the Yuanming Yuan heads again have a strong role in popular culture. Because here you have people affiliating themselves with a resurgent China, a China that deserves to hold onto its past in a big way. Just the link to history, to the Yuanming Yuan, becomes such a key touchstone—or a key flashpoint really—for the Chinese sense of national pride. And regaining pieces of art that had an affiliation with this particular site suddenly becomes a point of national pride. A site that looked to the West, was influenced by the West, now takes on a pivotal role in the Chinese conception of its own stature in the year 2010 in relation to the West.

Why is it that China begins to see itself in terms of objects again, and in terms of the validity of objects of its own national past? It's interesting to contrast that with China's more recent history, because you're getting a lot of people of an older generation who were Red Guards before, and successive generations who didn't have much in terms of physical possessions. Possessions were basically communal, and private ownership of anything was really not condoned. Once the society opens up through the mid-1980s and starts to focus on the right of individuals to own things, people start to have a sense of control over their own income, their career and family, the future of their children, their own destiny. Once they start having that level of individual ownership over their destiny and their future, you see them turning back to the past. A general re-evaluation of various objects and the connotations that these objects had.

It is interesting to note that it is during the 1980s you're starting to see domestic auction houses being founded in China itself. You're starting to see an art market supported by specific companies. Of course, art had been traded throughout China's history—scholars traded scrolls, people bought paintings and calligraphy. You're always going to have this trait of collecting in China's past.

There was an attempt to break that chain during the Cultural Revolution, with the destruction of many, many objects. But now, that tendency to focus on objects and what they can say about you and your status within society is starting to come back in a big way. People are now saying, Why don't I build a collection? Why can't my eye, the expression of my self and my interests, my own aesthetic taste—why can't that be an embellishment to my status as well?

In their own way, art objects that have lasted for many hundreds or thousands of years have endured cycles of natural disasters, multiple changes of ownerships, cycles of political structure and economic contraction, and various things. These art objects have an enduring sense of history, imbued in the objects themselves. Perhaps the act of owning these kinds of objects is an attempt to link directly into that sense of enduring. Art endures. Collections endure. Things, objects, in their own way last.

The Zodiac Heads and the Auction Block

8

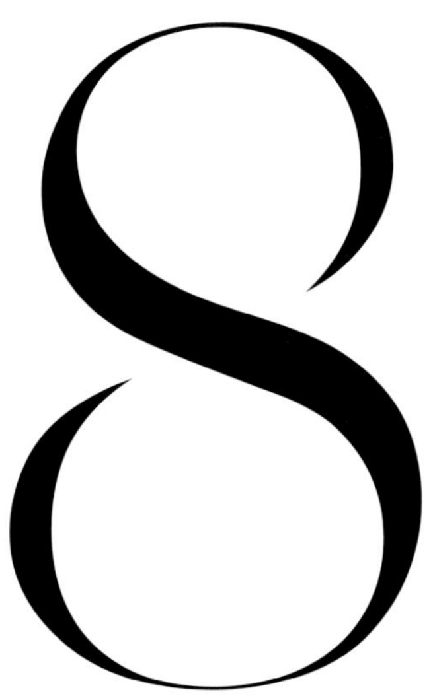

FIG. 82
The auction of the
bronze rat head from the
Yuanming Yuan fountain
on February 25, 2009,
during the Christie's
sale of the Yves Saint
Laurent estate

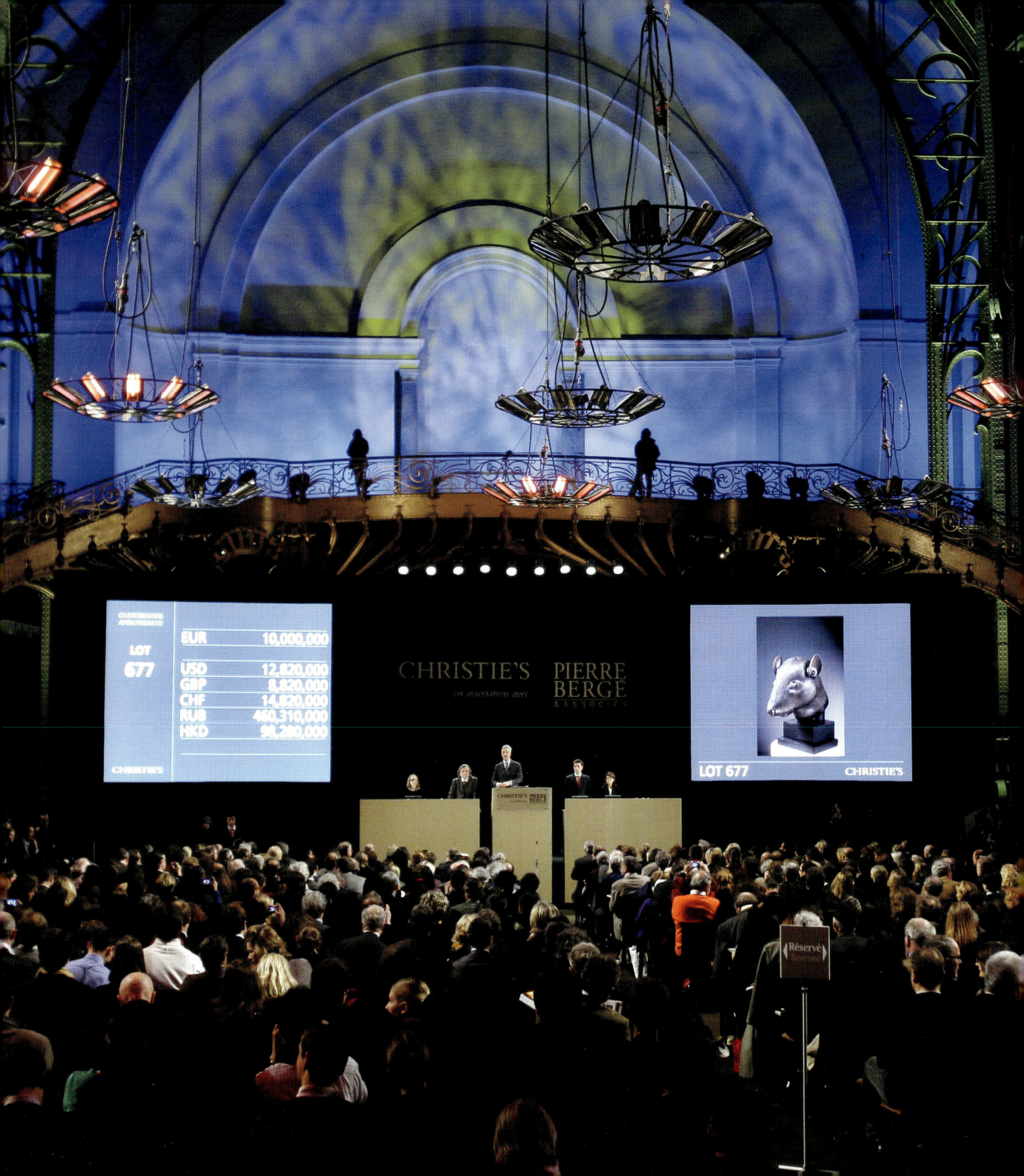
CONVERSIONS
APPROXIMATIVE
LOT
677
EUR   10,000,000
USD   12,820,000
GBP   8,820,000
CHF   14,820,000
RUB   460,310,000
HKD   98,200,000
CHRISTIE'S
CHRISTIE'S   PIERRE BERGÉ
en association avec   & ASSOCIÉS
LOT 677   CHRISTIE'S
Réservé

IN LATE FEBRUARY 2009, THE BRONZE HEADS OF A RAT and a rabbit went up for auction in Paris and quickly became a cause célèbre. Through the high tide of the Qing dynasty, these heads, along with ten others comprising the Chinese zodiac, had kept vigil over a carved stone fountain in the northeast corner of the Yuanming Yuan, an imperial getaway just outside Beijing. In 1860, the Yuanming Yuan was burned and looted by British and French troops. Its destruction was the last violent act of the Second Opium War (1856–60). In the aftermath, the heads slipped into anonymity. Some might have left China with the departing Europeans. Others may have been sold off by enterprising locals. Some might have been melted down— there's no way of knowing. For more than a century, the heads moved through private art markets. Then, in 1987, two appeared at a Sotheby's auction in New York. Since that time, for reasons only tenuously related to their artistic merit, these twelve sculptures have become to China what the Elgin Marbles are to Greece: the nation's most sought-after national treasures and a reminder of past ignominy at the hands of foreign power. As of February 2009, the whereabouts of only seven heads were known. Five of them had already been returned to Beijing. This made the rat and the rabbit into objects of international contention, even if, objectively speaking, they were little more than decorative art.

Before the Paris auction, the two heads had belonged to the late Yves Saint Laurent, the haute-couture luminary who introduced the suit jacket to women's fashion and had named every bulldog he owned Moujik. Saint Laurent's funeral in June 2008 was a somber event. French President Nicolas Sarkozy, Madame Bernadette Chirac, and one thousand others turned out. The eulogy was delivered by Saint Laurent's partner, Pierre Bergé. "It's the last time I speak to you, Yves," the aged industrialist began. "I remember your first collection under your name and the tears at the end. Then the years passed. Oh, how they passed quickly".[1]

Eight months later came the estate sale, and by then, the tone had become distinctly festive. Saint Laurent was gone, but his collection of art remained—and his collection was

marvelous! Since the designer launched his own fashion house in 1962, he and Bergé had accumulated a quantity of art and curios that could have easily rivaled a wing of Versailles. Their Left Bank flat and pied-à-terre in New York were caverns of luxury, storehouses for objects that spanned antiquity to Art Deco. There were works by Matisse, Picasso, and Duchamp, among others, and, of course, there were the rat and the rabbit. It would take three days to sell every piece, more than seven hundred objects in all. To house the anticipated crowds, Christie's rented a giant hall of ironwork and marble in the center of Paris, the Grand Palais. According to the auction house, the rat and the rabbit were the "superlative pieces of Asian art" in Saint Laurent's collection.[2] In fact, they were designed by a Jesuit missionary and only a fraction more Chinese than Saint Laurent's 1977 fragrance, Opium ("for those addicted to Yves Saint Laurent"). The irony didn't seem to register.

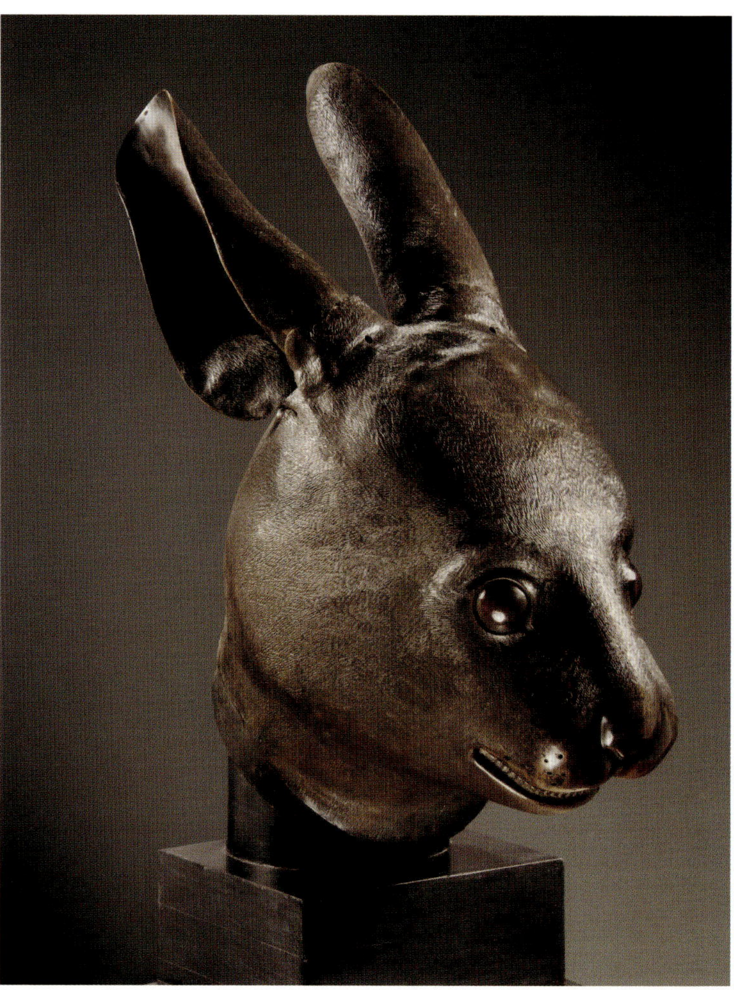

FIG. 83
Rabbit head made for the zodiac fountain of the Yuanming Yuan, Qing dynasty (1644–1911), Qianlong period (1711–99), on display prior to Christie's auction of the Yves Saint Laurent estate in February 2009

One week before the auction, China's State Administration of Cultural Heritage sent a letter of protest to Christie's demanding the sculptures' immediate return. The heads were cultural relics taken illegally from China during the Second Opium War, the administration argued, and buying them back would only condone the theft. A day later, some eighty Chinese lawyers joined the fray, filing an injunction in Paris on behalf of the descendants of Qing royalty.[3] Both of these actions were essentially performative. The same arguments had been made almost a decade earlier when three other zodiac heads—the monkey, ox, and tiger—had been auctioned in Hong Kong, and they now received the same ruling as they had then: Although the heads might have been taken from China during wartime, they were purchased lawfully; there were no legal grounds for repatriation. To this, Bergé added his own, less-than-politic postscript. "I would be very happy to go myself and bring these two Chinese heads to put them in the Summer Palace in Beijing," he told a press conference before the sale on February 23. "All they have to do is to declare they are going to apply human rights, give the Tibetans back their freedom, and agree to accept the Dalai Lama on their territory."

WITHOUT LEGAL PRESSURE FROM THE FRENCH courts, Christie's could claim that its hands were tied. "We understand that there are sensitivities in China that have been aroused by the sale of these objects," deputy chairman of Christie's America Jonathan Randall told the Agence France-Presse. "Our advice is that there is no legal restriction on them being bought or sold."[4] Randall's coolly phrased statement reflected a position that, in the past, China had more or less abided. While the government publicly rejected purchasing the zodiac heads, bidders with ties to the state had appeared

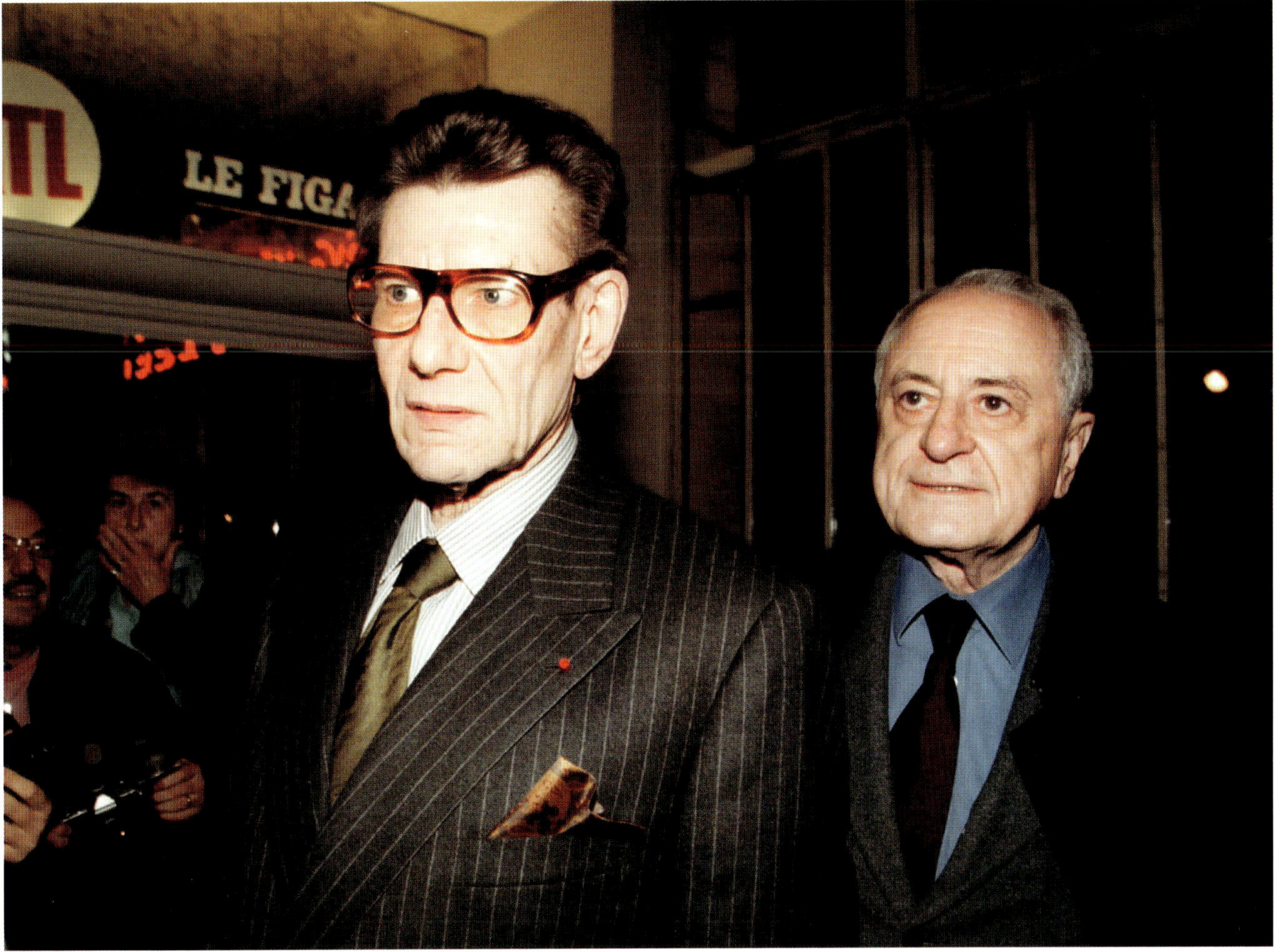

FIG. 84
Designer Yves Saint Laurent with partner Pierre Bergé in Paris, 1998

at just the right moment to snap up every head that had gone on the market since the Hong Kong auctions in 2000. All five of the zodiac sculptures in Beijing had been acquired this way, and all five had been donated to the same museum. But 2009 was a fraught year. The recent financial crash had sapped the enthusiasm and resources of potential buyers, and the price of the zodiac heads had climbed to astronomical heights. Christie's estimated the value of rat and the rabbit at $13 million each. They were almost guaranteed to sell for more.

As dire as the economy was, the political situation between China and France was even more severe. On March 14, 2008, as the Beijing Olympics approached, a demonstration in Lhasa erupted into rioting and was brutally suppressed by the People's Armed Police. Foreign reporters were barred from the region, paramilitary troops were sent in, and, based on the snippets of information that leaked out, Western journalists filed stories about a bloodbath occurring at the roof of the world. Meanwhile, the Olympic torch began its trip from Mount Olympus to Beijing. The "Journey of Harmony," as the Chinese dubbed it, arrived in London on April 6, where already the British media was reporting that the torch relay was a Nazi invention.[5] The next day, the relay reached Paris and found the metropolis up in arms.

A banner hanging from the city hall read, "Paris Defends Human Rights Everywhere in the World," and on the streets an angry crowd threw itself on the procession. The Olympic flame was extinguished three times that day, and to the horror of the Chinese public, one man tried to wrest the torch from a twenty-seven-year-old amputee named Jin Jing, an honorary carrier for the relay (fig. 85). In concert with Sarkozy's refusal to attend the Games, these events were interpreted as a tremendous slap in the face—proof that the French still thought they had the right to tell China what to do.[6] Nationalism swelled on the mainland, patriotic and at times ugly. Calls to boycott French companies circulated online and by text message, and in Qingdao, a crowd burned the *Tricolore* outside the entrance of Carrefour, which, aside from being a French retail chain, was rumored to have donated money to the Dalai Lama (fig. 86).[7]

The Beijing Olympics came off better than almost anyone had anticipated. Tibet stayed relatively calm. The fireworks were spectacular. Still, the rift that had opened between China and France remained unhealed that autumn as Bear Stearns and Lehman Brothers toppled and the world prepared to enter 2009. In December, Beijing postponed a sit-down with Sarkozy to

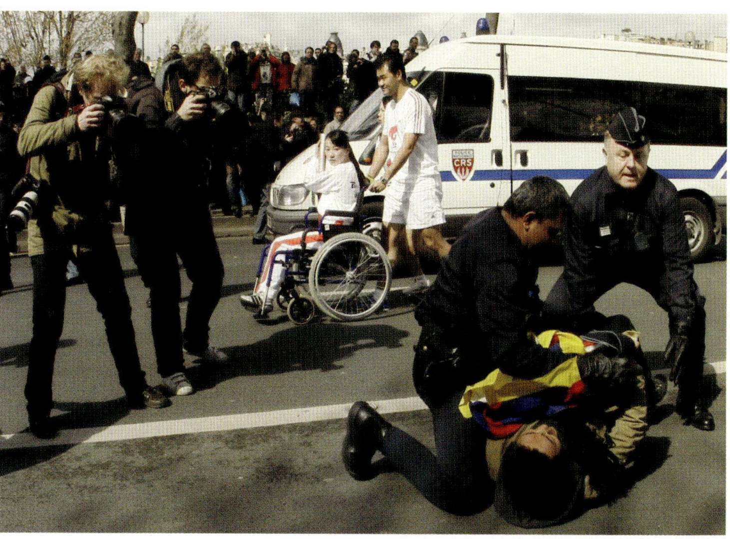

FIG. 85 French policemen hold down a pro-Tibet protestor attempting to reach a wheelchair-bound Olympic torch-bearer (in white), 2008.

protest his meeting with the Dalai Lama. Two months later came the Saint Laurent auction and a chance to rehash it all again.

On February 25, the last day of the auction, an anonymous bidder phoned Christie's and offered $19 million for each head. He won the lots, both heads were penciled in as sold, and China's state-sponsored news wire Xinhua ran a story suggesting that yet another Tibet-loving French billionaire, François Pinault, had secretly manipulated Bergé, Christie's, and the French government to keep the rat and rabbit out of Chinese hands.[8] Days later, the State Administration of Cultural Heritage held a press conference in Beijing. There, a small, middle-aged man took the podium to announce that it was he who had placed the winning bids, and that he had no intention of paying. Cai Mingchao was an antiques collector who had accrued minor fame in 2006 when he bought a Ming-dynasty Buddha sculpture for $15 million, the largest bid to date for a Chinese work of art. At the podium that day, he stressed that non-payment was his way of protesting the auction. "I believe that any Chinese person would have stood up at the time," said Cai. "I only did my duty."[9]

IF HOLDOVER ANIMOSITY FROM THE OLYMPICS ADDED tension to the Saint Laurent auction, the pivotal factor was the heads themselves. The zodiac fountain and the European-style buildings surrounding it were a mere fraction of some three thousand structures at the Yuanming Yuan, but because stone fares better with fire and age than wood, their ruins survived while vegetation and squatters took over the rest of the imperial grounds. The result, as historian Geremie Barmé writes, is that this broken rococo theme park has "become the ultimate icon in the Chinese mind of the vandalism of the West, and an abiding totem of national humiliation."[10] It took many years and some seismic ideological shifts for this transformation to occur. Suffice it to say that in the late 1980s, a small group of scholars and intellectuals were working diligently to preserve what was left of the ruins. By the mid-2000s, the notion that the Yuanming Yuan was one of the highest achievements of the Chinese people had gained the status of dogma.

The zodiac heads—finite, collectable, and overtly Chinese in a way comprehensible to Jesuits and Party members alike—eventually inherited the same talismanic power as their former home, lagging by about a decade. One can trace the metamorphosis by following the auction history. The first public record of a zodiac head being sold is from 1987, when Sotheby's offered the monkey and boar for sale in New York.[11]

In stark contrast to the posturing of 2009, this auction provoked no reaction from the mainland, neither from the media nor the government. When the hammer came down, the monkey had fetched $150,000 and the boar $90,000—both higher than expected but a far cry from the seven-figure sums that the heads would command a decade later. Three more zodiac heads—ox, horse, and tiger—were auctioned in London in 1989. The outcome was pretty much the same.[12]

The turning point came in Hong Kong in 2000, when the monkey, ox, and tiger were all slated for auction within the span of three days. This brought the first official protest from the Chinese government and generated enough media coverage to ensure that a crowd showed up on the first day and tried to storm Christie's front door. The protestors appeared again when Sotheby's auctioned the tiger but were contained by beefed-up security.[13] The sales went through, and at first all that was known was that an anonymous bidder from the mainland had won all three sculptures. That bidder, it soon came out, was an offshoot of the Chinese military called Poly Group. With protestors seething outside, a detachment of Poly's men had taken over the front row at each auction and started jumping bids, making it patently clear that they were going to take home the zodiac heads at any price. In this case, that meant $1 million (HK$7 million) each for the monkey and the ox, and $2 million for the tiger (HK$15 million). Following

Poly's coup, the three sculptures made a quick public tour around China before returning to Beijing. There, they became the principal attractions of the then-brand-new Poly Art Museum, a small operation on the second floor of the group's headquarters, which bears no sign outside the building and no posted hours.

The Chinese government had signaled that it wanted the heads back, and big money followed. In July 2003, Macao casino magnate and art collector Stanley Ho visited the Poly Art Museum and was approached about helping to buy back another head.[14] That fall, he negotiated the purchase of the boar from an American collector and donated it to the Poly.[15] Ho stepped in again in 2007 to buy the horse before Sotheby's auctioned it in Hong Kong. It cost him $10 million, five times what the tiger

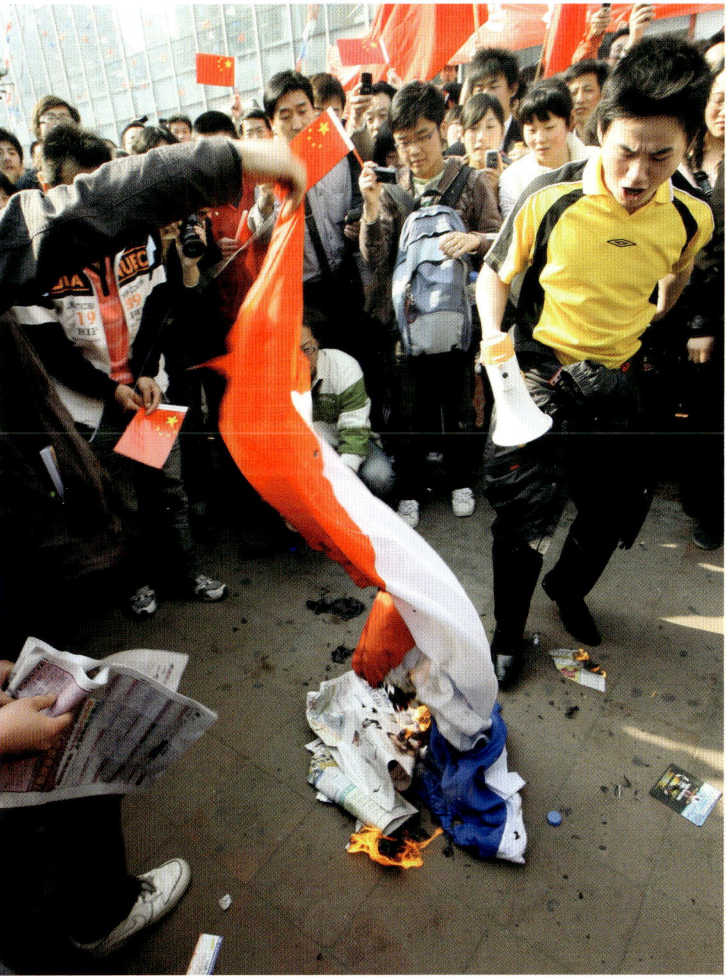

FIG. 86 Angry Chinese burn a French national flag outside a Carrefour supermarket in Qingdao, Shandong Province on April 18, 2008.

had gone for in 2000 and nearly seventy times what the monkey had cost in 1989. Based on the $19 million that the rat and rabbit each took at the Saint Laurent auction, this meant that the price of a zodiac head had increased more than 1,000 percent over twenty years, a profit margin worthy of a venture capitalist. Or it would have been, had the sale gone through.

CHRISTIE'S STILL REFUSES TO ADMIT THAT ANYTHING untoward happened, and as of February 2010, president of Asian operations François Curiel was claiming that the dispute with Cai Mingchao could be handled amicably. Cai, for his part, said he hadn't heard from the auction house since they threatened to sue him in 2009.[16] For a moment, there was speculation that the rat and rabbit would go to the second highest bidder.[17] Bergé quashed this rumor, saying that if Cai wouldn't pay, he himself would retain possession. "We will continue to live together in my home," Bergé told a French radio station.[18]

China's response was equally uncompromising. Immediately following the auction, the State Administration of Cultural Heritage issued a harshly worded statement charging Christie's with having defied the spirit of international conventions. "The State Administration of Cultural Heritage does not recognize the illegal ownership of looted cultural relics," the statement concluded. "It will continue . . . through every necessary channel to pursue artifacts that were looted or illegally exported [from China]."[19]

In December 2009, the government dispatched a team of researchers on a global hunt, for this exact purpose. If the rat and rabbit could not be recovered, propaganda was evidently the second-best option. Trailing in the wake of the researchers was a state-sponsored camera crew that dramatized the search in a series of television spots—a challenging task because, in the end, nothing was discovered. The biggest story the relic hunters generated might have been an article in the *New York Times* that depicted their mission as hypocritical and the researchers as rather bumbling.[20] The piece concluded with a brutal gaffe from a member of the Chinese research team:

> Even if [Mr. Liu] stumbled upon a palace relic, he said, he would be reluctant to take it back to an institution whose unheated exhibition space resembled little more than a military barracks. "To be honest, if you leave a thermos in our office, it gets broken," he said.

> "Maybe it's better these things stay where they are."

In the months that followed, it seemed as if things would settle back into the static, low-grade animosity between East and West that has accompanied China's economic ascendance over the years. But that fall brought one sign to suggest otherwise.

From September 14 through September 17, 2010, Christie's hosted an exhibition of Chinese contemporary art at its New York headquarters. Its title was *Trans-Realism*. Shows like this are not uncommon. They are usually presented to drum up excitement for an upcoming auction, and they normally open and close without raising eyebrows. This show, however, happened to be curated by the Chinese government. It featured seventeen Chinese artists who, according to co-curator Pan Qing, "go beyond what's happening in the country to express concerns about the world and humankind."[21] An affiliate of China's Ministry of Culture handpicked the curators. Christie's covered the transportation costs for the art, the exhibition catalogue, and travel expenses for the Chinese staff. It "is clearly a political move," long-time collector of Chinese art Joan Lebold Cohen told the *New York Times*. "This is to get back in the government's favor."[22] *Trans-Realism* was reportedly the first of several exhibitions that Christie's is considering financing as part of its new partnership with the Ministry of Culture subsidiary, the Center of International Cultural Exchange.

The works on display were not exactly apolitical—Song Kun's *Born in Garbage No. 3* and *No. 4* portrayed doe-eyed children set off against umbral backgrounds, suggesting life at the bottom of China's social bracket—but outright disaffection or social commentary was absent. If anything, *Trans-Realism* tended toward quietude. Qiao Xiaofei, a young artist who graduated from China's Central Academy of Fine Art, contributed a painting that depicted a ruddy, generational family crowded around an old television set, their faces awash in golden light from the screen. It is a scene from a simpler time, one that probably never existed. Another work, *Married for 50 Years*, by Xin Dongwang, shows an aged couple sitting contentedly side by side, the husband's eyes shut in peaceful resignation, the wife alert and contemplating something in the distance. This was not bad art, nor uninteresting. It was art that corresponded to the CCP's image of China.

In the same week that *Trans-Realism* was on view, Christie's New York auctioned some four hundred pieces of Chinese antiquities and artworks in its seasonal Asian Art Week sales. Many of these were Qing-dynasty objects, and it's likely that at least some came from the Yuanming Yuan.[23]

About this, China made no comment.

1. "Over 1000 Attend Yves Saint Laurent's Funeral," *New York*, June 5, 2008, http://nymag.com/daily/fashion/2008/06/over_1000_attend_yves_saint_la.html.

2. Edward Behrens, "Asian Art," *Christie's Magazine: Collection Yves Saint Laurent et Pierre Bergé*, February 2009, 194.

3. It took the lawyers some time before they found a plaintiff willing to join the suit. They eventually settled on a small organization whose title translates roughly as the "Global Society for Descendants of the Golden Manchu Clan." Li Jianya, "Zhuitao yuanmingyuan shoushou xu: Aixinjueluo jiazu zongqin hui (全球爱新觉罗家族宗亲会)," *China News Service*, February 10, 2009, http://news.china.com/zh_cn/domestic/945/20090210/15316528.html.

4. "China Offered 'Relics for Rights' in YSL Auction Row." *Agence France-Presse*, February 20, 2009, http://www.google.com/hostednews/afp/article/ALeqM5irGKB8T-5homX-zMbrq2ebtV5KfQ.

5. Chris Bowlby, "The Olympic Torch's Shadowy Past," *BBC News*, April 5, 2008, http://news.bbc.co.uk/2/hi/7330949.stm.

6. For an indication of just how strongly some Chinese citizens reacted to the Olympic protests and the way Western media covered the Tibet protests, see the following YouTube videos: "How China get your support? Never!" (http://www.youtube.com/watch?v=nxO-UElsaIU), and "We have nothing to fear!—We love China!" (http://www.youtube.com/watch?v=wz6epnlSWcc&feature=related).

7. Carol Matlack, "France's Carrefour Feels China's Ire," *BusinessWeek*, April 22, 2008, http://www.businessweek.com/globalbiz/content/apr2008/gb20080422_316128.htm?chan=top+news_top+news+index_global+business; Guo Shipeng, "Angry Chinese Burn French Flag Outside Carrefour," *Reuters*, April 18, 2008, http://ca.reuters.com/article/topNews/idCAPEK30252620080418.

8. "Jiashide yiyiguxing re haineiwai zhongnu, bijiang zishikuguo (佳士得一意孤行惹海内外众怒 必将自食苦果)," *Xinhuanet*, February 27, 2009, http://news.xinhuanet.com/collection/2009-02/27/content_10907843_1.htm.

9. Yang Jie, "Yuanmingyuan shoushou zhongguo paidezhe jujue paipinfuqian (圆明园兽首中国拍得者拒绝为拍品付钱)," *China Daily*, March 2, 2009. http://www.chinadaily.com.cn/hqgj/2009-03/02/content_7526715.htm.

10. Geremie Barmé, "The Garden of Perfect Brightness, A Life in Ruins." *China Heritage Quarterly*, no. 8 (December 2006): 127, http://www.chinaheritagequarterly.org/features.php?searchterm=008_morrison.inc&issue=008. This article is a reprint of one Barmé originally published in *East Asian History*, no. 11 (1996). The page number corresponds to the original printing.

11. Zodiac heads had been auctioned before 1987, but according to Lark E. Mason, the Sotheby's vice president who oversaw the 1987 sale, the heads were given only vague descriptions in the auction records—"eighteenth-century Chinese bronze," for example. This makes it next to impossible to trace their provenance back to the Yuanming Yuan. Author interview with Mason, former senior vice president in Sotheby's Chinese works of art department, New York, March 18, 2010.

12. "An Important Imperial Bronze Head of an Ox from the Zodiac Fountain in the Yuanming Yuan," Lot 517, Sale 2030 ("The Imperial Sale"), Christie's Hong Kong, April 30, 2000, http://www.christies.com/LotFinder/lot_details.aspx?from=searchresults&intObjectID=1789540&sid=cc28b5b1-ae52-401e-84ee-7e0c74bd606d.

13. It's worth pointing out that for all the patriotic zeal that attended the protests in Hong Kong, according to *Southern Weekly* the owner who put the heads up for sale was himself Chinese—a Taiwanese businessman named Cai Chennan. "Ding Buzhi. Shui zai caopan baibei baoli? (谁在操纵百倍暴利？)," *Nanfang Zhoumou*, April 1, 2009, http://www.infzm.com/content/26468.

14. Under Portuguese rule, Ho enjoyed a government-backed monopoly on Macau's gambling industry. Following the handover of the island to the Chinese state in 1999, the new regime stated publicly that it would allow foreign companies to move in when Ho's contract expired in 2004. Ho fought the change, but as of fall 2003, when he purchased the boar's head for the Poly Art Museum, he looked to be losing that battle, prompting speculation as to whether his motives were wholly disinterested. Damien McElroy, "Stakes High in Casino War: Billionaire Stanley Ho Controls Macau's Lucrative Gambling Industry and Is Unwilling to Give It Up without a Fight," *Financial Post*, Hong Kong, December 28, 2000, C12.

15. Deng Xinjian, "Guobao huigui guidian ye zhi, He Hongshen juanzeng mashou tongxiang qianqianhouhou (国宝回归贵点也值，何鸿燊捐赠马首铜像前前后后)," *Legal Daily*, September 24, 2007, http://big5.ce.cn/xwzx/gnsz/gdxw/200709/24/t20070924_13014771.shtml.

16. Le-Min Lim, "Sotheby's Sues Chinese Buyers for Nonpayment of Art Won at Sale," *Bloomberg*, February 10, 2010, http://www.bloomberg.com/apps/news?pid=newsarchive&sid=a6zUNWnEBNZQ.

17. The irony in this is that the next bidder in line allegedly planned to donate the heads to China. Cai Mingchao may have sabotaged the auction, but he also sabotaged a compatriot. The *Economist*, with a detectable note of schadenfreude, was happy to point this out. "Caveat venditor: the Fallout Continues," *Economist*, March 5, 2009.

18. "China 'Patriot' Sabotages Auction," *BBC News*, March 2, 2009, http://news.bbc.co.uk/2/hi/asia-pacific/7918128.stm.

19. "Guojia wenwuju guanyu jiashide gongsi paimai yuanmingyuan dongxiang shi dc biaotai (国家文物局关于佳士得公司拍卖圆明园铜像事的表态)" *Xinhuanet*, February 26, 2009, http://news.xinhuanet.com/politics/2009-02/26/content_10899951.htm.

20. Andrew Jacobs, "China Hunts for Art Treasures in U.S. Museums," *New York Times*, December 16, 2009, http://www.nytimes.com/2009/12/17/world/asia/1w7china.html?_r=1&scp=1&sq=china%20treasure&st=cse.

21. Lin Qi, "Marching to the Beat of the Auction Hammer," *China Daily*, September 7, 2010, http://www.chinadaily.com.cn/life/2010-09/07/content_11266385.htm.

22. David Barboza, "Christie's and China: An Artful Diplomacy," *New York Times*, November 19, 2010, http://www.nytimes.com/2010/11/20/arts/design/20realism.html.

23. "A Rare Pair of Gilt-Lacquered Wood Bodhisattvas," *Fine Chinese Ceramics and Works of Art*, September 17, 2010, Christie's New York. http://www.christies.com/eCatalogues/index.aspx?id=60C6169BE68916428525777E0058E7F7.

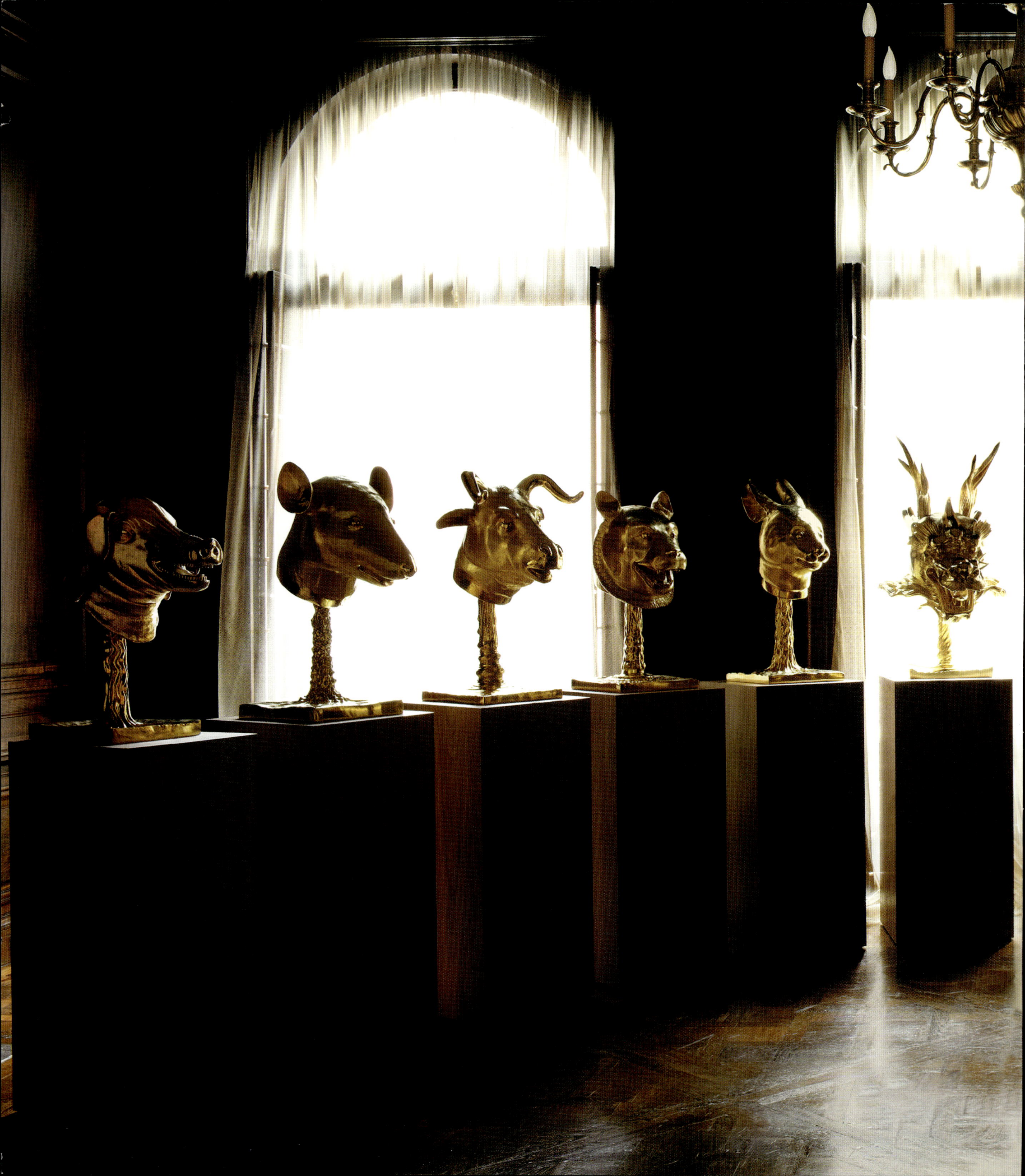

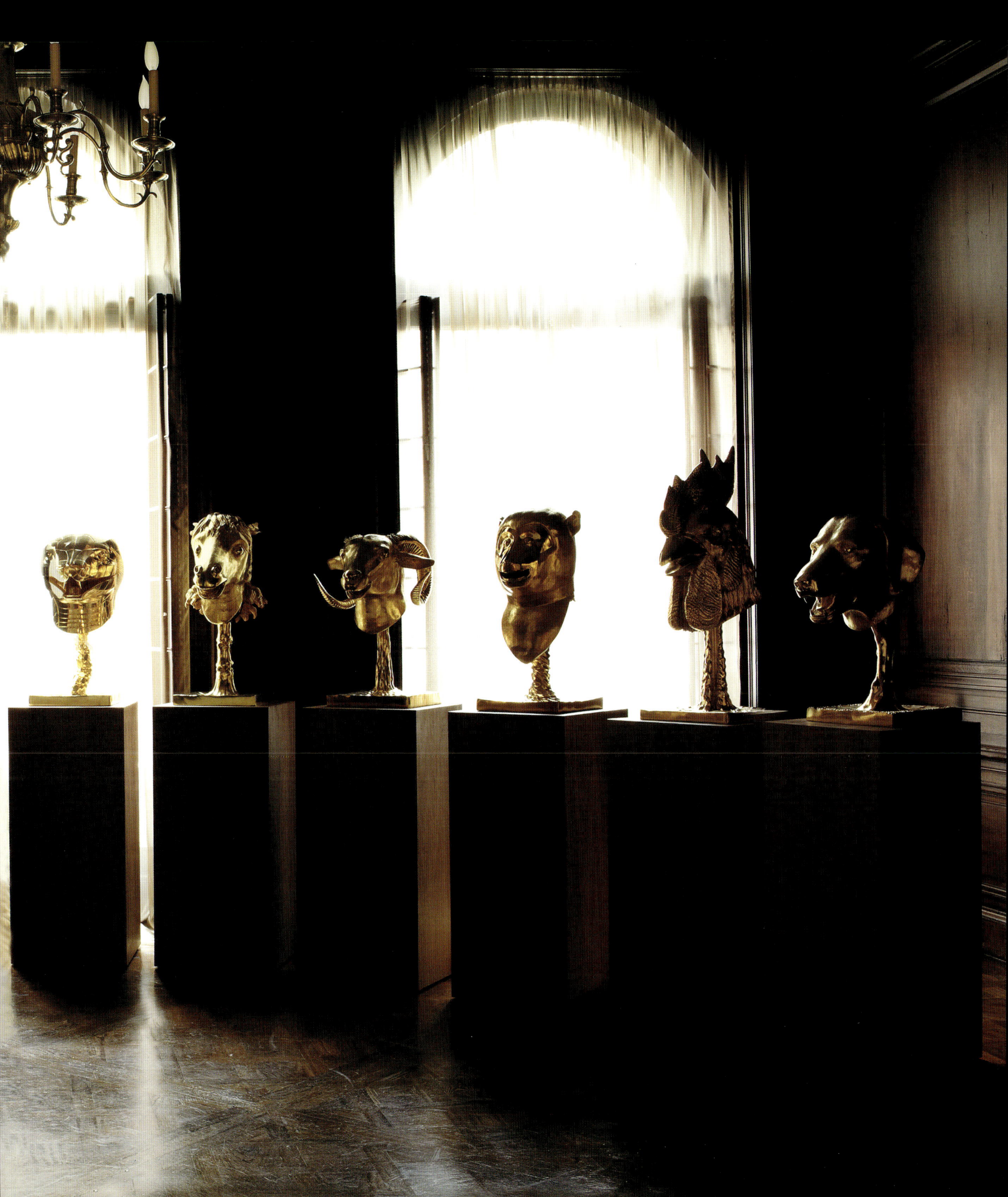

Acknowledgments

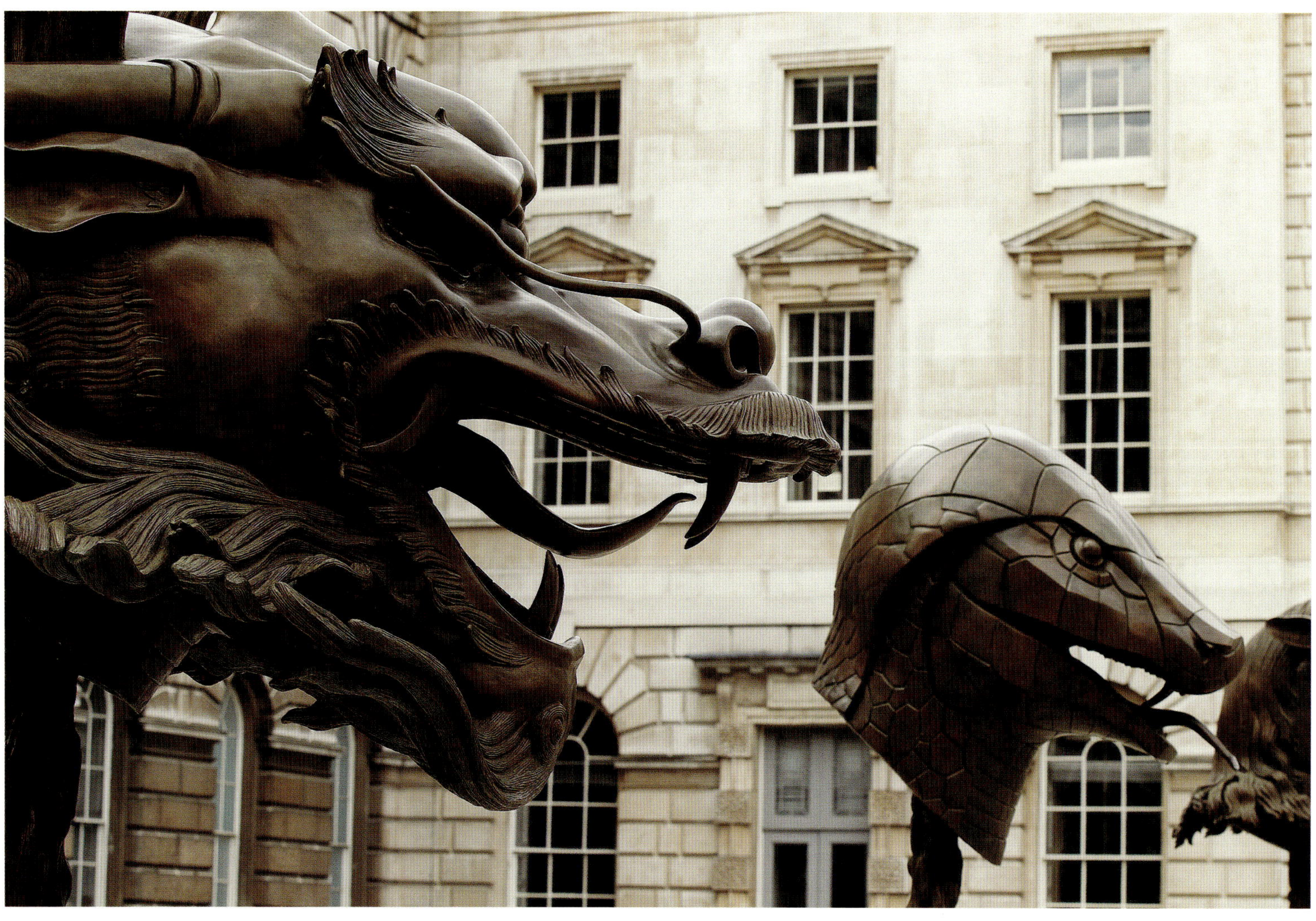

Installation detail view of *Circle of Animals/Zodiac Heads: Bronze* at the Somerset House, London, May 2011

PREVIOUS SPREAD: Installation view of *Circle of Animals/ Zodiac Heads: Gold*, 2011

THIS PROJECT WAS CONCEIVED WITH A SOMEWHAT unusual brief: to examine not only the work of a contemporary artist, but the reservoir of unfamiliar history that lay behind one work in particular. The contributors to this volume rose to that challenge with scholarly brio, and with enthusiasm, flexibility, and a patience for the editorial process that is deeply appreciated. Filmmaker Alison Klayman must be counted as an unofficial contributor as well, having generously shared transcripts of interviews shot for her 2011 feature-length documentary, *Ai Weiwei: Never Sorry*; these became source materials for Chapters 1 and 7. Phil Tinari, contemporary Chinese art scholar and editor of *Leap* magazine, was an invaluable sounding board in the project's early phases, and conducted several of the interviews with Ai Weiwei, as did Alison, Evan Osnos, Colin Jones, and Larry Warsh.

From its earliest stages, an informal circle of consultants, well-wishers, and friends has coalesced around this project, offering much-appreciated advice and encouragement. This invaluable group includes Melissa Chiu, vice president of global art programs and museum director for Asia Society; Alexandra Munroe, senior curator of Asian Art at the Solomon R. Guggenheim Museum; noted Chinese art expert James Lally; fine arts consultant Nadine Peyser; Gary Zarr and Cliff Sloan of Phil & Co.; marketing consultant Lou Sagar; graphic designer Alexandra Brand; Murray Pepper; Vicki Reynolds; and Katherine Grube.

Our profound thanks to the Honorable Mayor Michael R. Bloomberg and First Deputy Mayor Patricia E. Harris for their support in bringing *Circle of Animals/Zodiac Heads* to New York City. Thanks as well to Adrian Benepe, Commissioner of the New York City Department of Parks & Recreation, Douglas Blonsky and the Central Park Conservancy, and Jonathan Kuhn and Jennifer Lantzas of the Arsenal Gallery in Central Park for their support and assistance.

We would also like to thank the museum professionals whose vision and insights were so important in developing the installation tour: Michael Govan and Franklin Sirmans of the Los Angeles County Museum of Art, Kerry Brougher of the Hirshhorn Museum and Sculpture Garden, and Eric Shiner of the Andy Warhol Museum. As always, Agnes Gund remains a constant source of inspiration.

A smaller but no less enthusiastic circle of supporters also gathered around the book itself. Chief among them is China scholar John Finlay, who came to the project too late for an essay but has remained a generous and resourceful presence throughout. Jay Levenson, director of the International Program at the Museum of Modern Art, New York, was immensely helpful in early thinking about the book, and in recommending contributors. Lee Ambrozy—translator of the recently published *Ai Weiwei's Blog: Writings, Interviews, and Digital Rants 2006–2009*—was also very helpful. Katherine Don and George Wang of RedBox Studio and Eileen Boxer of Boxer Design contributed important initial thinking about the book's design.

Only those who have had to wrangle a hundred or so images (and attendant rights and permissions) can appreciate how vital the role of research coordinator can be. This project has been fortunate enough to have had two capable individuals in that position: Amara Antilla and Taliesin Thomas, director of AW Asia, assisted by Betty Chen, Avery Booker, and Steven Rodriguez. The staff of Ai Weiwei Studio were extremely supportive with image research, fact-checking, and other essentials; special thanks to Ragna van Doorn, Jennifer Ng, and E-Shyh Wong. Image research involved tapping museums and archives in China, Europe, and across the U.S., and in many cases, diligent and gracious individuals made light of this potentially time-consuming work. We are grateful for their help.

These days, setting a book before the public demands tenacity and resourcefulness well beyond what had been required in the past. With Prestel, this project has been particularly fortunate in its publisher, and in the dedication of the Prestel team to setting before the public the best book possible. Special thanks to Prestel's editor-in-chief, Christopher Lyon; editor Ryan Newbanks; designers David Heasty and Stefanie Weigler of Triboro; production managers Sue Medlicott and Nerissa Dominguez Vales; and copy editor John Farmer for their unstinting efforts on the book's behalf.

We cannot overlook the fact that this project originated in an artwork. I speak for AW Asia in thanking the many individuals involved in the development and production of *Circle of Animals/Zodiac Heads*, who helped communicate and give solid form to Ai Weiwei's vision: Yuan Gao; Jeremy Wingfield; Inserk Yang of FAKE Design; Chin Chin Yap; and Li Zhanyang & Studio. Our thanks as well to Simon Hornby, President of Art Services at Crozier Fine Arts.

Finally, on behalf of everyone associated with this book, our gratitude to Ai Weiwei for his unfailing support and encouragement in this effort to bring the history behind *Circle of Animals/Zodiac Heads* to new audiences.

Susan Delson
JUNE 2011

Contributors

PAOLA DEMATTÈ is associate professor of Chinese art and archaeology in the department of history of art and visual culture at the Rhode Island School of Design. She holds a Laurea in Chinese Language and Literature from the Università degli Studi di Venezia (Italy), and a Ph.D. in archaeology from the University of California, Los Angeles. Dr. Demattè specializes in the Neolithic and Bronze Age archaeology of China and has written on the origins of Chinese writing, early urbanism, archaic jades, and funerary art. She also has a keen interest in religion and East-West contacts. In this context, Dr. Demattè curated *China on Paper*, an exhibition at the Getty Center in Los Angeles and co-authored a related volume on Sino-European exchanges (*China on Paper: European and Chinese Works from the Late Sixteenth to the Early Nineteenth Century*, Getty Publications, 2007).

COLIN JONES is a Ph.D. candidate in the department of history at Columbia University, with a focus in interwar Pan-Asianism in China and Japan. He is a consulting producer of the documentary film *Ai Weiwei: Never Sorry* (2011). Before commencing his doctoral work, he was an editor at *Caijing* magazine in Beijing.

KRISTINA KLEUTGHEN is Assistant Professor of Art History and Archaeology at Washington University in St. Louis. Her areas of scholarly expertise include classical and modern Chinese painting, late imperial Chinese art and visual culture, and the role of Chinese art in global art history. She is now at work on her book *Imperial Illusions*, the first study of a monumental illusionistic genre of eighteenth-century Chinese court painting.

LARK E. MASON is an expert, curator, and advisor in Chinese art. He is the CEO of iGavel, Inc., an online art auction site, and an arts advisor with Timothy Sammons, Inc. He has appeared regularly as an expert on the Public Television series *The Antiques Roadshow* since 1996. He is the translator of *Connoisseurship of Chinese Furniture: Ming and Early Qing Dynasties* by Wang Shixiang, and *Classical Chinese Furniture of the Qing Dynasty* by Tian Jiaqing, and is the author of

numerous articles and the book, *Asian Art*. He was a senior expert at Sotheby's from 1979–2003 and a director of online auctions for Sothebys.com. He lives in New York.

CHARLES MEREWETHER is director of the Institute of Contemporary Arts Singapore. He is the author of *Ai Weiwei: Under Construction* (University of New South Wales Press, 2008) and co-editor of *After the Event: New Perspectives on Art History* (Manchester University Press, 2011). A former collections curator at the Getty Center in Los Angeles, Merewether was artistic director and curator of the 2006 Biennale of Sydney, and recently served as deputy director of the cultural district (Saadiyat Island) for the Tourist Development and Investment Company in Abu Dhabi. He has taught at the University of Sydney, Universitat Autònoma in Barcelona, the Ibero-Americana in Mexico City, and the University of Southern California.

MARCO MUSILLO is a scholar of Chinese art, Sino-Western encounters, and Baroque aesthetics. He has lectured and published on the Qing painter Giuseppe Castiglione, and on Qing court painting in the late modern period. He is the author of the forthcoming *Translating Italian Painting in China: Giuseppe Castiglione at the Qing Court 1715–1766*, and is currently conducting research on the display and reception of Chinese art in North American universal expositions and museums, with a focus on the twentieth century. He holds a Laurea in Chinese history from the Università degli Studi di Bologna and a Ph.D. in art history from the School of World Art and Museology, East Anglia University, Norwich. In 2009, he was the EDS-Stewart Chair Post-Doctoral Research Fellow at the Ricci Institute for Chinese Western Cultural History, USF, San Francisco. He is currently research associate of Chinese art at the Museum of Cultures in Lugano, Switzerland.

KAREN SMITH is an art historian and curator based in Beijing since 1992. She has written widely about the development of contemporary art in China for a range of publications and exhibition catalogues. Smith is the author of *Nine Lives: The Birth of Avant-Garde Art in New China* (Timezone

8, 2008), and is currently completing a second volume, *Bang to Boom: China's Contemporary Art in the 1990s*. Her curatorial work includes the group exhibitions *The Real Thing* (Tate Liverpool, 2007); *Subtlety* (Platform China, Beijing, 2008); *Music To My Eyes* (Today Art Museum, Beijing, 2009); and *Step into My World* (Today Art Museum, 2011). She has produced solo exhibitions by Ai Weiwei (*Illumination*) and Liu Xiaodong (*Tibetan Plateau and Beijing Girls*) at Mary Boone Gallery, New York City (2008), as well as an ongoing series of exhibition projects for young artists in China. Smith has written widely about Ai Weiwei. She was a contributor to the recent critical volume *Ai Weiwei* (Phaidon Press, 2009) and to *Utopias* (Whitechapel Gallery, 2009). Her monograph on Ai Weiwei is scheduled for publication in 2012. Smith was recently cited by *The New Yorker*'s Evan Osnos for her "invaluable work" in Chinese contemporary art.

JOE-HYNN YANG is founder and director of Courage & Joy, Inc., established in 2010 to deal in Chinese antiquities and provide advisory services in Asian art. From 2008 to mid-2009, he was senior vice president, Christie's, and head of the Chinese Works of Art department, New York. From 2001 to 2007 he was vice president, Sotheby's, and head of the Chinese Works of Art department, New York. He joined Sotheby's in 1998 as cataloguer in the Chinese Works of Art department, London, and transferred to New York as assistant vice president in November 2000. Yang was educated in Asian art through the 1997–98 Diploma Course jointly administered by the School of Oriental & African Studies (SOAS), University of London, and Sotheby's Institute, London. He graduated in Jurisprudence, BA (Hons.), at Brasenose College, Oxford University, winning the Martin Wronker Prize in Jurisprudence in 1996, and was called to the Bar at Grays' Inn, London.

LARRY WARSH is the founder of AW Asia, a private organization in New York City that promotes the field of Chinese contemporary art through institutional loans and acquisitions, curatorial projects, educational programs, and publications. Active in the New York art world for more than thirty years, he currently serves on the Contemporary Arts Council of Asia Society and the Contemporary Arts Committee of the China Institute. He is a member of the boards of the Alliance for the Arts, MUSE Film and Television, and The Getty Museum Photography Council, and serves on The Basquiat Authentication Committee. He is an honorary trustee of the Museum of Contemporary Art, Miami.

SUSAN DELSON (editor) is director of publications for AW Asia. She previously edited *Chinese Contemporary Art: 7 Things You Should Know* by Melissa Chiu, director of the Asia Society Museum (AW Asia, 2008), and was a consulting editor for *Contemporary Asian Art* (Thames & Hudson, 2010; in the U.S., *Asian Art Now*, Monacelli Press, 2010) and *Contemporary Art in Asia: A Critical Reader* (MIT Press, 2011), both by Chiu and Benjamin Genocchio. Prior publications as editor include *Cuba Avant-Garde: Contemporary Cuban Art from The Farber Collection* (University of Florida, 2006), and as author, *Dudley Murphy, Hollywood Wild Card* (University of Minnesota, 2006).

Bibliographies

KAREN SMITH

Ai Weiwei. *Ai Weiwei's Blog: Writings, Interviews, and Digital Rants, 2006–2009.* Edited and translated by Lee Ambrozy. Cambridge, MA: MIT Press, 2011.

Barmé, Geremie R. "Yuanming Yuan, the Garden of Perfect Brightness." *China Heritage Quarterly*, no. 8 (December 2006). http://www.chinaheritagequarterly.org/editorial.php?issue=008.

Fairbank, John K. *Trade and Diplomacy on the China Coast.* Cambridge, MA: Harvard University Press, 1953.

Gablik, Suzi. *Conversations before the End of Time.* London: Thames & Hudson, 1995.

Newsinger, John. "Elgin in China." *New Left Review*, no. 15 (May–June 2002).

Smith, Karen, Hans Ulrich Obrist, Bernard Fibicher, and Ai Weiwei. *Ai Weiwei.* Phaidon Contemporary Art Series. London: Phaidon Press, 2009.

CHARLES MEREWETHER

Beurdeley, Cécile, and Michel Beurdeley. *Giuseppe Castiglione: A Jesuit Painter at the Court of the Chinese Emperors.* Translated from the French by Michael Bullock. Rutland, VT: C. E. Tuttle Co., 1971.

Ledderose, Lothar. *Ten Thousand Things: Module and Mass Production in Chinese Art.* Princeton, NJ: Princeton University Press, 2000.

Merewether, Charles, ed. *The Archive.* London: Whitechapel Gallery and Cambridge, MA: MIT Press, 2006.

————. "Changing Perspective: Interview with Ai Weiwei." In Jonathan Napack, *Ai Weiwei: Works Beijing 1993–2003.* Beijing: Timezone 8 Books, 2003.

————. "Looting and Empire." *Grand Street*, no. 72 (Fall 2003): 82–94.

Pakesch, Peter. "A Bowl of Pearls." In *Ai Weiwei: Works 2004–2007*, edited by Urs Meile, Peter Pakesch, and Ai Weiwei. Lucerne: Galerie Urs Meile, 2007. Distributed by JRP Ringier Kunstverlag.

Reed, Marcia, and Paola Demattè, eds. *China on Paper: European and Chinese Works from the Late Sixteenth to the Early Nineteenth Century.* Los Angeles: Getty Research Institute, 2007.

Scott, Rosemary. "Les têtes en bronzes du Palais d'été de l'empereur Qianlong." In *Collection Yves Saint Laurent et Pierre Bergé.* Vol. 5, *Sculptures, objets d'art, art d'Asie, archéologie et mobilier*, 455–62. Paris: Christie's, 2009. Catalogue for February 25, 2009 sale.

Tinari, Philip. "The Leopard and the Tiger: Circular Narratives in Blue and White." In Waling Boers, Pi Li, Michael Ammann, et al., *Touching the Stones: China Art Now*, 134–39. Hong Kong: Timezone 8 Books, 2007.

PAOLA DEMATTÈ

An'guo, Pu. *Zhongguo sh er sheng xiao tu ji* (Patterns of the Twelve Animals). Xianggang: Wan li shu dian, 1987.

Attiret, Jean-Denis, S.J. "Attiret à M. de Assaut, 1er novembre 1743." *Lettres édifiantes et curieuses écrits des missions étrangères.* Vol. 28, 1–49. Paris: Les Frères Jésuites, 1749.

Barmé, Geremie R. "The Garden of Perfect Brightness, a Life in Ruins." *East Asian History*, no. 11 (June 1996): 111–58.

Chavannes, Éduoard. "Le cycle Turc des douze animaux." *T'oung Pao* 7, no. 1 (1906): 51–122.

Doolittle, Justus. *Social Life of the Chinese, with Some Account of Their Religious, Governmental, Educational, and Business Customs and Opinions, with Special but Not Exclusive Reference to Fuhchau.* New York: Harper, 1876.

Droguet, Vincent. "Les Palais Européens de l'empereur Qianlong et leurs sources italiennes." *Histoire de l'art* 25/26 (1994): 15–28.

Durand, Antoine, and Régine Thiriez. "Engraving the Emperor of China's European Palaces." *Biblion: The Bulletin of the New York Public Library* 1, no. 2 (1993): 81–107.

Fong, Mary H. "Antecedents of Sui-Tang Burial Practices in Shaanxi." *Artibus Asiae* 51, nos. 3–4 (1991): 147–98.

Gai, Shanlin. "*Zhongguo yanhua xue*" (Chinese Rock Art). Beijing: Shu mu wen xian chu ban she, 1995.

Goodkind, Daniel. "Chinese Lunar Birth Timing in Singapore: New Concerns for Child Quality Amidst Multicultural Modernity." *Journal of Marriage and Family* 58, no. 3 (1995): 784–95.

Harper, Donald. "Warring States: Natural Philosophy and Occult Thought." In *The Cambridge History of Ancient China: From the Origins of Civilization to 221 B.C.* Edited by M. Loewe and E. Shaughnessy, 813–84. Cambridge: Cambridge University Press, 1999.

Howard, Angela Falco, Li Song, Wu Hung, and Yang Hong, eds. *Chinese Sculpture.* New Haven: Yale University Press, 2006.

Institute of Archaeology, Chinese Academy of Social Sciences. *Tang Chang'an cheng jiao Sui Tang mu* (Sui and Tang tombs in the Suburbs of the Tang Capital Chang'an). Beijing: Wenwu, 1980.

Kelley, David H. "Calendar Animals and Deities." *Southwestern Journal of Anthropology* 16, no. 3 (1960): 317–37.

Keswick, Maggie, and Alison Hardie. *The Chinese Garden.* Cambridge, MA: Harvard University Press, 2003.

Little, Steven, with Shawn Eichman. *Taoism and the Arts of China.* Chicago: Art Institute of Chicago and Berkeley: University of California Press, 2000.

Liu, Lexian. *Shuihudi Qinjian rishu yanjiu* (Research on the Qin tablet almanac from Shuihudi). Taibei: Wenjin, 1993.

Loewe, Michael, ed. *Early Chinese Texts: A Bibliographical Guide.* Berkeley: Society for the Study of Early China & Institute of Asian Studies, University of California, 1993.

Los Angeles County Museum of Art, ed. *The Quest for Eternity: Ceramic Sculpture from the People's Republic of China.* San Francisco: Chronicle Books and Los Angeles: Los Angeles County Museum of Art, 1987.

Mission Palais d'Été. *Le Yuanmingyuan: Jeux d'eau et Palais Européens du XVIIe siècle à la Cour de Chine.* Paris: Éditions Recherche sur les civilisations, 1987.

Museo di Storia Cinese di Pechino, Seminario di Cinese dell'Università degli Studi di Venezia, Istituto Italiano per il Medio ed Estremo Oriente, eds. *Cina a Venezia.* Milan: Electa, 1986.

Nakayama, Shigeru. "Characteristics of Chinese Astrology." *Isis* 57, no. 4 (1966): 442–54.

Needham, Joseph. *Science and Civilisation in China.* Vol. 2, *History of Scientific Thought.* Cambridge: Cambridge University Press, 1956.

———. *Science and Civilisation in China.* Vol. 3, *Mathematics and the Sciences of Heaven and Earth.* Cambridge: Cambridge University Press, 1959.

Qing Qianlong. *Qinding xieji bianfang shu* (Treatise on Harmonizing Time and Distinguishing Directions, 36 juan). Translated by Thomas F. Aylward as *The Imperial Guide to Fengshui and Chinese Astrology.* UK: Watkins Publishing, 2007.

Reed, Marcia, and Paola Demattè, eds. *China on Paper: European and Chinese Works from the Late Sixteenth to the Early Nineteenth Century.* Los Angeles: Getty Research Institute, 2007.

Schafer, Edward H. *Pacing the Void: T'ang Approaches to the Stars.* Berkeley: University of California Press, 1977.

Shaanxi Institute of Archaeology. *Tang dai Xue Jing mu fajue baogao* (唐代薛儆墓发掘报告). Beijing: Kexue, 2000.

Smith, Richard J. *China's Cultural Heritage: The Qing Dynasty, 1644–1912.* Boulder, CO: Westview Press, 1994.

———. *Chinese Almanacs.* Oxford: Oxford University Press, 1992.

———. *Fortune Tellers and Philosophers: Divination in Traditional Chinese Society.* Boulder, CO: Westview Press, 1991.

Sterckx, Roel. *The Animal and the Daemon in Early China.* Albany: State University of New York Press, 2002.

Strassberg, Richard E. "War and Peace: Four Intercultural Landscapes." In *China on Paper: European and Chinese Works from the Late Sixteenth to the Early Nineteenth Century*, edited by Reed and Demattè, 89–137. Los Angeles: Getty Research Institute, 2007.

Wong Young-tsu. *A Paradise Lost: The Imperial Garden Yuanming Yuan.* Honolulu: University of Hawai'i Press, 2001.

Wu Yucheng. *Sheng xiao yu Zhongguo wen hua* (The Twelve Animals and Chinese Culture). Beijing: Renmin Press, 2003.

MARCO MUSILLO

Aimé, Henri Paulian. *Dizionario Portatile di Fisica.* Vol. 1. Venice: Silvestro Gatti, 1794.

Berger, Patricia. *Empire of Emptiness: Buddhist Art and Political Authority in Qing China.* Honolulu: University of Hawai'i Press, 2003.

Beurdeley, Cécile, and Michel Beurdeley. *Giuseppe Castiglione: A Jesuit Painter at the Court of the Chinese Emperors.* Translated from the French by Michael Bullock. Rutland, VT: C. E. Tuttle Co., 1971.

Choix des lettres édifiantes. Vol. 3. Paris: Imprimerie de Casimir, 1835.

Chung, Anita. *Drawing Boundaries: Architectural Images in Qing China.* Honolulu: University of Hawai'i Press, 2004.

Clossey, Luke. *Salvation and Globalization in the Early Jesuit Missions.* New York: Cambridge University Press, 2008.

Cohen, Joan Lebold. *The New Chinese Painting, 1949–1986.* New York: Harry N. Abrams, 1987.

Crossley, Pamela Kyle. *A Translucent Mirror: History and Identity in Qing Imperial Ideology.* Berkeley: University of California Press, 1999.

Du Halde, Jean Baptiste. *Description géographique, historique, chronologique, politique, et physique de l'Empire de la Chine et de la Tartarie chinoise.* Vol. 3. Paris: P. G. Le Mercier, 1736.

Ho, Wai-kam. *Eight Dynasties of Chinese Painting: The Collections of the Nelson Gallery-Atkins Museum, Kansas City, and the Cleveland Museum of Art.* Cleveland: Cleveland Museum of Art and Bloomington: Indiana University Press, 1980.

Finlay, John R. "The Qianlong Emperor's Western Vistas: Linear Perspective and Trompe l'Oeil Illusion in the European Palaces of the Yuanming Yuan." *Bulletin de l'École française d'Extrême-Orient* 94 (2007): 159–93.

Josson, Henry, and Leopold Willaert. *Correspondance de Ferdinand Verbiest de la Compagnie de Jésus (1623–1688) Directeur de l'Observatoire de Pékin.* Brussels: Palais des Académies, 1938.

Loehr, George Robert. *Giuseppe Castiglione (1688–1766) pittore di corte di Ch'ien-Lung, imperatore della Cina.* Rome: ISMEO, 1940.

Malone, Carroll Brown. *History of the Peking Summer Palaces under the Ch'ing Dynasty.* Urbana: University of Illinois, 1934.

Musillo, Marco. "Reconciling Two Careers: The Jesuit Memoir of Giuseppe Castiglione, Lay Brother and Qing Imperial Painter." *Eighteenth-Century Studies* 42, no. 1 (Fall 2008): 45–59. Baltimore: John Hopkins University Press.

Pagani, Catherine. *Eastern Magnificence and European Ingenuity: Clocks of Late Imperial China.* Ann Arbor: University of Michigan Press, 2001.

Pirazzoli-t'Serstevens, Michèle. "Europeomania at the Chinese Court: The Palace of the Delights of Harmony (1747–1751), Architecture and Interior Decoration." *Transactions of the Oriental Ceramic Society* 65 (2000–1): 47–60.

_______. *Giuseppe Castiglione 1688–1766: Peintre et architecte à la cour de Chine.* Paris: Thalia, 2007.

_______. "The Emperor Qianlong's European Palaces." *Orientations* 19, no. 11 (1988): 61–71.

Prandi, Fortunato. *Memoirs of Father Ripa, during thirteen years' residence at the court of Peking in the service of the emperor of China; with an account of the foundation of the college for the education of young Chinese at Naples.* London: John Murray, 1844.

Ripa, Matteo. *Storia della Fondazione della Congregazione e del Collegio dé Cinesi.* 3 vols. Naples: Manfredi, 1832.

Uitzinger, Ellen. "For the Man Who Had Everything: Western-Style Exotica in Birthday Celebrations at the Court of Ch'ien-lung." In *Conflict and Accommodation in Early Modern East Asia: Essays in Honour of Erik Zürcher.* Edited by Leonard Blussé and Harriet T. Zurndorfer, 216–39. Leiden: E. J. Brill, 1993.

Wu Hung. *The Double Screen: Medium and Representation in Chinese Painting.* London: Reaktion Books, 1996.

Yang Boda. "The Development of the Ch'ien-lung Painting Academy." In *Words and Images.* Edited by Alfreda Murck and Wen C. Fong, 333–56. New York: Metropolitan Museum of Art; Princeton: Princeton University Press, 1991.

Zhang Hongxing, ed. *The Qianlong Emperor: Treasures from the Forbidden City.* Edinburgh: National Museum of Scotland, 2002.

Zhu Jiajin. "Castiglione's *Tieluo* Paintings." *Orientations* 19, no. 11 (1988): 80–83.

MANUSCRIPT SOURCES

ARCHIVIO DI PROPAGANDA FIDE (APF), ROME:

Catalogus Missionariorum, qui actu existent in Imperio Sinarum, Scritture riferite nei congressi—Indie Orientali, Cina, 1723, 559 v.

Cina e Regni Adiacenti, *Copie manoscritte di vari scritti del Servo di Dio Matteo Ripa,* 1874, Miscellanea 16, 21 r., 26 December 1715.

Scritture riferite nei congressi—Indie Orientali, Cina Miscellanea 17, February 7, 1711, 33 r.

JESUIT ARCHIVE (ARCHIVUM ROMANUM SOCIETATIS IESU, ARSI), ROME:

Goa 9, vol. II, 500–501 r./v., 6 April 1713, 18 April 1713.

Memoria postuma, ARSI, Bras. 28, 92 r.- 93 v, 92.

NATIONAL LIBRARY, ROME:

Fondo Gesuitico, *Nuovi riscontri dalla Cina,* 1723, ms. 1254, n. 31, 315 r.-318 r., 315 v- 316 r.

KRISTINA KLEUTGHEN

Amiot, Jean Joseph Marie, S.J. "Extrait d'une lettre de M. Amiot, Missionaire," Beijing, January 25, 1787. *Mémoires concernant l'histoire, les sciences, les arts, les moeurs, les usages, etc., des chinois; par les missionaires de Pékin.* Vol. 14. Paris: 1789.

Attiret, Jean-Denis, S.J. "Letter to M. d'Assaut," November 1, 1743. *Lettres edifiantes et curieuses.* Vol. 3, 786–94. Paris: Les Frères Jésuites, 1749.

Barmé, Geremie R. "The Garden of Perfect Brightness, a Life in Ruins." *East Asian History,* no. 11 (June 1996): 111–58.

Callahan, William A. "The Cartography of National Humiliation and the Emergence of China's Geobody." *Public Culture* 21, no. 1 (2009): 141–73.

_______. "History, Identity and Security: Producing and Consuming Nationalism in China." *Critical Asian Studies* 38, no. 2 (2008): 179–208.

_______. "National Insecurities: Humiliation, Salvation, and Chinese Nationalism." *Alternatives* 29 (2004): 199–218.

d'Herrison, Maurice. "The Loot of the Imperial Summer Palace at Pekin." *Annual Report of the Smithsonian Institution,* 601–35. Washington, DC: US Government Printing Office, 1901.

Eckholm, Eric, and Mark Landler. "State Bidder Buys Relics for China." *New York Times,* May 3, 2000.

Hevia, James L. *Cherishing Men from Afar: Qing Guest Ritual and the Macartney Embassy of 1793.* Durham: Duke University Press, 1995.

_______. *English Lessons: The Pedagogy of Imperialism in Nineteenth-Century China.* Durham: Duke University Press, 2003.

_______. "Looting Beijing: 1860, 1900." In *Tokens of Exchange: The Problem of Translation in Global Circulations.* Edited by Lydia H. Liu, 192–213. Durham: Duke University Press, 1999.

_______. "Loot's Fate: The Economy of Plunder and the Moral Life of Objects 'From the Summer Palace of the Emperor of China.'" *History and Anthropology* 6, no. 4 (1994): 319–45.

______. "Plunder, Markets, and Museums: The Biographies of Chinese Imperial Objects in Europe and North America." In *What's the Use of Art? Asian Visual and Material Culture in Context*. Edited by Jan Mrázek and Morgan Pitelka, 129–41. Honolulu: University of Hawai'i Press, 2008.

Knollys, Henry, with Sir James Hope Grant. *Incidents in the China War of 1860, Compiled from the Private Journals of General Sir Hope Grant*. Edinburgh: William Blackwood and Sons, 1875.

Kraus, Richard Curt. "The Politics of Art Repatriation: Nationalism, State Legitimation, and Beijing's Looted Zodiac Animal Heads." In *Chinese Politics: State, Society and the Market*. Edited by Peter Gries and Stanley Rosen, 199–221. London: Routledge, 2010.

______. "The Repatriation of Plundered Chinese Art." *China Quarterly*, no. 199 (September 2009): 837–42.

Lucy, Armand. *Souvenirs de voyage: Lettres intimes sur la campagne de Chine en 1860*. Marseille: Jules Barile, 1861.

Malone, Carroll Brown. *History of the Peking Summer Palaces under the Ch'ing Dynasty*. Urbana: University of Illinois, 1934.

M'Ghee, Reverend R. J. L. *How We Got into Pekin: A Narrative of the Campaign in China of 1860*. London: Richard Bentley, 1862.

Merryman, John Henry. "Thinking about the Elgin Marbles." In *Thinking about the Elgin Marbles: Critical Essays on Cultural Property, Art and Law*. Edited by John Henry Merryman, 24–63. The Hague: Kluwer Law International, 2000.

Murphy, J. David. *Plunder and Preservation: Cultural Property Law and Practice in the People's Republic of China*. Oxford: Oxford University Press, 1995.

Mutrecy, Charles de. *Journal de la campagne de Chine*. Paris: A. Bourdilliat, 1861.

Pirazzoli-t'Serstevens, Michèle. "A Pluridisciplinary Research on Castiglione and the Emperor Ch'ien-lung's European Palaces, Part I." *National Palace Museum Bulletin* 24, no. 4 (September–October 1989): 1–12.

Swinhoe, Robert. *Narrative of the North China Campaign of 1860*. London: Smith, Elder, 1861.

Thiriez, Régine. *Barbarian Lens: Western Photographers of the Qianlong Emperor's European Palaces*. Amsterdam: Gordon and Breach Publishers, 1998.

Thomas, Greg M. "The Looting of Yuanming and the Translation of Chinese Art in Europe." *Nineteenth-Century Art Worldwide* 7, no. 2 (Autumn 2008). http://www.19thc-artworldwide.org/index.php/autumn08/93-the-looting-of-yuanming-and-the-translation-of-chinese-art-in-europe.

Varin, Paul [Charles Dupin]. *Expédition de Chine*. Paris: Michel Lévy Frères, 1862.

Wong, Young-tsu. *Paradise Lost: The Imperial Garden Yuanmingyuan*. Honolulu: University of Hawai'i Press, 2001.

Wu Hung. "Ruins, Fragmentation, and the Chinese Modern/Postmodern." In *Inside Out: New Chinese Art*. Edited by Gao Minglu, 59–66. San Francisco: San Francisco Museum of Modern Art, New York: Asia Society Galleries, and Berkeley: University of California Press, 1998.

COLIN JONES

Barboza, David. "Christie's and China: An Artful Diplomacy." *New York Times*, November 19, 2010. http://www.nytimes.com/2010/11/20/arts/design/20realism.html.

Barmé, Geremie R. "The Garden of Perfect Brightness, a Life in Ruins." *East Asian History*, no. 11 (June 1996): 111–58. Reprint, "Yuanming Yuan, the Garden of Perfect Brightness." *China Heritage Quarterly*, no. 8 (December 2006): 127. http://www.chinaheritagequarterly.org/editorial.php?issue=008.

Behrens, Edward. "Asian Art." *Christie's Magazine: Collection Yves Saint Laurent et Pierre Bergé*, February 2009, 194.

Bowlby, Chris. "The Olympic Torch's Shadowy Past." *BBC News*, April 5, 2008. http://news.bbc.co.uk/2/hi/7330949.stm.

"Caveat Venditor: The Fallout Continues." *Economist*, March 5, 2009. http://www.economist.com/node/13226433?story_id=13226433.

"China Offered 'Relics for Rights' in YSL Auction Row." *Agence France-Presse*, February 20, 2009. http://www.google.com/hostednews/afp/article/ALeqM5irGKB8T5homX-zMbrq2ebtV5KfQ.

"China 'Patriot' Sabotages Auction." *BBC News*, March 2, 2009. http://news.bbc.co.uk/2/hi/asia-pacific/7918128.stm.

Deng Xinjian. "Guobao huigui guidian ye zhi, He Hongshen juanzeng mashou tongxiang qianqianhouhou." *Legal Daily*, September 24, 2007. http://big5.ce.cn/xwzx/gnsz/gdxw/200709/24/t20070924_13014771.shtml.

"Ding Buzhi. Shei zai caopan baibai baoli." *Nanfang Zhoumou*, April 1, 2009. http://www.infzm.com/content/26468.

Guo Shipeng. "Angry Chinese Burn French Flag Outside Carrefour." *Reuters*, April 18, 2008. http://ca.reuters.com/article/topNews/idCAPEK30252620080418.

"Guojia wenwuju guanyu jiashide gongsi paimai yuanmingyuan dongxiang shi de biaotai." *Xinhuanet*, February 26, 2009. http://news.xinhuanet.com/politics/200902/26/content_10899951.htm.

"An Important Imperial Bronze Head of an Ox from the Zodiac Fountain in the Yuanming Yuan." Lot 517. Hong Kong: Christie's, 2009. Catalogue for Sale 2030 ("The Imperial Sale"), April 30, 2000. http://www.christies.com/LotFinder/lot_details.aspx?from=searchresults&int

ObjectID=789540&sid=cc28b5b1-ae52-401e-84ee-7e0c74bd606d.

Jacobs, Andrew. "China Hunts for Art Treasures in U.S. Museums." *New York Times*, December 16, 2009. http://www.nytimes.com/2009/12/17/world/asia/17china.html?_r=1&scp=1&sq=china%0treasure&st=cse.

"Jiashide yiyiguxing re haineiwai zhongnu, bijiang zishikuguo." *Xinhuanet*, February 27, 2009. http://news.xinhuanet.com/collection/2009-02/27/content_10907843_1.htm.

Li Jianya. "Zhuitao yuanmingyuan shouhsou xu: Aixinjueluo jiazu zongqin hui." *China News Service*, February 10, 2009. http://news.china.com/zh_cn/domestic/945/20090210/15316528.html.

Lim Le-Min. "Sotheby's Sues Chinese Buyers for Nonpayment of Art Won at Sale." *Bloomberg*, February 10, 2010. http://www.bloomberg.com/apps/news?pid=newsarchive&sid=a6zUNWnEBNZQaccess.

Lin Qi. "Marching to the Beat of the Auction Hammer." *China Daily*, September 7, 2010. http://www.chinadaily.com.cn/life/2010-09/07/content_11266385.htm.

Matlack, Carol. "France's Carrefour Feels China's Ire." *BusinessWeek*, April 22, 2008. http://www.businessweek.com/globalbiz/content/apr2008/gb20080422_316128.htm?cha=top+news_top+news+index_global+business.

McElroy, Damien. "Stakes High in Casino War: Billionaire Stanley Ho Controls Macau's Lucrative Gambling Industry and Is Unwilling to Give It Up without a Fight." *Financial Post*, Hong Kong, December 28, 2000, C12.

"Over 1000 Attend Yves Saint Laurent's Funeral." *New York*, June 5, 2008. http://nymag.com/daily/fashion/2008/06/over_1000_attend_yves_saint_la.html.

"A Rare Pair of Gilt-Lacquered Wood Bodhisattvas." In *Fine Chinese Ceramics and Works of Art*. Christie's New York (September 17, 2010).

Yang Jie. "Yuanmingyuan shoushou zhongguo paidezhe jujue paipinfuqian." *China Daily*, March 2, 2009). http://www.chinadaily.com.cn/hqgj/2009 03/02/content_7526715.htm.

YOUTUBE VIDEOS

"How China get your support? Never!" http://www.youtube.com/watch?v=nxO-UElsaIU.

"We have nothing to fear!—We love China!" http://www.youtube.com/watch?v=wz6epnlSWcc&feature=related.

Image Credits

Courtesy Ai Weiwei Studio, Bejing: 50, 53, 57, 59, 69 (top), 70 (top left), 73, 74, 75, 78, 79, 80, 90–91, 92, 93, 94, 96, 97, 100, 106–29 (*Gold* portfolio)

Courtesy AW Asia: frontispiece, 48–49, 54, 58, 63, 65

Courtesy University of Alberta Museums, University of Alberta, Edmonton, Canada: 176

Courtesy American Museum of Natural History Library, New York: 132–33

Courtesy Art Resource, New York: 138, 157, 177

Courtesy Asian Art Museum of San Francisco: 146–47, 151

Courtesy Bibliothèque Nationale de France, Paris: 163, 164, 168–69, 170–71, 176 (bottom)

Courtesy Mary Boone Gallery: 66, 81

Courtesy Christie's: 187, 198

Courtesy Dreamstime: 141

Courtesy Sidney D. Gamble Photographs, Duke University Rare Book, Manuscript, and Special Collections Library: 192

Courtesy Getty Images, Photo by Benhamou & Valente/Prestige: 199

Courtesy Getty Images, Photo by Frederic J. Brown/AFP: 140–41

Courtesy Getty Images, Photo by Thomas Coex/AFP: 200

Courtesy Getty Images, Photo by Patrick Kovarik/AFP: 197

Courtesy Getty Research Institute, Research Library: 14–15, 89, 136, 143, 190

Photo by Marcus Ginns Photography: 13

Courtesy Harvard College Library: 191

Photos by Aaron Igler/Matt Suib (Greenhouse Media): 76, 77

From Jin Yufeng, "*Yuanming yuan xiyanglou pingxi*" in *Yuanmingyuan* 3 (1984): 86–87

Courtesy Library and Archives Canada, Ottawa: 167 (left)

Image copyright © The Metropolitan Museum of Art / Art Resource, NY: 139, 157

Photo by Marco Musillo: 148

Photos by Tim Nighswander/IMAGING4ART: Front cover, 22–45 (*Bronze* portfolio)

Courtesy Palace Museum, Beijing: 56, 152, 154

Courtesy Philadelphia Museum of Art: 138

Photos by Adam Reich: 2–3, 60, 61, 62, 69 (bottom), 70 (bottom left, right), 71, 72, 98–99

Courtesy Reuters: 201

Courtesy The Royal Collection, England: 167 (right), 189

Courtesy Shaanxi History Museum, Xi'an, China: 51, 137

Courtesy Smithsonian Institution, Freer Gallery of Art, Washington, D.C.: 155

Courtesy Smithsonian Institution, Arthur M. Sackler Gallery, Washington, D.C.: 158, 159

Courtesy University of Illinois Archives: 178

Photo by Cari Vuong, courtesy Kasmin/Holzer: 204–5

X

Y

Z

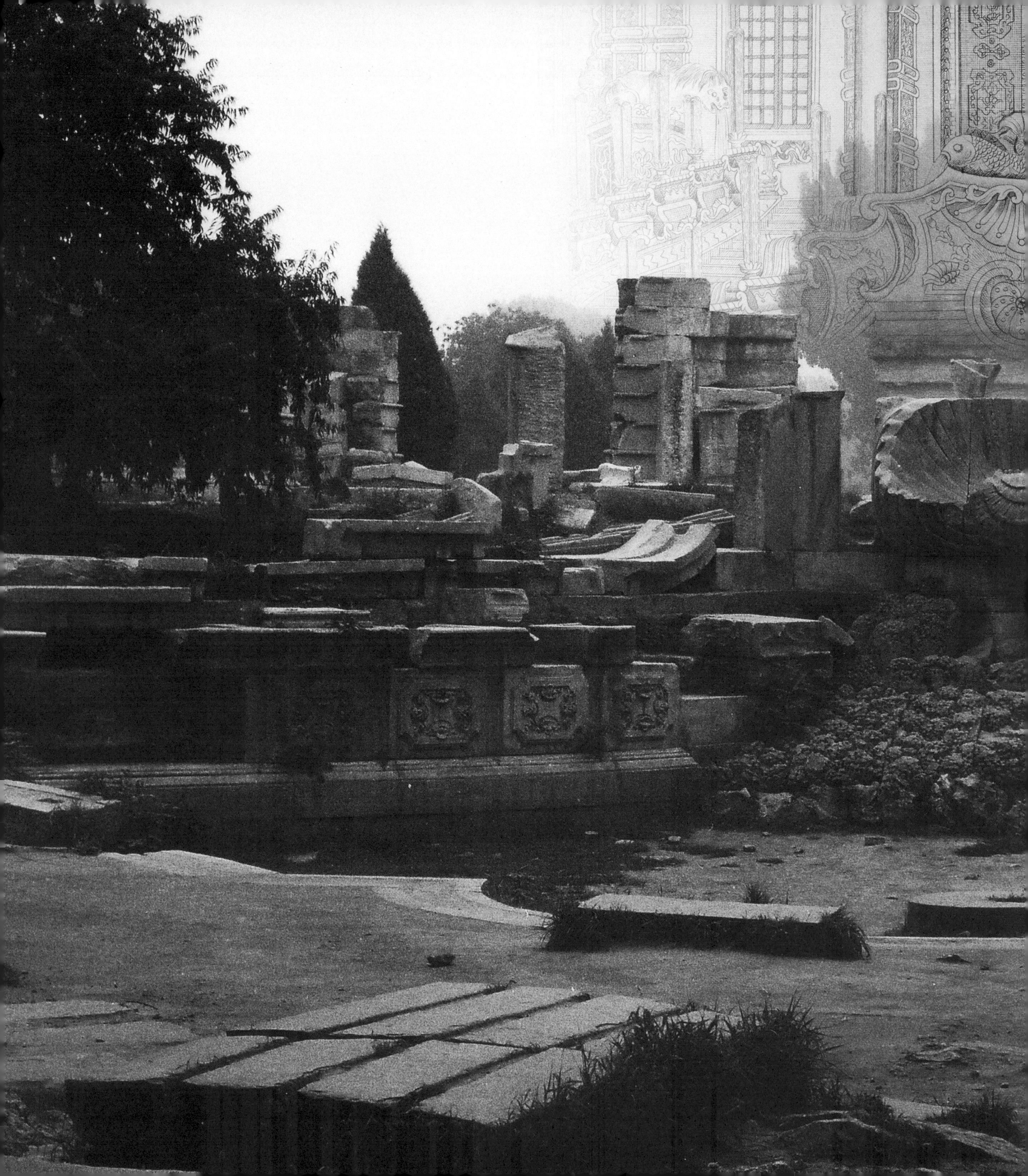